The Russian Social Democratic Labour Party 1898–October 1917

The four volumes in this series are edited as an integral set. Each contains a subject index in which Russian abbreviations and acronymic names are translated. Tables summarizing the personnel of the main party executive bodies since 1917 are also provided. At the same time each of the volumes is built around a coherent period in the development of Russian Communism, and each reflects the special features of its time.

Volume 1 treats the period before the October Revolution of 1917. It is the first colletion of materials on the early evolution of the Russian Social Democratic Party that deals with the entire movement, so that the interaction of the various factions of the party may be understood as a whole and not merely in a partisan Leninist framework. This volume also breaks new ground in publishing in English vital records of Communist activity during the Revolution of 1917.

RALPH CARTER ELWOOD is Associate Professor of Russian History at Carleton University, Ottawa. He is associate editor of *Canadian Slavonic Papers* and author of *Russian Social Democracy in the Underground: A study of the RSDRP in the Ukraine, 1907–1914*.

**Resolutions and decisions of the
Communist Party of the Soviet Union**

Volume 1
The Russian Social Democratic Labour Party
1898–October 1917

Editor: Ralph Carter Elwood

University of Toronto Press

© University of Toronto Press 1974
Toronto and Buffalo
Reprinted in paperback 2017
ISBN 978-0-8020-2157-1 (cloth)
ISBN 978-1-4875-9169-4 (paper)
LC 74-81931

TO

The late Vladimir Ilyich Lenin, who summed up the feelings of the present editors, upon completion of this task, when he wrote to Maxim Gorky in 1913:

Resolutions, they say, are the most boring of all forms of literature.
I am a man who has consumed too many resolutions.

Publications the research and writing of which have been supported by the Centre for Russian and East European Studies, University of Toronto

Feeding the Russian Fur Trade by James R. Gibson (Madison: University of Wisconsin Press, 1969)

The Czech Renascence of the Nineteenth Century: Essays in Honour of Otakar Odložilík edited by Peter Brock and H. Gordon Skilling (Toronto: University of Toronto Press, 1970)

The Soviet Wood-Processing Industry: A Linear Programming Analysis of the Role of Transportation Costs in Location and Flow Patterns by Brenton M. Barr (Toronto: University of Toronto Press, 1970)

Between Gogoľ and Ševčenko by George S.N. Luckyj, Harvard Series in Ukrainian Studies (Munich: Wilhelm Fink Verlag, 1971)

Interest Groups in Soviet Politics edited by H. Gordon Skilling and Franklyn Griffiths (Princeton: Princeton University Press, 1971)

The Collective Farm in Soviet Agriculture by Robert C. Stuart (Lexington, Mass.: D.C. Heath and Company, 1972)

Leon Trotsky and the Politics of Economic Isolation by Richard B. Day (Cambridge: Cambridge University Press, 1973)

Literature and Ideology in Soviet Education by Norman Shneidman (Lexington, Mass.: D.C. Heath and Company, 1973)

Narrative Modes in Czech Literature by Lubomir Doležel (Toronto: University of Toronto Press, 1973)

Soviet Urban Politics by Michael B. Frolic (Cambridge, Mass.: The MIT Press, forthcoming)

General Editor's Introduction

These books attempt to fill a major gap in the documentary material available in English on the development of the Communist Party of the Soviet Union (CPSU). At present there is a substantial body of translated ideological material, based on the collected works of Lenin and Stalin, running to 72 volumes in full, but reduced to more manageable proportions in various anthologies. This is undoubtedly valuable, but it slights a large and equally important kind of documentary material that has long been readily available in Russian and emphasized in Soviet publications on the CPSU. This category may be summarized under the label 'decisions' (resheniia), which has had a fairly definite meaning in Russian communism since the early days of the party. The party decision as a document appears under diverse labels, principally rezoliutsiia, postanovlenie, and polozhenie, and is at least closely allied to the programma and ustav, which have equivalent or greater authority. (Not all such labels suggest any particular English translation. Rezoliutsiia is clearly 'resolution' and programma is 'programme,' but the others might be variously translated.) All decisions of the party are considered to be formal and binding expressions of the authority of the whole party; they, and not the classics of marxism-leninism, are the operating commands. Decisions that represent the party as a whole and that are binding on the entire party are always issued in the name of the party congress, conference, or Central Committee. The former two bodies scarcely differ, both being relatively large, infrequent assemblies that purport to represent the party as a whole. However, the authority of the Central Committee may be imparted to a decision in either of two ways: by an assembly of the entire Central Committee (a 'plenum'), which has grown from a handful to several hundred in membership, or (in the post-revolutionary years) by some part of its executive apparatus: the Politburo, Secretariat, or Orgburo. Just which of these latter bodies has acted in the name of the Central Committee usually is not revealed, nor are these decisions ratified by the Central Committee plenum or the party congress. All decisions have equal, absolute authority for party members.

The importance of party decisions is emphasized by the special place they have occupied in Soviet publications. The main case in point, which is one of the most widely used reference works concerning Soviet affairs, is

Kommunisticheskaia Partiia Sovetskogo Soiuza v rezoliustiiakh i resheniiakh s"ezdov, konferentsii i plenumov TsK (The Communist Party of the Soviet Union in Resolutions and Decisions of Congresses, Conferences, and Plenums of the Central Committee), the seventh edition of which consisted of four substantial volumes (vols I-III, 1954; vol. IV, 1960). In 1970–72 an eighth edition appeared, covering the period 1898–1971 in ten volumes. Some indication of the importance of this work is its editorship, which began with L.B. Kamenev in 1923, later included Stalin's personal secretary, A.N. Poskrebyshev, and finally assumed the imposing anonymity of the 'Institute of Marxism-Leninism of the Central Committee.'

While this work has never been suppressed, it appears that in Khrushchev's Russia it was supplanted as an active project by a 17-volume series bearing the general heading *V pomoshch' izuchaiushcham po istorii KPSS* (An Aid to Students of the History of the CPSU), which reprinted many party decisions along with other materials.

Other major publications have also signalized the importance of decisions. From 1921 to 1935 nine volumes appeared in a series entitled *Spravochnik partiinogo rabotnika* (The Party Worker's Handbook). This contained almost all party decisions published from the October Revolution until the end of 1934, and also a list of so-called 'circulars,' which were of lower stature and were not published. It is probably significant that this was discontinued on the flowering of Stalin's arbitrary authority, and also that the series was resumed in somewhat different form but with the same title after the destalinization campaign in 1956. While the revived *Spravochnik partiinogo rabotnika* is an important Soviet reference work, stressing the importance of party decisions, it is far less complete than the original series of this name and also differs from it by including many non-party documents.

Another type of important Soviet publication emphasizing party decisions is the thematic anthology, a few of which appeared in the period before 1953 and many more thereafter. The weightiest of these is a continuing multi-volume reference work entitled *Resheniia partii i pravitel'stva po khoziaistvennym voprosam* (Decisions of the Party and Government on Economic Questions). Other collections of decisions deal with such varied themes as the press, the military, education, trade unions, and the youth movement.

Although we know specifically who drafted some party decisions, the majority of them are published in the name of anonymous party bodies, and draw their authority from these bodies rather than from any individual, no matter how prestigious. This has enabled the party to treat its decisions as the durable, continuous expression of its will from the nineteenth century to the present, unlike the 'classics' of individual leaders. While Lenin's works have long occupied a crucial position as classics, they can hardly be said to represent the will of the party since his death in 1924. The fate of Stalin's and Khrushchev's writings and the personal reticence of the post-Khrushchev leadership has increased the significance of party decisions as the fundamental record of the institution.

It is significant that party decisions, unlike ideological classics, have not been widely translated into major foreign languages by Soviet publishers. While the entire fourth edition of Lenin's works in 42 volumes has been translated into English, no substantial part of *KPSS v rezoliutsiiakh i resheniiakh s''ezdov, konferentsii i plenumov TsK* has been translated into a non-Soviet language, nor have many of the individual documents in it been translated. These materials are mainly operational instructions for internal use by the party. While some of the published decisions are to a large extent hortatory and all are couched in marxist-leninist terms, the style of party decisions is generally intended more for command than propaganda. An important function of decisions is to point out and correct short-comings, which often makes rather grim reading, not very attractive to the outsider.

Some decisions have never been published, and are not included in our collection. Although the party leadership is capable of disseminating directives secretly, it does not appear that they choose to operate in this way very frequently as far as formal decisions are concerned. To support the compilation of the present anthology, an attempt was made to prepare a checklist of all decisions that have appeared in print or have been alluded to in Soviet sources since the October Revolution (Robert H. McNeal, *Guide to the Decisions of the Communist Party of the Soviet Union*, University of Toronto Press, 1972). While the total number of entries in this list exceeds 3000, only a few dozen more or less secret decisions could be identified through allusions in a wide range of Soviet books and periodicals.

Here it must be noted that the definition of secrecy poses some problem. We must presume that we do not know at all about the existence of some decisions. Then there are some that were not known at all outside official circles for some time after their adoption, but were published in full or in part a while later. The modest number of these suggests that fully secret decisions are not very numerous.

Finally, there are some decisions, especially of recent years, that are not published verbatim in the Soviet Union but are summarized more or less fully in the press soon after their adoption. All in all, the compilers of the present work feel that they have had a good opportunity to consider nearly all decisions made by the CPSU.

The study of party decisions alone does not provide an adequate basis for the study of the CPSU. There are other categories of documents, many of which also remain little known in translation, and which are at least equally valuable. There are, for example, speeches, letters, and authoritative statements of policy in the form of articles in periodicals. (A particularly valuable assortment of such materials from the pre-revolutionary period was compiled by the late Boris Nicolaevsky and was kindly made available to me by Professor Leonard Schapiro and Dr. Harold Shukman. This material deserves publication, but it contains no otherwise unknown party decisions.) It would certainly be useful to have an anthology of these materials, but we concluded that the present collection would lose focus, though gaining in coverage, if we were to include such items.

It was particularly difficult to establish a reasonably consistent policy on the inclusion of decrees by the Soviet state. The complex interconnection of the party and the state in the Soviet Union for over fifty years has made it impossible to segregate completely the decisions of these two political structures. Some of the Soviet anthologies referred to above mingle party and state decisions, and many important decisions bear the joint authority of party and state organs, such as the Central Committee and Council of Ministers. No solution to the problem could be wholly satisfactory, but the editors of the present volumes decided that the best course would be to follow the general pattern of the standard Soviet work, *KPSS v rezoliutsiiakh i resheniiakh s"ezdov, konferentsii i plenumov TsK*. The focus of that collection and the present one is the party, not the whole range of Soviet political institutions. Accordingly we have included no purely state (Soviet government) documents and only those joint decisions of party and state that have a particularly direct connection with party policy. These occur in the final, post-Stalin section of the book. It was quite easy to omit the joint party-state decisions of the Stalin period, because these seem to have been essentially state documents to which party approval was given as a matter of form.

In another question, however, the standard Soviet collection could not serve as an adequate model, precisely because of our desire to focus on the party as an institution. As the title of *The CPSU in Resolutions and Decisions of Congresses, Conferences, and Plenums of the Central Committee* suggests, decisions issued in the name of the Central Committee but *not* on the authority of a plenum are generally excluded from that work. There are a few exceptions to this, but they are drawn mainly from the later Stalin period, in which congresses, conferences, and plenums were exceedingly rare. However, as noted above, many of the most important party decisions have been issued in the name of the Central Committee but have in practice been the work of its standing executive organs, the Secretariat, Politburo, and Orgburo. It would be impossible to provide a fair impression of the record of party decisions without including numerous selections of this sort, and we have chosen those we found important. When a given document appeared as a decision of a congress, conference, or plenum of the Central Committee, this is indicated by the headings supplied by the editors. Decisions that bear the authority of the Central Committee in the absence of a plenum lack such headings.

A special problem is posed by the successive party resolutions concerning the economic plans, starting with the directive that was issued in 1927 concerning the first plan. Excepting the Fourth Five-Year Plan, covering 1946–50, all eight of the plans have been approved by major party meetings, although the plan itself is specifically a state, not a party, document. In view of the party's stress on the importance of the plans and its role in their composition and execution, it was necessary to include some of the relevant party documentation concerning them. On the other hand, party resolutions on the plans are fat with statistical data and related technical information which is generally too detailed for the purposes of the student of history or political science who may consult our work and which is not particularly helpful to the economist. The study of the Soviet economy has gone far beyond reliance on the data in the plans, and the student in this field is more likely to want to start with the rich secondary literature in English, with its statistical material, than with the party resolutions on the plans. Therefore we have applied a compromise solution, which is not always easy to carry out. We have included only relatively short excerpts from the resolutions on the plans, covering the broadest policy directives without much of the statistical material.

A related editorial problem concerns the reports on the work of the Central Committee that have been presented to each party congress, except the twenty-first (1959), since the October Revolution, usually by the principal party leader of the day. Acceptance of this report (otchetnyi doklad) by the congress constitutes a blanket vote of confidence for the decisions taken by the Central Committee and its executive organs in the interval since the preceding congress. The format of these resolutions of approval has, however, varied markedly over the years. When there has been a single party leader of unchallenged authority (during Lenin's post-revolutionary years and Stalin's maturity as dictator), the resolutions approving their reports for the Central Committee were brief formal statements that in themselves conveyed almost nothing. The reports themselves were lengthy and general discourses on the state of the union; technically they are not party decisions and are better considered part of the body of Lenin-Stalin classics already available in English. We have therefore included neither these speeches (reports) nor the empty, short resolutions of approval.

In other periods in party history there have been rather substantial resolutions, passed by congresses in approval of the report of the Central Committee. Perhaps the implication of this practice is that the party leaders wish to emphasize that the authority of the party secretary does not stand so high that his report itself can simply be rubber-stamped. The congress therefore chose to symbolize the corporate authority of the party by issuing its own resolution on the work of the Central Committee. These resolutions do form an integral and important part of the documentation with which this anthology is concerned, and they are included, with abridgements.

Another problem of definition concerns the foreign relations of the CPSU and the USSR. In claiming the prerogative of guiding all forms of policy, the CPSU has for years been concerned with matters of foreign policy. An interpretation of the world situation and position of the USSR occurs in various decisions of a general character, such as resolutions on the reports of the Central Committee to congresses and the party Programme of 1961. While the Comintern existed, resolutions on the report of the Russian representatives to its executive committee also formed substantial statements on foreign policy, as have some later party decisions, such as one of February 1964, concerning the Sino-Soviet dispute. The importance of such material should not be minimized, and it could be included in the present volume in keeping with the basic criteria concerning the definition of party decisions. With some reluctance, however, we have decided to omit material bearing on foreign affairs, primarily because it has already received substantial attention in specialized documentary anthologies. (See especially: Jane Degras, ed, *Soviet Documents on Foreign Policy*, vols I–III, covering 1917–41, New York, 1951, 1952, 1953; Degras, ed., *The Communist International, 1919–1943: Documents*, 2 vols, New York, 1956, 1960; and Xenia Joukoff Eudin and Robert M. Slusser, eds., *Soviet Foreign Policy 1928–1934: Documents and Materials*, vols I–II, University Park, 1966, 1967.)

The pre-revolutionary years of party history pose still another question of definition for this volume. This arises from the schisms that plagued the Russian Social Democratic Labour Party beginning with its Second Congress in 1903. While Soviet documentary publications in this field have naturally followed the leninist interpretation of socialist legitimacy in the pre-revolutionary period, the editors of the present collection are not committed to this partisan approach. Despite their serious disagreements, the Bolsheviks and Mensheviks were generally regarded as being part of a single party. Even Lenin's more high-handed schismatic meetings (in London in 1905 and Prague in 1912) did not dare to exclude unconditionally all of the Mensheviks from the party. The pre-revolutionary section of the present collection has therefore attempted to represent the party as a whole as it existed in this period. It is, however, clear that a full and final split between Bolsheviks and Mensheviks occurred in 1917, and from that time we regard the party as the equivalent of its leninist branch. For this reason the various formal statements of oppositional groups of the 1920s fail to qualify for inclusion as party decisions.

If the compilers of this anthology faced numerous difficulties in dealing with party decisions, the student who attempts to analyse them will as well. Although party decisions have maintained a considerable degree of consistency in their general character for over seventy years, their historical environment has altered markedly, not only when the small revolutionary party emerged from the underground and emigration in 1917 to become the ruling force in a vast country, but at two major junctures since that time. Both the Stalin Revolution of about 1930 and the end of the Stalin era are usually regarded in and outside the Soviet Union as fundamental historical demarcations. With this in mind, and not just as a matter of division of labour, the editors have therefore divided the history of the CPSU into four periods: to October, 1917; 1918–29; 1929–52; and 1953–64. Each editor has provided an essay characterizing the history and politics of the party in a given period, with special reference to the decisions published here. He has also provided more specific background information on individual congresses, conferences, and plenums of the Central Committee, and editorial notes in square brackets in the text of documents to deal with more detailed problems.

It is not easy to characterize the problems of analysis that the student of party decisions faces. Inevitably, the exercise of critical imagination is the prime requisite for penetrating interpretation of any human record, and this elusive quality cannot be summarized. One of the broad problems that the student faces is the emphasis of literal or concealed meanings. In any polity, and especially in the Soviet Union, it is a mistake to assume that all official norms and commands are observed in reality. Rules may be violated, orders may be unfulfilled, rhetorical boasts may be empty, and the most important communications may be cloaked in 'esoteric language' or left unsaid. Insofar as party decisions resemble law, establishing norms for conduct, they should be read with the critical judgment that inevitably must be applied to such evidence. Even granting this shortcoming, laws can be a vital form of evidence about the goals of a polity. In some cases party decisions represent a form of super-law, standing above the legislative enactments of the state or usurping the constitutional prerogatives of the state. In other cases party and state authorities have jointly issued decisions, which are usually regarded as a species of Soviet law, hence endowing the party with a share in legislative prerogatives. In a literal sense this may be the only example of party decisions as law, but it is important to bear in mind that the party itself is in effect a state within a state. Its internal life is in practice excluded from the authority of the state and is regulated only by party decisions, never by state law. Not only the party rules but also other party decisions attempt to establish norms for this community. This practice grew out of the pre-revolutionary, social democratic period in the history of the party, when it was assumed that only the procedures of parliamentary democracy could legitimize the self-government of the party. Throughout the Soviet period there have been strivings, at least by some party officials, to establish a kind of rule of law within the party through the observance of democratic procedures and the publication of definite norms in such collections as *The Party Worker's Handbook*. Against this there has been the leninist tradition of arbitrary centralized authority, approximating an autocracy that is not bound by its own laws. In this spirit Khrushchev ignored the party rules when reorganizing the party apparatus on separate agricultural and industrial lines of command in 1962, without submitting this decision to a party congress. This mixture of rule of law and autocratic fiat in party decisions requires discriminating critical judgment of the student of these materials. Some decisions represent the former tendency, and may be read as ideal norms that will not be observed. Other decisions represent the commands of the autocracy, which should be observed to avoid severe penalties (even though all orders are not in fact obeyed, even in the best of armies).

Although it is true that party decisions are generally more business-like than other media in Soviet politics, there is still an element of rhetoric in them. Unlike law and like Napoleon's famous orders, some party decisions (or portions of them) are intended more as exhortation than as operational commands. In this connection it should be noted that the compilers of these volumes have excluded from their interpretation of the category 'decision' the borderline species called 'obrashchenie' (appeal), which contains a high proportion of verbal froth as compared to serious orders. In most party decisions the reader will readily be able to distinguish between the elements of pure propaganda or marxist-leninist incantation and the practical business of the party. The propaganda may, of course, be important in its own right, reflecting the current emphasis in party policy, but it should usually be treated symbolically rather than literally.

This raises the question of the non-explicit content of party decisions, which some western observers call 'esoteric language.' Compared to some other Soviet media that are often analysed (such as newspaper articles), party decisions appear to contain rather little of this interesting but sometimes baffling communication. There are, however, occasions when it is important to understand the meaning of a given phrase in a particular context. For example, Lenin's use of the term 'liquidator' in the decisions of the Prague Conference of 1912 was meant to imply condemnation of all Mensheviks, even though the groups that were specifically expelled from the party were but a minor fringe of menshevism. In the Stalin era 'expulsion from the party' was a euphemism for 'arrest as an enemy of the people,' and in the Khrushchev era 'cult of personality' implied a far broader range of misdeeds than mere egoism. It is also true that the silences in party decisions may be particularly significant. The representation of the great purges in party decisions offers food for thought in this connection.

GENERAL INTRODUCTION

The present series of four volumes covers the years from the founding of the Russian Social Democratic Labour Party to the retirement of Khrushchev in 1964. This was not the editors' original intention. It had been hoped to bring the work as close as possible to the present, which meant the late 1960s. Two forces, however, dissuaded us from this plan. The difficulties in preparing and publishing such a work were such that it proved impossible to terminate volume 4 at any point in history proximate to the date of publication. Moreover, the character of the Brezhnev administration appeared less an intermission between major performances, as it had seemed to many informed observers in its first years, and more an era with its own integrity and weight, deserving a separate volume. The preparation of such a volume in fact began in the course of compiling and editing the present volume 4, and with this head start it is hoped that volume 5, tentatively entitled 'The Brezhnev Years,' can be published fairly soon after the conclusion of his period at the head of the Communist Party of the Soviet Union.

Robert H. McNeal

Acknowledgments

In the course of almost a decade from their conception to publication, these volumes have incurred weighty and varied debts. Among institutions that helped, the Canada Council must be cited with special gratitude for its grants in support of the research, translation, and technical services which made these volumes possible. Certain technical services in the later stages of the work were supported by the Centre for Russian and East European Studies of the University of Toronto and by the University of Massachusetts at Amherst. The book has been published with the help of a grant from the Social Science Research Council of Canada, using funds provided by the Canada Council. Finally, the editors are exceedingly grateful to the University of Toronto Press for its support of the project.

Among individuals to whom these volumes owe much, Professor H. Gordon Skilling, Director of the Centre for Russian and East European Studies of the University of Toronto, has been an unfailing source of encouragement from the outset. Professor Leonard Schapiro and Dr. Harold Shukman were most helpful in making available some special materials in their possession and in offering suggestions. The late Professor Merle Fainsod kindly gave permission for the use of the Harvard University Library copy of the Smolensk archives of the Soviet Communist Party. Professor T.H. Rigby provided counsel and information. Various kinds of valuable editorial assistance were rendered by Nelly Arakcheyev, Alexandra Elez, Philip Cronenwett, Carol Hagglund, and Thomas Poole.

The main labour of translation in these volumes was performed by Harris Coulter and Robert Ehlers, working separately. Any praise that the translation may deserve should be attributed to them. In the later stages of the work some relatively short passages of translation were added by Susan Wobst, and the general editor. A very few documents were adapted from Soviet translations. As a result of the passage of years and the shunting of parts of the manuscript among various editors and translators, it is no longer simple to identify particular translated documents as the work of this or that individual. Suffice it to say that the original work of Harris Coulter and Robert Ehlers has passed through various editorial hands, and it would be unfair to attribute to them errors that may exist in the published text. It would also be unfair to attribute to the translators the ponderous style that generally characterizes party resolutions and decisions, and which we have attempted to convey in translation, believing that the medium is at least part of the message.

A simplified form of the Library of Congress system of transliteration has been followed in treating Russian words, with exceptions for words and names that seem to have conventional English spellings that do not conform to this system.

Without the insight, good humour and patience of R.I.K. Davidson of the University of Toronto Press, these volumes would not exist.

R.H.M.

Editor's Preface

Russian terms are translated if a generally accepted English form exists, but are transliterated otherwise. In the latter case, the term (e.g., guberniia) is treated as an anglicized expression, without the use of hard and soft signs (except in titles of publications), to simplify the appearance of the text. The index of the volume provides parenthetical translations of transliterated terms. Translations of newspaper titles appear with the first occurrence of a given title and in the index.

All dates in this volume follow the Old Style, which was thirteen days behind the dates used in western countries. It is not possible to determine the precise date on which some resolutions were adopted, although the inclusive dates of the meetings at which such resolutions were adopted are given. The order in which the resolutions appear is not necessarily the order in which they were passed. Document numbers (e.g., 1.42) are supplied by the editor of the volume; the prefix '1.' indicates the volume number in the present series.

The denomination of meetings adheres to original official forms as much as possible, though this does not necessarily concur with later Soviet practice. The Central Committee resolutions of 1917 have been arranged in several chronological and topical groups by the editor.

Square brackets [ ] enclose material added by the editor of this volume, while parentheses appearing in documents are in the original. Brackets are used in titles of documents if the original version of a given resolution lacked a definite title. Ellipses (...) indicate omissions of part of the original document by the editor. To assist the reader in identifying changes in successive versions of the party Rules, bracketed notes are inserted with each article, indicating whether it is a new, revised, or unchanged article, with respect to the previous version of the Rules. In the case of the 1906 version of the Rules, reference is made to the 1905 version as the previous one, although it should be kept in mind that the Mensheviks did not recognize the legitimacy of the 1905 version.

At the end of each meeting, or – in 1917 – each group of resolutions, source attributions are provided. On the left is cited the earliest published source, which in almost all cases has been consulted by the present editor. On the right is cited the location of the material in a standard Soviet reference work: *Kommunisticheskaia Partiia Sovetskogo Soiuza v rezoliutsiiakh i resheniiakh s "ezdov, konferentsii i plenumov TsK* (Communist Party of the Soviet Union in Resolutions and Decisions of Congresses, Conferences and Plenums of the Central Committee), 8th edition, Moscow, 1970–72 (hereafter abbreviated to *KPSS v rezoliutsiiakh*). Not all documents published in the present work appear in *KPSS v rezoliutsiiakh*; thus other readily available sources are cited in its absence.

The end of each meeting of a party body or of each grouping of documents devised by the editor of this volume is indicated by the following symbol: ✺.

Contents

	General Editor's Introduction	vii
	Acknowledgments	xvii
	Editor's Preface	xix
	Introduction	3
	1898 **I Party Congress** (March)	33
1.1	Manifesto of the Russian Social Democratic Labour Party	34
1.2	Decisions of the Congress	36
	1903 **II Party Congress** (July–August)	38
1.3	Programme of the RSDRP	39
1.4	Organizational Rules of the RSDRP	45
1.5	On Local Organizations	47
1.6	On the Place of the Bund in the Party	48
1.7	On the Withdrawal of the Bund from the Party	48
1.8	On the Central Organ of the Party	49
1.9	On Party Literature	49
1.10	On the Presentation of Propaganda	50
1.11	On the Attitude toward the Liberals	50
1.12	On the Party of the Socialist Revolutionaries	51
1.13	On Demonstrations	52
1.14	On the Trade Union Struggle	53
1.15	On the Attitude toward Students	54

1905

	III Party Congress (April)	54
1.16	Party Rules (21 April 1905)	56
1.17	On Propaganda and Agitation	58
1.18	On the Central Organ of the Party	59
1.19	On the Armed Uprising	59
1.20	On a Provisional Revolutionary Government	60
1.21	On the Attitude toward the Government's Tactics on the Eve of the Revolution	61
1.22	On the Question of Overt Political Activity by the RSDRP	62
1.23	On Support of the Peasant Movement	63
1.24	On Practical Agreements with Socialist Revolutionaries	64
1.25	On the Attitude toward the National Social Democratic Organizations	64
1.26	On Divergent Parts of the Party	64
1.27	On Preparing Conditions for Unity with the Mensheviks	65
1.28	On the Dissolution of Committees which Refuse to Accept the Decisions of the III Congress	65
	I All-Russian Menshevik Conference (April)	66
1.29	On Relations Between the Two Parts of the Party	67
1.30	Organizational Rules	69
1.31	On Party Literature	70
1.32	On the Armed Uprising	71
1.33	On the Seizure of Power and Participation in a Provisional Government	72
1.34	On Participation in Elections to Representative Institutions	73
1.35	On the Attitude toward Other Revolutionary and Opposition Parties	74
1.36	On Trade Unions	75
1.37	On Informal Organizations	76
1.38	On Work with the Peasantry	76

	Conference of Social Democratic Organizations in Russia (September)	79
1.39	On the State Duma	80
	II All-Russian Menshevik Conference (November)	82
1.40	On Party Membership	82
1.41	On the Organization of the Party	83
1.42	On the Unification of the Bolshevik and Menshevik Factions	83
	Conference of the Majority (December)	85
1.43	On Merging the Centres	85
1.44	[On the Rapid Merger of Parallel Local Organizations]	86
1.45	On the Calling of a Unification Congress of the RSDRP	86
1.46	On Party Reorganization	87
1.47	Agrarian Resolution	87
1.48	On the State Duma	88
	1906 **Unified Central Committee** (January)	89
1.49	[On Party Unity]	89
	Unification Congress (April)	92
1.50	Organizational Rules	93
1.51	Agrarian Programme	95
1.52	Tactical Resolution on the Agrarian Question	95
1.53	On the Attitude toward the Peasant Movement	96
1.54	On the Armed Uprising	97
1.55	On Partisan Activities	99
1.56	On the Attitude toward the State Duma	100
1.57	On Trade Unions	102
1.58	Conditions for the Merger of the Social Democrats of Poland and Lithuania with the RSDRP	102
1.59	Draft Conditions for the Unification of the Bund with the RSDRP	104

I All-Russian Conference of the RSDRP (November) — 105

1.60 On the Tactics of the RSDRP during the Election Campaign — 105
1.61 On Electoral Unity at the Local Level — 107

1907
London Congress (April–May) — 107

1.62 Organizational Rules — 109
1.63 On Attitudes toward Non-Proletarian Parties — 110
1.64 On the Workers' Congress and Non-Party Workers' Organizations — 112
1.65 On the State Duma — 113
1.66 On Relations between the Duma Fraction and the Central Committee — 114
1.67 On Partisan Activities — 114
1.68 On Trade Unions — 115

II All-Russian Conference of the RSDRP (July) — 115

1.69 [On Participation in the Elections to the III Duma] — 116
1.70 [On Alliances in the Duma Elections] — 117

III All-Russian Conference of the RSDRP (November) — 117

1.71 On Factional Centres and Strengthening of Ties between the Central Committee and the Local Organizations — 118
1.72 On Participation in the Bourgeois Press — 119

1908
Central Committee on Legal Activities (February–March) — 120

1.73 On Trade Unions — 121
1.74 [On Co-operatives] — 122

Plenum of the Central Committee (August) — 124

1.75 The Organization of the Central Committee — 125

December All-Russian Conference of the RSDRP (December) — 127

1.76	On the Tasks of the Party at the Present Moment	128
1.77	On the Reports to the Conference	129
1.78	On the Work of the Central Committee	129
1.79	On the Organizational Question	130
1.80	On the Unification of National Organizations at the Local Level	131
1.81	On the Social Democratic Duma Fraction	131

1910
Plenum of the Central Committee (January) — 134

1.82	Rules of the Central Committee	136
1.83	On the Central Organ	137
1.84	On Factional Centres	137
1.85	On the Newspaper *Pravda*	138
1.86	On the *Vpered* Group	138
1.87	On the Party School	138
1.88	On Derogations from Party Discipline	139
1.89	On Convening the Next All-Party Conference	139

1911
Meeting of Members of the Central Committee (May–June) — 141

1.90	On Calling a Party Conference	142
1.91	On Creating a Technical Commission	143

Bern Meeting (August) — 144

1.92	On the Attitude toward the Technical and Organizational Commissions	144
1.93	On the Party Conference	145

1912
Prague Conference of the RSDRP (January) — 146

1.94	Changes in the Organizational Rules of the Party	147
1.95	On the Party's Tasks at the Present Moment	148

1.96	On the Reports from the Local Organizations	148
1.97	On the Character and Organizational Forms of Party Work	149
1.98	On the Elections to the IV State Duma	150
1.99	On the Social Democratic Tasks in the Fight against Hunger	153
1.100	On the Attitude toward the Draft Duma Law on State Insurance for Workers	153
1.101	On the Central Organ	155
1.102	On Liquidationism and the Group of Liquidators	155
1.103	On the Party Organization Abroad	157

Paris Meeting (February) — 157

1.104	[On the Prague Conference]	158

August Conference (August) — 159

1.105	On the Organizational Committee	160
1.106	On Organizational Unity	160
1.107	On the Polish Socialist Party	161
1.108	On the Organizational Forms of Party Development	162
1.109	On the Economic Struggle	162
1.110	On Electoral Tactics	163
1.111	On Unity in the Election Campaign	164
1.112	On the Insurance Laws of 23 June 1912	165
1.113	On the Recent Events in the Army and the Navy	166
1.114	On the Question of National-Cultural Autonomy	167

1913
Cracow Meeting of the Central Committee (December 1912–January) — 168

1.115	On the Revolutionary Resurgence, Strikes, and the Party's Tasks	169
1.116	On the Structure of the Illegal Organization	170
1.117	On the Attitude toward Liquidationism and on Unity	172

1.118	On the 'National' Social Democratic Organizations	173
1.119	On the Insurance Campaign	174
1.120	On the Reorganization and Work of the *Pravda* Editorial Board	175

Poronin Meeting of the Central Committee (September–October)   177

1.121	On the Strike Movement	178
1.122	On the Party Press	179
1.123	On the Social Democratic Duma Fraction	180
1.124	On Work in Legal Organizations	180
1.125	On the Nationality Question	181
1.126	On the Organizational Question and the Party Congress	183

Meeting of the Central Committee (December)   183

1.127	On the Activities of the Russian Social Democratic Workers' Fraction	184
1.128	For the Guidance of *Pravda*'s Editors	186

1914
Meeting of the Central Committee (April)   187

1.129	On Calling the Party Congress	188
1.130	On Establishing an Organizational Section of the Central Committee for the Leadership of Underground Work	190

Central Committee on the War (September)   191

1.131	The War and Russian Social Democracy	192

1917
Russian Bureau of the Central Committee (February–March)   196

1.132	To All Citizens of Russia	198
1.133	On Tactical Tasks	199
1.134	[On the Question of the Publication of a Party Organ]	200
1.135	[On the Attitude toward the Soviet]	200

1.136	[On Relations between the Soviet of Workers' and Soldiers' Deputies and the Provisional Government]	200
1.137	On the War	201
1.138	[On the Return of Stalin, Kamenev, and Muranov]	202
1.139	[On the Question of *Pravda*]	203
1.140	[On the Editorial Board of *Pravda*]	203
1.141	[On Party Unity]	203
1.142	On Party Membership	204
1.143	On the Provisional Government	204
1.144	On War and Peace	205
	Menshevik Organizational Committee (March)	206
1.145	On the Attitude toward War and Peace	207
1.146	[On the Attitude toward the Provisional Government]	208
	All-Russian Meeting of Party Workers (March–April)	209
1.147	On the War	211
1.148	On the Attitude toward the Provisional Government	212
	Central Committee on the April Crisis (April)	213
1.149	On the Provisional Government's Note of 18 April 1917	214
1.150	[On Peaceful Demonstrations]	215
1.151	[On Dual Power]	216
	VII All-Russian Conference of the RSDRP (April)	217
1.152	On the War	218
1.153	On Uniting with the Internationalists against the Petty Bourgeois Defencist Bloc	219
1.154	On the Attitude toward the Provisional Government	220
1.155	On a Coalition Ministry	222
1.156	On the Soviets of Workers' and Soldiers' Deputies	222
1.157	On the Agrarian Question	224
1.158	On the Nationality Question	225

All-Russian Conference of Menshevik and United Organizations of the RSDRP (May) — 226

1.159 On the Attitude toward the Provisional Government — 228
1.160 On the War — 229
1.161 On Fraternization — 230
1.162 On the Attitude toward the Soviets of Workers' and Soldiers' Deputies — 230
1.163 On Labour Policy — 231
1.164 On Agrarian Policy — 232
1.165 On Party Unity — 233

Central Committee on Worker Control of Industry (May) — 234

1.166 On Measures to Cope with Economic Dislocation — 235

Central Committee on the June Demonstrations (June) — 236

1.167 Appeal to All Toilers, Workers, and Soldiers of Petrograd — 238
1.168 [On the Cancellation of the Planned Demonstration] — 239

Central Committee on the July Days (July) — 239

1.169 Appeal to the Workers and Soldiers of Petrograd — 240
1.170 On the Demonstration — 241
1.171 [On Accusations that Lenin is a German Agent] — 242

Menshevik Organizational Committee (July) — 243

1.172 [On the Current Situation] — 243

Expanded Meeting of the Central Committee (July) — 246

1.173 On the Current Situation — 247

VI Party Congress (July–August) — 249

1.174 Rules of the Russian Social Democratic Labour Party — 251
1.175 On the Current Situation and the War — 253
1.176 On the Political Situation — 254
1.177 On the Economic Situation — 255

1.178	On the Party and the Trade Union Movement	257
1.179	On the Electoral Campaign for the Constituent Assembly	257
1.180	On Propaganda	259
1.181	On Party Unification	260
1.182	On Comrade Lenin's Failure to Appear before the Court	260

Central Committee on the Subordination of the Military Organization (August) — 261

1.183	[On *Rabochii i soldat*]	262
1.184	[On the Publication of *Soldat*]	263
1.185	[On the Central Bureau of Military Organizations]	263

Menshevik 'Unification' Congress (August) — 264

1.186	On the Organization of the Party	265
1.187	On the Political Situation and the Tasks of the Party	267
1.188	On War and Peace	270
1.189	On Election Tactics and the Organization of the Election Campaign	271

Central Committee on the Kornilov Revolt (August) — 273

1.190	[Appeal Not to Yield to Provocation]	274
1.191	[Telegram to Local Party Organizations]	275
1.192	[On Activities in the Committee for the Struggle against Counter-Revolution]	275
1.193	[Appeal to All the Toilers, Workers, and Soldiers of Petrograd]	275

Central Committee on Preparations for the October Revolution (August–October) — 277

1.194	On Power	279
1.195	[Report of the Organizational Bureau]	281
1.196	[On a New Presidium for the Soviet of Workers' and Soldiers' Deputies]	281
1.197	[On Lenin's Suggestion to Seize Power]	282

CONTENTS xxxi

1.198	[On Participation in the Democratic Conference]	282
1.199	[On the Peace Declaration of the Democratic Conference]	283
1.200	[On Use of the Term 'Comrade']	283
1.201	[On the Pre-Parliament]	284
1.202	[On the Soviet of Workers' and Soldiers' Deputies]	284
1.203	On the Current Situation and the Tasks of the Proletariat	285
1.204	[On Calling an Extraordinary Party Congress]	286
1.205	[On Bolshevik Candidates for the Constituent Assembly]	287
1.206	[On the Situation in Moscow and the Return of Lenin]	287
1.207	[On Establishing a Bureau for Information on the Struggle against Counter-Revolution]	288
1.208	[On an Armed Uprising]	288
1.209	[On Establishing a Politburo]	289
1.210	[On the Armed Uprising]	289
1.211	[On the Military Revolutionary Centre]	289
1.212	[On the Actions of Zinoviev and Kamenev]	290
1.213	[Debate on the Military Revolutionary Committee]	290
1.214	[On the Executive Committee of the Petrograd Soviet]	291
1.215	[Debate on the II Congress of Soviets]	291
1.216	[On Defensive Preparations]	292
1.217	[Debate on Relations with the Central Executive Committee and on the Assignment of Central Committee Members]	292
1.218	[Debate on Establishing an Auxiliary Headquarters]	293
	Index	295

**The Russian Social Democratic Labour Party
1898–October 1917**

Introduction

In contrast to most revolutionary movements in western Europe and imperial Russia during the nineteenth century, the Russian Social Democratic Labour Party was not a temporary phenomenon with limited class and geographical appeal.[1] Whether one dates its beginnings from the formation of G.V. Plekhanov's Emancipation of Labour Group in 1883, or from its abortive I Congress in 1898, or from its truly constituent convention in 1903, the fact remains that the RSDRP was in existence for a relatively long period of time prior to its seizure of power in October 1917. During this period of gestation, the party's leadership formulated a theoretical programme in which they sought to adapt western marxism to Russian conditions; they established an organizational structure which sought to take into account police pressures in imperial Russia; and they developed various modes of operation in both illegal and legal institutions so as to broaden the party's influence. In the course of arriving at these programmatic, organizational, and functional decisions, disputes arose inside the party hierarchy which resulted in the formation of numerous factional and competing groups. While the ultimate success of one of these factions was more a consequence of the factors at play in 1917 than of pre-revolutionary developments, the fact remains that the Bolsheviks, after they achieved power, continued to be influenced by ideological and organizational principles formulated at congresses and conferences held long before the revolution.

I

The first official Programme of the RSDRP was drafted by the II Congress of the party in 1903 (1.3). It, however, was built on principles developed in the Emancipation of Labour programme of 1884[2] and in the Manifesto of the I Party Congress (1.1). These documents asserted that Russian economic development would indeed follow the pattern of the more advanced countries of western Europe, that Marx's precepts were therefore valid for

---

[1] In Russian the name of the party is Rossiiskaia Sotsial-demokraticheskaia Rabochaia Partiia, hereafter abbreviated as RSDRP.

[2] In G.V. Plekhanov, *Selected Philosophical Works* I (Moscow, 1959), 400–5.

Russia, but that differing social conditions and differing rates of development would cause variations in the Programme of the RSDRP from those of other social democratic parties. In particular, Plekhanov asserted that the masses of Russia were fettered by a double yoke – that of nascent capitalism and obsolescent patriarchial feudalism – and that the underdeveloped Russian middle class was incapable of taking the initiative (as it had done elsewhere in Europe) in the struggle against absolutism. Therefore, he concluded, 'the socialist intelligentsia' should not wait passively for the bourgeois revolution but rather 'has the obligation to organize the workers and prepare them as far as possible for the struggle against the present-day system of government as well as against the future bourgeois parties.'

The II Congress reiterated that the RSDRP had the same long-term objectives as the other European socialist parties: i.e., a 'social revolution' that would abolish private property, initiate a planned economy, eliminate class distinctions and economic exploitation, and result in the dictatorship of the proletariat. The Congress, however, devoted most of its Programme to elaborating its short-term tasks which might differ from those of other social democratic parties owing to the presence in Russia of remnants of the pre-capitalist order. The immediate task was seen as the overthrow of the autocracy and its replacement by a democratic republic. This republic would have a unicameral legislature elected by universal, direct, and secret suffrage; it would guarantee the basic freedoms, grant broad local self-government, and recognize the equality of all citizens.

Among the other short-term goals of the Programme were better labour legislation, agrarian reform, and recognition of the rights of the national minorities. The party's 'labour plank' called for an eight-hour day, limited night work, no overtime work, no child labour, no payment in kind, better factory health and safety inspection, and workers' insurance. The major agrarian objectives were the cancellation of the remaining redemption payments, confiscation of church and appanage land, return of lands cut off from peasant holdings at the time of the Emancipation, and removal of restrictions on peasant sale of land. The nationality programme was less precise but more sweeping. It called for the recognition of 'the right of self-determination for all nations forming part of the state,' the right to education in one's native language, and self-government for particular ethnic regions. In achieving these immediate goals, the party said it was willing 'to support any oppositional or revolutionary movement directed against the existing social and political order in Russia.'

Despite suggestions in 1914 and August 1917 that a new programme was needed, the 1903 document remained the party's basic theoretical statement of policy until March 1919. Subsequent congresses and conferences acknowledged the correctness of its theoretical assumptions and repeated its various slogans (1.76, 1.95). On occasion, certain aspects of the Programme were modified or expanded to fit current circumstances. The agrarian demands, for example, were expanded at the III and IV Party Congresses in light of the unexpected peasant unrest during the Revolution of 1905. The party supported seizure of noble land (1.23) and the transfer of all land to undefined municipal organizations (1.51). At what stage this was to take place and the ultimate fate of the land was never made clear. Similarly, the revival of national consciousness among the Russian minorities just before the war caused the Social Democrats to re-examine the nationality demands in their 1903 Programme. While the Mensheviks talked about recognizing the right of national-cultural autonomy at the Vienna Conference, they postponed action on the issue (1.114). The Bolsheviks, on the other hand, produced a sweeping resolution in September 1913 which recognized the right of regional autonomy and local self-government as well as defining self-determination to mean the 'right to secede and to form an independent state' (1.125). The privilege of exercising this right, however, was reserved to the centralized Social Democratic Party. Once again one notes a vagueness concerning when these rights were to be operative – before or after the socialist revolution.

Indeed, the party was vague throughout all its programmatic statements concerning the timing and alliances of the bourgeois and socialist revolutions as well as the policies that would follow each. It can be argued that this vagueness was intentional since the party wanted the support of all discontented groups in the overthrow of the autocracy and later of the bourgeoisie, but it did not want to be bound by precise principles at any stage of revolutionary development. Thus the 1903 Programme, as modified by subsequent pre-revolutionary congresses and conferences, remained a series of opportunistic slogans that in no way offered a blueprint of how the party was to operate once it came to power.

II

Perhaps more important than the theoretical task of adapting marxism to Russian conditions was the practical task of creating a revolutionary organization. Unlike most western European social democratic parties, the RSDRP could not operate legally and openly in tsarist Russia but instead had to adjust itself to very stringent police conditions. Just as Marx had little to say about the objectives of a socialist party in a pre-capitalistic order, so also he offered little guidance for Social Democrats seeking to build an underground organization. The organizational principles and practices of the RSDRP, therefore, had to be developed on a trial-and-error basis before the revolution and were in turn a significant contribution to revolutionary marxism of the twentieth century.

Prior to the II Party Congress, Russian social democracy had very little cohesion. Scattered groups, patterned after the St Petersburg Union of Struggle for the Emancipation of Labour, grew up in various Russian cities during the 1890s. The I Party Congress in 1898 tried with very limited success to give them a focal point through the establishment of a Central Committee. During the first three years of the twentieth century, the distribution network of the émigré newspaper *Iskra* (The Spark) served to unite and to co-ordinate these scattered groups as well as to call a second congress that would create a firmer organizational structure. This Congress, when it met in 1903, adopted Rules that defined party membership, the responsibilities of party officers, and the structure of the party from its congress at the top to the factory organization on the local level. These Rules, as amended by subsequent congresses and Central Committee plenums, offer an interesting picture of how an illegal underground party should be built.

'The supreme organ of the party,' according to the Rules (1.4, 1.16, 1.50, 1.174), was its congress. Congresses were to be called annually or biennially by the Central Committee or, failing this, at the request of local organizations representing at least one-half of the party's membership. These were the great gatherings of the clan when up to 300 underground leaders met for two or three weeks in western Europe with their émigré bosses. The norms of representation varied from one or two delegates per local committee meeting certain membership and longevity requirements to one delegate for every 500 or 1000 local party members. Elections were supervised in most cases by a local control commission and verified in all cases by a congressional Mandates Commission. Delegates were elected by factional affiliation, they were seated by faction, and they were subject to factional discipline during the debates of the congress.

While the powers of a congress were never clearly defined, they were by implication unlimited. In theory, a congress could pass binding legislation, decide future policy, change party Rules, and appoint a Central Committee and other central institutions to execute these decisions. In practice, it delegated many of these responsibilities to the bodies it created and indeed it gradually delegated its powers of appointment as well. One of the reasons for this abdication of authority was that because of size, length, factional differences, and police pressures, congresses were difficult to call and expensive to run. Thus, despite statutory regulations, no party congresses met in the decade preceding the revolution.[3]

The party, nevertheless, needed some form of national meeting that could make interim decisions. A partial solution was found in party conferences which could be called with less attention to formal election require-

---

3 Attempts were made to call congresses in 1909 and 1914 (1.129) but because of factional disagreements and the advent of the war both initiatives failed.

ments. While the III Congress in 1905 had recognized the need for 'periodic conferences,' no provisions for them were incorporated into the party Rules until the London Congress requested that the Central Committee call a meeting every three or four months of representatives of regional and national party organizations (1.62; see also 1.89). These were to be purely deliberative gatherings whose resolutions required Central Committee approval. By implication, they did not possess the power of a congress to change the composition of national committees or the wording of party Rules.

The party held six 'official' pre-revolutionary conferences. These, in comparison with party congresses, had the distinct advantages of being smaller (average number of voting delegates was 26), shorter (average length was seven days), and cheaper. Four of these more or less satisfied the requirements set down by the London Congress while the so-called I and VI (Prague) conferences were convened by bodies other than the Central Committee and were less representative. At least as valid as these two gatherings were the three Menshevik conferences held in Geneva (April 1905, 1.29–1.38), St Petersburg (November 1905, 1.40–1.42), and Vienna (August 1912, 1.105–1.114).

Between party congresses and conferences, the RSDRP was run by the Central Committee and its auxiliary bodies. The I Congress had designated the Central Committee as the chief 'executive organ' of the party (1.2) and it retained this pre-eminent position through most of the pre-war period.[4] Its far-ranging powers included convening party congresses and conferences, appointing one or more editors of the Central Organ, managing the party treasury, publishing and distributing certain types of party literature, resolving conflicts between different party institutions, representing the RSDRP in relations with other revolutionary groups, and 'generally co-ordinating and directing all the activity of the party' (1.4, 1.16, 1.50). The Committee was appointed by the party congress and reflected on the basis of proportional representation the factional composition of the congress. The size of the body varied from three members in 1903 to fifteen in 1907 with provisions being added at the Unification and London Congresses for an additional fifteen and thirty candidate members.

One of the major difficulties facing the Central Committee was the local insistence that it function inside imperial Russia rather than abroad. Owing to police surveillance and the reluctance of some party leaders to work in the underground, activity by the Committee in Russia was extremely difficult. As already noted, the party tried to compensate for anticipated decimation of the Committee by increasing its size and provid-

---

4 Briefly, from 1903 to 1905, the Central Committee was subordinate to the party Council. The latter body, however, was abolished at the III Congress (see 1.4, 1.16).

ing for candidate members. After 1910, the restrictions on co-opting additional members were relaxed somewhat (1.82) so as to keep the Committee operative. Nevertheless, despite these measures and statutory requirements that it meet every month or three months (1.75, 1.82), the Committee convened very irregularly. The editors of *KPSS v rezoliutsiiakh*, for instance, include the resolutions of only three formal plenums in the prerevolutionary period (August and December 1908 and January 1910, all of which met abroad). Unquestionably, the body met more frequently on an informal basis and its members from time to time also issued letters, leaflets, and resolutions in its name (see 1.49, 1.73, 1.74, 1.131). This relative inactivity, however, was noted by several party conferences and it also invited other groups to act in its place, as was the case with V.I. Lenin's 1911 'meeting of Central Committee members living abroad' (1.90, 1.91) and the resultant Menshevik meeting in Bern (1.92, 1.93). After the Prague Conference, Lenin's restructured Central Committee conferred on some twelve occasions; while four of these meetings included representatives from the Duma and the Social Democratic underground (1.115–1.130), none satisfied the statutory requirements for formal party plenums.

Because of its diversified responsibilities and its inability to meet regularly, the Central Committee found it necessary to create several auxiliary bodies in Russia and western Europe. If the Central Committee itself could not operate effectively in Russia, it was hoped that at least a small portion of that body could be physically present so as to co-ordinate the activities of the scattered Social Democratic groups, provide a modicum of revolutionary leadership, and generally serve as the focal point for underground operations. For these reasons, a five- to seven-man subcommittee of the Central Committee – variously entitled the uzkii sostav, the suzhennyi sostav, the Russian Board, and the Russian Bureau – was appointed by the parent body to serve as its liaison with the underground inside imperial Russia.[5] This subcommittee, which existed on paper from 1908 to 1914, was plagued throughout its existence by police pressures and factional differences. It is doubtful whether it ever achieved any of its stated objectives before the Bolshevik deputies to the IV Duma took advantage of their parliamentary immunities to serve as a de facto Russian revolutionary centre on the eve of the First World War.

The August 1908 Plenum, which first established the above-mentioned subcommittee, also created a Foreign Bureau of the Central

---

5 See the elaborate operating rules drafted by the August 1908 (1.75) and the January 1910 (1.82) plenums of the Central Committee for more detail on the composition and functions of this body.

Committee to co-ordinate the activities of the numerous Social Democratic groups in western Europe (1.75). The Foreign Bureau had ample precedent in the Union of Russian Social Democrats Abroad (1894), the Foreign League of Russian Revolutionary Social Democrats (1901), and the Committee of Foreign Organizations (1904), all of which tried to organize and discipline the factious groups in emigration. The Bureau, which was subordinate to the subcommittee and through it to the Central Committee, was composed of three to five members of the Central Committee, usually living in the same western European city. Their specific responsibilities included, in addition to supervising the various émigré groups, collecting membership dues abroad, representing the Central Committee in dealings with other social democratic parties, and maintaining contact with the subcommittee. After 1910 it also printed and transported illegal party literature to Russia and had the right to call meetings of the Central Committee (1.82). In 1911 Lenin used its failure to exercise this right to establish a competing Foreign Organizational Commission and a Technical Commission (1.90, 1.91) which assumed the Foreign Bureau's various responsibilities and worked to convene the Prague Conference. These ad hoc bodies were in turn replaced by a Committee of Foreign Organizations which was duly confirmed by the Prague Conference as the official co-ordinating body for all émigré groups wishing to have contacts with the underground (1.103).

One of the most important national-level bodies of the RSDRP was its Central Organ or official party newspaper. 'The editorial board of the Central Organ,' according to the Rules of the II Congress, 'provides ideological leadership for the party' (1.4) through a discussion of the theoretical issues confronting the RSDRP. In addition, the Central Organ could unite isolated underground groups through its distribution network and by publishing accounts about what other organizations were doing; it could inform local units of central party decisions in the long intervals between congresses and conferences; it could print sample leaflets suitable for local reproduction; it could expose suspected provocateurs; and it could publicize instances of political or economic abuse.

The party had a variety of pre-revolutionary Central Organs: *Rabochaia gazeta* (The Worker's Newspaper, 1.2), the short-lived Kievan journal named by the I Congress; *Iskra*, the de facto organ before the II Congress and the de jure after (1.8); *Proletarii* (The Proletarian), the Bolshevik creation of the III Congress to challenge the 'new' or Menshevik *Iskra* (1.18); and *Sotsial-demokrat* (The Social Democrat), the irregularly published Central Organ from 1906 to 1917. The editorial boards of these papers varied in size from three to six members who were appointed either by a party congress or, as was the case after 1907, by the Central Committee. Because of the paper's far-ranging responsibilities and its potentially great influence over the party, some of the leading pre-revolutionary Social Democrats sat on its board: Plekhanov, Lenin, I.O. Martov, F.I. Dan, L.B. Kamenev, G.E. Zinoviev, and A.A. Bogdanov.

With the exception of a brief period during and after the 1905 Revolution, the Central Organ was published abroad so as to avoid police interference and was then smuggled into imperial Russia. As a result of the unavoidable time lapse and physical separation, workers in the underground often complained that the party's chief newspaper was irrelevant to local needs and conditions. They also criticized with just cause the excessively intellectual tone and theoretical approach of the newspaper which made it difficult reading for many of the poorly educated rank-and-file party members.[6] The party leadership recognized these weaknesses and sought rather unsuccessfully to correct them by passing resolutions on the question (1.9, 1.31, 1.101) or by establishing 'organs of the Central Committee' that would be more popular in tone and broader in appeal (1.85). In part to compensate for the short-comings in the Central Organ and in part to express their own divergent views, most of the factions of the party after 1903 published their own newspapers which they dispatched to the local organizations. Among these were the Bolshevik *Proletarii*, the left-Bolshevik *Vpered* (Forward), L.D. Trotsky's *Pravda* (Truth), Plekhanov's *Dnevnik Sotsial-demokrata* (Diary of a Social Democrat), and the Mensheviks' *Golos Sotsial-demokrata* (The Voice of a Social Democrat).

Besides organizing on the national level, the RSDRP also tried to create regional bodies inside imperial Russia that could co-ordinate more directly the activities of the local organizations. These bodies, which were made up of representatives from the city committees in their region, were known as unions (soiuz) or after 1906 as regional (oblast) committees and were most notably operative in the Urals, the Caucasus, the Crimea, the Donets Basin, and in the Central Industrial Region. In addition to co-ordinating local activities and providing ideological leadership, these regional bodies also approved the formation of new committees, shored up weak committees, held their own conferences, in some cases published their own newspapers, and elected representatives to party congresses and conferences (1.79). Like the subcommittees of the Central Committee, however, these regional groups proved vulnerable to police infiltration and factional manipulation. As a result, few were in existence after 1907 and, despite Lenin's

---

6 These criticisms were voiced in a candid fashion in the very interesting local correspondence to the editors of the various émigré presses. See, for instance, *Sotsial-demokrat*, nos 7/8 (9 August 1909): 10; *Sotsial-demokrat*, no. 9 (31 October 1909): 6; *Golos Sotsial-demokrata*, no. 12 (March 1909): 16.

efforts to revive them on the eve of the war (1.129), most local organizations were left to their own devices.[7]

If the superstructure of the Social Democratic Party were the regional and national organizations, then the base was made up of its factory cells, raion collectives, and city committees. The congresses and conferences of the RSDRP gave surprisingly little attention to the structure of these grassroots organizations. Outside of several resolutions (1.5, 1.25, 1.80) calling for the co-ordination or unification of the various national parties (the Polish Social Democrats, the Latvian Social Democrats, and the members of the Jewish Bund) with their Russian counterparts on the local level, only the Menshevik Conferences of April and November 1905 passed guidelines to help underground committees in building their illegal organization (1.30, 1.41). These committees, therefore, usually drew up their own variable statutes which very often expressed organizational aspirations rather than operational reality.[8]

To be a member of the RSDRP a worker had to accept the party Programme, subordinate himself to party decisions, pay party dues, and belong to a party cell (iacheika) which was usually located in his place of employment. These cells, which had from five to thirty members, met weekly or bi-weekly to hear reports, to discuss party literature, and to elect representatives to a raion collective.[9] The cell representatives in turn took responsibility for arranging cell meetings, collecting dues, distributing literature and generally serving as a liaison between the cell and the collective.

7 The party on occasion also tried to form provincial (guberniia) or district (okrug) organizations to co-ordinate activities on a smaller scale than the regional bodies. These intermediary organizations, however, were not as widespread and were equally unsuccessful.

8 Examples of these rules, which are not reproduced herein, can be found in *Bol'sheviki Ukrainy v period mezhdu pervoi i vtoroi burzhuazno-demokraticheskimi revoliutsiiami v Rossii: sbornik dokumentov i materialov* (Kiev, 1960) for Ekaterinoslav, Nikolaev, and the Donets Basin; *Golos Sotsial-demokrata*, nos 8/9 (July/September 1908): 38 for Kharkov; and *Sotsial-demokrat*, nos 7/8 (8 August 1909): 9 for St Petersburg. The following description of the underground structure on the local level is a composite of these rules. Very often the names of particular bodies would vary from city to city and indeed the presence of party bodies on all three local levels at any one time was problematical.

9 If a factory had several cells, each would elect a representative to a factory committee; if the city itself were large and had many cells, each cell would also elect a representative to a subraion committee. These intermediary bodies met every two weeks to co-ordinate party work in their factories or districts.

Most Russian cities were divided for party and administrative purposes into three to five geographical raions, each of which was serviced by a raion collective composed of six to twelve cell representatives. The collective, which was supposed to meet bi-weekly, was responsible for all technical work in the raion: collecting dues, recruiting new members, authorizing strikes, arranging for local agitation and propaganda. In practice, it usually delegated these responsibilities to its executive or leadership commission composed of the secretary-organizer, treasurer, propagandist, and perhaps the party printing press manager or librarian. These salaried officers, ideally professional revolutionaries drawn from the ranks of the intelligentsia, represented the core of the underground organization and their efficiency or lack of it usually determined the success or failure of local party operations.

At the apex of the local organization stood the city-wide (obshchegorodskoi) committee which in theory provided overall ideological and political leadership as well as co-ordinating the technical and organizational work of the raion collectives. These committees were also responsible for publishing local leaflets and underground newspapers, establishing contacts with other city committees and the émigré centres, and electing representatives to party congresses and conferences. They were composed of a half-dozen or so elected members, chosen either directly by the cells or (as was usually the case) indirectly by the raion collectives or their executive commissions, plus several co-opted non-voting members. City-wide committees might be assisted in their operations by auxiliary groups, such as a College of Propagandists or a Military Organization (see 1.5, 1.54, 1.183–1.185), and were guided by their own executive commissions and by the decisions of infrequent city-wide conferences.

While these committees functioned in many areas of Russia from 1900 to 1906, their obvious importance and conspicuousness made them logical targets for police attention. Thus, from 1907 to 1917, many were inoperative and their responsibilities for guiding the party's illegal and legal activities on the local level very often devolved upon the raion collectives.

III
Besides formulating a theoretical programme and creating a revolutionary organization, the leaders of the RSDRP also had to find ways of developing class consciousness among the Russian proletariat and of broadening the party's appeal among the Russian population as a whole. The presence of censorship and the absence of legal trade unions and parliamentary institutions before 1906 meant that the RSDRP could not achieve these ends by using the usual legal means employed by the social democratic parties in most western European countries. The party therefore devoted considerable attention at its congresses to developing illegal forms of propaganda

and agitation by which it might spread the social democratic idea (see 1.10, 1.17, 1.79, 1.97, 1.122).

One way of popularizing the party's slogans and elucidating its ideological concepts was through the distribution in the underground of the Central Organ and the various émigré factional newspapers. As already noted, however, these journalistic efforts were handicapped by their infrequent appearance, excessively intellectual tone, factional content, and lack of local relevance. Thus, many of the larger underground organizations attempted to publish their own illegal newspapers. The mere appearance of an underground newspaper gave the workers renewed confidence in their movement as well as fulfilling in a more timely and topical fashion the organizational, agitational, and propagandistic functions of the émigré press. These ventures, however, were difficult, dangerous, and expensive. The organization had to have access to a large and costly typographical press; it needed supplies of ink, paper, and type; it required someone who knew how to run the press, set the type and compose the articles; and it had to be adept at conspiratorial techniques so as to conceal these activities from the police and to distribute the final product among the workers. As a result, the life of such papers was usually short. Only a very few, such as *Iuzhnyi rabochii* (The Southern Worker), stayed in existence for more than a year; most would publish only three or four issues before being closed by the police. By the spring of 1910, all of the underground papers in Russia had disappeared. Although a few revived in the two years before the war, most local organizations looked to other means of propaganda.

A more practical alternative was to publish illegal leaflets which were easier and less expensive to produce. Leaflets required less education and experience to compose; indeed, they could be copied if necessary from samples sent by other organizations or from abroad. They could be run off simply and cheaply on a hectograph or mimeograph machine if a typographical press was unavailable. And several thousand one-page leaflets could be distributed rapidly outside factory gates, in workers' quarters, or even on street corners. Leaflets played an organizational role in calling on the proletariat to join the party and trade unions and in popularizing the party's Programme and slogans. They served a propaganda function by explaining the theoretical and historical significance of such events as May Day, Bloody Sunday, and the Lena massacre. Above all, they provided a good means of agitating the workers by calling attention to examples of police brutality, mine disasters, construction accidents, and the prevalence of famine. Leaflets could also be used to agitate against particular economic abuses, to foment new strikes, and to rally support for existing strikes.

One of the most important forms of illegal activity carried out by the party was kruzhkovshchina or circle work. Many leaders of the RSDRP never accepted the marxian postulate that workers could acquire class consciousness through their economic and social environment alone. They stressed instead the need to accelerate this process by increasing class awareness through systematic study and instruction. This was done through propaganda circles where party workers heard lectures, read books, and discussed social questions. The larger organizations subdivided their circles by age, sex, occupation, education, or most commonly, by number of years in the party. The latter delineation resulted in 'circles of the lower type,' which had an elementary curriculum designed to inform participants about the basic tenets of socialism and the party Programme; 'circles of the middle type'; and 'circles of the higher type,' which read and discussed works by contemporary socialists as well as by Marx and Engels. These study circles usually were small, ranging in size from six to fifteen workers who ideally met conspiratorially once a week. Since the success of these ventures depended on the availability of adequate reading material and of trained propagandists, the II and III Party Congresses suggested that the Central Committee develop study guides and pamphlets as well as sending experienced propagandists from city to city (1.10, 1.17).

Most Social Democrats felt that propaganda alone was not enough and that it had to be supplemented with practical agitation aimed at a broader audience. Agitation was intended to arouse popular emotions over specific grievances and to produce more immediate results in the form of resolutions, demonstrations, or strikes. Agitation took various forms. As already noted, underground leaflets and newspapers were used to call the workers' attention to specific instances of economic exploitation or political oppression. Agitation was also carried out at two types of public meetings: letuchki and massovki. A letuchka or 'flying meeting' was usually held in the courtyard or outside the gates of a factory. Occasionally these meetings would attract several thousand workers who would receive leaflets, hear an impromptu speech by an agitator, and perhaps pass a resolution on some particular question. Massovki were customarily held in a wood or other isolated spot outside an industrial city where several hundred workers would gather on Sunday or a holiday for a picnic augmented by speeches calling on them to join the party or to participate in some party project, demonstration, or strike.

The demonstrations which agitational leaflets and meetings tried to provoke 'constituted one of the most important techniques for the political education of the broad mass of the people and for spreading and strengthening the influence of the Social Democratic Party' (1.13). The party stressed that these demonstrations should not be incited artificially, that extensive preliminary agitation was necessary, and that the local organization should organize the hard core of the demonstrators which would try to control events. Suitable occasions for such demonstrations were May Day, the anniversaries of Bloody Sunday, and the Lena massacre, and in periods of revolutionary unrest such as in St Petersburg during 1905 and July 1914.

Except under unusual circumstances, the party sought to avoid armed clashes with the police and the army during these demonstrations. It also traditionally opposed armed expropriations of funds from banks or post offices, the assassination of political figures, and the destruction of public or private property. Most Social Democrats before 1905 felt that these acts of spontaneous and senseless violence or terrorism could in no way strengthen class consciousness; indeed, they only diverted the workers' attention and expended their resources. In 1905, however, circumstances changed. The planning and execution of an armed uprising became 'one of the most important and urgent tasks' facing the party (1.19). The workers were armed; 'fighting squads' (boevye druzhiny) were organized; counter-terror against the Black Hundreds and expropriations were tacitly justified (1.21, 1.32, 1.54) and openly executed. As the chances for a successful revolution receded in 1906 and 1907, however, the party officially reverted to its original position by condemning expropriations and assassinations as 'anarchistic methods of struggle [which] disorganize the ranks of the proletariat [and] obscure its class-consciousness' (1.67; see also 1.55, 1.88). At the same time 'fighting squads,' which had continued these activities in some areas, were ordered disbanded as the party sought to return to more peaceful forms of illegal activity.

The Revolution of 1905 had two other profound effects on the party's operations. First, many of the Social Democratic intelligentsia, who had provided the party with the majority of its organizers, agitators, and propagandists, chose not to return to the underground after the failure of the long-sought revolution (1.79). Many were in prison or had emigrated; others resumed their education or sought new legal forms of political activity. This meant that the underground newspapers, propaganda circles, and agitational efforts which had depended so heavily on the intelligentsia would be hard-pressed unless new worker cadres could be trained through party schools (1.87) or other means. The second effect of 1905 was that the concessions forced from the tsar during that year opened up new opportunities for the party to broaden its influence. The legalization of workers' associations or trade unions, the establishment of the State Duma, the easing of restrictions on the worker press, and the later formation of workers' insurance organizations meant that the party could now carry out much of its agitation and propaganda through legal institutions and by legal means. This, together with the loss of the underground leadership, caused the RSDRP to concentrate more of its attention on the type of legal activity traditionally carried out by other social democratic parties.

The term 'legal activity' was in some respects a misnomer since the work the party conducted within the Duma, trade unions, the legal press, insurance groups, and other so-called 'legal' worker organizations was in many cases implicitly illegal and aimed at promoting revolutionary change. In this sense, these groups can best be understood as 'front organizations' through which the party sought to broaden its appeal and disguise its operations. The party stressed on numerous occasions that agitational, propagandistic, and organizational activities within these legal groups should remain under the strict guidance of the illegal party organization and if possible of party cells within them (see 1.22, 1.37, 1.79, 1.97, 1.124).

The legal activity that received the most attention at party congresses and conferences was work within the State Duma. At first, the party recommended boycotting the proposed Duma on the grounds that it was a constitutional illusion that could only create false hopes among the workers (1.48). But after it became evident that the workers and peasants had voted nevertheless, often returning the most radical candidates available, the party reversed its position and participated in the elections to the II, III and IV Dumas (1.56, 1.69, 1.98, 1.110). The RSDRP and especially the Bolsheviks never had much faith in the Duma's ability or desire to pass constructive labour legislation. Rather, they sought to use the Duma as a forum from which they could expose the true nature of the autocracy, the hypocrisy of the liberals, the oppression of the masses, and the futility of parliamentary institutions in contemporary Russian society (1.69). Through the interpellation of ministers and the presentation of motions, Social Democratic deputies could also disseminate revolutionary slogans and offer socialist solutions for social and economic problems. The agitational value of these speeches was enhanced by the fact that newspapers were allowed to print the stenographic reports of Duma debates. Thus, close ties developed between workers' newspapers and the deputies who in addition served as editors, contributors, and solicitors of subscriptions. Through correspondence and personal visits, the deputies used their political immunity to help co-ordinate Social Democratic activity in their constituencies and generally to further the illegal interests of the party (1.127). The Bolshevik deputies to the IV Duma even functioned as an unofficial Russian Bureau of the Central Committee. Because of the agitational and organizational importance of the fraction, the Central Committee sought to insure that the deputies operated under the constant supervision and direction of the party's central institutions (1.56, 1.66 and 1.81) and that they would not become an extra-party organization as was the case with most socialist parliamentary groups in western Europe.

The party was somewhat ambivalent concerning its attitude toward trade unions. Prior to 1906, many Social Democrats felt that the western type of unions, with their emphasis on improving economic conditions, would distract the workers from more important political tasks.[10] But the spontaneous growth of these organizations during 1905 and their legalization in 1906 forced the Unification Congress to recommend that Social Democrats join non-party unions which would remain neutral on political issues. A year later, the London Congress rejected trade union neutrality and called instead for the formation of 'party unions' which would be controlled by the underground and would emphasize political agitation (1.57, 1.68). However, the restrictive nature of the 4 March 1906 law permitting 'worker associations,' the strict police interpretation of this law, and the legalistic sentiments of many of the trade union leaders made party unions virtually impossible. About the best the RSDRP could hope for was the formation of a Social Democratic fraction within existing unions that would try to influence the union leadership and to carry out indoctrinational work through worker libraries, discussion groups, and occasionally propaganda circles within the union (1.97). Trade unions also provided a convenient cover for party meetings and a place to recruit new party members. The natural alliance between trade unionism and social democracy that developed in many western European countries, however, was not evident in Russia before 1917.

During 1912, two other possibilities for legal activity – legal journalism and penetration of worker insurance groups – assumed new importance. Social Democrats had, of course, used legally published books and journals as a means for marxian elaboration and theoretical disputation since the 1890s. The propagandistic value of these efforts, however, was diminished by the fact that authors had to be circumspect through the use of Aesopian language and that censorship imposed severe limitations on subject matter. As a result of police conditions after 1906, only two Social Democratic journals – *Prosveshchenie* (Enlightenment) and *Nasha zaria* (Our Dawn) – managed to publish for more than two years. Legally published workers' newspapers, which concentrated more on agitation than propaganda by calling attention to economic abuses and worker protests, suffered the same fate between 1906 and 1911. As a result, Social Democrats were forced to utilize trade union or liberal bourgeois papers which the party rarely controlled but which accepted Social Democratic contributions and occasionally included party members on their editorial boards (see 1.72 for party restrictions on this type of activity).

After 1911, a relaxation of the censorship laws and a dissatisfaction with other legal and illegal alternatives resulted in renewed party interest in

---

[10] See, for instance, Lenin's view in his *Polnoe Sobranie Sochinenii* XI (Moscow, 1960), 111–12, and the hesitant resolution of the II Congress (1.14).

publishing both local and national workers newspapers (see 1.122). Among the latter the most notable were *Zvezda* (Star), published once to three times a week from December 1910 to April 1912; *Luch* (The Ray), the Menshevik daily published in St Petersburg from September 1912 to July 1913; and *Luch*'s more famous competitor, *Pravda* (April 1912 to July 1914 with variations in title). The editors of *Pravda*, in particular, tried to put out a popular product that in contrast to the émigré papers was less theoretical and more relevant. It carried regular columns on the trade union movement, Duma activity, and worker insurance matters as well as voluminous correspondence from worker organizations. In contrast to the émigré journals and earlier legal newspapers, *Pravda*'s content was less explicitly agitational and propagandistic. Perhaps for this reason, it appealed to a broader audience and was circulated to over a thousand points in European Russia, thereby providing a degree of national co-ordination and communication that had been lacking since 1905. Perhaps for the same reason, Lenin criticized the paper for trying to be too popular and conciliatory. On several occasions his Central Committee either criticized the content of the paper, changed its editorial board, or sought to bring it under more direct central party control (1.120, 1.127, 1.128). The censor, however, was sufficiently aware of the paper's popularity and national scope, and of party influence on it, that he confiscated 155 of its 645 editions, fined its editors on 36 occasions, and jailed them on several others.

The two workers' insurance acts which received imperial approval on 23 June 1912 offered a new opportunity for the RSDRP to organize and influence the proletariat through legal means. The sickness funds, insurance councils, and provincial insurance offices which the acts set up were to have elected worker representatives. The party utilized these election campaigns to attack the limited scope and the class nature of the law as well as to promote its own candidates (1.100, 1.112, 1.119). Numerous party members were in fact elected and often used their new positions as a legitimate 'cover' for distributing Social Democratic literature, conducting propaganda circles, and revitalizing local party operations.

While the Duma, trade unions, workers' newspapers, and the insurance organizations were the most prominent legitimate outlets available to the party, they were by no means the only legal opportunities. Indeed, the RSDRP found that any group which brought workers together without overtly violating tsarist regulations could be used to organize or at least to propagandize the non-Social Democratic masses (see 1.97). Among the other legal groups which the party tried to exploit before the war were: co-operatives (1.74); congresses of various types (anti-prostitution, anti-alcohol, factory doctors, artisans, women's groups, adult education and co-operative institutions); mutual aid, enlightenment, thrift, fire protection and temperance societies; workers' clubs, technical schools, workers' banks, and the 'political' Red Cross.[11]

IV

It was almost inevitable that differences of opinion among the party leadership would arise during the course of arriving at the programmatic, organizational, and functional decisions discussed above. These differences were subsequently magnified by the hothouse atmosphere of émigré life and by personality clashes, with the result that they all too often received organizational expression.

One of the principal and continuing areas of disagreement concerned the relationship between legal and illegal activity. One of its earliest manifestations was the controversy over 'Legal Marxism.' While most of the Social Democratic leaders in the 1890s had used legal publications to spread marxian ideas in a circumspect fashion, several Russian counterparts of Eduard Bernstein (most notably P.B. Struve and S.N. Bulgakov) wanted to restrict party activity to legal journalism and eventually to the achieving of socialism through evolutionary and solely constitutional means. At the turn of the century, another group of marxists known as the 'Economists' sought to concentrate the party's attentions on winning economic improvements for the workers through spontaneous strikes rather than developing their class consciousness through agitation and propaganda that would lead to lasting political change. Both of these tendencies were opposed by the orthodox marxists on *Iskra*'s editorial board and were condemned as heresies by the II and III Party Congresses (1.3, 1.11, 1.14 and 1.26).

A variation of this argument emerged after the 1905 Revolution had forced the government to grant certain legal concessions. Some right-wing Mensheviks, whom Lenin labelled the 'Liquidators,' advocated using the Duma, trade unions, co-operatives, workers' clubs, and the popular press to further the workers' interests through legal means at the expense of illegal agitation and propaganda within these groups which might have compromised their existence. Lenin charged incorrectly that they thereby sought to 'liquidate' the underground party and cited their reluctance to participate in the illegal Russian subcommittee of the Central Committee as

[11] This organization gave financial assistance to political prisoners or exiles and occasionally smuggled manuscripts out of prison or gave money directly to the party for disbursement among needy Social Democrats. Originally composed of sympathetic but non-party intellectuals, the RSDRP took steps after 1911 to infiltrate the 'political' Red Cross and to subordinate its branches to local party organizations (see *KPSS v rezoliutsiiakh* 1, 343).

evidence (see 1.77). The opposite viewpoint, that is, that the party should function only through illegal organizations, also found adherents after 1906. These left-wing Bolsheviks, who later become known collectively as the Vperedists, felt that participation in bodies like the Duma[12] and trade unions would only result in the workers gaining the mistaken impression that they could achieve their political goals through legal means. The party condemned both liquidationism and Vperedism at the January 1910 Plenum of the Central Committee but stopped short of expelling their adherents as Lenin desired.

There were also differences over organizational matters within the party. The most notable of these was, of course, between the Mensheviks and the Bolsheviks. The attempt to implement the organizational principles inherent in Lenin's *What Is To Be Done?* at the II Congress led to the well-known split in 1903. Lenin's emphasis on a conspiratorial, highly centralized, and rigidly disciplined party, while alien to Marx and to western European marxism, had lasting effects on the Russian revolutionary movement[13] and on the structure of the future Communist Party of the Soviet Union.

One of the most vexing organizational problems for the RSDRP was its relationship with non-Russian socialists in the various parts of the empire. At one time or another between 1898 and 1914 the party entered into negotiations concerning organizational unity with social democratic groups in Poland, Lithuania, the Latvian Region, the Ukraine, Armenia, Finland, and of course with the Jewish Bund. Differences of opinion usually occurred over two questions: the degree of autonomy these groups would have within the RSDRP and the degree of independence their nations would have within the post-revolutionary Russian state.

On the first question, the Russian Social Democrats in general (and Lenin in particular) wished to limit the federative status the minorities

---

12 Some left-wing Bolsheviks felt that the party should 'boycott' the Duma elections altogether (Boycotters), others that the Central Committee should 'recall' elected deputies (Otzovists). Some of these same individuals also held religious ('God-contructionism') and philosophical (Machism) views at variance with those of the orthodox marxists, or at least with those of Lenin. For a more detailed discussion of these left-Bolshevik beliefs, see Dietrich Grille's *Lenins Rivale* (Cologne, 1966).

13 Readers might profitably compare the organizational resolutions of the Bolshevik III Congress (1.16, 1.28), so-called I (1.46) and VI (1.94, 1.97, 1.102, 1.103) conferences with the nearly concurrent resolutions of the Menshevik conferences in April 1905 (1.29, 1.30), November 1905 (1.41), and August 1912 (1.106, 1.108). The Menshevik resolutions to date have only been available in scarce Russian editions published shortly after the respective conferences.

sought within the RSDRP (1.6, 1.25). The Bund (the General Jewish Workers Union of Russia and Poland, changed in 1901 to the General Jewish Workers' Union of Lithuania, Poland, and Russia), which had been formed in 1897 and a year later was one of the constituent forces in the founding of the RSDRP, left the party in 1903 when it was denied the right to speak for all Jewish proletarians in Russia (1.7). When the federative limitations were relaxed somewhat at the Unification Congress, the Bund rejoined the party (1.59). This also led to merger with Social Democracy of Poland and Lithuania[14] (1.58), the Latvian Social Democratic Labour Party,[15] and the Ukrainian Social Democratic Union ('Spilka').[16] All but Spilka were given the right to have their own Central Committees, central organs, and congresses as well as to participate in the central institutions of the RSDRP. Given the virtual parity of Menshevik and Bolshevik forces between 1906 and 1911, this participation put the national organizations in a position to determine party policy. At first, this worked to the advantage of the Bolsheviks since they had the backing of the Poles and the Latvians while the Bund usually lined up behind the Mensheviks. In 1911 and 1912, however, the Poles and the Latvians began to waver owing to a dislike of Lenin's overt centralism, his growing factionalism, his meddling in the internal affairs of their parties, and his rethinking of Social Democratic nationality policy.

Most of these ethnic regions also had more nationalistic wings to their socialist parties which occasionally flirted with the RSDRP in the hope that they might gain some assurances concerning the future independence of their nations in return for joining forces with the RSDRP. Since the Russian Social Democrats for a long time refused to go beyond the vague slogans of

---

14 Social Democracy of the Kingdom of Poland, which had been formed in 1894 as an offshoot of the more nationalistic Polish Socialist Party (PPS) and had merged in 1899 with the Union of Workers of Lithuania, first sought to join the RSDRP at the latter's II Congress. This attempt failed, however, when the RSDRP refused to modify its position on self-determination which the Poles considered to be a violation of socialist internationalism.

15 This party, which had been established in June 1904, joined the RSDRP in 1906 as an 'autonomous territorial organization' but was exempt from following the agrarian portion of the party's Programme because of 'special local conditions.'

16 Spilka was a splinter of the Revolutionary Ukrainian Party (RUP) which had been formed in 1900 to promote peasant socialism and Ukrainian nationalism. In 1904, when the emphasis had switched to the latter, Spilka left the RUP and a year later joined the RSDRP as 'an organization of Ukrainian-speaking workers' with the rights of an autonomous regional organization (see 1.38).

the II Party Congress (1.3), this kept the Polish Socialist Party-Levitsa,[17] the Ukrainian Social Democratic Labour Party,[18] the Lithuanian Social Democratic Party, the Armenian Social Democratic Workers' Organization,[19] and the Finnish Workers Party out of the RSDRP before the war.

Despite the prevalence of factional sentiments among the party leadership in emigration, a strong desire for Social Democratic unity existed among the party rank and file in the underground. Indeed, the local groups rarely gave organizational expression to these various factional trends (except in the capitals), preferring instead to operate within a unified underground structure. This sentiment, plus the revolutionary events of 1905 (1.42–1.45, 1.49), forced the Mensheviks and Bolsheviks to unify at the national level in 1906 and to take the steps noted above to admit the various national bodies (see the resolutions of the Unification Congress, 1.50–1.59). This unity, however, was superficial. In 1910, a 'unification' plenum of the Central Committee had to be held in an attempt to divest some of the competing factions of their organizational machinery (1.84). At the same time certain factional groups developed – the Bolshevik 'conciliators,' Trotsky's 'non-factionalists,' and Plekhanov's Party Mensheviks – whose sole raison d'être was to promote party unity in their own factional fashions. Lenin, however, considered unity 'a noose around the neck of the party' and used the Prague Conference to complete the schismatic work begun at the II Congress. This Conference condemned union with the national Social Democratic parties as 'a federation of the worst type' (see also 1.118), it declared that the Liquidators 'had once and for all placed [themselves] outside the party' (1.102), and it set up solely Bol-

17 The Polish Socialist Party (PPS), which had been established in 1892 and had spawned Social Democracy of the Kingdom of Poland two years later (see note 14), split again in 1906 with PPS-Levitsa agreeing to replace the prior demand for Polish independence with one for autonomy within the future Russian state. It accordingly sought closer relations with the RSDRP and with the Mensheviks in particular (see 1.107).

18 The Revolutionary Ukrainian Party, after the departure of Spilka in 1904, came under the influence of the Bund and in 1905 changed its name to the Ukrainian Social Democratic Labour Party. It sent an observer to the Unification Congress who unsuccessfully sought a federated status for his group within the RSDRP.

19 Both the Lithuanian Social Democratic Party, which had been formed in 1895 and had seen the less nationalistic Union of Workers of Lithuania split off in 1899, and the Armenian Social Democratic Workers Organization had received agreements in principle at the London Congress to join the RSDRP. Owing to mutual suspicions concerning nationality policy, neither of these mergers materialized. The Lithuanians did, however, send a representative to the Mensheviks' 1912 Conference and both they and the Armenians were included in Lenin's plans for a congress in 1914 (1.129).

INTRODUCTION   23

shevik organizational machinery to compete with the Menshevik committees approved by the August Conference shortly thereafter (1.105). In 1913 and 1914, Menshevik-Bolshevik differences became more evident in the underground itself, in trade union and insurance directorates, in competing legal workers' newspapers, and eventually in the splitting of the Social Democratic Duma fraction (1.123).

V

Despite a decade of planning, the RSDRP contributed little to the immediate causes of the revolution in February 1917, and indeed was largely unprepared for the long-awaited upheaval. The party was split more than ever along Menshevik-Bolshevik lines as well as intrafactionally over the proper response to Russia's participation in the Great War. Its leaders were scattered throughout western Europe, North America, and Siberia. And its underground organization, while recovering somewhat from the debilitating effects of patriotism and suppression during the opening stages of the war, was poorly equipped to guide the revolutionary discontent caused by the war, inept tsarist leadership, and long-standing socio-political grievances. The party faced two immediate problems of paramount importance. First, as a result of the overthrow of the autocracy, social democracy was now a legitimate political movement and as such had to transform its illegal organization into a more conventional, visible, and legal political structure. And secondly, it had to adopt new policies with respect to the exercise of state power, the continuation of the war, and the implementation of domestic reforms since orthodox marxism and pre-war programmatic formulations were soon found to be of little use in a rapidly changing revolutionary situation.

After nearly two decades of underground existence, the RSDRP suddenly became a legal entity in February 1917. Curiously, the new party Rules adopted by both the Mensheviks and the Bolsheviks in August of that year (1.174, 1.186) did not noticeably reflect this change. While more attention was given to the structure of the local organizations than was the case earlier, this merely formalized pre-war structural patterns. On the national level, the party found itself able for the first time to convene its congresses and conferences openly and legally. Again it is curious, given the pressing need for new policy decisions, that only two congresses and three conferences were called[20] and that the resolutions of these gatherings were so

    20 These included the Bolsheviks' March Conference (27 March-2 April), VII Conference (24-29 April), VI Congress (26 July-3 August), and the Mensheviks' May Conference (7-12 May) and Unification Congress (19-26 August). The Bolsheviks also planned to call an extraordinary party congress on the eve of the II Congress of Soviets (1.204) but this was postponed because of differences within the leadership.

uninformative and nebulous. In comparison to several pre-war congresses held under much more difficult conditions, the accomplishments and contributions of the 1917 meetings were minimal. It should be noted, for instance, that despite radically changed circumstances and several insistent resolutions, the party was unable to come up with a new programme in 1917 to replace the one drafted 14 years earlier. This inability of the congresses and conferences to set policy and to make programmatic decisions is probably explained by the fact that political forces were constantly in flux during 1917 and that long debates over policy were inappropriate, especially when they might reveal sharp divisions within the various factions. As a result, most of the important formulations of policy were made in secret and on an ad hoc basis by executive bodies created by the ineffectual congresses. This in turn has resulted in a dearth of conventional documentary material on the party's activities during the revolutionary year and a need to rely on leaflets, reports, and telegraphic protocols in order to document the events of 1917.[21]

As in the pre-war period, both the Mensheviks and the Bolsheviks had competing executive bodies. The Mensheviks' Organizational Committee, which had been established in 1912, was operative again in March 1917, enlarged to seventeen members at the May Conference, and replaced by a Central Committee of twenty-five in August. Throughout its existence, however, the Organizational (Central) Committee was overshadowed and often overruled by prestigious Menshevik leaders within either the Soviet or the Provisional Government itself.

The Bolsheviks also utilized a pre-war creation, the Russian Bureau of the Central Committee, to guide the party immediately after the February Revolution. Originally composed of three second-echelon Bolsheviks, it was enlarged to twelve and then to eighteen members in March 1917. Its larger size necessitated the formation of a more manageable five-man presidium, but with the return of Lenin from Switzerland in early April the Russian Bureau went into limbo and was replaced by the old Central Committee. The Central Committee in turn grew from nine mem-

---

[21] Prior to its 8th edition, published in 1970, *KPSS v rezoliutsiiakh* included only the resolutions of the VII Conference, VI Congress (though not in its entirety), the July Central Committee meeting, and three well-known decisions of the Central Committee during the fall of 1917 (1.194, 1.208, 1.210). The resolutions of the Menshevik Organizational Committee, May Conference, and Unification Congress were omitted for obvious reasons. The resolutions and indeed the very existence of the Bolsheviks' March Conference as well as the protocols of the Russian Bureau in March and of the Central Committee during September–October were ignored because they revealed the vacillation, hesitation, and often anti-leninist stand of the party that was contrary to official stalinist hagiology of the revolution.

bers and five candidates elected at the VII Conference to twenty-one members and ten candidates chosen by the VI Congress. Following prewar precedents, it created an eleven-man subcommittee which met on an average of three times a week throughout the autumn. The faction's tenfold increase in size during 1917 resulted in bookkeeping problems which E.D. Stasova and her several assistants could not manage, and thus a five-man secretariat under I.M. Sverdlov was established by the Central Committee in August. In an attempt to delegate and distribute its many added responsibilities, the Central Committee also created several new bodies – an Auditing Commission (1.174), an Orgburo (1.195), and a Politburo (1.209) – whose functions, membership, and viability during 1917 are questionable but which later became very important elements in the party's organizational structure. The Central Committee continued to appoint the editors of the faction's newly legal but frequently suppressed Central Organ[22] as well as setting up in haphazard fashion a number of auxiliary groups to deal with legitimate party work in trade unions, insurance bodies, municipal groups, and in the elections to the Constituent Assembly (1.179, 1.195). Perhaps the most important of these auxiliary bodies was the reconstituted Military Organization which was to co-ordinate party activities in the army. While this body at times operated more independently and more recklessly than the Central Committee might have wished (see 1.183–1.185), its leaders subsequently were instrumental in the Central Committee's Military Revolutionary Centre and in the Petrograd Soviet's Military Revolutionary Committee (1.211, 1.213).

The success of the February Revolution and the mere existence of parallel and competing central committees and central organs created pressures in 1917, just as in 1905, for organizational unity. Indeed, by the end of March, as Menshevik and Bolshevik policies toward the war and the Provisional Government became increasingly similar, such diverse leaders as I.G. Tseretelli and J.V. Stalin began promoting unity and plans were laid for a true unification congress. With the return of Lenin, however, the policies of the two factions once again began to diverge and broad party unity became unrealistic. The Mensheviks still espoused it in principle in

---

22 *Pravda*, the Bolsheviks' Central Organ from 5 March until its suppression on 8 July, was succeeded by *Rabochii i soldat* (Worker and Soldier, 4–9 August), *Proletarii* (13–24 August), *Rabochii* (The Worker, 25 August–2 September), and *Rabochii put'* (The Worker's Path, 3 September–26 October). *Rabochaia gazeta*, which was the official organ of the Menshevik Organizational (Central) Committee from 7 March to 17 November 1917, is a largely untapped mine of information about Menshevik operations during the revolution and includes the resolutions reproduced herein of the faction's long-obscured May Conference and Unification Congress as well as those of the Organizational Committee itself.

May (1.165) and some centrist groups still advocated a joint congress in June, but in the aftermath of the July Days these ideas were largely forgotten (see 1.172). By the end of August the two factions were irrevocably split (1.181). The Bolsheviks did, however, win over some very valuable allies in the Inter-District Committee (Mezhraionka), which formally joined the faction at the VI Congress, and made overtures toward Martov's Menshevik Internationalists (1.141, 1.153). The latter, while most uncomfortable within Menshevik ranks, could not forget long-standing differences and chose to remain the unofficial conscience of their own faction.

The second problem facing the RSDRP in February 1917 and the one which intensified these organizational differences was the need to formulate policies concerning relations with the Provisional Government, the continuation of the war, and the introduction of economic, agrarian, and nationality reforms. As already noted, neither Marx nor the pre-war congresses offered a reliable guide. Nor could lessons be drawn from the so-called 'dress rehearsal' of 1905 since in 1917 power had passed to the bourgeoisie and a war of catastrophic proportions was still being waged.

On the key question of who should exercise political power, the Bolsheviks vacillated. At first the Russian Bureau merely repeated 1905 slogans by calling for the establishment of a provisional revolutionary government and for the overthrow of the recently established liberal Provisional Government (1.132, 1.133). During the course of the next month, however, it modified this position – first calling for non-cooperation with the Provisional Government, then advocating putting pressure on it for reform, and finally virtually recognizing the right of the government to rule (1.136, 1.143, 1.148). In April, at Lenin's prodding, the party reversed this trend. While recognizing that the slogan 'Down with the Provisional Government' was inappropriate (1.151), the Bolsheviks nevertheless refused to give further support to the government and approved in principle the eventual and presumably peaceful transfer of political power to the Soviets of Workers' and Soldiers' Deputies (1.154). As Lenin feared, the attempt by more militant Bolsheviks to put this into immediate effect during July proved premature since his party still lacked a majority in the key Soviets. At his insistence and as a result of the July Days, the VI Congress dropped the slogan of a peaceful transfer of power to the Soviets and instead called in vague terms for the assumption of power by the 'revolutionary proletariat' (1.176). With the collapse of the Kornilov revolt and the Bolsheviks' acquisition of majorities in the Petrograd and Moscow Soviets, the Central Committee revived the slogan 'All Power to the Soviets' (1.203) and on 10 October indicated that this would be achieved by means of an 'armed insurrection' (1.208).

Menshevik policy on the question of political power was significantly different. Their initial reaction to the creation of the Provisional Government was to see it in classical marxian terms as a bourgeois government that had a legitimate right to rule after the bourgeois February Revolution. As a proletarian party, social democracy would remain in loyal opposition through the Soviets which in no case should attempt to seize power in their own right (1.146). As the internal and external threats to the gains of the revolution appeared to increase during the spring of 1917, the Mensheviks not only gave their 'full and unconditional support' to the Provisional Government but also in May agreed to participate in it (1.159). Three months later their Unification Congress once again approved both rule by the Provisional Government and, over Martov's strenuous objections, continued Menshevik membership in Kerensky's coalition (1.187). This solution, of course, made them responsible for the government's policies should they prove unsuccessful.

The most unpopular of these policies and the one which split the Mensheviks and perhaps ultimately resulted in their downfall was the active continuance of the war. The faction was far from unanimous on this question. One group, led by Plekhanov and A.N. Potresov, continued to support Russian war efforts and traditional war aims; at the other extreme, Martov and the Menshevik Internationalists urged the immediate end of the war through pacifistic action by all of Europe's proletarian parties; and in the middle stood the majority of the faction behind the Organizational Committee which, while once basically internationalist in approach, now favoured the protection of the new régime through 'revolutionary defencism.' At first its emphasis was on pressuring the Provisional Government to start peace negotiations while opposing any aggressive military moves (1.145). By May the Mensheviks had switched their emphasis to strengthening the army's 'combat readiness' while opposing Bolshevik agitation for fraternization (1.160, 1.161). And in August, despite the failure of the Provisional Government to make any concrete moves toward peace, the Unification Congress still supported its policies and concluded that 'the entire will of the Russian proletariat must be directed toward repulsing the enemy invasion' (1.188).

In contrast with this, the Bolsheviks began by calling for the transformation of 'the imperialist war into a civil war,' for the formation of soldiers' committees at the front, and for fraternization between the soldiers in the opposing trenches (1.137). While this stand was modified somewhat in late March so as to repudiate disorganization within the Russian forces and to call on the troops 'to remain at their posts' (1.147), Lenin succeeded in bringing his party back to a policy of fraternization (1.152) and to a recognition that peace could only be achieved through the overthrow of the Russian bourgeoisie (1.175). His unqualified slogan of 'peace' was much more successful than the Mensheviks' qualified and hesitant support of revolutionary defencism which all too often turned into unsuccessful offensive actions.

The Bolsheviks were also successful in exploiting the failure of the Provisional Government to make much-needed domestic reform and the propensity of the Mensheviks to defer offering solutions to the nationality and agrarian questions until the Constituent Assembly. Rather than opposing the seizure of arable land, as the Mensheviks did at their May Conference (1.164), the Bolsheviks called for the immediate confiscation and nationalization of all land holdings (1.157). Rather than ignoring the problem of the national minorities, as the Mensheviks did in May and August, the Bolsheviks recognized the right of 'every nation forming part of Russia ... to secede freely and to form an independent state' (1.158). Only on the question of labour legislation did the Mensheviks come out for immediate reform (1.163), but here too the Bolsheviks' slogan of 'worker control' through factory committees (1.166, 1.177) probably was more effective in eliciting worker support.

One problem faced by Mensheviks and Bolsheviks alike was the rising expectations and revolutionary momentum of the urban masses which had tasted power in February. The Mensheviks, now that their own power was institutionalized through the Soviets and later the Provisional Government, experienced the realities of exercising power and came to fear the anarchic spirit of the masses just as had the liberals after the October General Strike in 1905. They wanted to maintain domestic order and a stable war effort while making haste very slowly, democratically, and methodically on the major problems facing Russia. They avoided popular slogans which might excite the crowds, telling them instead to put their faith in the eventual Constituent Assembly (1.172).

The Bolsheviks were restrained neither by the responsibilities of governing nor by the liberal-democratic sensibilities of their rivals. They used the slogans of 'bread,' 'peace,' 'land,' 'self-determination,' 'worker control,' and 'All Power to the Soviets' to good agitational advantage. But they too had acquired vested interests in the form of their newly legal newspapers, committee headquarters, and personal freedoms. Many members of the Central Committee also came to fear the anarchic mood of their sometime followers and more particularly that premature mass action would result in the crushing of the party, either by the government or by counter-revolutionary forces. They were thus in a dilemma when their slogans were acted upon by the crowds in the street. During the April Crisis, the Bolshevik leadership supported the Soviet's ban on demonstrations (1.151) which their own propaganda had caused. In June the hesitant Central Committee agreed to peaceful demonstrations but then rescinded its decision (1.167, 1.168). In July, it was forced most reluctantly to acquiesce to mass demonstrations against the Provisional Government which the more militant Bolsheviks in the Military Organization had promoted (1.169, 1.170). The temporary suppression of the Bolsheviks as a result of the failure of the July Days had a lasting effect on the Bolshevik leadership. During the Kornilov threat, it caused the Central Committee to pay more attention to avoiding provocations than to exploiting the government's embarrassment (1.190). In September, it resulted in the burning of Lenin's demand for armed insurrection and in a ban on unauthorized demonstrations (1.197). And in October, it led Zinoviev and Kamenev to publicize plans for the insurrection in an effort to head one off (1.212). Even after Lenin had enforced his will on the Central Committee (1.208, 1.210), his colleagues were reluctant to go beyond adopting the slogan 'All Power to the Soviets' by specifying how and when power was to be seized. On the eve of the October Revolution, they were more concerned with the threat of government counter-action and with protecting their own persons (1.216–1.218) than they were in putting their own slogan into effect. In the end, the 'weakness of the Provisional Government exceeded all expectations,' as Trotsky said, and the party merely filled the power vacuum by backing into the Winter Palace.

R.C.E.

Documents

I Party Congress   1 – 3 March 1898

The inaugural congress of the Russian Social Democratic Labour Party was not a very impressive affair. Called on the initiative of some Kievan Social Democrats with the assistance of the Jewish Bund, it attracted only nine relatively unknown delegates from a half-dozen organizations: three from the Bund, two from Kiev's illegal *Rabochaia gazeta*, and one each from the Unions of Struggle for the Emancipation of Labour in Moscow, St Petersburg, Kiev, and Ekaterinoslav. The Congress, which met under conspiratorial conditions in Minsk, was the shortest in the history of the party and the only one before the revolution to convene inside imperial Russia.

The principal achievement of the gathering was to establish the party as a formal entity with provisions for periodic congresses, a three-man Central Committee, an official newspaper (*Rabochaia gazeta*), and a series of local committees. In contrast to later developments, the party envisaged by the delegates was remarkably decentralized. The Central Committee was to be closely guided by the decisions of past party congresses and if possible was to defer contentious questions to future congresses. Local committees were given freedom of action in all areas not explicitly covered by central directives and could reject or adapt to fit local conditions those directives that they did receive. Moreover, the Bund was recognized as an 'autonomous organization' independent in matters concerning Jewish workers.

Contrary to the expectations of many Social Democrats, the Congress never discussed a formal party programme but rather delegated the task without any specific instructions. Even more surprising, the author selected was not Plekhanov but rather P.B. Struve, a theoretician and publicist living in St Petersburg. The document that he produced several months after the Congress adjourned was in fact a 'Manifesto' rather than a systematic programme. It sought to apply marxism to Russian conditions and especially to emphasize the special role the proletariat would play in the absence of a strong bourgeoisie in Russia's political development. It is interesting to note that Struve took considerable liberties with the name of the new party. He inserted the term 'Labour,' which the delegates had earlier rejected (perhaps because only one of their number was a worker), into the party's official appellation. He also continually used the word 'Russkaia,' which has a narrow ethnic connotation, rather than the broader political or geographic term 'Rossiiskaia' which the delegates had purposefully incorporated into their title.

Neither the creators of the Congress nor their creations had much influence after March 1898. Within a few months, eight of the nine delegates including two of the Central Committee members-designate were under arrest; the Central Committee itself failed to co-opt new members and passed temporarily out of existence; the printing press of *Rabochaia gazeta* was soon seized; and ideological differences began appearing abroad and inside the growing but scattered and still unco-ordinated local committees.

1.1
Manifesto of the Russian Social Democratic Labour Party

Fifty years ago the life-giving storm of the Revolution of 1848 swept across Europe.

The modern working class for the first time appeared on the scene as a major historical force. Through its efforts, the bourgeoisie succeeded in sweeping away many antiquated feudal-monarchial customs and usages. But the bourgeoisie soon perceived in its new ally its bitterest enemy, and betrayed both it and itself and the cause of freedom, to the reaction. It was already too late, however. Temporarily suppressed, the working class would in ten or fifteen years again appear on the stage of history with redoubled strength and heightened consciousness, as a fully mature fighter for its own ultimate liberation.

During this time Russia, to all appearances, remained apart from the mainstream of historical development. The class struggle could not be seen, but it was there and, what is important, continued to grow and mature. The Russian government, with commendable zeal, itself sowed the seeds of the class struggle, depriving the peasants of their livelihood, patronizing the landowners, nursing and pampering the big capitalists at the expense of the working population. But the bourgeois-capitalist order is inconceivable without a proletariat or working class. The latter is born at the same time as capitalism, grows up with it, becomes stronger, and as it grows, is increasingly thrown into conflict with the bourgeoisie.

The Russian factory worker, both serf and free, has always waged a secret and an open struggle against his exploiters. The scope of this struggle has grown with the development of capitalism, encompassing increasingly broader layers of the working population. The awakening of class consciousness in the Russian proletariat and the growth of a spontaneous workers' movement has coincided with the final development of international social democracy as the vehicle of the class struggle and of the class ideal of conscious workers throughout the world. The newest Russian workers' organizations have always, consciously or unconsciously, conducted their activities in the spirit of social democratic ideas. The power and significance of the workers' movement, and of social democracy which it supports, were most vividly revealed by the recent series of strikes in Russia and Poland, in particular the famous strikes of the St Petersburg weavers and spinners in 1896 and 1897. These strikes compelled the government to promulgate the law of 2 June 1897 [regulating] the length of the working day. This law – no matter how great its inadequacies – will ever remain a memorable demonstration of the mighty pressure which the combined efforts of the workers can bring to bear on the legislative and other functions of the government. In vain the government imagines that it can appease the workers with concessions. The working class everywhere becomes more demanding the more it is given, and the Russian proletariat will do the same. In the past it has obtained something only when it *made the demand*, and in the future it will get only what it *demands* as well.

And what does the Russian working class not need? It is totally deprived of that which its foreign comrades enjoy freely and peacefully: a share in the state administration, freedom of speech and the press, freedom of assembly and of association – in a word, all the instruments and means with which the western European and American proletariat improve their position and at the same time battle for their ultimate liberation, against private property and capitalism – for socialism. Political liberty is as necessary to the Russain proletariat as clean air is for healthy breathing. It is the basic condition of its free development and of success in the struggle for partial improvements and final liberation.

But only the Russian proletariat *itself* can win the political liberty which it needs.

The further east one goes in Europe, the more cowardly, mean, and politically weak is the bourgeoisie, and the greater are the cultural and political tasks confronting the proletariat. The Russian working class must and will bear on its own sturdy shoulders the cause of winning political freedom. This is an essential, but only an initial step in discharging the great historic mission of the proletariat – creating a social order in which there will be no exploitation of man by man. The Russian proletariat will throw off the yoke of autocracy, and thus with greater energy will continue the struggle against capitalism and the bourgeoisie for the complete victory of socialism.

The first steps of the Russian workers' movement and of Russian social democracy could not help being unco-ordinated and somewhat random, devoid of unity and plan. The time has now come to unite the local forces, circles, and organizations of Russian social democracy into a single 'Russian Social Democratic Labour Party.' Mindful of this, the representatives of the Unions of Struggle for the Emancipation of Labour, the group publishing *Rabochaia gazeta*, and the General Jewish Workers' Union of Russia and Poland [the 'Bund'] have held a congress whose decisions are given below.

In uniting to form a party, the local groups are fully conscious of the importance of this step and of the responsibility which it entails. They thereby confirm, once and for all, the transition of the Russian revolutionary movement to a new epoch of conscious class struggle. As a socialist trend and movement, the Russian Social Democratic Party carries on the cause and traditions of the entire preceding Russian revolutionary movement; in defining the principal immediate task of the party as the complete conquest of political liberty, social democracy pursues the goal which was already clearly outlined by the glorious figures of the old Narodnaia Volia [a populist group established in 1879 for the purpose of achieving peasant socialism by means of political terror]. But social democracy selects other ways and means. This selection is determined by its conscious desire to be, and to remain, a class movement of the organized working masses. It is firmly convinced that 'the liberation of the working class can only be its own affair' and will steadfastly conduct all its activities in conformity with this basic principle of international social democracy.

Long live Russian, long live international social democracy!

1.2
Decisions of the Congress

1   The Unions of Struggle for the Emancipation of Labour, the *Rabochaia gazeta* group, and the General Jewish Workers' Union of Russia and Poland hereby form a single organization called the Russian Social Democratic [Labour] Party; the General Jewish Workers' Union of Russia and Poland enters the party as an autonomous organization, independent only in matters specially affecting the Jewish proletariat.

2   The executive organ of the party is the Central Committee which is elected by the party congress and reports to it on its activities.

3   The duties of the Central Committee include:

a concern for the regular operation of the party (the distribution of personnel and funds, submission and follow-up of routine requests, etc.); in this the Central Committee is guided by the general directives issued by party congresses;

b issuing literature and supplying it to the local committees;

c the organization of any measures of general significance for the whole of Russia (celebrating the First of May, issuing leaflets on important occasions, giving assistance to strikers, etc.).

I PARTY CONGRESS 37

4   In particularly important cases the Central Committee is guided by the following principles:

  a when the matter can be postponed, the Central Committee must seek instructions from the party congress;

  b when the matter cannot be postponed, the Central Committee acts independently and by unanimous vote, reporting on its actions to the next regular or extraordinary party congress.

5   The Central Committee has the right to co-opt new members.

6   The party funds at the disposal of the Central Committee are made up of:

  a voluntary single donations of the local committees made at the time the party is formed;

  b periodic voluntary deductions from the funds of local committees;

  c special party assessments.

7   Local committees carry out Central Committee decrees in the form which they find most suited to local conditions. In exceptional cases local committees have the right to refuse to fulfil Central Committee demands, notifying the latter of the reason for such refusal. In all other matters local committees act with complete autonomy, guided only by the party Programme.

8   The Central Committee represents the party in relations with other revolutionary organizations in so far as this does not violate the principles of its programme and its tactical methods. The party recognizes the right of each nationality to self-determination.

Note   Local committees enter into relations with [other revolutionary] organizations only with the knowledge of the Central Committee and following its instructions.

9   The highest organ of the party is the congress of representatives of local committees. Regular and extraordinary congresses are held. Each regular congress designates the date of the ensuing regular congress. Extraordinary congresses are convened by the Central Committee both upon its own initiative and upon the demand of two-thirds of the local committees.

10   The Union of Russian Social Democrats Abroad [formed by Plekhanov in 1894] is a part of the party and is its foreign representative.

11   *Rabochaia gazeta* is to be the official organ of the party.

Manifest Rossiiskoi Sotsial-demokraticheskoi Rabochei Partii (Geneva, 1903), 1–5

KPSS v rezoliutsiiakh 1, 13–17

II Party Congress   17 July – 10 August 1903

One reflection of the growth of Russian social democracy after the I Congress was the fact that fifty-seven delegates turned up at the party's II Congress five years later: thirty-two of them represented twenty underground organizations; eleven represented various émigré publishing or administrative groups; and fourteen attended in a consultative capacity. The composition of the Congress also reflected, though in a somewhat distorted fashion, the organizational dominance and ideological conformity that the émigré journal *Iskra* had imposed upon the party. The Legal Marxists were totally absent, the once influential 'economist' tendency had only three representatives, and the numerically large Jewish Bund had but five delegates. On the other hand, all but one of the local organizations sent delegates thought to be of *Iskra*'s persuasion.

The first objective of the organizers of the Congress was to formalize this apparent doctrinal agreement through the adoption of a formal party programme. Plekhanov's draft had been subject to considerable acrimony within *Iskra*'s editorial board a year earlier. Its author had argued unsuccessfully that capitalism was only 'becoming' but had not 'already become the dominant mode of production' in Russia as Lenin insisted. Behind the semantics was the unstated but all-important question of whether the party was working toward the bourgeois or the socialist revolution. The final draft, however, was accepted with only minor modifications by all but one of the delegates. This document, which had more merit as agitational material than as a blueprint for future action, embodied a theoretical preface describing the impending crisis of capitalism and the transition to socialism as well as a set of minimum demands to be put forward at the time of the bourgeois revolution. Perhaps the most interesting of these are the concessions which Lenin, particularly, sought for the Russian peasantry. Modest as these are, they represent the first incorporation of peasant demands into a European social democratic programme.

The Congress also sought to formalize and centralize the organizational structure of the party. The binding Rules which it adopted after much debate revoked the organizational autonomy granted the Bund five years earlier and made central decisions mandatory for all local organizations. Indeed, differences over the degree of élitism and centralization implicit in the definition of party membership caused the well-known split between Lenin and Martov. Lenin's definition ('A member of the party is one who recognizes its Programme, and supports it both financially and by personal participation in one of the party organizations') went down to defeat 23 to 28 while Martov's formulation (1.4, art. 1), which closely resembled similar clauses in other European social democratic rules, was passed 28 to 22 with one abstention.

After being defeated on several additional but less significant parts of the Rules dealing with the right of co-optation, Lenin suddenly gained a tenuous majority and a factional name for his followers when the five Bundists and two Economists decided to walk out over other grievances. The departure of the Bund was hastened both by the passage of a resolution (1.6) which restricted rights given to that body at the I Congress, and by the defeat on 5 August of its own resolution (41 to 5 with 5 abstentions) calling for the party to be organized along federative lines with its groups having the power to speak for all Jewish workers. The Economists left on that same day when the Congress recognized the *Iskra*-controlled Foreign League of Russian Revolutionary Social Democrats as 'the only foreign organization of the RSDRP' and dissolved their own Union of Russian Social Democrats Abroad (see doc. 1.2). Lenin then used his new majority to recoup his position by electing his followers to the new central party institutions: the party Council, the Central Organ *Iskra* (three former editors – Potresov, P.B. Akselrod, V.I. Zasulich – were purposefully not re-elected, Martov refused to serve, thus leaving the paper in the hands of Lenin and Plekhanov), and the Central Committee (F.V. Lengnik, G.M. Krzhizhanovsky, V.A. Noskov; before the end of the year, Lenin and five other Bolsheviks were co-opted to the Committee).

So much time and energy had been spent on the Programme and Rules and on moving from Brussels to London because of police pressures in the Belgian city, that the Congress agenda had to be foreshortened and most of the remaining resolutions crammed into the last day. Of particular interest are the three resolutions dealing with new challenges to social democracy's bid for popular support: 'police socialism' was rejected in a resolution on trade unions; the Party of the Socialist Revolutionaries was branded a 'bourgeois-democratic faction'; and the liberal resurgence among the intelligentsia and in zemstvo circles was 'unmasked.' One suspects, however, that the average worker reading these resolutions and the others passed by the Congress found little of relevance or guidance. What was relevant to him was the fact that the party at its moment of consolidation had split into competing Menshevik and Bolshevik factions.

1.3
Programme of the Russian Social Democratic Labour Party   1 August 1903

The development of trade has established such close ties between the peoples of the civilized world that the great movement of proletarian liberation had to become, and has long since become, international.

Considering itself one detachment of the world-wide army of the proletariat, Russian social democracy pursues the same ultimate goal as the social democrats of all other countries.

This ultimate goal is determined by the character of contemporary bourgeois society and by the course of its development.

The chief characteristic of this society is commodity production on the basis of capitalist production relations. The largest and most significant part of the means of production and the exchange of commodities belongs to a numerically small class of persons while the overwhelming majority of the population consists of proletarians and semi-proletarians whose economic position obliges them, continuously or periodically, to sell their labour, i.e., to hire themselves out to the capitalists, and by their labour to create the income of the higher classes of society.

The area ruled by capitalist production relations expands continually as the constant improvement of technology, increasing the economic significance of large enterprises, squeezes out the small independent producers, transforming part of them into proletarians, narrowing the socio-economic functions of the remainder, and in places making them more or less fully, more or less openly, more or less heavily dependent upon capital.

In addition, this same technological progress enables the entrepreneurs to make even greater use of female and child labour in the production and circulation of commodities. And since, on the other hand, it leads to a relative diminution in the needs of management for human labour power, the demand for labour inevitably lags behind its supply; consequently, the dependence of hired labour upon capital is increased, and the level of its exploitation is heightened.

This situation in the bourgeois countries, as well as the increasingly fierce competition among these countries on the world market, makes it more and more difficult to sell the commodities which are being produced in steadily increasing quantities. Over-production, manifested in the form of more or less acute industrial crises followed by more or less extended periods of industrial stagnation, represents an inescapable consequence of the development of productive forces in bourgeois society. Crises and periods of industrial stagnation, in their turn, ruin the small producers still further; increase even further the dependence of hired labour upon capital; lead even more rapidly to the relative – and sometimes even to the absolute – deterioration of the position of the working class.

Thus the improvement of technology, signifying an increase in the productivity of labour and the growth of social wealth, causes an increase in social inequality in bourgeois society, a widening of the gap between the haves and the have-nots, a more precarious existence, a rise in unemployment, and increased privations of various sorts for ever wider sections of the labouring masses.

But as all these contradictions which are inherent in bourgeois society grow and develop, the dissatisfaction of the toiling and exploited masses with the existing order also grows; the size and the solidarity of the proletariat increases; and its struggle with its exploiters becomes more intensified. At the same time the improvement of technology, which concentrates the means of production and of distribution and which socializes the labour process in capitalist enterprises, creates ever more rapidly the material conditions for replacing capitalist production relations with socialist ones; i.e., of bringing about the social revolution which represents the ultimate goal of all the activity of the international social democratic movement, as the conscious spokesman for the class movement of the proletariat.

By substituting public for private ownership of the means of production and distribution and by instituting the planned organization of the social productive process so as to ensure the well-being and the comprehensive development of all members of society, the social revolution of the proletariat will abolish the class division of society and thereby liberate all oppressed humanity, since it will end all forms of exploitation of one part of society by another.

The essential condition for this social revolution is the dictatorship of the proletariat; i.e., the conquest by the proletariat of such political power as will enable it to suppress any resistance on the part of the exploiters.

In setting itself the task of making the proletariat capable of fulfilling its great historical mission, international social democracy organizes the proletariat into an independent political party opposed to all bourgeois parties, guides all the manifestations of its class struggle, lays bare the irreconcilable conflict between the interests of the exploiters and the exploited, and teaches the proletariat the historical significance and the necessary conditions for the imminent social revolution. At the same time, it reveals to the rest of the toiling and exploited masses the hopelessness of their position in a capitalist society and the necessity of a social revolution for their own liberation from the capitalist yoke. The party of the working class, the Social Democratic Party, calls to its ranks all strata of the toiling and exploited population in so far as they accept the point of view of the proletariat.

On the way to their common ultimate goal, which is dictated by the dominance of the capitalist method of production throughout the civilized world, Social Democrats of different countries are obliged to set themselves different short-term tasks, both because this method of production is not developed everywhere to the same extent and because it is developing in each country in a different socio-political environment.

In Russia, where capitalism has already become the dominant mode of production, there are still very many remnants of our old pre-capitalist order which was based on the enserfment of the toiling masses to the landowners, the state, or the sovereign. These remnants are the greatest possible obstacle to economic progress; they inhibit a comprehensive development of the class struggle of the proletariat; they help to maintain and to intensify the most barbarous forms of exploitation of millions of peasants by the state and by the propertied classes; and they keep all the people in ignorance and subjection.

The most striking of these remnants, and the mightiest buttress of this whole barbarous order, is the tsarist autocracy. By its very nature it is hostile to any social change, and can hardly fail to be the bitterest opponent of all aspirations of the proletariat for freedom.

Therefore, the Russian Social Democratic Labour Party sets as its immediate political task the overthrow of the tsarist autocracy and its replacement by a democratic republic whose constitution would guarantee:

1 The sovereignty of the people; i.e., the concentration of the supreme power of the state in a unicameral legislative assembly composed of representatives of the people.

2 Universal, equal, and direct suffrage for all citizens, male and female, who have reached the age of twenty, in the elections to both the legislative assembly and all local organs of self-government; a secret ballot in these elections; the right of every voter to be elected to any representative institution; a two-year parliamentary term; salaries to be paid to the people's representatives.

3 Broad local self-government; regional self-government for localities with particular conditions of life or a particular make-up of the population.

4 Inviolability of person and dwelling.

5 Unrestricted freedom of conscience, speech, press, and assembly; freedom to strike and to form trade unions.

6 Freedom of movement and occupation.

7 The elimination of class privileges and the complete equality of all citizens regardless of sex, religion, race, or nationality.

8 The right of any people to obtain an education in their native language, to be guaranteed by setting up the necessary schools at the expense of the state and the organs of self-government; the right of each citizen to employ his native language in public meetings; the use of the native language on an equal basis with the state language in all local, public and state institutions.

9 The right of self-determination for all nations forming part of the state.

10 The right of every person through normal channels to prosecute before a jury any official.

11   The popular election of judges.
12   The replacement of the standing army by the general arming of the population [i.e., the formation of a people's militia].
13   Separation of church and state, and of school and church.
14   Free and compulsory general or vocational education for all children of both sexes up to the age of sixteen; provision by the state of food, clothes, and school supplies for poor children.

As a fundamental condition for the democratization of our national economy, the RSDRP demands *the abolition of all indirect taxation and the introduction of a graduated tax on incomes and inheritances.*

To protect the working class from physical and moral degradation, and also to develop its capacity for the liberation struggle, the party demands:
1   Limitation of the working day to eight hours for all hired workers.
2   Legal provision for a weekly rest period of not less than 42 consecutive hours for wage earners of both sexes in all branches of the national economy.
3   A complete ban on overtime work.
4   A ban on night work (from 9.00 p.m. until 6.00 a.m.) in all branches of the economy with the exception of those which absolutely require it for technical reasons that have been approved by workers' organizations.
5   The prohibition of the employment of children of school age (up to 16 years of age) and the restriction of the working day of minors (16 to 18 years of age) to six hours.
6   A ban on the use of female labour in occupations which are harmful to the health of women; maternity leave from four weeks prior to childbirth until six weeks after birth, with wages to be paid at the usual rate throughout this period.
7   The provision of nurseries for infants and young children in all shops, factories and other enterprises employing women; the freeing of nursing mothers from work for not less than half an hour in every three hours.
8   State insurance for workers against old age and partial or complete disability through a special fund supported by a tax on capitalists.
9   A ban on the payment of wages in kind; the establishment in all hiring arrangements of a weekly time during working hours when cash payment will be made.
10   The prohibition of management from making deductions from wages, regardless of the reason or the purpose of such deductions (fines, defective work, etc.).
11   The appointment of an adequate number of factory inspectors in all branches of the economy and the extension of inspection to all enterprises employing hired labour including state-run enterprises (the work of domestic servants is also subject to this inspection); the appointment of female

inspectors in those industries employing female labour; the participation of representatives elected by the workers and paid by the government in checking on the enforcement of factory legislation, in establishing wage rates, and in accepting or rejecting finished goods and other work.

12   The supervision by organs of local self-government, together with elected workers' representatives, of sanitary conditions in factory housing as well as of the rules governing use of these accommodations and the conditions of lease so as to protect the workers from the interference of employers in their lives and activities as private persons and citizens.

13   The establishment of properly organized health inspection in all enterprises employing hired labour, this medical health organization to be entirely independent of the management; free medical services for workers at the employer's expense, with wages to be paid during time of illness.

14   Establishment of criminal responsibility of employers for violations of laws intended to protect workers.

15   The establishment in all branches of the economy of industrial tribunals made up equally of representatives of the workers and of management.

16   The requiring of organs of local self-government to establish employment bureaus (labour exchanges) for the hiring of local and out-of-town labour in all branches of the economy, with representatives of workers' organizations participating in their administration.

In order to eliminate the remnants of serfdom, which lie as an oppressive burden on the peasantry, and to further the free development of the class struggle in the countryside, the party demands above all:

1   The cancellation of redemption payments [for land received as a result of the 1861 Emancipation] and quitrents, together with all obligations presently falling upon the peasantry as a tax-paying class.

2   The repeal of all laws hampering the peasant's disposal of his own land.

3   The return to the peasants of all monies taken from them in the form of redemption payments and quitrents; the confiscation, for this purpose, of monastic and church property as well as of lands owned by the emperor, government agencies, and members of the tsar's family; the imposition of a special tax on estates of the landowning nobility who have availed themselves of the redemption loans; the deposit of sums obtained in this way into a special public fund for the cultural and charitable needs of the village communities.

4   The institution of peasant committees:
   a for the return to village communities (through expropriation or, if the lands have passed into other hands, through purchase by the state at the

expense of the large holdings of the nobility) of lands cut off from peasant holdings at the time of the abolition of serfdom and which now are used by the landowners as a means of keeping the peasants in bondage;

   b for the return to peasants in the Caucasus of lands which they presently hold under temporary obligation [to their landlord], as khizani [i.e., landless tenant farmers in Georgia who had not been covered by the reforms of 1861], etc.;

   c for doing away with those remnants of serfdom which have been preserved in the Urals, the Altai, in the Western Region, and in other areas of the country.

5   The granting to the courts of the right to reduce excessively high rents and to declare null and void all transactions reflecting relations of servitude.

In striving to achieve its immediate goals, the RSDRP will support any oppositional or revolutionary movement directed against the existing social and political order in Russia. At the same time, it resolutely rejects all reformist projects involving any broadening or strengthening of police or bureaucratic tutelage over the toiling classes.

The RSDRP, for its part, is firmly convinced that the complete, consistent, and lasting realization of these political and social changes can only be achieved *through the overthrow of the autocracy* and the convocation of *a constituent assembly* freely elected by the entire nation.

1.4
Organizational Rules of the RSDRP   5 August 1903

1   A member of the Russian Social Democratic Labour Party is one who accepts its Programme, supports it financially, and extends it regular personal assistance under the guidance of one of its organizations.

2   The supreme organ of the party is the party congress. It is summoned (if possible, at least once every two years) by the party Council. The party Council must call a congress if this is demanded by party organizations which jointly would be entitled to one-half of the votes at the congress. A congress is considered valid if at it are represented organizations which jointly are entitled to more than one-half of the [party's total eligible] votes.

3   The following are entitled to representation at a congress:

   a the party Council;
   b the Central Committee;
   c the Central Organ;
   d all local committees which do not belong to special unions;
   e other organizations which are equivalent to committees;
   f all unions of committees recognized by the party. [On 6 August the

Congress passed an additional resolution approving the formation of unions of committees 'in those regions of Russia which differ markedly with respect to language, make-up of population, etc.' Most were in fact established on a geographic rather than on an ethnic basis.]

Each of these organizations is represented at a congress by a single delegate with two votes; the party Council is represented by all of its members, each possessing a single vote.

Representation of the unions is defined by special rules.

Note 1 Only those organizations have the right to representation which have been confirmed [by the Central Committee] at least one year before the congress.

Note 2 The Central Committee may invite to the congress, in an advisory capacity, delegates of organizations which do not meet the conditions set forth in Note 1.

4   The congress appoints the fifth member of the Council, the Central Committee, and the editorial board of the Central Organ.

5   The party Council is made up of two members each from the editorial board of the Central Organ and the Central Committee; arrested members of the Council are replaced by the institutions which have appointed them, and the fifth member is replaced by the Council itself.

The party Council is the highest party institution. The task of the Council is to co-ordinate and unify the activities of the Central Committee and the editorial board of the Central Organ and to represent the party in its relations with other parties. The party Council has the right to replace the Central Committee and the editorial board of the Central Organ if all the members of either of these bodies are arrested.

The Council meets whenever this is demanded by one of the party centres; i.e., the editorial board of the Central Organ, the Central Committee, or two members of the Council.

6   The Central Committee organizes committees, unions of committees, and all other party institutions, and guides their activities; it organizes and conducts undertakings of significance for the party as a whole; it allocates party personnel and funds and has charge of the central party treasury; it settles conflicts both between and within various party institutions; and it generally co-ordinates and directs all the practical activity of the party.

Note Central Committee members may not belong at the same time to any other party organization except the party Council.

7   The editorial board of the Central Organ provides ideological leadership for the party.

8   Each party organization is autonomous in all matters falling specially and exclusively in the area of party activity for whose conduct the organization has been created.

9   All party organizations are confirmed by the Central Committee except those which are approved by the party congress. All decisions of the Central Committee are binding on all party organizations. The latter are also obligated to contribute amounts determined by the Central Committee to the central party treasury.

10   Each party member and any person having any contact with the party has the right to demand that any statements made by him should be submitted in the original to the Central Committee, the Central Organ, or the party congress.

11   Each party organization is obliged to make available to the Central Committee and to the editorial board of the Central Organ all materials bearing on their activities and personnel.

12   All party organizations and collegial bodies [i.e., the Central Committee and the Central Organ] resolve questions by simple majority vote and possess the right of co-optation. In the absence of a substantiated protest, a two-thirds majority is required for co-optation of new members [to organizations other then the Central Committee and the Central Organ] or for expulsion. Any decision of an organization co-opting or expelling a member may be appealed to the party Council.

Co-optation of new members to the Central Committee or to the editorial board of the Central Organ is by unanimous vote. If unanimity is not attained in co-opting to the Central Committee or the editorial board of the Central Organ, the matter may be appealed to the Council, and such appeals from the decision of one of these bodies are resolved in the Council by a simple majority.

The Central Committee and the editorial board of the Central Organ will keep each other informed about newly co-opted members.

13   The Foreign League of Russian Revolutionary Social Democrats, the only foreign organization of the RSDRP, has as its purpose agitation and propaganda abroad and also assistance to the movement in Russia. The League enjoys all the rights of a committee with the single exception that it extends assistance to the movement in Russia only through persons and groups specially appointed by the Central Committee.

1.5
On Local Organizations   6 August 1903

With respect to local organizations, the Congress recognizes as essential that only a single guiding organization exist in each centre of party activity and charges the Central Committee with the adoption of measures to bring about such unity. As regards groups outside the local organizations – in the armed forces, in publishing houses, etc. – the Congress recognizes the existence of such groups on the condition that they be approved by the Central Committee of the party.

1.6
On the Place of the Bund in the Party 21 July 1903

Considering:
 a that the closest union of the Jewish proletariat and the proletariat of those races in whose midst it is living is absolutely essential in its struggle for political and economic freedom;
 b that only such a close union guarantees the success of social democracy in the struggle against all forms of chauvinism and anti-semitism;
 c that such a union in no way excludes the independence of the Jewish workers' movement in anything relating to the particular tasks of agitation among the Jewish population, owing to the special character of its language and living conditions —

The II Congress of the RSDRP is deeply convinced that restructuring the organizational relations between the Jewish and Russian proletariat along federative lines would be a substantial obstacle in the way of the fuller organizational rapprochement of conscious proletarians of different races and would inevitably cause enormous damage to the interests of the proletariat generally, and of the Jewish proletariat in particular; and, therefore, emphatically rejecting as absolutely unacceptable in principle any possibility of federative relations between the RSDRP and its component, the Bund, the Congress resolves that within the united RSDRP the Bund occupies the position of an autonomous component, the limits of whose autonomy are to be defined in the working out of the party Rules ...

1.7
On the Withdrawal of the Bund from the Party 10 August 1903

Considering:
 a that the II Congress of the RSDRP set itself the goal of uniting in a single integrated party all active Social Democrats in Russia;
 b that, in particular, one of its tasks was to institute very close ties between the 'General Jewish Workers' Union' and the other sections of our party;
 c that, despite the Bund's recognition of the party programme, such unification could not take place owing to differences in principle over the Bund's place in the party, and recognizing the very severe loss which the

Bund's departure from the party will inevitably mean for the progress of unification —

The II Congress of the RSDRP therefore expresses its deepest regret [concerning the walkout of the Bund] and at the same time expresses its firm conviction that these differences will disappear with the further growth of the movement, and that in the interests of the working class struggle for liberation there will of necessity take place a coalescence of the proletarians of all nationalities into a single RSDRP.

1.8
On the Central Organ of the Party   22 July 1903

Considering:

a the services of *Iskra* in promoting ideological unity, in developing and defending the principles of revolutionary social democracy, and in struggling on the basis of these principles with every kind of opportunist tendency in our party as well as with tendencies striving to deflect the movement of the working class from the only correct course;

b the role of *Iskra* in directing the practical work of the party; and

c the guiding role of *Iskra* in the work for [party] unification —

The II Congress therefore declares *Iskra* to be its Central Organ.

1.9
On Party Literature   10 August 1903

Considering:

a that the broadening of the workers' movement must be paralleled by the clearest possible understanding, on the part of the working masses, of the short- and long-range goals of the Social Democratic Party;

b that at the present time the party faces the urgent task of creating a strictly consistent literature, intelligible to the largest possible number of readers, and with due regard for the present state of the party's resources—

The Congress therefore recognizes as essential:

1 that the Central Organ of the party devote the utmost space to questions of political and social life written in a form understandable to the broadest possible circle of readers, leaving out wherever possible articles of a purely theoretical nature;

2 that with this in mind and to ensure a more systematic elucidation of questions of socialist theory, *Zaria* [Dawn] should be transformed into a

party organ; the Congress instructs the Central Committee to reach agreement with the editors of the Central Organ with regard to the conditions of publication of *Zaria*;

3   that an extensive pamphlet literature be created, its task being to popularize systematically the party Programme and the tactical resolutions of the Congress.

I.10
On the Presentation of Propaganda   10 August 1903

Considering:

a   that the workers' movement in Russia is growing far more rapidly than the cadre of conscious worker Social Democrats capable of acting as leaders in the ever more complex struggle of the Russian proletariat;

b   that conspiratorial-police conditions hinder very greatly the correct presentation of propaganda in all but the very smallest study circles;

c   that the lack of a sufficient number of experienced and skilled propagandists causes considerable obstacles to this kind of propaganda —

The Congress therefore recognizes the necessity of local committees giving very serious attention to the correct presentation of propaganda, being guided above all by the goal of developing class-conscious and aggressive agitators with a well-defined revolutionary outlook. The Congress orders local committees to devote special attention to the selection of skilful propagandists and instructs the Central Committee to adopt all necessary measures to systematize and unify propaganda work at the local level by [preparing] systematic guides for study circles, series of systematically selected propaganda pamphlets, etc.

I.11
On the Attitude toward the Liberals   10 August 1903

Considering:

a   that social democracy must support the bourgeoisie in so far as it is revolutionary or even oppositional in its struggle with tsarism;

b   that, therefore, social democracy must welcome the awakening of political consciousness in the Russian bourgeoisie; but that, on the other hand, it is obliged to unmask before the proletariat the limited and inadequate nature of the bourgeois movement for liberation wherever these limitations and inadequacies are evident —

The II Congress of the RSDRP, therefore, urgently recommends that all comrades in their propaganda direct the attention of the workers to the anti-revolutionary and anti-proletarian character of the trend represented by [*Osvobozhdenie* (Liberation), the liberal] organ of Mr P. Struve.

1.12
On the Party of the Socialist Revolutionaries 10 August 1903

Considering:
 a that the interests of the Russian proletariat generally and of its emancipation movement in particular require it to act as a fully independent political force in the struggle with tsarism;
 b that only activity aimed at uniting the proletariat into such a force possesses a socialist-revolutionary content in the struggle with absolutism.
  Considering further:
 c that the [Party of the] 'Socialist Revolutionaries' in theory and practice opposes the efforts of the Social Democrats to weld the workers into an independent political party and, on the contrary, strives to keep them in the condition of a politically shapeless mass capable only of serving as the weapon of the liberal bourgeoisie —
  The Congress hereby states that the 'Socialist Revolutionaries' are nothing more than a bourgeois-democratic faction and that Social Democrats can in principle have no different an attitude toward them than toward liberal representatives of the bourgeoisie generally.
  Considering further:
 a that the 'Socialist Revolutionaries' pursue their bourgeois tendencies under the flag of socialism and
 b that, in addition or more precisely for the same reason, as a bourgeois-revolutionary faction they are utterly bankrupt —
  The Congress therefore considers their activity harmful not only to the political development of the proletariat but also to the overall democratic struggle against absolutism.
  For all of these reasons, the Congress condemns unconditionally any attempt to hide the political and principled significance of the differences between 'Socialist Revolutionaries' and Social Democrats. On the contrary, it recognizes as indispensable, both for the development of the political independence of the Russian proletariat and for the particular benefit of the liberation movement against absolutism, that Social Democrats elucidate and stress the bourgeois tendencies of the 'Socialist Revolutionaries' and their bankruptcy from the overall democratic point of view.
  In the light of the above considerations, the Congress decisively condemns any attempts at unifying the Social Democrats with the 'Socialist Revolutionaries' and recognizes as possible only private agree-

ments with them in particular instances of the struggle with tsarism, the conditions of such agreements to be subject to the supervision of the Central Committee.

1.13
On Demonstrations
10 August 1903

Considering:

a that under existing conditions in Russia, political demonstrations constitute one of the most important techniques for the political education of the broad mass of the people and for spreading and strengthening the influence of the Social Democratic Party;

b that demonstrations are at the same time the best instrument for the systematic disorganization of governmental machinery;

c that, gradually increasing in scope, these demonstrations should lead and, in part, are already leading to a series of armed clashes between the people and the governmental power, thus preparing the masses of the people for a Russia-wide uprising against the existing order —

The Congress therefore recognizes as indispensable that local committees take advantage of suitable occasions for organizing political demonstrations.

At the same time, the Congress hereby states that the previous approach to this question gave rise to considerable mistakes in practice and recommends the following steps for their elimination:

1   through extensive preliminary agitation, committees should endeavour to ensure that the broadest strata of the population are sympathetic to the purposes of the demonstration and are informed of the aims of the party;

2   demonstrations should be organized at times when the mood of the working masses is favourable; demonstrations are not to be artificially incited in the absence of this prior condition;

3   the active core of demonstrators should be sufficiently numerous, well organized, and prepared for their role;

4   measures should be taken to ensure that, in case of necessity, demonstrators will be able to repulse the police hordes aggressively and, if possible, with arms;

5   in view of the fact that regular troops are increasingly being used against the people in demonstrations, steps should be taken to acquaint the soldiers with the character and purpose of the demonstrations, and they should be invited to fraternize with the people; the demonstrators should not be allowed to antagonize them unduly.

The II Congress of the RSDRP recognizes the desirability of the

Central Committee directing and co-ordinating the efforts of local committees in organizing demonstrations as well as taking into its own hands the organization of Russia-wide political demonstrations in accordance with an overall plan.

1.14
On the Trade Union Struggle   10 August 1903

Considering:

a that the trade union struggle of the workers is the necessary consequence of the position of the proletariat in a capitalist society;

b that this struggle of the workers is one of the principal means of countering the tendency in the capitalist system toward a decline in the living standard of the workers;

c that in so far as this struggle develops in isolation from the political struggle of the proletariat led by the Social Democratic Party, it leads to the fragmentation of the proletarian forces and to subordination of the workers' movement to the interests of the propertied classes —

The Congress therefore recognizes that, with respect to the trade union movement, the task of the RSDRP is to lead the daily struggle of the workers for improved working conditions and to agitate for the removal of all the obstacles placed in the way of the trade union movement by the legislation of the Russian autocracy; in a word, to consolidate the individual clashes of isolated groups of workers into a single, organized, class struggle.

At the same time, in view of the increasingly apparent attempt of the tsarist government to take into its own hands the economic struggle of the working class – under the guise of 'legalization of the workers' movement' – and, distorting it politically, to make it the pawn of its own policies; in view of the fact that this so-called 'Zubatov policy' [S.V. Zubatov, high official in the Ministry of the Interior from 1889 to 1903 and primarily responsible for the formation of workers' associations under police guidance] is, besides its reactionary-political underpinning and the police-provocateur methods of its implementation, a policy of systematic betrayal of the interests of the working class for the benefit of the capitalists —

The Congress recommends that all comrades continue the unremitting struggle against Zubatovism in all its aspects, that they unmask before the workers the self-seeking and treacherous character of the tactics of the Zubatovist demagogues, and that they appeal to all workers to unite in a single class struggle for the political and economic liberation of the proletariat. To this end, the Congress recognizes as desirable that party organizations give support and guidance to strikes by legal workers' organizations and at the same time avail themselves of these clashes to unmask the reactionary character of the union between the workers and the autocracy.

1.15
On the Attitude toward Students
10 August 1903

The II Congress of RSDRP welcomes the quickening of revolutionary activity among students and calls on all party organizations to co-operate in every way with the efforts of these students to organize themselves. It recommends that all student groups and study circles should, firstly, accord priority in their activities to developing among their members an integrated and consistent socialist outlook so as to give them a thorough knowledge of marxism, on the one hand, and of Russian populism and western European opportunism, on the other, these being the principal trends among the leading conflicting tendencies of today; secondly, that they should try, when undertaking practical activity, to establish prior relations with Social Democratic organizations so as to benefit from their advice and, when possible, to avoid major errors at the very outset of their work.

All except 1.7 in *Vtoroi ocherednoi s"ezd Ross. Sots.-Dem. Rabochei Partii* (Geneva, 1904), 1–18

KPSS v rezoliutsiiakh 1, 60–83

III Party Congress
12–27 April 1905

Lenin's victory at the II Congress turned out to be of the Pyrrhic variety. By the end of 1903 he had lost control of the Council, the Central Organ, and the Foreign League; shortly thereafter, the Bolshevik-controlled Central Committee began to doubt his intentions and in early 1905 expelled him from that body. Lenin sought to recoup his losses by turning to the underground committees with the suggestion that they demand the calling of an extraordinary congress under article 2 of the party Rules. Despite the Council's refusal to comply, twenty-four delegates representing twenty-one local committees and two émigré bodies as well as fourteen guests showed up in London for the 'First Bolshevik' or III Party Congress. The mandates of many of these delegates were questionable. Some represented specially created splinter groups; others, such as Lenin and Kamenev, who 'represented' Odessa and the Caucasus Union respectively, were supposedly sent by cities they had rarely visited. While the Council denied the validity of the gathering and the Mensheviks refused to accept its resolutions as binding, the Congress nevertheless enabled Lenin to regain the initiative and the influence he had lost in the aftermath of the II Congress.

In organizational matters, the Congress accepted Lenin's version of the party Rules; it abolished the Council; it created a new all-powerful, all-Bolshevik Central Committee (Lenin, Bogdanov, L.B. Krasin, A.I. Rykov, D.S. Postolovsky); and it redefined the relationship of the local committees to the central party bodies abroad and to the peripheral organizations in the underground. It also gave Lenin more organizational flexibility and control by instructing Central Committee members working in Russia to meet abroad at least every four months with their 'foreign section' (i.e., Lenin) and by permitting the Committee to call periodic but ill-defined 'conferences of representatives from various party organizations.'

While all the delegates at the Congress were Bolsheviks, they were not necessarily all Leninists. Many of the local committeemen in fact were opposed both to émigré domination of the underground and to Lenin's attempts to increase the participation of workers at the expense of the intelligentsia in the underground structure. Moreover, despite the questionable mode of their own elections, many of the delegates sincerely wanted party unity. Thus they defeated Lenin's effort to condemn Plekhanov (who refused to attend) and they forced the Bolshevik leader to hold back his prepared resolution expelling the Mensheviks from the party. A secret resolution was instead passed instructing the Central Committee to explore conditions of unity with the Mensheviks but at the same time that body was given the authority to dissolve Menshevik committees that refused to accept the decisions of the Congress.

In the background of these factional manoeuvres was the fact that revolution had broken out in Russia during January of 1905. The Congress spent nearly a week discussing the party's attitude to the government's concessions as well as the RSDRP's role in leading an armed uprising and its possible participation in a future provisional revolutionary government. It also recognized that the time had come to pass from propaganda to agitation and to acknowledge the revolutionary potential of the Russian peasantry by enlarging the party's agrarian programme.

1.16
Party Rules 21 April 1905
[Replaces Rules adopted 1903; see 1.4]

1   [Revises 1.4, art. 1] A member of the party is one who accepts its Programme, supports the party financially, and participates through personal work in one of its organizations.

2   [Revises art. 2] The supreme organ of the party is the party congress. It is summoned annually by the Central Committee of the party. The Central Committee must call a congress within two months if this is demanded by party organizations which jointly would be entitled to one-half of the votes at the congress. A congress is considered valid if at it are represented organizations which jointly are entitled to more than one-half of the [party's total eligible] votes.

Note 1 If the Central Committee refuses to convoke a congress at the demand of one-half of the committees, the congress is to be called by an Organizational Committee elected at a conference of the representatives of qualified committees. In calling a congress, the Organizational Committee has all of the rights of the Central Committee.

Note 2 A list of newly confirmed organizations is to be published immediately in the Central Organ of the party with an indication of the date of their approval by the Central Committee.

3   [Revises art. 3] The following are entitled to representation at a congress:
   a   the Central Committee;
   b   all local committees which do not belong to special unions;
   c   other organizations which are equivalent to committees;
   d   all unions of committees recognized by the party.

Each of the above organizations is represented at a congress by a single delegate with a single vote; the Central Committee is represented by two delegates, each with a single vote; one of these delegates must be the chief editor of the Central Organ.

Representation of the unions is determined by special statutes.

Note 1 Only those organizations have the right to representation which have been approved at least six months before the congress.

Note 2 The Central Committee may invite to the congress, in an advisory capacity, delegates of organizations which do not meet the conditions set forth in Note 1.

4   [New] The congress elects the Central Committee.

5   [Revises art. 6] The Central Committee represents the party in relations with other parties; it appoints one of its members as chief editor of the Central Organ; it organizes committees, unions of committees and other party institutions, and guides their activities; it organizes and conducts

undertakings of significance for the party as a whole; it allocates party personnel and funds and has charge of the central party treasury; it settles conflicts both between and within various party institutions; and it generally co-ordinates and directs all the activity of the party.

6 [Revises art. 8] All basic party organizations (local, raion, factory committees, etc.) are autonomous in all matters falling specially and exclusively in the area of party activity for whose conduct they have been created; the degree of autonomy of groups (publishing groups, agitation groups, etc.) fulfilling particular and special functions is determined by the centres which have created them.

7 [New] Any organization which has been approved by the congress or the Central Committee has the right to issue party literature in its own name. The Central Committee must distribute the publications of any organization if five qualified [local] committees so demand. All party periodicals are obliged to publish statements by the Central Committee on the latter's demand.

8 [Revises art. 9] Party organizations, other than those confirmed by the party congress, are approved by the Central Committee; local peripheral organizations [i.e., cells, factory, and raion committees, etc.] are approved by the local centres. All decisions of the Central Committee are binding on all party organizations. The latter must also contribute to the central treasury 20 per cent of their receipts with the exception of the Committee of Foreign Organizations [created by émigré Bolsheviks in March 1905 to compete with the Menshevik-controlled Foreign League; see 1.4, art. 13] which must forward 90 per cent of its receipts to the Central Committee.

9 [New] A local committee must be dissolved by the Central Committee if two-thirds of the members of the Central Committee and two-thirds of the workers belonging to the local party organizations favour such a dissolution.

10 [New] Each party member and any person having any contact with the party has the right to demand that any statements made by him should be submitted in the original to the Central Committee, the Central Organ, or the party congress.

11 [Revises art. 11] Each party organization is obliged to make available to the Central Committee and to the editorial board of the Central Organ all materials bearing on their activities and personnel, submitting to the Central Committee detailed reports on their activities at least once every two weeks.

12 [Revises art. 12] All party organizations resolve questions by simple majority vote; autonomous organizations [see art. 6 above] have the right of co-optation. A two-thirds majority is required for co-optation and expulsion of party members. [Local] committees have the right to place their

members in autonomous peripheral organizations. Decisions on co-optation or expulsion of members may be appealed to the Central Committee.

Co-optation of members to the Central Committee must be unanimous. In [local] committees and similar organizations co-optation of official candidates proposed by the Central Committee or by autonomous peripheral organizations is by simple majority.

1.17
On Propaganda and Agitation   25 April 1905

Considering:
1   that the tasks of a planned and harmoniously organized revolutionary-proletarian movement, in view of its present colossal rate of growth, demand an incomparably greater number of Social Democratic personnel than was ever the case in the past;
2   that it is exceptionally important therefore to attract to the leading roles in the movement – as agitators, propagandists, and particularly as members of local and national party centres – the largest possible number of class-conscious workers since they are the people most closely associated with this movement and who bind it most tightly to the party. The inadequacies of such political leaders among the workers is explained precisely by the relative domination up to now of the party centres by intellectuals;
3   that under these conditions only a considerable expansion and improvement of agitation and propaganda will produce the necessary cadres of party workers —

The III Congress of the RSDRP therefore confirms the resolution of the II Congress on propaganda [1.10] and instructs the Central Committee:

    a   to organize a literary-propaganda group with the functions of working out an overall propaganda programme and of developing a companion series of popular brochures on the main questions of the party Programme, tactics, and organization; giving particular attention to pamphlet literature for use among the peasantry;

    b   to take steps to issue a popular organ in Russia;

    c   to see to the organization of travelling groups of agitators and propagandists for assisting the local [party] centres;

    d   to take steps to issue propaganda and agitational literature in Yiddish and in other [non-Russian] languages; for this purpose, entering when necessary into agreements with local committees.

1.18
On the Central Organ of the Party 25 April 1905

Considering:
1 that the editors of *Iskra* [since 12 November 1903: Martov, Plekhanov, Potresov, Akselrod, Zasulich] did not appear at the Congress and have not taken steps to co-ordinate its further activity with the decisions and directives of the III Party Congress;
2 that the activities of the editorial board of the new *Iskra* in no way guarantee a correct solution of tactical problems in the future —

The III Congress of the RSDRP therefore resolves that the newspaper *Iskra* is henceforward no longer the Central Organ of the party and instructs the Central Committee to establish, in accordance with the party Rules, a new Central Organ called *Proletarii*.

1.19
On the Armed Uprising 16 April 1905

Considering:
1 that the proletariat, by virtue of its position the most advanced and only consistently revolutionary class, is therefore called upon to play the leading role in the general democratic revolutionary movement in Russia;
2 that this movement has at the present time already given rise to the need for an armed uprising;
3 that in this uprising, which will determine the fate of the revolution in Russia, the proletariat will inevitably be the most active participant;
4 that the proletariat can assume the commanding role in this revolution only if solidly united into a single and independent political force under the banner of the Social Democratic Labour Party, which will direct its struggle both ideologically and practically;
5 that only assumption of this role can assure the proletariat of the most favourable conditions for the struggle for socialism against the propertied classes of bourgeois-democratic Russia —

The III Congress of the RSDRP recognizes that the task of organizing the proletariat for direct struggle against the autocracy by means of an armed uprising is one of the most important and urgent tasks of the party at the present revolutionary moment.

Therefore, the Congress instructs all party organizations:
a to explain to the proletariat through propaganda and agitation not only the political significance, but also the practical organizational side of the impending armed uprising;

b to explain in this propaganda and agitation the role of mass political strikes which may be of major significance at the onset and during the actual course of the uprising;

c to take the most energetic measures to arm the proletariat, and also to develop a plan for the armed uprising and for its direct guidance, creating for this purpose special groups of party workers whenever necessary.

1.20
On a Provisional Revolutionary Government
19 April 1905

Considering:

1 that both the immediate interests of the proletariat and the interests of its struggle for the ultimate goals of socialism require the fullest possible measure of political freedom and, consequently, the replacement of the autocratic form of government by a democratic republic;

2 that a democratic republic can be established in Russia only as the result of a victorious popular uprising whose agency will be a provisional revolutionary government which alone is capable of ensuring completely free pre-electoral agitation and of convening a constituent assembly, elected by secret ballot on the basis of universal, equal, and direct suffrage, that will genuinely express the will of the people;

3 that with Russia's present socio-economic structure this democratic revolution will not weaken, but rather will strengthen, the domination of the bourgeoisie which, stopping at nothing, will inevitably attempt at some moment to snatch away from the Russian proletariat the largest possible part of the gains of the revolutionary period —

The III Congress of the RSDRP therefore resolves that:

a it is necessary to disseminate among the working class a concrete idea of the most probable course the revolution will take and of the necessity for the emergence at a given moment in the revolution of a provisional revolutionary government from which the proletariat will demand the implementation of all the immediate political and economic demands of our Programme (the minimum programme) [see second half of 1.3];

b depending upon the alignment of forces and other factors which cannot be precisely defined in advance, representatives of our party may be allowed to take part in the provisional revolutionary government so as to conduct a relentless struggle against all counter-revolutionary attempts and to uphold the independent interests of the working class;

c as an essential condition of such participation, our party will maintain strict control over its representatives and will constantly safeguard the independence of the Social Democratic Party which strives for a complete socialist revolution and hence is irreconcilably opposed to all bourgeois parties;

d regardless of whether or not the Social Democrats will be able to participate in the provisional revolutionary government, we must propagandize among the broadest sections of the proletariat the idea that the proletariat, armed and led by the Social Democratic Party, must keep constant pressure on the provisional government with the aim of preserving, consolidating, and extending the gains of the revolution.

1.21
On the Attitude toward the Government's Tactics
on the Eve of the Revolution   19 April 1905

Considering that in the present revolutionary period the [tsarist] government, for purposes of self-preservation, is intensifying its customary repressive measures aimed primarily against class-conscious elements of the proletariat and at the same time:

1   through concessions and promised reforms is trying to corrupt the working class politically in order to divert it from the revolutionary struggle;

2   for the same reason, is dressing up its hypocritical policy of concessions with pseudo-democratic trappings, starting with the invitation to workers to elect their representatives to commissions and conferences [i.e., the Shidlovsky Commission to investigate worker grievances] and ending with the creation of such caricatures of popular representation as the so-called 'Zemskii Sobor' [a consultative assembly which met sporadically during the sixteenth and seventeenth centuries; see 1.39 for its 1905 application];

3   is organizing the so-called Black Hundreds [i.e., arch–reactionary, anti-semitic groups which sought to suppress all signs of revolutionary sentiment] and is arousing against the revolution all elements of the population which are just generally reactionary, lacking in consciousness, or blinded by racial or religious hatred —

The III Congress of the RSDRP therefore resolves to call on all party organizations:

a to unmask through propaganda and agitation the reactionary purposes of the government's concessions emphasizing, on the one hand, that they were granted under compulsion, and on the other, the absolute impossibility of the autocracy granting reforms satisfactory to the proletariat;

b to use the electoral campaign [for the proposed consultative assembly] to explain to the workers the true significance of such governmental measures and to prove the proletariat's need for the calling of a constituent assembly by revolutionary means and on the basis of an electoral law granting universal, equal, and direct suffrage with secret ballot;

  c to organize the proletariat for the immediate revolutionary implementation of the eight-hour working day and the other immediate demands of the working class;

  d to organize the armed repulse of the Black Hundreds and of all-reactionary elements led by the government.

1.22
On the Question of Overt Political Activity by the RSDRP   19 April 1905

Considering:

1 that the revolutionary movement in Russia has already considerably shaken and disorganized the autocratic government, which has been compelled to permit limited freedom of political activity to classes which are hostile to it;

2 that this freedom of political activity is now being enjoyed primarily by the bourgeois classes, which thereby intensify still further their economic and political domination of the proletariat and increase the danger that the working class will be transformed into a mere appendage of bourgeois democracy;

3 that increasingly broader segments of the working masses are showing a desire for independent and overt activity in the political arena, even without the participation of the Social Democratic Party —

The III Congress of the RSDRP therefore draws the attention of all party organizations to the necessity:

  a of using every opportunity for legal activity to contrast the independent class demands of the proletariat with general democratic demands, so as to organize the proletariat during the course of these activities into an independent Social Democratic force;

  b of exploiting all legal or semi-legal workers' societies, trade unions, and other organizations, so as to secure in them predominant Social Democratic influence and to transform them as much as possible into bases for the future openly functioning Social Democratic Labour Party in Russia;

  c of seeing to it that our party organizations not only maintain and expand their own conspiratorial apparatus but also immediately undertake, wherever and whenever possible, the preparation of suitable arrangements for the Social Democratic Party's transition to open activity; in this they should not stop short of clashes with the armed forces of the government.

1.23
On Support of the Peasant Movement 20 April 1905

Considering:

1 that the growing peasant movement, although spontaneous and politically unconscious, will none the less inevitably turn against the existing order and against all remnants of serfdom generally;

2 that one of the tasks of social democracy is to support every revolutionary movement against the existing social and political order;

3 that by virtue of this, Social Democrats must strive to cleanse the revolutionary-democratic content of the peasant movement of all reactionary admixtures, developing the revolutionary consciousness of the peasantry and carrying through their democratic demands;

4 that the Social Democratic Party, as the party of the proletariat, must at all times and under all circumstances steadfastly work for the independent organization of the rural proletariat and explain to [this group] the irreconcilable antagonism between its interests and those of the peasant bourgeoisie —

The III Congress of the RSDRP therefore instructs all party organizations:

a to state in propaganda among broad segments of the population that the Social Democratic Party undertakes to give utmost support to all peasant revolutionary initiatives that are capable of improving their condition, up to the confiscation of land owned by the landlords, the state, the church, the monasteries and the imperial family;

b as a practical slogan for agitation among the peasants and as a means of instilling the highest degree of consciousness in the peasant movement, to raise the issue of the immediate organization of revolutionary peasant committees that will have as their aim the carrying out of all revolutionary-democratic reforms so as to rescue the peasantry from the yoke of the police, the bureaucracy, and the landowners;

c with the aim of disorganizing the autocracy and maintaining revolutionary pressure on it, to arouse among the peasantry and rural proletariat all kinds of political demonstrations as well as collective refusals to pay assessments and taxes, to perform military service, and to obey the decrees and orders of the government or its agents;

d to strive for an independent organization of the rural proletariat, for its merger with the urban proletariat under the banner of the Social Democratic Party, and for the inclusion of its representatives in peasant committees.

1.24
On Practical Agreements with Socialist Revolutionaries   23 April 1905

Confirming the attitude of the RSDRP toward the Party of the Socialist Revolutionaries as defined by the resolution of the II Congress [1.12], and considering:

1   that temporary combat agreements between Social Democrats and Socialist Revolutionary organizations, for purposes of combatting the autocracy, may in some cases be useful;

2   that such agreements may under no circumstances limit the complete independence of the Social Democratic Party, nor may they encroach on the integrity and purity of its proletarian tactics and principles —

The III Congress of the RSDRP therefore instructs the Central Committee and the local committees to enter if necessary into temporary combat agreements with Socialist Revolutionary organizations, provided that these are concluded only under the supervision of the Central Committee.

1.25
On the Attitude toward the National Social Democratic Organizations   23 April 1905

Considering:

1   that the interests of the proletariat's economic and political struggle require the unification of the Social Democratic organizations of all nationalities in Russia;

2   that the beginning of the openly revolutionary struggle against the autocratic order and the nearness of the armed uprising makes such a unification especially necessary —

The III Congress therefore confirms the attitude of the II Congress on the question of federalism [1.6] and instructs both the Central Committee and the local committees to make every effort to reach agreement with national Social Democratic organizations [such as the Bund] with the aim of co-ordinating local work and thus preparing the ground for the unification of all Social Democratic parties in a single RSDRP.

1.26
On Divergent Parts of the Party   23 April 1905

The Congress notes that since the period of struggle with 'economism' [1899 to 1903] there have remained within the RSDRP ... various nuances [e.g., menshevism, which Lenin called an 'imitation of economism'] characterized by a general tendency to belittle the significance of consciousness, which they subordinate to spontaneity, in the proletarian struggle ... In tactical matters [the supporters of this view] manifest a desire to narrow the scope of party work; speaking out against the party pursuing completely independent tactics in relation to the bourgeois-liberal parties, against the possibility and the desirability of our party undertaking an organizational role in the popular uprising, and against the party's participation under any conditions in a provisional democratic-revolutionary government.

The Congress therefore instructs all party members everywhere to carry out an energetic ideological struggle against such partial deviations from revolutionary Social Democratic principles, but at the same time finds that persons to some extent espousing these views may participate in party organizations on the essential condition that they recognize the [decisions of the] party congresses and the party Rules and in all matters subordinate themselves to party discipline.

1.27
On Preparing Conditions for Unity with the Mensheviks   23 April 1905

The III Congress of the RSDRP instructs the Central Committee to take all steps to prepare and work out the conditions for unity with the part of the RSDRP which has split off, these conditions to be submitted to a new party congress for final approval.

1.28
On the Dissolution of Committees Which Refuse to
Accept the Decisions of the III Congress   23 April 1905

Considering the possibility that some Menshevik organizations will refuse to accept the decisions of the III Congress, the Congress orders the Central Committee, after careful elucidation has fully established the refusal of these Menshevik organizations and committees to accept party discipline, to dissolve such organizations and to approve as committees parallel organizations which accept the authority of the Congress.

  Tretii ocherednoi s"ezd Ross.   *KPSS v rezoliutsiiakh* I, 111–27
  sots.-dem. rabochei partii: Polnyi
  tekst protokolov (Geneva, 1905),
  xvi–xxix; 1.27 and 1.28 in 'Novye
  materialy o III s"ezde RSDRP,'
  Proletarskaia revoliutsiia, no. 25
  (1924), 187–90

I All-Russian Menshevik Conference April 1905

The Mensheviks readily acknowledged that their 'first all-Russian conference of party workers' came about largely 'by chance.' Shortly before the convocation of the III Congress, the representatives of eight underground organizations came to the conclusion that the Bolshevik gathering was going to be of questionable legality and unrepresentative of true party opinion. They therefore left the Congress, probably in the company of two of the guests, and went to Geneva where they joined with several other underground workers who happened to be abroad and with some Menshevik émigrés to hold their concurrent conference.

Despite the fact that they claimed to represent fifteen local organizations and had in attendance most of the prominent figures of Russian social democracy (Plekhanov, Martov, Akselrod, Zasulich, Potresov, Dan, A.S. Martynov), the Mensheviks refused to call their meeting a congress or to make their decisions binding for the underground organizations. While criticizing the growing tendency 'for the direction of party policy to be in the hands of a bunch of "professional revolutionaries" more or less estranged from the local organizations,' they ineffectually combatted Bolshevik control of the Central Committee by establishing their own Organizational Commission (V.N. Gutovsky, M.S. Makadziub, L.M. Khinchuk, I.M. Grintser, A.A. Tarasevich) which was entrusted with tying together the Menshevik groups in Russia and within conducting preliminary negotiations with the Bolsheviks concerning party unity. The Mensheviks thus sat on the fence: they refused to challenge the Bolsheviks with a united RSDRP by fighting it out at the III Congress and they refused to go to the opposite extreme of setting themselves up as a separate party.

Many of the resolutions of the Conference were equally vague and ill-formulated. The delegates sought to modify the highly centralized edifice the II Congress had set up by suggesting more democratic procedures for local organizations. But as Lenin noted, nothing was said about the central party institutions and the resulting local structure was like 'a six-decker bus which would not be able to budge an inch even if it could be built.' Despite the revolutionary events occurring in Russia, the Mensheviks gave far less attention and importance to the question of an armed uprising; indeed, the resolution on arming the workers was never discussed owing to a 'lack of time.' In contrast to the Bolsheviks, the Mensheviks refused to advocate either the seizure of power in the imminent revolution or Social Democratic participation in any resulting provisional government. They followed the more orthodox but less attractive alternative of remaining 'the party of the extreme revolutionary opposition' unless socialist revolutions should spread to the more advanced countries of western Europe. (For a detailed if one-sided comparison of this argument as reflected in 1.33 below with the Bolshevik position at the III Congress, [1.20 above], see Lenin's *Two Tactics of Social Democracy in the Democratic Revolution*.) The Mensheviks continued to stress the historical role of the liberal bourgeoisie in the overthrow of the autocracy, unlike the Bolsheviks who had come to see the peasantry as the proletariat's principal ally in the democratic revolution. Thus the Conference suggested leaving the ultimate solution of the land question to a future constituent assembly – a policy which could hardly attract peasant support and which was to have profound consequences twelve years later. On the other hand, the Mensheviks realized more clearly than their rivals that the rapidly developing trade unions and other legal worker organizations offered not only a new and fertile field for Social Democratic activity but also the prospect for moving toward a mass workers' party.

1.29
On Relations between the Two Parts of the Party

I
Considering that, despite the protest lodged against the so-called [III] 'Congress' by one-half of the party organizations, the comrades who went to this 'Congress' declared it a congress of the party and thereby accomplished the division of the party into two parts grouped around differing conceptions of the party's immediate tactical and organizational tasks; considering also that the only real tie preserving the party from disintegration is the unity conferred by a recognized Programme and the intention of both parts of the party to remain under the banner of the RSDRP;

Considering also that this situation makes it somewhat easier to restore organizational unity throughout in that it affords the opportunity to eliminate arguments about competence and formal rights which have accumulated on the basis of these divergent views —

The Conference therefore resolves as follows:

To facilitate the restoration of party unity, that part of the party which adheres to the [Menshevik] Conference decisions hereby rejects any claim to represent all party organizations and invites the other part of the party [i.e., the Bolsheviks] to do the same.

The Conference hereby ceases to consider the Rules worked out at the II Congress [1.4], which were abolished by the other part of the party [1.16], as binding upon party members.

The Conference hereby empowers the Organizational Commission to accept and follow up any initiative emanating from the ranks of international social democracy [e.g., August Bebel's offer in late January 1905 to head a five-man independent tribunal that would mediate Russian factional differences] aimed at drawing together and unifying the two parts of the party in accordance with the [1904] decision of the Amsterdam Congress of the [Second] International.

In the name of that part of the party which it represents, the Conference invites Comrade Plekhanov to remain as the party's representative in the International [Socialist] Bureau, as authorized by the united delegation of the party at the [Amsterdam] Congress, and expresses the hope that the other part of the party will join in this invitation.

II

Regarding the decisions of the [III] Congress convoked by the Bureau of the Committees of the Majority and the Central Committee as not binding upon the party, the Conference views the institutions elected by that Congress as representing only a particular section of the party.

Considering that, despite the existence of differing views on tactical and organizational questions, unification of the party is both entirely possible and necessary, the Conference orders the newly elected Organizational Commission, as soon as it is constituted, to undertake in the name of those organizations which adhere to the decisions of the Conference negotiations with the central institutions of the other side so as to elucidate the bases of agreement between the two parts of the party.

This agreement must be based on the following:
1   Both centres will promote attempts to unify and co-ordinate political and organizational work on the local level.
2   The centres agree on joint action to restore party unity.
3   The literary organs of both tendencies will continue to exist in parallel, and their interests will be concerted in matters of the transportation and dissemination of literature.

It is further recommended that the Organizational Commission reach particular agreements, through conferences or discussions or in other ways, with the central institutions of the other section of the party on the various other questions of party work.

Regardless of any overall agreement, the Conference advises comrades, in those places where organizations of the two party factions exist in parallel, to agree among themselves on joint action to promote the complete fusion of the two factions through the fullest possible co-ordination and unification of political and organizational work on the local level.

Note Any permanent agreements to co-ordinate or unify party work must be concluded with the entire local party organization, not just with the [local city] committee.

The Organizational Commission is advised to be of service to all party organizations which agree to make use of these services. Similarly, organizations accepting the decisions of the Conference may not refuse the services of the centre of the other part of the party to the extent that the latter does not set as an obligatory condition the recognition of its jurisdictional rights with respect to themselves.

1.30
Organizational Rules

Striving to guarantee to a broader circle of party workers a share in the development and direction of party policy, the Conference proposes a series of organizational standards for reforming local work. The Conference finds it necessary to point out that through the standards proposed for local organizations it is striving to introduce into the organizational life of the party that degree of democratization for which the time is ripe and which can already be implemented in all advanced organizations. At the same time, the Conference recommends that local organizations, wherever conditions are favourable, proceed further along the path of such democratization; on the one hand, increasing the degree of influence of lower level organizational cells on the party's practical activity and, on the other, gradually introducing the elective principle into the local organizational system [i.e., the election by rank-and-file members of local party officials and representatives].

1   The guiding political collective in each city is made up of the [city] committee together with its raion committees.
Note Groups working with particular sections of the population, such as peasant or military groups, enter into the guiding collective of a given area along with the raion committees and have the same rights.
2   A raion committee is made up of persons taking an active part in the work of the organization of the given raion.
3   A raion committee also contains a representative of the [city] committee. The [city] committee must recall its representative and replace him with another at the demand of a majority of the members of the raion committee.
4   *a* All decisions determining the attitude of the entire organization, as the party's local representative, on political or party questions are made by a majority vote of the members of the raion committees and the [city] committee.
   b In all cases of practical activity requiring the active and compulsory participation of all members of the organization, the entire local organization must take part in the discussion and the vote.
Note 1 In exceptional cases, which cannot be postponed and which require the [city] committee to act at once before obtaining the opinion of the raion committees, the [city] committee has the right to act independently but must then report on its activities to the raion committees.

Note 2 Any proposal to the [city] committee made by any group of a local organization must be discussed and voted upon by the whole guiding collective.

5   The [city] committee must report periodically to the raion committees on its activities. Such reports must also be submitted on an ad hoc basis at the demand of members of a raion committee.

6   If a majority of the members of the raion committees express a lack of confidence in the [city] committee, the latter will be reorganized by mutual agreement between the oblast committee and the raion committees.

7   If a [city] committee is completely arrested or has its membership reduced to two persons, it is to be restored in the way indicated in the preceding paragraph.

8   When a [city] committee is being formed in a place where none has previously existed, it is established by mutual agreement between the oblast committee and a meeting of responsible [party] workers.

9   Raion committees are reorganized by agreement between the guiding collective and the lower level organizations of the given raion.

10   Delegates to oblast and all-party congresses are elected following the procedure laid down by the guiding collective of the given locality.

Note If there are two tendencies in the organization, the minority has the right to special representation [at the congress] if it is supported by not less than one-third of the members of the guiding collective.

11   Oblast committees, consisting of 3 to 5 persons elected by oblast congresses, act as permanent organs unifying the work of the local organizations and linking them together.

Note 1 St Petersburg is considered to be an autonomous oblast organization.

Note 2 If possible, all members of oblast committees take part in local work.

[12   This article was omitted, perhaps for conspiratorial reasons.]

13   The regular conference, consisting of the Executive Commission and the representatives of all oblast committees, is the body which unifies all party work. These conferences fulfil the functions of the Central Committee.

Note The Executive Commission is located in St Petersburg and if possible all its members participate in local work. The Executive Commission is elected at general conferences of all Central Committee members.

1.31
On Party Literature

The Conference recognizes as essential:
1   that the Organizational Commission take steps to increase the oppor-

tunities for party publicists to conduct a struggle in the legal press for the party's theoretical principles;
2   that *Sotsial-demokrat* be issued more frequently and assume a more militant and agitational character;
3   that *Iskra* set as its main task the development of general issues in the Social Democratic Programme and tactics, making it easier for party workers to analyse independently current questions involved in the party's practical policy;
4   that *Letuchii listok Sotsial-demokrata* [Leaflet of a Social Democrat] be issued in St Petersburg, with the support of the central party institutions, as an agitational organ capable, with the further development of the party organizations, of compensating for the short-comings of Social Democratic literature published abroad;
5   that regional organizations, wherever they are in a position to do so, set up regional organs to deal with those requirements of the proletariat that remain unsatisfied in the current literary situation;
6   that party organizations give thought to bringing under their influence those democratic newspapers which pursue the aim of assisting the workers' movement.

1.32
On the Armed Uprising

In setting itself the task of preparing the masses for an uprising, the Social Democratic Party strives to bring the uprising under its influence and leadership and to use it in the interests of the working class.
Considering that:
1   a simultaneous and widespread uprising cannot be timed to occur at a precise moment or be prepared by conspiratorial-organizational means, if only because of the organizational weakness of the more advanced proletariat and the inevitable spontaneous character of the revolutionary movement among precisely those popular masses whose rapid involvement in the struggle against tsarism is the guarantee of our victory;
2   it is, above all, the unceasing fermentation among the masses and the increasing disorganization of the forces of reaction which create favourable conditions for a victorious uprising —
To prepare for the uprising social democracy must, first of all:
a   extend its agitation among the masses by exploiting current political developments;
b   tie to its political organization and subject to its influence, those social and economic movements which are arising independently among the proletarian masses;
c   reinforce among the masses the realization of the inevitability of

revolution, the need to be always prepared for armed defence, and the possibility at any given moment of transforming this confrontation into an uprising;

d establish closest ties among the fighting proletarians of various localities so as to enable social democracy to take the initiative in transforming the spontaneous preparations of these movements into planned uprisings. It must associate to the fullest possible extent the proletarian movement in the cities with the revolutionary movement in the countryside;

e arouse the interest, through extensive agitation, of the broadest possible segments of the population in the proletariat's revolutionary struggle for a democratic republic, thus eliciting the active support of non-proletarian groups for the militant actions of the proletariat guided by its independent class party.

Only if preceded by such comprehensive work by the Social Democratic Party can the moment of the uprising be advanced, can its subordination to our leadership be facilitated, and can the technical and military preparations of our party organizations for the uprising take on any real significance.

1.33
On the Seizure of Power and Participation in a Provisional Government

The decisive victory of the revolution over tsarism may be marked either by the establishment of a provisional government – issuing from the victorious popular uprising – or by the revolutionary initiative of one or another representative institution which will decide, under the direct revolutionary pressure of the people, to organize a national constituent assembly.

In either case, such a victory will inaugurate a new phase in the revolutionary epoch.

The objective conditions of social development confront this new phase, in the most immediate manner, with the task of liquidating once and for all the whole monarchial régime of social estates through the internecine struggle among the elements of the politically liberated bourgeois society for the realization of their own social interests and for the direct acquisition of power.

Therefore, the provisional government that would undertake to carry out the tasks of this revolution (bourgeois in its historical character) would be compelled, in regulating the mutual struggle of the opposed classes of the self-liberating nation, not only to promote revolutionary development but also to combat those factors which threaten the foundations of the capitalist order.

Under these conditions, social democracy must strive to retain for itself, throughout the entire [bourgeois] revolution, a position which would best afford it the opportunity of furthering the revolution, which would not bind its hands in the struggle against the inconsistent and self-seeking policies of the bourgeois parties, and which would prevent it from losing its identity in bourgeois democracy.

Therefore, social democracy should not set itself the goal of seizing or sharing power in the provisional government but must remain the party of the extreme revolutionary opposition.

Of course, this tactic in no way excludes the expediency of partial or episodic seizures of power and the formation of revolutionary communes in one city or another, or in one region or another, solely for the purpose of furthering the spread of the uprising and the disorganization of the government.

In only one case should social democracy take the initiative and direct its efforts toward seizing power and holding it as long as possible – and that is if the revolution should spread to the advanced countries of western Europe where conditions for the realization of socialism have already attained a certain degree of maturity. In such a case, the limited historical scope of the Russian revolution may be considerably broadened, and it may become possible to set out on the path of socialist reforms.

By basing its tactics on the expectation that throughout the entire revolutionary period the Social Democratic Party will maintain a position of extreme revolutionary opposition to all the governments which may succeed one another during the course of the revolution, social democracy can best prepare itself for wielding governmental power if it should fall into its hands.

1.34
On Participation in Elections to Representative Institutions

In demanding the convocation of a national constituent assembly, the Social Democratic Party, as an independent political party, must also exploit those representative institutions [such as the proposed Bulygin Duma, see 1.39] which may in the immediate future be convoked by the declining autocracy.

In such cases, the slogan used in electoral agitation must be the demand for replacement of such representative institutions by a national constituent assembly.

The working class must confront with this same demand any constituent assembly convoked on the basis of estates or of a restricted electoral law.

In the case of a bicameral representational system, with the lower chamber elected democratically, Social Democrats should pressure the lower chamber to overthrow the upper chamber and declare itself a constituent assembly.

The Social Democratic Party should act in all elections as an independent class party, rejecting any agreements with non-proletarian parties and groups on submission of joint candidates, and pursuing in the electoral campaign the primary goal of a class organization of the proletarian masses so as to exert revolutionary pressure on the representative organs which will do the work of renovating the Russian state and social order.

1.35
On the Attitude toward Other Revolutionary and Opposition Parties

Considering that:

1   the present moment is characterized by the formation of a whole series of political parties and groups which are introducing a certain differentiation into the hitherto more or less homogeneous mass of the bourgeois and petty bourgeois opposition;

2   in the struggle for its existence the autocratic monarchy is attempting to exploit this fragmentation to maintain power through compromises with certain groups;

3   the temporary success of such attempts by the autocracy can have only one outcome — that the process of liberating Russia will become more extended and more painful for the masses of the people and will be accompanied by an unleashing of the dark forces of reaction as exemplified by the events in Baku [where bloody racial clashes took place between Muslims and Armenians during February 1905] and elsewhere;

4   from this it follows that a genuine fusion of all social forces anxious for a democratic reconstruction, and the most rapid and complete rescue of Russia from tsarism, can be achieved only through a relentless revolutionary war against all the foundations of the monarchial system of social estates;

Considering all of this, social democracy demands the following from all enemies of tsarism, in the interests of a successful struggle against it:

1   energetic and unequivocal support for any determined action by the organized proletariat designed to strike new blows against tsarism;

2   open recognition and unreserved support for the demand for a national constituent assembly on the basis of universal, equal, and direct suffrage with the secret ballot, and an open attack on all parties and groups

striving to curtail the rights of the people, whether by limiting the suffrage or by replacing the constituent assembly with a constitution conceded by the monarchy;
3   decisive support for the struggle of the working class against the government and the magnates of capital for the freedom to hold strikes and to form trade unions;
4   open opposition to all attempts by the government and the feudal nobility to crush the peasant revolutionary movement by using measures of barbarous violence against the persons and property of peasants;
5   refusal to support any measures designed to perpetuate in a free Russia either limitations on the rights of separate nationalities or traces of national oppression;
6   active participation in the cause of the people arming themselves for the struggle against the reaction and active support for social democracy's efforts to organize a mass armed struggle.

In presenting these demands, revolutionary social democracy declares that in the interests of liberating the people it will continue, as before, to oppose as hypocritical friends of the people all those political parties which, while holding up the banner of liberalism and democracy, refuse to give genuine support to the revolutionary struggle of the proletariat.

1.36
On Trade Unions

Considering:
that the revolution through which our country will have to pass will not only fail to eliminate capitalist production relations but will even give a new and powerful stimulus to their development; that the proletariat which has to sell its labour in the market must organize into trade unions to struggle for the most favourable possible conditions of employment and work;
that one of the most important eventual conquests of the Russian proletariat in the forthcoming revolution will be the right to organize freely such trade unions and also the collective right to refuse to work under conditions which are not advantageous for the workers;
that our party would not be fulfilling its duty to the workers if it did not stress the enormous importance to them of these rights and did not, at the opportune time, lead them to a conquest of these rights;
that this conquest is greatly facilitated by the atmosphere of revolutionary fermentation —
   The Conference therefore advises all party organizations immediately to undertake extensive agitation among the workers for the or-

ganization of trade unions, whose very creation would signify that the time is near for the final achievement of these rights, and recommends:

1   the encouragement of all efforts by the workers to create unions for the defence of their economic interests, and an appeal for the organization of such unions despite the existing prohibitory laws;
2   the setting up of regular meetings of representatives of the various trade unions or of representatives of industrial establishments (foremen, deputies, etc.) so as to establish continuous contact among them;
3   the maintaining of permanent ties between party organizations and trade unions, and extending constant assistance to the latter by means of the personnel and technical resources available in the party organizations;
4   the compulsory participation of all workers who are party members in the existing trade unions or those which may arise at their places of employment;
5   representation of those trade unions which recognize the party Programme in the general party organization.

1.37
On Informal Organizations

In the present atmosphere of revolutionary ferment among the broad masses there are arising various kinds of informal associations of workers.

By uniting the workers without distinction as to trade, on the ground of social, economic, and political needs common to the entire working class, these associations by virtue of historical circumstances have become the starting points for the political unification of the proletariat.

Taking into account that the development of these associations creates the basis for the quick expansion and strengthening of an independent party of the working class under the banner of social democracy, the conference recommends:

1   assisting such associations to emerge and to multiply; and
2   trying to turn them into permanent revolutionary organizations of the proletariat (workers' clubs), under the leadership of the Social Democratic Party, which will have as their aim direct intervention in political and social affairs in the interests of the working class.

1.38
On Work with the Peasantry

1

The Russian Social Democratic Party, as a proletarian party, strives to organize the workers, both industrial and agricultural, into a single political party to struggle for their immediate demands and for the ultimate goal of the world-wide workers' movement, i.e., the annihilation of capitalist production relations and their replacement by socialist production relations.

The activities of the Social Democratic Party among agricultural workers are especially facilitated by the awakening which has recently affected the whole population of the country and has even extended to the peasantry.

The necessity of such activities, which is understandable in itself, is felt with particular strength now that the agricultural entrepreneurs are making unambiguous attempts to consolidate the dependent position of the rural workers and, even in their reformist plans, are calling for a limitation of the rights which the workers need to defend their interests as sellers of labour power.

The Conference calls upon comrades to take advantage of these circumstances in order to intensify agitation among rural workers, to organize a strike movement, and to consolidate the workers into unions for the struggle to protect their trade interests.

In the course of such agitation comrades must explain to the village proletariat the extreme importance for it of all the demands of our Programme, which aims at defending the interests of hired labour.

Organizations must devote attention to hiring points for seasonal agricultural labour, taking advantage of the times when a number of workers are gathered there for the most energetic agitation.

II

But in addition to the struggle between hired labour and capital, in the village today there is also a movement for liberating the peasantry as an estate which has been put in a particularly difficult and humiliating position by the now rapidly crumbling system of serfdom.

Agitating on the basis of its agrarian programme [1.3], social democracy contrasts the demands contained therein to all attempts under the guise of agrarian reform which impose new burdens on the peasantry for the benefit of the landowning nobility (plans for a new purchase of their estates); it unmasks reactionary illusions predicated on the idea that the tsar is the supreme owner of all the land in the state, or those which idealize small-scale farming, or those which encourage the village poor to think that they can be liberated from capitalist exploitation by some redistribution of landed property.

At the same time, social democracy supports any attempts by the peasants at forcible seizure of the land, explaining to the peasantry that its conquests in the struggle with the landowners can be firmly secured only by a freely elected national constituent assembly which must be required to form, on a democratic basis, special committees (peasant committees) which will bring about the final elimination of the old rural regulations which are so oppressive for the peasantry.

Proceeding from the fact that the attitudes of serfdom in the village are perpetuated not only by the present distribution of landed property but also by the whole structure of state and social life, the Social Democratic Party conducts unceasing agitation among the peasants on the basis of its democratic demands and, in particular, points out the prime importance to the peasantry of:

a the replacement of all indirect taxes by a single direct and progressive tax on incomes and inheritances;

b the destruction of all estate restrictions and of the passport system;

c the full democratization not only of the state order but also of all organs of local and community self-government; and

d the replacement of the standing army by a people's militia.

III

Rejecting, in its agitational activity, the use of agrarian terror as an instrument of systematic struggle and viewing this as an unsuitable means which distracts attention from genuinely revolutionary tasks, the Social Democratic Party considers the following to be necessary:

1 the village must be informed to the fullest possible extent of the course of the revolutionary movement in Russia and, in particular, of the tasks and the manifestations of the working-class movement; the closest possible co-operation must be established between the revolutionary movement in the cities and in the countryside;

2 all governmental efforts to make the peasantry into an instrument for crushing the liberation movement must be unmasked, and the anti-popular and reactionary nature of such attempts must be explained;

3 agitation must be conducted on behalf of:

a the open voicing of political demands in village and volost assemblies;

b the arming of everyone for self-defence against governmental violence;

c the refusal to pay taxes or to carry out obligations;

d the refusal to supply recruits, to report for training, or to rally to the flag if the reserves are called up;

e the refusal to recognize any governmental powers or the powers of those elected by governmental pressure;

f the free election of officials and, as a result,

g the revolutionary self-government of villages and revolutionary unions of self-governing rural communities as the organization of the peasant uprising against tsarism.

IV

The Conference feels that it would be a timely measure to convoke a special conference of agitators occupied in village work for a detailed elaboration of the practical issues involved in this work. The Conference orders the Ukrainian Social Democratic Union [or Spilka, which joined the RSDRP in early 1905] to take upon itself the organization of such a conference, with the co-operation of the Organizational Commission, and resolves that it be requested to publish in Russian all literature issued in Ukrainian provided that such literature possess more than purely local interest.

Pervaia obshcherusskaia konferentsiia partiinykh rabotnikov, supplement to *Iskra*, no. 100 (Geneva, 1905), 17–28

Conference of Social Democratic Organizations in Russia   7–9 September 1905

On 6 August 1905 the imperial government finally announced the details concerning the consultative assembly or 'Bulygin Duma' which was to convene before 15 January 1906. While the Mensheviks and Bolsheviks had known about the intention to call such an assembly since February and had made some passing references to it in their respective April conferences (1.21 and 1.34), they nevertheless needed to formulate a clear-cut policy in view of the imminent elections. It was for this purpose as well as to promote Social Democratic unity that the Bund arranged for a conspiratorial meeting in Riga of eight representatives from both major factions and from four national Social Democratic bodies that were not at this time part of the RSDRP. All except the representative of the Menshevik Organizational Commission, Gutovsky, agreed that the Duma should be actively boycotted and the elections used as a pretext for a possible general strike. Gutovsky suggested instead that not only should oppositional groups participate in the elections and in the Duma but also that parallel elections should be held by disenfranchised voters who would elect a 'people's duma.' The election of this body would lead, in his opinion, to the formation of 'organizations of revolutionary self-government' on the local level and to revolutionary pressure for a constituent assembly on the national level.

All of these debates were soon overtaken by revolutionary events, however. The massive general strike a month after the Conference led to the October Manifesto which promised to replace Bulygin's consultative assembly with a truly legislative duma. The discussion of the relative merits of participation or boycott in legal institutions was only just beginning.

1.39
On the State Duma

We, the representatives of the central institutions of the General Jewish Workers' Union of Lithuania, Poland and Russia (the Bund), the Latvian Social Democratic Labour Party, the Polish Social Democratic Party, the Revolutionary Ukrainian Party, and the Central Committee of the RSDRP, having discussed at this Conference the question of the attitude to be taken toward the State Duma, have come to the following conclusion. The State Duma to be convoked by the tsarist government is a crude imitation of popular representation whose purpose is to preserve and strengthen the power of the autocracy, which has been shaken by the revolutionary movement of the proletariat, as well as to form in the hands of the government and the bourgeoisie an instrument for consolidating their political domination of the proletariat and the poor peasantry.

By the illusion of popular representation, the autocracy is striving for a political rapprochement with a considerable part of the bourgeoisie – which is worn out by the workers' movement and yearning for order – and after ensuring bourgeois sympathy and support intends through alliance with it to overwhelm the revolutionary movement of the proletariat and the peasantry.

All the fundamental provisions of the law of 6 August are in full accord with this designation of the State Duma as a new organ of the tsarist government.

1   *The electoral system*, based on a high property qualification, completely excludes from participation in the elections the entire proletariat, all women, more than nine-tenths of the peasants, the greater part of the toiling intelligentsia and of the urban petty bourgeoisie; with respect to that part of the population which is not kept from participating, the multi-stage electoral system transforms the right to vote into a simple fiction.

2   *The competence* with which the State Duma is endowed transforms it into an exclusively advisory assembly with no legislative power, thereby depriving it of any positive political significance for the people and lowering it to the level of a simple appendage of the bureaucratic mechanism of Russian absolutism.

3   *Elementary civil rights* – freedom of speech and of the press, of assembly and the right to form unions, inviolability of person and dwelling

– are absent. Along with this, the increasingly extensive application of the most severe repressions in the form of martial law, mass executions, the organization of Black Hundreds, and the fomentation of animosity among nationalities will transform the elections themselves into a brazen comedy fully guaranteeing the government the make-up of the State Duma which it desires.

In view of this, the Conference has recognized:

I   By its very essence the State Duma is incapable of adopting even the least satisfactory measures for improving the economic and legal position of the broad popular masses; any hopes along these lines, so energetically instilled in the people by the government and a part of the bourgeoisie, can only serve to promote the views of the autocracy, weakening the revolutionary energy and depressing the militant mood of the proletariat and peasantry.

II   By confirming the correctness of our *tactical slogan* that only a victorious popular uprising led by the proletariat will put an end to the autocratic régime and create the state structure most conducive to the broad development of the proletarian class struggle, i.e., a democratic republic, the law on the State Duma has once again confronted Russian social democracy with the urgent task of preparing for a popular armed uprising.

Therefore, the Conference has resolved as follows:

I   The forthcoming period of the electoral campaign is to be used for purposes of broadest agitation.

Meetings are to be held and all electoral assemblies are to be infiltrated in the greatest possible numbers in order, by disclosing at them the true character and aims of the State Duma, to contrast the Duma with the need for the revolutionary convocation of a constituent assembly on the basis of universal, equal, and direct suffrage with the secret ballot.

All truly democratic elements of society are to be called on to actively boycott the Duma, and those who participate in the elections are to be branded as shameful traitors to the cause of popular freedom.

At all assemblies, appropriate resolutions are to be adopted on the attitude toward the State Duma and on adherence to the revolutionary struggle of the proletariat.

II   Open mass demonstrations by the proletariat are to be organized in protest against institution of the State Duma and in order to exert pressure on the electors.

III   General political strikes, protests and demonstrations are to be timed to occur everywhere on the day of the final elections to the State Duma, and every technique is to be used to ensure that the elections do not take place, including when necessary the violent disruption of electoral assemblies.

II All-Russian Menshevik Conference 20 November 1905

In the aftermath of the successful October General Strike and the granting of the October Manifesto, both the Menshevik and the Bolshevik leaderships felt pressure for party unity from their rank-and-file members. On 10 November 1905, shortly after Lenin returned to Russia, the Bolshevik Central Committee finally called for the convocation a month hence of a unification congress. This congress, however, was to be preceded by separate but concurrent Menshevik and Bolshevik congresses or conferences which would work out factional platforms and then come together in equal numbers at the unification congress.

The Mensheviks, while disapproving of the built-in factionalism of this scheme, were in fact well-advanced in planning their own II All-Russian Conference which duly met on 20 November in St Petersburg. Menshevik elements favouring the transition to a broad workers' party were successful in attracting to their Conference the chairmen of the Petersburg Soviet (G.S. Khrustalev-Nosar) and of the Central Bureau of Trade Unions (Smelov) in advisory capacities. Even Lenin stopped in for some of the debates. The delegates gave their post facto approval to the merger of parallel factional groups on the local level and to the calling of a unification congress but on the basis of proportional representation rather than numerical equality. They also called for the merger of their Organizational Commission with the Bolsheviks' Central Committee and of their organ *Iskra* with the Bolsheviks' *Proletarii*. The editorial board of the new Central Organ, however, was not to contain any member of the unified Central Committee; a stipulation clearly aimed at Lenin who was both an editor of *Proletarii* and a ranking member of his faction's Central Committee (cf., 1.42, 1.43, 1.49). Nevertheless, in an ecumenical spirit, the Mensheviks agreed to accept Lenin's demand that a Social Democrat would have to be a member of a party organization although they did not adopt his exact wording for this article of the party Rules over which the RSDRP had split two years earlier. Perhaps the most interesting of the Menshevik resolutions concerned 'democratic centralism.' This term, which usually is associated with Lenin's organizational principles inherent in *What Is To Be Done?* (1902) and is considered his major contribution to party organizational theory, had not in fact been used either by Lenin himself or by the Bolsheviks in their own resolutions prior to this Conference.

1.40
On Party Membership 20 November 1905

Anyone may be a member of the RSDRP who: *a*/recognizes its Programme, *b*/participates in one of the party organizations, *c*/pays various dues to the organization.

1.41
On the Organization of the Party   20 November 1905

The RSDRP must be organized according to the principle of democratic centralism.
All party members take part in the election of party institutions.
All party institutions are elected for a [specified] period, are subject to recall and obligated to account for their actions both periodically and at any time upon demand of the organizations which elected them.
Decisions of the guiding collectives are binding on the members of those organizations of which the collective is the organ. Actions affecting the organization as a whole (i.e., congresses, reorganizations) must be decided upon by all of the members of the organization. Decisions of lower-level organizations are not to be implemented if they contradict decisions of higher organizations. The foundation of the organization is the party union, whether unified for a given locality or subdivided into raion and subraion unions. Raion and subraion unions are autonomous within the limits of their activities. All party members vote directly in elections to general party congresses; congress delegates are elected by organizations in proportion to the number of their members. No delegate may have more than one vote at a congress. The agenda [of a congress] must be published beforehand so that organizations will have an opportunity to discuss it.

1.42
On the Unification of the Bolshevik
and Menshevik Factions   20 November 1905

1   The Conference strongly supports the immediate merger of all 'Bolshevik' and 'Menshevik' organizations at the local level, on the basis of democratic centralism. Considering the merger of the parallel 'Bolshevik' and 'Menshevik' organizations to be the most important prerequisite for the success of a unification congress, the Conference appeals to all 'Bolshevik' and 'Menshevik' organizations to effect an immediate merger and, for its part, instructs the central institution which it has elected [i.e., the Organizational Commission] to co-operate in this merger.
2   The Conference considers it essential to undertake immediate preparation of a unification congress whose principal task will be the liquidation of the party schism.

The Conference strongly opposes the equal representation of factions at the unification congress, since this could split the congress into two halves and thus harm the cause of unity. The Conference considers it essential that the number of delegates from each locality correspond to the number of party members there, irrespective of adherence to one faction or the other. Therefore, the Conference recommends that joint electoral meetings be held in those localities where parallel organizations are still in existence at the time of the elections. To guarantee the rights of the minority, the Conference considers it essential that the right of special representation be granted to any minority which has collected not less than two-thirds of the number of votes needed to send a delegate.

3   The merger of the practical centres [i.e., the Bolshevik Central Committee and the Menshevik Organizational Commission] is possible and necessary, both to unify political leadership and to further unification of the parallel organizations on the local level, as well as to organize the unification congress. Merger of the practical centres is necessary and possible regardless of whether or not the literary organs will be merged.

The two practical centres are to be merged on the basis of equality of the two factions. If by chance, during the formation of the merged centre, the Organizational Commission has fewer members than the Central Committee of the Bolshevik faction, then the Organizational Commission will enlarge its membership from among the candidates elected at the Conference in the order of the number of votes received by each; if the list of candidates is exhausted, the Organizational Commission will be granted the right of co-optation. The resulting board will be a common collective reaching its decisions by simple majority vote. The unified practical centre will be given the right of co-optation only to replace members who for some reason or other leave the centre. Co-optation will be by majority vote. Members of the editorial board of the Central Organ cannot at the same time be in the practical centre.

4   The Conference considers it desirable that a common Central Organ be formed and considers it necessary to impose upon the Unified Centre the obligation of devoting every effort toward the immediate organization of a common editorial board for the Central Organ; the Conference further states that the 'Mensheviks' should not strive for the numerical predominance of its adherents on the editorial board.

The Conference proposes to the 'Bolshevik' faction that it issue directives along the above lines to its part of the Unified Centre.

V.I. Lenin, *Sochineniia* VIII (3rd ed. Moscow, 1935), 466–7

Conference of the Majority   12–17 December 1905

To offset the Mensheviks' II Conference and to lay plans for the forthcoming unification congress, forty Bolsheviks representing twenty-six organizations and one Menshevik took advantage of Finnish autonomy to meet in Tammerfors during December 1905. Since the concurrent Moscow insurrection cut down on the number of Bolsheviks who could attend, the delegates decided to constitute themselves as a 'Conference of the Majority' rather than as a Bolshevik congress as the Central Committee had proposed a month earlier. Subsequent Soviet historians have mislabelled this gathering the 'First Conference of the RSDRP.'

Four of the resolutions of the Conference dealt with aspects of party unity. The delegates agreed with the Mensheviks that the two factional centres and the central literary organs should be merged; that parallel organizations should unite on the local level; and that a unification congress should be convened as soon as possible so as to formalize this unity. The Conference did not, however, accept Lenin's formula that there should be factional parity at the congress and that delegates should be elected en bloc by their respective factions. The other two resolutions passed by the Conference were tactical statements on issues that would undoubtedly come before the congress. One of these, 'On the State Duma,' is interesting because it witnessed a clash between Lenin and Stalin, who was making his first appearance on the national level of party politics. Lenin apparently came to the conclusion that the Duma could serve a useful agitational purpose. Faced with opposition from Stalin and others in the drafting committee, the Bolshevik leader announced that he was 'withdrawing in good order' (thereby admitting his 'blunder' according to Stalin fifteen years later) and subsequently voted in favour of boycotting the forthcoming elections to the I Duma.

The general mood of this Conference was militant and optimistic. Between sessions, the delegates even held revolver practice. And, according to the current official party history, 'on a motion from Lenin, the Conference hastened to conclude its work so that the delegates could return home to take part in the insurrection.'

1.43
On Merging the Centres

For purposes of practical [party] unity and as a temporary measure before the unification congress, the Conference orders the immediate and simultaneous merger of the practical centres [i.e., the Bolshevik Central Committee and the Menshevik Organizational Commission] and the literary central organs on a basis of [factional] equality; members of the editorial board can also be members of a practical centre.

The editorial board is guided by the directives of the overall centre. Whenever one-third of the editors so desire, the editorial board will be obliged to print their particular opinion with an appropriate editorial disclaimer.

I.44
[On the Rapid Merger of Parallel Local Organizations]

The Conference favours the immediate merger of parallel organizations on the local level.

I.45
On the Calling of a Unification Congress of the RSDRP

The merged Central Committee and Organizational Commission (or the united council of the Central Committee and Organizational Commission, if no merger takes place) should immediately announce the convocation of a unification congress of the RSDRP to be held at the earliest possible date. Representation at the unification congress is to be proportional and on the basis of elections. All members of the party organization are to participate in the election of delegates by direct and secret vote. There will be one delegate for every 300 party members. Autonomous local organizations with a total membership of less than 300 but more than 100 may also send a single delegate. Autonomous local organizations with a total membership of less than 100 but more than 50 may send delegates in an advisory capacity. Delegates will stand on tactical platforms in these elections. Votes cast in different localities or raions for a single person may be put together only if all of the organizations are unified under a single local centre.

Note 1 Members who have entered the party after the announcement of the convocation of the congress may not participate in the elections.

Note 2 Delegates to the party congress may not have more than one mandate. Detailed rules governing elections to the unification congress (with instructions that they are absolutely binding upon all party members), together with an agenda for the congress, are to be published by the merged centre not later than three weeks after announcement of the convocation of the congress. Each local organization with more than 100 members is to establish an electoral commission for settling all questions of party membership and electoral procedure. Electoral commissions are elected by majority vote of the local organization and must contain representatives of the factional minority. In places where parallel organizations do not merge before the congress, representatives of both factions are appointed in equal numbers to the electoral commission. All disputes about elections to the unification congress, which have not been resolved by the electoral commissions, will be referred for final solution to the merged centre.

1.46
On Party Reorganization

1   Recognizing as indisputable the principle of democratic centralism, the Conference considers the broad implementation of the elective principle necessary; and, while granting elected centres full powers in matters of ideological and practical leadership, they are at the same time subject to recall, their actions are to be given broad publicity, and they are to be strictly accountable for these activities.
2   The Conference recommends the formation of oblast conferences and unions with oblast organs for purposes of unifying and stimulating local work.
3   The Conference orders all party organizations quickly and energetically to reorganize their local organizations on the basis of the elective principle; while it is not necessary for the moment to seek complete uniformity of all systems for electing institutions, departures (two-stage elections, etc.,) from fully democratic procedures are permitted only in the event of insurmountable practical obstacles.

1.47
Agrarian Resolution

1   The Conference recognizes that the development of the peasant movement entirely confirms the fundamental principles of revolutionary marxism both as to the revolutionary character and as to the true social and economic essence of this movement which is shattering the remnants of serfdom and creating free bourgeois relationships in the countryside. The Conference views as desirable the alteration of our party's agrarian programme [1.3] along the following lines: the article on lands cut off [from peasant holdings at the time of the Emancipation] is to be deleted and replaced by a statement to the effect that the party supports the revolutionary measures of the peasantry up to and including the confiscation of all state, church and monastic, crown and privately owned land; and also that the party's principal and constant task is the independent organization of the rural proletariat, explaining to the rural proletariat the irreconcilable conflict between its interests and those of the rural bourgeoisie, showing it that the ultimate goal of socialism is the only one capable of doing away

with the class division of society and of all exploitation of man by man.

2   The Conference expresses the hope that the demand for return of the land redemption payments and the formation of a special fund from the money thus collected will be dropped from the agrarian programme. The demand for confiscation of state and monastic lands, etc., is to be moved to another paragraph.

1.48
On the State Duma

Ever since [the Manifesto of] 17 October, the autocratic government has been trampling all the fundamental civil liberties won by the proletariat. The government has covered the whole country with blood, shooting down with machine guns and cannon the workers, peasants, soldiers, and sailors fighting for their freedom. The government mocks the national demand for the convocation of a constituent assembly and by its law of 11 December [concerning the mode of election of Duma deputies] attempts once again to deceive the proletariat and the peasantry and to postpone its own ultimate downfall. The law of 11 December actually excludes the proletariat and the peasant masses from participation in the State Duma and attempts to ensure ahead of time, using various ruses and police restrictions, that the Duma will be dominated by Black Hundred elements and the exploiting classes.

The Conference expresses its confidence that the entire class-conscious proletariat in Russia will reply to this new tsarist law by a resolute struggle against this, as against any other, imitation of popular representation. The Conference is of the view that social democracy should strive to defeat this police Duma and reject any participation in it. The Conference advises all party organizations to make extensive use of electoral assemblies, not for the sake of conducting any elections to the State Duma in deference to the police restrictions, but to expand the revolutionary organization of the proletariat and to conduct agitation for an armed uprising among all sections of the population. The uprising must be prepared at once, without delay and organized everywhere, for its victory alone will create the possibility of convoking a truly popular representative body, i.e., a freely elected constituent assembly on the basis of universal, direct, and equal suffrage, and with a secret ballot.

'Rezoliutsiia konferentsii bol'shinstva,' leaflet (Moscow, 1905)   *KPSS v rezoliutsiiakh* I, 135–8

Unified Central Committee January 1906

In late December 1905, the decisions of the II Menshevik Conference and the Conference of the Majority concerning the need for party unity were put into effect. The Bolshevik Central Committee and Menshevik Organizational Commission were merged into a Unified Central Committee consisting of three Bolsheviks (Krasin, I.K. Lalaiants, I.A. Sammer) and three Mensheviks (Tarasevich, V.N. Krokhmal, N.I. Iordansky). The factional journals *Proletarii* and *Iskra* were superseded by a single Central Organ *Partiinye izvestiia* (News of the Party) with three Bolshevik editors (Lenin, A.V. Lunarcharsky, V.A. Bazarov) and three Mensheviks (Dan, Martov, Martynov). Two issues of this paper appeared illegally in St Petersburg during the interval before the Unification Congress. These decisions, which probably reflect the greatest degree of organizational unity the party was ever to achieve, were communicated by the Unified Central Committee in the following leaflet entitled 'To the Party.'

1.49
[On Party Unity]

COMRADES! The Central Committee of the 'majority' and the Organizational Commission of the 'minority' have merged into a single Unified Central Committee made up of an equal number of representatives of the former centres of both factions. At the same time the Unified Central Committee has formed a unified editorial board for the Central Organ, also made up of an equal number of editors of the former organs of the two factions. Even in times of very strained relations between the party's two factions, members have always been conscious of the necessity of establishing organizational unity, despite the presence of disagreements over certain questions of tactics and organization, and have endeavoured not to weaken the party by a split. And at precisely the time when the division into two factions was formalized – at the III Congress of the 'majority' and the I Conference of the 'minority' – both sides adopted analogous resolutions on the need for undertaking immediate preparations for party unification [1.27, 1.29]. The mighty revolutionary struggle of the proletariat for the liberation of Russia, which since that time has been spreading with great rapidity, more and more urgently demands the merger of the RSDRP into a single 'organization.' And the merger has in fact started from below – in the broad circles of 'peripheral' party workers. At the same time, the party's local and national centres have been collaborating on the basis of agreements and federations which have become increasingly close.

The course of the revolution has to some extent eliminated many of the tactical and organizational disagreements which had previously divided our party into two factions. The question of the attitude toward the Bulygin State Duma fell into abeyance after [the Manifesto of] 17 October. The armed uprising became a fact in certain places in Russia and with the development of the revolutionary struggle the question of the convocation of a constituent assembly by the revolutionary government has taken on real significance. In the organizational area, the transition from the tight framework of conspiratorial institutions to more or less open elective organizations has unified the party on the principle of democratic centralism. The establishment on the local level of elective party institutions, which at the same time and within the limits of their competence possess the powers of guiding centres, has confronted the party with the concrete question of a more accurate and strict registration of its members. And the former problem of party membership, by the way, has been uniformly resolved in the sense of compulsory participation by party members in one or another party organization [i.e., by the adoption of Lenin's version of article 1 of the Rules; see 1.4, 1.16, 1.40]. The urge for party unification, which has been prepared by the course of the joint revolutionary struggle of the factions against the autocratic government, has found expression in the resolutions of the conferences of the 'majority' [1.43–1.45] and the 'minority' [1.42]. Both conferences recognized the urgent need for a merger of both the central and the local party institutions, for a reorganization of local institutions on the basis of democratic centralism, and for the immediate convocation of a unification congress of the entire party which would finally consolidate the merger of the two factions and create a party organization which will be unified from top to bottom. The task which the party is now entrusting to the Unified Central Committee consists, in addition to those functions which it has inherited from the Central Committee and the Organizational Commission, principally in organizing this unification congress of the party. The congress will adopt directives, which will be binding on party members, on those tactical issues which are at present still being resolved in a somewhat different manner by the representatives of the two factions. The first of these issues, which has again taken on important tactical significance thanks to the [election] law of 11 December, is the attitude toward the State Duma. Discussion of this issue in a joint meeting of the Unified Central Committee and the editorial board of the Central Organ demonstrated that the representatives of the two factions were in agreement in their basic attitude toward the Duma: the attempt of the government to falsify the representation of the people and substitute the Duma for a constituent assembly, as before, should be opposed by the slogan calling for the revolutionary convocation of a national constituent assembly and by the most energetic preparation for an armed uprising. According to this view, the party's participation in the last stage of the electoral campaign, i.e., in the election of the Duma deputies themselves, is under the present circumstances recognized as inadmissible. Opinion was divided only with respect to the party's participation in the first stages of the electoral campaign, i.e., participation in the election of representatives and electors.

In view of the disagreement thus revealed, the Unified Central Committee has decided to permit a comradely discussion of this issue in party literature and to advise the local organizations to adopt one or the other tactic with respect to exploiting the early stages of the elections, but this decision must be uniform for the entire area of activity of the given organization and must be made by majority vote of the organization with the minority being compelled to bow to the general decision. In announcing the convocation of a party unification congress, the Unified Central Committee orders all party organizations immediately to begin its preparation. Detailed instructions on the procedure for electing representatives to the congress will be published in the near future by the Unified Central Committee [see *KPSS v rezoliutsiiakh* I, 143–9, for leaflet issued in February 1906].

For the time being the Unified Central Committee limits itself to transmitting the decrees of the conferences of the 'majority' and the 'minority' calling for the organization of a party unification congress on the basis of elective representation from all party members participating in local organizations.

The preliminary merger of the local organizations is the guarantee of the success of the unification congress. The central organizations have unified, thus bowing to the will of the whole party as clearly expressed in the decrees of the conferences of both party factions and in a whole series of declarations by local organizations. Now the Unified Central Committee urgently appeals that all party organizations immediately effect the merger of parallel local organizations and reorganize party institutions on the principle of democratic centralism. Both one and the other will enhance the power of the party in the continuing revolutionary struggle with the autocracy and will create the necessary conditions for the full and correct expression of the party's will at the forthcoming unification congress.

Chetvertyi (ob"edinitel'nyi) s"ezd RSDRP: Protokoly (Moscow, 1959), 556–7

KPSS v rezoliutsiiakh I, 140–3

Unification Congress   10–25 April 1906

The forces working for party unity that were evident at the 1905 factional conferences and in the Unified Central Committee culminated in a Unification Congress which met in Stockholm during the spring of 1906. This gathering, which the Mensheviks informally referred to as the III Congress since they refused to accept the legality of Lenin's 1905 congress of the same name, has subsequently been given the appellation 'Fourth' by Soviet historians. Since the factions were represented proportional to their local voting strength rather than equally as the Bolshevik Central Committee had suggested, the Mensheviks' numerical superiority in the underground was rewarded. Of the 112 voting delegates from fifty-seven local organizations, 66 were 'former' Mensheviks and 46 were 'former' Bolsheviks. There were in addition some 45 persons attending in an advisory capacity, as observers, or as guests.

The Mensheviks' majority was reflected in the election of Plekhanov and Dan to the Congress' two-man steering committee and in the composition of the party's new central institutions. The editorial board of the Central Organ (*Sotsial-demokrat*), which once again was chosen by the Congress against Lenin's wishes, was composed solely of Mensheviks: Martov, Martynov, Dan, Potresov, and P.P. Maslov. The new Central Committee consisted of seven Mensheviks (V.N. Rozanov, L.I. Goldman, L.N. Radchenko, Khinchuk, Krokhmal, B.A. Bakhmetev, and P.N. Kolokolnikov), three Bolsheviks (Krasin, Rykov who was soon replaced by Bogdanov, and V.A. Desnitsky), two members of the Bund (R.A. Abramovich, A.I. Kremer), two Polish Social Democrats (A.S. Warski, F.E. Dzerzhinsky), and one Latvian Social Democrat (K.K. Danishevsky). The election of the representatives from the three national organizations was in fact deferred until the summer of 1906 when their parent organizations approved the conditions of merger with the RSDRP that had been worked out at the Unification Congress (1.58, 1.59). While the party restated its 'resolute opposition to the organization of the proletariat by nationality' and 'decisively opposed the principle of organizing trade unions by nationality,' the Congress nevertheless granted these three national groups a privileged autonomous status and skirted the question of national self-determination which in 1903 had prevented union with the Poles and had led to the withdrawal of the Bund (1.7). Some of Lenin's critics suggested that the reason he suddenly favoured the admittance of these groups was that he hoped they could help him offset the Menshevik majority in the Central Committee and at future congresses.

It is quite evident that the Congress merely papered over differences within the party concerning both tactics and strategy. As Lenin noted at the close of the gathering, 'the three most important resolutions of the Congress clearly bear the stamp of the erroneous views of the former Menshevik faction.'

These decisions concerned a revision of the agrarian section of the party's 1903 Programme in light of peasant unrest in 1905; participation in the remaining elections to the I State Duma; and the role of the party in restricting 'inopportune armed outbursts' (1.54) and in containing para-military tactics developed during the revolution of the previous year. The Menshevik agrarian programme (1.51), which was sponsored by Plekhanov, Maslov, and N.N. Zhordaniia and passed by a vote of 62 to 42 with 7 abstentions, called for the 'municipalization' of state and large private land holdings through their transfer to local zemstvo-type assemblies. Lenin opposed this by advocating the 'nationalization' of all land, including the 'small holdings' of the peasantry, and its transfer to the state. The Bolsheviks were split on the question of Duma participation (1.56). Most of them were among the 46 delegates who unsuccessfully opposed participation in general despite the fact that many peasants and workers had already ignored their earlier appeal to boycott the elections (1.48). When the time came to consider specific participation in the few remaining elections in the Caucasus, however, Lenin and 16 other Bolsheviks joined the Menshevik majority in favouring participation. They were opposed by 11 die-hard Bolsheviks; Stalin and 15 others abstained. The resolution 'On Partisan Activities' (1.55) was principally aimed at curtailing the widespread 'expropriation' of tsarist banks and post offices conducted by para-military Bolshevik groups. Despite the fact that this resolution was passed 64 to 4 with 20 abstentions (Lenin was conveniently out of the room when the vote was taken), many Bolsheviks opposed its spirit and expropriations continued until 1910 (see 1.67 and 1.88). Each of these resolutions provoked heated and prolonged debate as well as Bolshevik defeat. Subsequently, Lenin called on his followers to 'fight ideologically' against these decisions but within the framework of a united party.

In comparison with the furor at the II Congress, the revision of the party Rules passed very smoothly. Even the majority of the Mensheviks were content to keep the organizational emphasis on the illegal underground rather than moving toward a mass workers' party as some of their right-wing elements desired. The only contentious question concerned the Menshevik suggestion that two-thirds of the party should be required to call extraordinary congresses. Lenin, realizing that he would not be able to muster this much support and that only a new congress would allow him to reverse the above decisions, threatened to renew the split unless the right to call a congress was restored to a simple majority of the party membership.

1.50
Organizational Rules 25 April 1906
[Replaces Rules adopted 1905; see 1.16]

1   [Revises 1.16, art. 1] A member of the party is one who accepts the

party programme, supports the party financially, and belongs to some party organization.

2 [New] All party organizations are built on the principles of democratic centralism.

3 [Revises arts. 6, 7] All party organizations are autonomous with respect to their internal activities. Every approved party organization has the right to issue party literature in its own name.

4 [Revises art. 8] New party organizations are approved by oblast conferences or by two neighbouring organizations. The Central Committee exercises supervisory power over such approvals.

5 [New] The organizations of a given region may unite to form oblast unions. An oblast centre is elected at the oblast conference or congress.

6 [Revises art. 8] All party organizations must contribute 10 per cent of all income received to the Central Committee.

7 [Revises art. 5] The Central Committee and the editorial board of the Central Organ are elected at the congress. The Central Committee represents the party in relations with other parties; it organizes various party institutions and guides their activities; it organizes and conducts undertakings of significance for the party as a whole; it allocates party personnel and funds, and has charge of the central party treasury; it settles conflicts between and within various party institutions and it generally co-ordinates all the activity of the party. When questions of policy are being resolved, the Central Committee is also to include the editorial board of the Central Organ. Members leaving the Central Committee [by arrest, retirement, etc.] are replaced by candidates appointed by the congress and in the order established by the congress. Members leaving the editorial board of the Central Organ are replaced by the Central Committee acting jointly with the remaining editors.

8 [Revises art. 2] The congress is the supreme organ of the party. Regular congresses are summoned annually by the Central Committee. An extraordinary congress must be called within two months upon the demand of not less than one-half of the party membership.

If the Central Committee refuses to convoke a congress under these circumstances, the half of the party which demanded it has the right to form an Organizational Committee which enjoys all the rights of the Central Committee with respect to convening the congress.

All approved party organizations are represented at the congress by one delegate for each 500 members participating in the election of the delegates. Organizations with at least 300 voting members are entitled to a single delegate. Organizations with an insufficient number of members can unite with neighbouring organizations to send a common delegate if jointly they have at least 500 voting members. Elections to a congress are conducted on democratic principles.

UNIFICATION (IV) CONGRESS

A congress is considered valid if more than one-half of all party members are represented at it.

The convocation of any congress and its agenda are to be announced by the Central Committee of the party, or under appropriate circumstances by the Organizational Committee, at least one and a half months before the date of the congress.

1.51
Agrarian Programme

In order to eliminate the remnants of serfdom, which lie as an oppressive burden directly on the peasantry, and to further the free development of the class struggle in the countryside, the RSDRP demands:

1   the abolition of all class constraints on the persons and property of the peasants;
2   the abolition of all payments and obligations connected with the peasantry as a class and the elimination of all indebtedness involving an element of bondage;
3   the confiscation of church, monastic, crown and state lands and their transfer ... to large local self-governing bodies uniting urban and rural districts; lands needed for colonization as well as forests and waters of national significance are to be transferred to the democratic state;
4   the confiscation of privately owned land, except for small holdings, and the placing of this land at the disposal of large local self-governing bodies which are to be democratically elected; the minimum size of the holdings subject to confiscation is to be determined by the large local self-governing bodies.

1.52
Tactical Resolution on the Agrarian Question

While supporting revolutionary initiatives of the peasantry up to and including confiscation of landlords' estates, the RSDRP will always and unswervingly oppose any attempts to hinder the course of economic development. Striving, with the victorious development of the revolution, to transfer the confiscated lands to the democratic institutions of local self-government, the RSDRP, in the event of conditions unfavourable for this purpose, will support a division among the peasants of those landlord properties upon which small-scale agriculture is in fact being conducted or which are needed for rounding off [peasant] holdings. In such a case the party will be in all circumstances, regardless of the course of the democratic agrarian reforms, set itself the task of steadfastly working for the independent class organization of the rural proletariat, of explaining to the rural proletariat the irreconcilable conflict between its interests and those of the peasant bourgeoisie, of warning it against being seduced by a system of small-scale farming which, under conditions of commodity production, is never capable of eliminating the poverty of the masses and, finally, of pointing out the necessity of a complete socialist revolution as the only way to abolish all poverty and all exploitation.

1.53
On the Attitude toward the Peasant Movement 25 April 1906

Considering:
1   that the peasantry, in its struggle for land and against the police-bureaucratic order, is at the present time a revolutionary class;
2   that, on the one hand, the implementation of peasant demands concerning both agricultural and legal relations is possible only in the event of a general democratic reconstruction of the state and that, on the other hand, such a reconstruction is possible only with the active participation of the peasant masses in the revolution;
3   that, at the same time, the peasant movement is essentially petty-bourgeois and that classes of rural proletariat and rural bourgeoisie have already been formed in the countryside, the struggle between them having been concealed only by the general yoke of serfdom which has burdened the peasantry in general and its lowest, semi-free class in particular;
4   that the bourgeois parties are striving to make use of the peasant movement and to subordinate it to their own purposes – one (the Socialist Revolutionary Party) for the sake of a utopian petty-bourgeois socialism, the other (the Constitutional Democratic Party) for maintaining a significant degree of large private land-ownership while satisfying at the same time the possessive instincts of the peasantry through partial concessions, thus weakening the revolutionary movement —

The Unification Congress of the RSDRP therefore resolves:
1   by giving detailed attention to the peasantry, to associate its economic demands with the political tasks of the present revolutionary moment;
2   to create, wherever possible, independent Social Democratic organizations of farm labourers (both proletarian and semi-proletarian) which will be part of the RSDRP, and at the same time to promote the organization of the peasantry as a whole, both through its entry into the Peasant Union [formed under the influence of the Socialist Revolutionaries in the summer

of 1905] (which for the time being will remain non–party) and through the formation of peasant committees, Soviets of Peasants' Deputies, etc., which will unite peasants with one another and bind them to the urban proletarian organizations; and to strive to influence their programmes and tactics along lines favourable to social democracy;

3   to intensify the clashes of the peasants with the government and the landlords, which will lead the peasants to an awareness that their agrarian and political demands can only be satisfied by a national constituent assembly; and for this purpose, to put forward the revolutionary demands of the peasants in the form of instructions and orders [to peasant deputies] and by sending deputations to all public institutions up to and including the State Duma;

4   to restrain the peasants from agrarian terror, arson, etc., controlling their sporadic outbursts, making every effort to expand and co-ordinate these acts with the advance of the proletariat against tsarism;

5   to recommend, together with the revolutionary upsurge of the peasantry against their landlords, the boycott of the local authorities and their replacement by new and, wherever possible, elected authorities;

6   to instil in the revolutionary peasantry, in connection with their mass actions, an awareness of the necessity for an armed uprising, occurring simultaneously and in concert with the uprising of the proletariat and the urban petty bourgeoisie, as the only means presently available for securing the convocation of the national constituent assembly;

7   to advance the following slogans, in order to ensure a systematic struggle by the peasantry: harvest of grain by tenants without payment of rent, refuse to pay taxes, boycott governmental institutions, refuse to supply recruits, etc.

With respect to farm labourers, the Congress considers it necessary, in addition to organizing them by bringing them into the ranks of the RSDRP, to form trade unions to stand up for the occupational interests of these workers. As a means of organizing farm labourers and welding them together, the Congress recommends a strike for higher wages to day and seasonal workers and for a reduction in the labour rent owed by tenant farmers.

To ensure successful propaganda and agitation among the peasants, the Congress considers it necessary to issue appropriate literature.

1.54
On the Armed Uprising

Considering:
1   that the revolutionary struggle, in bringing to the forefront the im-

mediate task of wresting state power from the hands of the autocratic-feudal government, has already confronted the people and will continue to confront them with the necessity of an armed uprising;

2   that the victory of a popular uprising is conceivable only if the troops are disorganized and at least a part of them pass over to the side of the people;

3   that the troops will cease being an obedient instrument in the hands of the government, and a more or less significant part of them will pass over to the side of the people, only if broad layers of the urban bourgeoisie and the peasantry participate actively and decisively in the uprising beside the proletariat;

4   that broad layers of the population will participate actively in the uprising only if these same layers of the population have been gradually drawn into active struggle with the government as a result of the extreme intensification of social and political contradictions during the course of this struggle —

The Congress therefore recognizes:

a   that the fundamental task of the party at present is the development of the revolution by means of expanding and strengthening agitational activity among the broad layers of the proletariat, peasantry, urban petty bourgeoisie, and the troops as well as involving them in the aggressive struggle against the government through the constant intervention of the Social Democratic Party and the proletariat which is led by it in all manifestations of the country's political life; that, in carrying out this basic task, the party at the same time also furthers the preparation of the conditions for the victory of the uprising, leading the mass of the population to the realization of the impossibility of any agreement with the tsar and his government and of the necessity of achieving their political demands through armed force;

b   that the party, as an organization, cannot assume the responsibility of arming the people, which would arouse false hopes, and must limit itself to promoting the self-arming of the population and to organizing and arming of fighting squads [i.e., small and highly conspiratorial groups formed within local party organizations to deal with spies and Black Hundred terrorism] capable of initiating and planning the insurrectionary struggle;

c   that the party is obliged to oppose all attempts to involve the proletariat in an armed clash under unfavourable conditions, regardless of the motivation of such attempts;

d   that party committees must make combat agreements with other revolutionary and oppositional organizations to ensure that the process of arming will go forward successfully and that the actions of the insurgents will receive maximum co-ordination.

At the same time, the Congress resolves that propaganda and organizational activities among the troops and in military schools must be intensified and made more systematic.

The activities of local Military Organizations [i.e., conspiratorial auxiliary groups composed of several propagandists from the local underground committee and an equal number of Social Democratic soldiers who carried out agitational work within military units during the revolutions of 1905 and 1917; see also 1.183–1.185] are to be governed by the directives of the Central Committee and the local party committees to whom the Congress, from the experience of recent years, hereby points out that inopportune armed outbursts lead only to a fruitless waste of revolutionary energy.

1.55
On Partisan Activities

Considering that the tsarist government – convinced that the revolution will array against it all levels of population and leave as its only allies the police, the bureaucracy, military commanders discredited in the war [with Japan], and parasitic social elements – is striving to disorganize and demoralize the forces of revolution, and to this end:

   a is undertaking measures of intimidation in the form of punitive expeditions, mass executions, hangings, torturing, and bestial outrages against the individual;

   b is inflaming national hatred, organizing pogroms against the Jews, slaughters of Armenians and Muslims;

   c is organizing armed raids by members of the Black Hundreds on the intelligentsia and the workers, encouraging killings and robberies in order to create social anarchy and to turn the struggle against the government into a fight of each against all and all against each.

Considering, further, that déclassé layers of society, criminals, and the dregs of the urban population have always used revolutionary upheavals for their own anti-social purposes and that the revolutionary populace has always had to take stern measures against the bacchanalia of thievery and brigandage; finally, that a very important element in revolution is its moral and political effect on the revolutionary masses, on society, and on the whole army, and that by disorganizing the state power the revolution aims not at social anarchy but at organizing the forces of society —

    The Congress therefore resolves:

1   recognizing, together with the preparation for the forthcoming uprising of revolutionary forces based on the organization of the working masses and the inevitability of an active struggle against governmental terror and the violence of the Black Hundreds, that it is necessary:

a to combat the actions of persons or groups aimed at seizing money in the name of or using the slogans of the Social Democratic Party;

b to avoid any violations of the personal security or private property of peaceful citizens except for those cases which are the involuntary consequence of the struggle with the government or which – as, for example, in the construction of barricades – are due to the immediate needs of the struggle. The Congress rejects the expropriation of money from private banks as well as all forms of compulsory contributions [from private individuals] for revolutionary purposes;

c to destroy or damage government buildings, railroads, and other structures, public and private, only in fulfilment of an immediate military objective;

d to seize the capital of the State Bank, the Treasury, and other governmental institutions only when this is associated with the formation of revolutionary organs of power in a particular place and is done under their direction; in this case, the confiscation of public funds from official institutions must be done openly and with complete accountability.

Arms and military uniforms belonging to the government should be seized at every opportunity.

1.56
On the Attitude toward the State Duma

Considering that:

1   the tsarist government has summoned the State Duma, under the revolutionary impetus of the proletariat and the pressure of the bourgeois opposition, in order to weaken the revolutionary upsurgence and, hoisting the banner of pseudo-constitutionalism, to secure for itself victory in the battle for its existence;

2   stubbornly defending the existence of the old régime, the government and its reactionary allies – as a force irreconcilably hostile to any manifestation of spontaneous political activity by the people – will be compelled to engage in a decisive struggle with the State Duma at the very outset of its activity and will refuse to grant it the possibility of undertaking any serious initiative, no matter how small, in the transformation of the Russian state structure;

3   the antagonism between the inherent interests and needs of the new bourgeois society in Russia and the old régime which binds it hand and foot has become so intense, that conflicts have become inevitable between the Duma and the tsarist government, as well as between various elements within the Duma itself;

4   these conflicts, compelling the opposition elements in the State Duma

to seek support among the broad masses, concentrate the attention of these masses even more than before on the struggle with autocracy and thus transform even a mock-constitutional institution like the Duma from an instrument of the counter-revolution into an instrument of the revolution;

5 in the present revolutionary atmosphere clashes between the State Duma and the government will also exert a disrupting and revolutionizing influence upon the army which will be shaken in its fealty to the throne and will perceive for the first time on Russian soil a new authority, emerging from the bosom of the nation, speaking in her name, and trampled by arbitrary tsarist rule —

The Congress therefore recognizes that the social democracy must:

1 exploit methodically all conflicts arising between the government and the Duma, and within the Duma itself, so as to broaden and deepen the revolutionary movement, and to this end:

a must strive to broaden and intensify these conflicts to the point where they will become the starting point for general mass movements aimed at overthrowing the present political order;

b must endeavour at each particular stage to associate the political tasks of the movement with the socio-economic demands of the worker and peasant masses;

c must organize, through broad agitation among the popular masses for the presentation of revolutionary demands to the Duma, outside pressure upon the State Duma with the aim of revolutionizing it;

2 conduct its intervention in such a way that these aggravated conflicts:

a make clear to the masses the inconsistency of all the bourgeois parties which in the Duma lay claim to the role of spokesmen for the popular will; and

b make the broad masses (the proletariat, the peasantry, and the urban petty bourgeoisie) aware of the total unsuitability of the Duma as a representative institution and of the need to convoke a national constituent assembly on the basis of universal, equal, direct, and secret suffrage.

Furthermore, without resolving for the present the question of the party's official representation in the State Duma, it must be recognized as desirable that future Social Democratic deputies working in the party organization and subject to its directives will form a Social Democratic group which, acting under the constant supervision and direction of the party's central institutions, will use its criticism [of the government] to push all the bourgeois parties toward more resolute opposition, to weld all revolutionary elements around itself, to raise socio-economic issues and associate them with political issues, to intensify the conflict between the Duma and the government, and through the agency of the party organization, to maintain a constant tie with the broad working masses.

Therefore, wherever elections are still being held [e.g., in the

Caucasus] and the RSDRP can put forward its candidates, without entering into blocs with other parties, the party must strive to secure the election of these candidates.

1.57
On Trade Unions

Considering:
1   that the trade union movement is a necessary component of the class struggle and that trade unions are an essential element in the class organization of the proletariat;
2   that by the very nature of the aims which they pursue, trade unions should endeavour to organize the broadest masses of the proletariat;
3   that, in particular, the proletariat of Russia has shown a strong desire to organize trade unions;
4   that the economic struggle will lead to a real improvement in the position of the working masses and to a strengthening of their genuinely class organization only if it is properly combined with the political struggle of the proletariat;
5   that in the atmosphere of the revolutionary epoch, the trade unions not only defend the economic interests of the working class but also involve the proletariat in the immediate political struggle and promote the general organization and political unification of the working class;
6   that in such a revolutionary atmosphere the working masses, in the process of becoming organized and politically united, come increasingly under the banner of social democracy —
    The Congress therefore recognizes:
1   that the party must support the workers' aspirations for professional organizations and give every assistance to the formation of non-party trade unions;
2   that, to this end, the legal framework must be steadily extended and an undeviating struggle for complete trade union freedom must be conducted by using all legal opportunities, particularly the law [of 4 March 1906 which legalized the formation of] trade unions;
3   that all party members should enter trade unions, participate actively in all union functions, and constantly strengthen the class solidarity and class consciousness of their members, in order to bind the trade unions and the party organically through struggle and agitation.

1.58
Conditions for the Merger of the Social Democrats of Poland and Lithuania with the RSDRP

1   The Social Democratic Party of Poland and Lithuania is a territorial

organization of the RSDRP which works with proletarians of all nationalities in its area and unifies the activities of all party organizations in this territory.

Note 1 Socialist organizations in Poland can come into the RSDRP only by entering the Social Democratic Party of Poland and Lithuania. Agreements, both permanent and temporary, between such organizations and the RSDRP are concluded only with the assent of the Social Democratic Party of Poland and Lithuania.

Note 2 The relations between the Social Democratic Party of Poland and Lithuania and the Bund are determined in agreement with the RSDRP. Within the limits of this overall relationship, the Social Democratic Party of Poland and Lithuania can decide on specific cases of joint local action.

2   The question of retaining Lithuania within the area of activity of the Social Democratic Party of Poland and Lithuania is to be decided by the Central Committee of the RSDRP and by the Main Presidium of the Social Democratic Party of Poland and Lithuania with the participation of all local organizations which have an interest in the matter.

3   Within the area of its activity, the Social Democratic Party of Poland and Lithuania independently resolves all questions relating to kinds of agitation and forms of organization and also determines its own relations with other parties conducting activities in their territory.

4   The Social Democratic Party of Poland and Lithuania holds its own congresses.

5   The Social Democratic Party of Poland and Lithuania retains the right, within the limits of its own activities, to resolve independently the question of the relations between trade unions and the party organization.

6   The Social Democratic Party of Poland and Lithuania participates in general party congresses on the same basis as all other organizations of the RSDRP.

7   The editorial board of the Central Organ includes a member of the Social Democratic Party of Poland and Lithuania who has the same rights as all other editors to participate in general editorial work and who will direct the Polish section [of the newspaper].

8   The Social Democratic Party of Poland and Lithuania is represented independently at international socialist congresses and in the International Socialist Bureau as long as Poland remains an independent section at these congresses.

9   The Social Democratic Party of Poland and Lithuania retains its own name, which follows 'RSDRP' as a subheading.

10   Special representatives of the Social Democratic Party of Poland and Lithuania must participate, on terms of equality with representatives of the RSDRP as a whole, in all inter-party conferences involving the participation of any other party [e.g., Polish Socialist Party] working in Poland.

1.59
Draft Conditions for the Unification of the Bund with the RSDRP

1   The Bund enters the RSDRP as the Social Democratic organization of the Jewish proletariat; its activities are not limited to any particular region.
2   The Bund accepts the Programme of the RSDRP.
Note The question of the nationality programme remains open since it was not examined by the Unification Congress.
3   All decrees of party congresses are binding upon the Bund.
4   Within the limits of the general decrees of RSDRP congresses and of the general directives of the Central Committee, the Bund retains its independence in matters of agitation, organization, and propaganda.
5   The Bund has its own local organizations and central institutions, holds its own congresses, and independently handles the affairs of its own organization.
6   All local organizations in the RSDRP form a single guiding city committee of the RSDRP on the basis of general elections, regardless of the nationality of the party members.
Note This committee resolves all questions common to the proletariat of the particular city by simple majority vote. The mode of electing the city committee is determined by the general principles accepted in the party.
7   The organizations of the Bund send their representatives to party congresses and conferences on the same basis as the other organizations of the RSDRP.
Note Elections to a congress may be held at general electoral meetings if the local organizations so agree.
8   The Bund is represented in the Central Committee of the RSDRP.
Note The manner in which the Bund is represented in the Central Committee is determined by agreement between the Central Committee of the Bund and the Central Committee of the RSDRP.
    Representatives of the Bund are included in all RSDRP delegations to international socialist congresses.

Protokoly Ob" edinitel' nogo s"ezda Rossiiskoi Sotsial' demokraticheskoi Rabochei Partii (Moscow, 1907), 413–19; 1.51, 1.52, 1.58, 1.59 in *Chetvertyi (Ob"edinitel'nyi) s"ezd RSDRP: Protokoly* (Moscow, 1934), 541–53

KPSS v rezoliutsiiakh 1, 170–84

I All-Russian Conference of the RSDRP 3–7 November 1906

Very shortly after the conclusion of the Unification Congress, the Bolsheviks began agitating for the convocation of still another congress which would, so they hoped, reassert their factional superiority. They justified this on the grounds that the dismissal of the I Duma on 8 July 1906 had sufficiently shown the illusory character of tsarist concessions. Thus broader participation in the elections to the II Duma scheduled for January 1907 was warranted than was allowed under the resolution passed in Stockholm (1.56). The Menshevik-controlled Central Committee apparently accepted this rather tortured argument but called an 'All-Russian Conference' in Tammerfors (Soviet historians refer to this as the II Conference thus legitimizing the Bolsheviks' earlier 'First' Conference in the same city) rather than the proposed extraordinary congress. Since the delegates were chosen by the Central Committee, it is not surprising that the Mensheviks predominated. Of the seventeen representatives from eleven local Russian organizations, eleven were Mensheviks. Of the representatives from the newly-admitted national organizations, the eight Polish and Latvian Social Democrats supported Lenin while the seven Bundists voted Menshevik. The delegates agreed, much to Lenin's pleasure, that their decisions would not be binding on the local organizations.

This factional composition was reflected in the 18 to 14 acceptance of the Menshevik resolution on Duma election tactics and alliances (1.60). Lenin was particularly upset that the Conference approved 'local agreements' with 'democratic opposition parties' which he believed opened the door for wholesale election alliances with the Constitutional Democrats. He felt that this mistake was only partially corrected by document 1.61, which noted that the Central Committee could not force local organizations into alliances which they did not want. In another decision, the Conference duly favoured the calling of a party congress in the next three months. Unfortunately, a lack of time prevented what would have been a very interesting discussion of expropriations which had continued despite the Unification Congress' prohibition (1.55).

1.60
On the Tactics of the RSDRP during the Election Campaign

I

In its electoral campaign the RSDRP, acting as an independent proletarian party, sets itself the following goals:
1 to give the broadest possible publicity to the programme of revolu-

tionary social democracy and to organize the broadest possible strata of the proletariat on the basis of the class struggle;

2   to explain to the masses the illusory nature of any hopes for a peaceful outcome in the struggle for power between the people and the autocratic government; to expose the bankruptcy and the half-way nature of the tactical methods and programmatic slogans of the bourgeois opposition parties, contrasting them with the revolutionary methods and goals of the proletariat and impelling the democratic elements along the path of revolutionary struggle;

3   to defeat the counter-revolutionary plans of the reactionaries who are endeavouring to dominate the Duma in order to use it to group backward social elements around the monarchy; and

4   to heighten the political activity of the masses and, organizing the forces of revolution both outside and inside the Duma, to create the conditions for transforming the Duma into a bastion of the revolution; to reveal the total impotence of the State Duma as a legislative institution under an autocratic monarch and the need to struggle for a sovereign constituent assembly.

II

1   In its electoral agitation, the Social Democratic Party everywhere stands on an independent party platform.

2   According to the resolution of the Unification Congress [1.56], all alliances are rejected which are concluded between parties as a whole or which bind individual party groups for the entire election campaign.

3   During the first stage of the elections in the workers' curia [according to the election law of 11 December 1905, eligible voters in the workers' curia elected 'representatives' (first stage), who in district electoral assemblies chose 'electors' (second stage), who finally in guberniia electoral assemblies with electors from the other curiae picked the actual Duma deputies], absolutely no partial or local agreements are permitted with groups or parties which do not adhere to the viewpoint of the proletarian class struggle.

4   In all other curiae [i.e., landowners', peasants', and other urban residents'], if during the course of the election campaign there appears to be a danger that the lists of the right-wing parties will win, local agreements are permitted with revolutionary and democratic opposition parties in accordance with local conditions and under the general supervision of the central [party] institutions. In such cases, however, party candidates and organizations are absolutely forbidden to commit themselves to any concessions of principle with respect to the other parties entering into the agreement.

5   The forms of such agreements must correspond to the local condi-

tions and may involve either a territorial distribution of candidacies within a single electoral district or the composition of joint lists of elector candidates.

Note When this is done, an effort should be made to compile joint lists only at the last moment before the elections, when the electoral agitation is coming to an end.

1.61
On Electoral Unity at the Local Level

The Conference is convinced that all members of a single organization must carry out all decisions relating to the electoral campaign which have been adopted by the competent bodies of local organizations, within the limits of the general directives of the Central Committee; the Central Committee may prohibit local organizations from presenting lists [of candidates] which are not purely Social Democratic but should not compel them to present lists which are not purely Social Democratic.

'Vserossiiskaia konferentsiia RSDRP,' *Proletarii*, no. 8 (23 November 1906), 1–3

KPSS v rezoliutsiiakh I, 188–91

London Congress   30 April – 19 May 1907

The congress which met in the spring of 1907 was the largest and the last of the pre-revolutionary gatherings of this type. Originally, it was to have convened in Copenhagen, but police pressure forced the assembled delegates to leave Denmark on twelve hours' notice, whence they went to London via Sweden. Officially known as the London Congress, it has subsequently been given the appellation 'Fifth' by Soviet historians. While the exact number of delegates varied from day to day and indeed from account to account, the current Soviet calculation is that some 392 Social Democrats were in attendance. Of these, 303 had voting privileges and supposedly represented 138 local organizations; another 39, including such luminaries as Bogdanov, Dan, Trotsky, Stalin, A.M. Gorky, and ten members of the Social Democratic Duma fraction, attended in an advisory capacity; and there were fifty invited guests. In all, the Congress claimed to represent some 150,000 Social Democrats inside imperial Russia.

Of the voting delegates, 89 belonged to the Bolshevik faction, 88 to the Menshevik, 55 to the Bund, 45 to the Polish and Lithuanian Social Democrats, and 26 to the Latvian Social Democrats. Since the latter two groups tended to vote with the Bolsheviks, Lenin had his long-sought majority – at least on paper. In practice, however, his Polish and Latvian allies refused to go along with his more factional manoeuvres. Moreover, they held the deciding votes in the new Central Committee elected by the Congress inasmuch as that body was composed of only five Bolsheviks (I.P. Goldenberg, N.A. Rozhkov, I.F. Dubrovinsky, I.A. Teodorovich, V.P. Nogin), four Mensheviks (Martynov, Zhordaniia, Nikifor, I.A. Isuv), two Poles (Warski and Dzerzhinsky), two Latvians (Danishevsky and another to be named by the Latvian Central Committee), and two Bundists to be named later by their organization. Since the Committee was expected to operate under hazardous conditions inside Russia, the more important and prestigious Social Democrats such as Lenin, Bogdanov, Zinoviev, Krasin, and Rykov were included only among the thirty candidate members.

Despite its length and size, the London Congress contributed nothing to the party Programme and very little to its organizational structure other than to re-subordinate the Central Organ (*Sotsial-demokrat*) to the Central Committee and to approve in principle the admittance of the Armenian Social Democratic Workers' Organization and the Lithuanian Social Democratic Party into the RSDRP. This relatively small contribution was partially a result of spending twenty-two of the Congress' thirty-five sessions uselessly debating the reports of the former Central Committee and the Duma fraction. In the end, the conciliatory attitude of Lenin's national allies kept the Bolshevik leader from pushing through resolutions critical of these two Menshevik-controlled bodies. Indeed, most of the tactical resolutions (which the Congress crowded into its last few days) tended to be conciliatory in tone even if they were basically Bolshevik in content. Perhaps the most interesting of these concerned non-party workers' organizations and partisan activities which served to delineate the limits of party operations and also to split the two main factions internally. On the question of non-party organizations, the RSDRP recognized for the first time the usefulness of the Soviets of Workers' Deputies which had sprung up in 1905 but at the same time condemned the idea of a supra-party workers' congress composed of representatives of trade unions, co-operatives, and other worker organizations which Akselrod and some right-wing Mensheviks hoped would lead to the formation of a mass workers' party. The other extreme, that of a para–military semi-anarchistic party, was also ruled out when the Congress voted 120 to 35, with 52 Bolshevik abstentions, to disband the 'fighting squads' and to condemn the expropriations that the left-wing of the Bolshevik faction had continued to carry out to the benefit of their factional treasury.

1.62
Organizational Rules 19 May 1907
[Replaces Rules adopted 1906; see 1.50]

1   [As in 1.50, art. 1] A member of the party is one who accepts the party Programme, supports the party financially, and belongs to some party organization.
2   [As in art. 2] All party organizations are built on the principles of democratic centralism.
3   [As in art. 3] All party organizations are autonomous with respect to their internal activities. Every approved party organization has the right to issue party literature in its own name.
4   [Revises art. 4] New party organizations are approved by oblast conferences or by two neighbouring organizations. The Central Committee exercises supervisory power over such approvals. The Central Committee should in due course publish in the party press the names of newly confirmed organizations.
5   [As in art. 5] The organizations of a given region may unite to form oblast unions. An oblast centre is elected at the oblast conference or congress.
6   [As in art. 6] All party organizations must contribute 10 per cent of all income received to the Central Committee.
7   [Revises art. 7] The Central Committee is elected at the congress. The Central Committee represents the party in relations with other parties; it organizes various party institutions and guides their activities; it appoints the editorial board of the Central Organ, which works under its supervision; it organizes and conducts undertakings of significance for the party as a whole; it allocates party personnel and funds, and has charge of the central party treasury; it settles conflicts between and within various party institutions and it generally co-ordinates all the activity of the party. Members leaving the Central Committee [by arrest, retirement, etc.] are replaced by candidates appointed by the congress and in the order established by the congress.
8   [New] For discussion of the major questions of party life, the Central Committee at least once every three or four months convokes periodic conferences of representatives of oblast unions, the Bund, the Social Democratic Party of Poland and Lithuania, and the Social Democratic Party of the Latvian Region, on the basis of one delegate for each 5000 organized workers participating in the elections to the most recent congress.

All organizations not included in oblast unions elect delegates in the same way at their own conferences. Decisions of the [periodic] conferences become binding only after they have been approved by the Central Committee.

9 [As in art. 8 except the third paragraph, which is revised] The congress is the supreme organ of the party. Regular congresses are summoned annually by the Central Committee. An extraordinary congress must be called within two months upon the demand of not less than one-half of the party membership.

If the Central Committee refuses to convoke a congress under these circumstances, the half of the party that demanded it has the right to form an Organizational Committee which enjoys all the rights of the Central Committee with respect to convening the congress.

All party organizations that have been approved at least three months before the date of the congress have the right to be represented at it, on the basis of one delegate for each 1000 members participating in the elections of the delegates. Organizations with an insufficient number of members may unite with neighbouring organizations to send a common delegate if together they have at least 1000 voting members. Elections to a congress are to be conducted on democratic principles.

A congress is considered valid if more than one-half of all party members are represented at it.

The convocation of any congress and its agenda are to be announced by the Central Committee of the party, or under appropriate circumstances by the Organizational Committee, at least one and a half months before the date of the congress.

1.63
On Attitudes toward Non-Proletarian Parties   16 May 1907

Considering:
1   that the RSDRP is at present faced with the particularly urgent task of defining the class character of the various non-proletarian parties, of evaluating class relations at the present moment and, in accordance with this, of defining its attitude toward these other parties;
2   that the Social Democratic Party has always recognized the necessity of supporting the oppositon and revolutionary movement directed against the existing social and political order in Russia;
3   that the Social Democratic Party, while maintaining a completely independent class position, is obliged to do everything in its power to enable the proletariat to carry out its role as the leader of the bourgeois-democratic revolution –

Considering this, the Congress recognizes:
1   That the reactionary and Black Hundred parties (the Union of Rus-

sian Men, the Monarchist Party, the Council of the United Nobility, etc.) are more and more resolutely and definitely setting themselves up as class organizations of the feudal-minded landowners, are endeavouring through nationalist incitement and the organization of pogroms to drown the revolution in the blood of internecine warfare; that the Social Democratic Party must [therefore] point out the extremely close connection between these parties and tsarism and explain the necessity for an uncompromising struggle aimed at the total abolition of all social and political remnants of feudal barbarism.

2   That such parties as the Union of the 17th of October [the Octobrists], the Party of Commerce and Industry, to some extent the Party of Peaceful Reform, etc., represent organizations relying on a section of the landowners and the more backward strata of the bourgeoisie which have entirely gone over to the side of the counter-revolution, are clearly supporting the government, and are advocating the most undemocratic constitution possible, based on property qualification; that the Social Democratic Party must [therefore] conduct a most relentless fight against these parties.

3   That the parties of the liberal-monarchist bourgeoisie, headed by the Constitutional Democratic Party [Kadets], have now definitely turned aside from the revolution and endeavour to halt it through a deal with the counter-revolution; that the social basis of these parties is made up of the economically more progressive segments of the bourgeoisie, especially the bourgeois intelligentsia, while a section of the urban and rural petty bourgeoisie continues to follow these parties only through tradition and because they are deliberately deceived by the liberals; that the political aims of these parties do not go beyond a constitutional monarchy protected from the inroads of the proletariat by the police, the bicameral legislative system, and the standing army, etc.; that the Social Democratic Party must [therefore] use the activities of these parties to educate the people politically, drawing the contrast between their hypocritically democratic phraseology and the consistently democratic approach of the proletariat, unmasking the constitutional illusions which they are disseminating, and fighting without mercy against their hegemony over the democratic petty bourgeoisie.

4   That the populist or labour parties (the Popular Socialists, the Labour Group [Trudoviks], the Socialist Revolutionaries) more or less adequately express the interests and viewpoint of the broad masses of the rural and urban petty bourgeoisie, vacillating between submission to the hegemony of the liberals and a resolute struggle against the landowners and the feudal state; these parties envelop their essentially bourgeois-democratic aims in a more or less nebulous socialist ideology; the Social Democratic Party should [therefore] persistently unmask their pseudo-socialist character and fight against their endeavours to play down the opposition between the

proletarian and the small property-owner; on the other hand, the Social Democratic Party must make every effort to tear these parties away from the influence and leadership of the liberals, compelling them to make a choice between the policies of the Constitutional Democrats and those of the revolutionary proletariat – thus forcing them to take the side of the Social Democrats against the Black Hundreds and the Kadets in the struggle to carry the democratic revolution through to a consistent conclusion.

5   The resulting joint efforts must preclude all possibility of deviation from the Social Democratic Programme and tactics, and must serve merely to ensure a common onslaught against both the reaction and the treacherous tactics of the liberal bourgeoisie.

1.64
On the Workers' Congress and Non-Party Workers' Organizations   18 May 1907

Considering:

1   that the Social Democratic Labour Party is the only organization uniting the conscious part of the proletariat and, as its vanguard, leading the struggle of the working class for a socialist order and for the political and economic conditions needed to realize it;

2   that, besides the Social Democratic Party, the principal forms of organization for defending and serving the economic interests of the working masses are the trade unions and, after them, the other types of workers' organizations such as co-operatives, etc.;

3   that at the moment of revolutionary upsurge it becomes possible to organize and use such non-party representative institutions of the working class as the Soviets of Workers' Deputies, the Soviets of Workers' Delegates, etc., to develop social democracy;

4   that the idea of a workers' congress leads by its very essence to the ultimate substitution of non-party workers' organizations for the Social Democratic Party, while the organizational and agitational preparation of a workers' congress will inevitably lead to the party's disorganization, promoting the subordination of the broad working masses to the influence of bourgeois democracy –

The Congress therefore recognizes that:

a   To broaden and strengthen the Social Democratic influence on the broad proletarian masses it is necessary, on the one hand, to intensify the work of organizing trade unions and of developing Social Democratic propaganda and agitation within them; and on the other, to attract increasingly broader segments of the working class to participation in party organizations of all kinds.

b It is desirable for organizations of the Social Democratic Party to participate in non-party Soviets of Workers' Deputies, Soviets of Workers' Delegates, and in congresses of their representatives, and also to organize such institutions, on the condition that this be done along strict party lines for the purposes of strengthening and developing the Social Democratic Labour Party.

c Agitation for a non-party workers' congress, which has been snatched up by the anarcho-syndicalists as a weapon for use against the Social Democratic influence on the working masses, is harmful to the class development of the proletariat.

1.65
On the State Duma   19 May 1907

1   The immediate political tasks of the Social Democratic Party in the Duma are:

a explaining to the people the Duma's complete lack of suitability as an instrument for realizing the demands of the proletariat, the revolutionary petty bourgeoisie, and especially the peasantry;

b explaining to the people the impossibility of achieving political liberty by parliamentary means as long as the real power remains in the hands of the tsarist government, and the inevitability of an open struggle between the masses of the nation and the armed power of absolutism – a struggle whose aim will be total victory, meaning the transfer of power into the hands of the people's representatives and the calling of a constituent assembly on the basis of universal and equal suffrage, direct elections, and the secret ballot.

2   The fault-finding, propagandistic, agitational, and organizational role of the Social Democratic Duma fraction, as one of the organizations of our party, should be put in the forefront. It is precisely this role, and not any immediate legislative purpose, that is to govern the submission of draft laws by the Social Democratic fraction in the Duma. The overall character of the struggle in the Duma must be subordinated to the proletariat's struggle outside the Duma; the tactics of mass economic struggle and the support of these tactics are of particular importance.

3   Fighting not only against the autocracy, but also against the treacherous policy of bourgeois liberalism which, under the slogan 'Safeguard the Duma,' in fact sacrifices the popular interests to the Black Hundreds, the Social Democratic fraction and the Social Democratic Party, guided exclusively by the course of the revolutionary crisis developing on the basis of objective conditions outside the Duma, should neither provoke a premature conflict nor artificially prevent or postpone conflict by a deprecatory

attitude toward its own slogans, as this can only discredit the Social Democratic Party in the eyes of the masses and cut it off from the revolutionary struggle of the proletariat.

4   Considering that the 'subordination' of the executive power to the present Duma (in the form of the so-called 'ministerial responsibility,' etc.), which clearly expresses the striving of the liberal bourgeoisie for a deal with the autocracy, could come about only in the event that revolutionary pressure was too weak to effect total victory, the Social Democratic Party can neither put forward nor adopt such slogans – which serve only to becloud the democratic consciousness of the masses and thereby to impede their struggle.

1.66
On Relations between the Duma Fraction and the Central Committee
19 May 1907

The Central Committee must have an official representative in the fraction who will communicate to the fraction the directives of the Central Committee.

All Central Committee members have the right to participate in meetings of the fraction in an advisory capacity.

1.67
On Partisan Activities
19 May 1907

Considering:
1   that the intensified economic struggle, unemployment, and the bloody policies of tsarism have impelled certain strata of the proletariat to adopt the partisan form of struggle; that is, individual and group attacks on the lives of government agents and representatives of the bourgeoisie;
2   that expropriations of government and private property are developing and intensifying for the same reasons;
3   that these anarchistic methods of struggle disorganize the ranks of the proletariat, obscuring its class-consciousness and generating in it illusions about the possibility of substituting for its own organized struggle the efforts of selfless individuals, thus deadening in the proletariat the striving for and the habit of independent mass activity;
4   that, furthermore, the partisan activities and expropriations, which the government then uses to heighten its repressive measures against the peaceful population, prepare the soil for Black Hundred agitation among the popular masses and, in particular, among the troops;
5   that participation by party members in partisan activities and expropriations not only hampers the party's struggle with anarchistic tendencies

among the working masses, but also compromises it in the eyes of the broad masses of the population and demoralizes its own ranks —

Considering all of this, the Congress therefore resolves:

1 that party organizations must conduct an energetic struggle against partisan activities and expropriations, explaining to the working masses the complete bankruptcy of these methods of struggling for the political and economic interests of the working class and the harm they do to the cause of revolution;

2 that party members are forbidden to participate in any way at all in the partisan activities and expropriations, or to give them assistance.

At the same time, and without prejudging the question of the forms of organizing the arming of the masses in periods of open attack as well as for self-defence, the Congress finds that fighting squads attached to party organizations as permanent institutions with special military functions and of necessity isolated from workers' organizations [see 1.54], are inclined to expand the use of terrorist tactics in the revolutionary struggle and are a contributing factor to the spread of partisan activities and expropriations.

In view of the above, the Congress resolves that all specialized fighting squads attached to party organizations are to be disbanded.

1.68
On Trade Unions   19 May 1907

Confirming the resolution of the Unification Congress on work in trade unions [1.57], the Congress calls the attention of party organizations and Social Democrats working in trade unions to one of the principal purposes of Social Democratic work in them – promoting trade union recognition of the ideological leadership of the Social Democratic Party and also establishing organizational ties with the party – and to the necessity of implementing this aim where local conditions permit.

> *Londonskii s"ezd Rossiiskoi Sots.–*   *KPSS v rezoliutsiiakh* 1, 212-21
> *Demokr. Rab. Partii (sostoiavshiisia*
> *v 1907 g.): Polnyi tekst protokolov*
> (Paris, 1909)

II All-Russian Conference of the RSDRP   21–23 July 1907

The London Congress had no sooner resolved the vexing Duma question by favouring future Social Democratic participation than the government reopened the issue by dismissing the II Duma on 3 June 1907 and radically changing the election law to the disadvantage of the urban proletariat. At the instigation of the Central Committee, the II All-Russian (or III by Bolshevik nomenclature) Conference met in Kotka, Finland, to reassess the situation. Besides members and candidates of the Central Committee, some twenty-six local representatives attended. Of these, nine were Bolsheviks, five Mensheviks, five Bundists, five Polish, and two Latvian Social Democrats. The Bolsheviks, however, were far from united on the Duma issue. Their left-wing, led by Lenin's former colleague Bogdanov, once again called for a boycott of the body. Lenin, with the assistance of the Mensheviks, defeated this move 15 to 9 and then with Bogdanov's help defeated Dan's counter-proposal before having his own resolution (1.69) adopted by a 15 to 11 margin.

The Conference also discussed the party's relationship to the trade union movement. The Mensheviks favoured a return to the Unification Congress' espousal of party neutrality within trade unions (1.57); the Bolsheviks stuck to the London resolution (1.68) calling for unions to recognize the ideological leadership of the party. In the end, the problem in the form of four conflicting draft resolutions was left for the Central Committee to resolve.

1.69
[On Participation in the Elections to the III Duma]

... Finding that:
1   boycotting [the Duma elections] would be a correct tactic only in the event of a broad, universal, and rapid revolutionary upsurge associated with some direct attack on the old régime, or in order to combat widespread constitutional illusions (as was done in the boycotts of the Bulygin Duma and Witte [or I] Duma [1.39, 1.48]);
2   the conditions enabling revolutionary social democracy to participate in the II Duma [1.60, 1.65] have not changed substantially, since the new electoral law [of 3 June 1907] only promises to replace the Duma which talked like a Kadet one and acted like an Octobrist Duma with one which will be openly Octobrist;
3   that the government coup of 3 June 1907 is the direct and inevitable result of the defeat of the December 1905 [Moscow] uprising, the treachery of the liberal bourgeoisie, and the activities of the two Dumas which perverted the revolutionary consciousness of the masses and depressed their revolutionary mood by their policy of deals and agreements with the old régime (e.g., slogans of 'ministerial responsibility,' 'Safeguard the Duma,' etc.); and that the lesson of the second period of the Russian revolution – the years 1906 and 1907 – is that the same advance of the reaction and retreat of the revolution which has occurred throughout this

entire period is inevitable as long as faith in the constitution and in Kadet hegemony prevails in the liberation movement —

The Conference therefore recognizes that:

a it is necessary to participate in the electoral campaign and in the III Duma;

b during the electoral campaign and in the Duma itself the Social Democratic Party must disseminate and instil in the popular consciousness the idea of socialism and the revolutionary slogans, and must struggle resolutely against the reaction and against Kadet hegemony, both in the liberation movement generally and in the Duma in particular.

1.70
[On Alliances in the Duma Elections]

1   In the elections, the Social Democratic Party is independent and does not enter into any electoral agreements in the first stage [see 1.60].
2   If there is a second ballot, agreements are permitted with all parties to the left of the Constitutional Democrats.
3   In the second and subsequent stages agreements are permitted with all revolutionary and opposition parties up to and including the Constitutional Democrats (and related groups, such as the Muslims, cossacks, etc.).
4   In such agreements Social Democrats must be guided by the following order of non-socialist parties listed by the degree of their adherence to democratic principles: 1 / Socialist Revolutionaries, 2 / Popular Socialists, 3 / Trudoviks, 4 / Constitutional Democrats.
5   In the workers' curia, no agreements are permitted with other parties or organizations, except the Polish Socialist Party and the national Social Democratic organizations which are not part of the RSDRP.
6   The only agreements permitted are those of a purely technical nature.

'Izveshchenie o partiinoi   *KPSS v rezoliutsiiakh* 1, 227-35
konferentsii 21, 22, i 23
iiulia 1907 goda,' leaflet (1907)

III All-Russian Conference of the RSDRP   5–12 November 1907

The III All-Russian Conference (or IV Conference by Bolshevik calculations) met in Helsingfors (Helsinki) and was attended by twenty-seven delegates: ten Bolsheviks, four Mensheviks, five Bundists, five Polish, and three Latvian Social Democrats. Lenin gave a lengthy report on Social Democratic tactics in the III Duma which resulted in a resolution being passed, over Menshevik and Bundist objections, that more or less repeated the instructions of the London Congress (1.65). Of more interest was the resolution criticizing the activities of the various factional centres. While Soviet historians indicate that this was aimed at a Menshevik offshoot of the old Organizational Commission which tried to circumvent the new unified Central Committee, it stands to reason that the main target of this resolution was in fact the Bolshevik Centre formed at the time of the Unification Congress. This fifteen-man group, which operated under the guise of being the expanded editorial board of the Bolshevik paper *Proletarii*, was very active throughout 1907, co-ordinating forbidden expropriations and managing factional affairs. In all likelihood, the desires for party unity on the part of the underground representatives coincided with those of the national organizations to push this resolution through the Conference. The gathering also passed a motion limiting the freedom of Social Democrats to publish in bourgeois journals. According to Lenin, this was aimed at Plekhanov and certain Menshevik publicists who had criticized the decisions of the II All-Russian Conference in the liberal newspaper *Tovarishch* (Comrade). Since the Bolshevik Centre continued to operate until 1910 and since the virtual absence of Social Democratic newspapers in Russia after 1907 made publication in bourgeois papers unavoidable, these resolutions had little actual effect other than to express the temper of the times.

1.71
On Factional Centres and Strengthening of Ties between the Central Committee and the Local Organizations

Although the Conference considers that the existence of different tactical tendencies within the party and of different interpretations of the party's tasks is natural and inevitable in view of the past history of the Russian Social Democratic movement, none the less it finds:

1   that the joining together of local Bolshevik or Menshevik organizations into separate factional organizations within the party and the existence of separate factional centres whose functions compete with those of the Central Committee, are impermissible and opposed to the existence of a unified party;

2   that the dissemination of directives through the party organizations by anonymous groups which are not responsible before the party is equally impermissible;

3   that the guiding bodies of local, regional, and national organizations

III CONFERENCE 119

must make every effort to ensure that the ideological struggle being conducted by the various sections of the party under no circumstances takes the form of an organizational struggle, i.e., the organizational suppression of one section of the party in the given locality by another.

The Conference draws to the attention of the local organizations the fact that the Central Committee, whose actions implement a particular tactical line on the basis of the resolutions of the London Congress, is an all-party and non-factional institution, and that it alone is supposed to lead the party.

The Conference, therefore, imposes on all party organizations the obligation of turning to the Central Committee, and only to the Central Committee, for assistance and instructions whenever needed, and demands that they place the maintenance of party unity at the local level above all else.

The Conference finds that to establish close ties between the Central Committee and the local organizations, it is necessary:

1   to do everything possible to ensure the immediate issuance of the Central Organ [*Sotsial-demokrat*, which ceased publication in December 1906 and did not reappear until February 1908];
2   to organize contacts with local organizations by means of periodic personal visits by members of the Central Committee and its representatives;
3   to remind all local and national organizations of their duty to support the Central Committee financially;
4   to remind all local and national organizations of their obligation to send detailed monthly reports on their activities to the Central Committee;
5   to do everything possible for the rapid unification of national organizations [with local units of the RSDRP where they exist side-by-side] on the local level;
6   to take steps to maintain and reinforce party discipline.

Finally, the Conference calls the attention of the Central Committee to the necessity of ending the schism which is evident in several local party organizations and which has manifested itself in the formation of local factional organizations.

1.72
On Participation in the Bourgeois Press

1   The Conference believes that the participation of Social Democrats in the liberal and liberal-democratic press at the present time in Russia has assumed a character such that it does serious harm to the party and that continued development of this participation is capable of leading to serious

ideological and organizational disruption in the Social Democratic Labour Party.

2   The Conference believes that participation in the non-party press is impermissible if connected with a direct or indirect struggle against the Russian Social Democratic Labour Party and its leading institutions or against the tactical views of one or another element of the party.

3   The Conference believes that it is also impermissible for Social Democrats to participate in the non-party press under conditions such that the themes and interpretations involved in the working out of political questions are limited by the interests of the bourgeois editorial staff; this leads in fact to the creation of an ideological and political bloc of socialists and non-socialists who hold common views on crucial questions of international socialism.

4   The Conference proposes that the participation of Social Democrats in the non-party press under conditions other than those outlined above is permissible, but must be placed under the supervision of organizations of the RSDRP in all cases where such participation is capable of having any practical political significance and influence whatsoever on the masses.

5   It is impermissible for Social Democrats to participate in the bourgeois press in an editorial capacity or to publish unsigned articles.

6   The Conference believes that news reports on party affairs should be written only by persons empowered to do so by party organizations.

'Rezoliutsii 3-i obshcherossiiskoi konferentsii,' *Proletarii*, no. 20 (19 November 1907), 4–5

KPSS v rezoliutsiiakh 1, 236–40

Central Committee on Legal Activities February – March 1908

Although the concessions won in 1905 had opened up new opportunities for Social Democrats in a variety of legal workers' organizations, most of the party's attention immediately after the revolution was centred on factional matters or Duma activity. As a result, these organizations grew rapidly during 1906 and 1907 but without the guidance or even the formal approval of the RSDRP. The Unification and London Congresses, for instance, passed only brief and contradictory resolutions on the question of party operations in trade unions. This situation was further complicated by the fact that the II

All-Russian Conference submitted no less than four draft resolutions on the question for the Central Committee to reconcile and elucidate. Similarly, in the absence of clear party directives, many Social Democrats had simply joined co-operatives and some trade unions had become financially embroiled in them. It took over two and a half years for the Central Committee to come to the conclusion that the co-operative movement could indeed 'be of quite considerable use to the proletariat.'

To resolve these difficulties and uncertainties, the Central Committee in 1908 established a Trade Union–Co-operative Commission. This Commission rather belatedly formulated the following guidelines for party activities in these mass worker organizations. It should be noted, however, that by this time many of the more than 600 legal trade unions which had existed a year earlier had been closed by the authorities. This, of necessity, led to the formation of some 95 illegal unions, but these generally were small, short-lived and not particularly influential among the workers. The situation was the same, if not worse, in the few remaining co-operatives.

1.73
On Trade Unions   February 1908

1   Intensified work by the Social Democratic Party in the trade union movement, as demanded by the contemporary situation, must be conducted in the spirit of the resolutions of the London Congress [1.68] and the Stuttgart Congress [of the Second International in 1907]; i.e., in the spirit of an undeviating drive for the closest possible rapprochement between the unions and the Social Democratic Party and under no circumstances in the spirit of recognizing in principle trade union neutrality or non-party affiliation.

Recognition of trade unions as Social Democratic should be the result solely of Social Democratic propaganda and organization within the trade unions and should not disrupt the unity of the proletariat's economic struggle.

2   In most cases trade unions have not succeeded in creating tightly knit organizational cells in the various enterprises, as became evident both during and after the various actions of the proletariat [in the 1905 Revolution]. Therefore, the government's repressions led not only to the closing of the bulk of the unions but to the complete destruction of certain of them; in view of this, the task of creating tightly knit organizational cells is paramount at the present time. Without such cells it is impossible either to construct stable trade unions or to guide the economic struggle of the proletariat.

3   Where legal trade unions exist or can be re-established, these cells or

primary trade organizations ought to be created in all factories and plants, artisanal, and commercial enterprises. Members of the Social Democratic Party should form tightly knit groups in all such primary organizations in order to influence them systematically in the Social Democratic spirit under the guidance of the local party centres.

And in places where police repressions have completely shattered the legal trade unions, and where all opportunities for restoring them on a legal basis have been exhausted, the organization of illegal trade unions must be undertaken immediately. Each illegal union, like each legal one, must be based on organizing the largest possible number of workers into a trade cell in a given enterprise, and inside this cell it is necessary to organize in particular a trade union group of Social Democrats in that enterprise.

4   In order to unite all Social Democratic work in trade unions, it is necessary to organize trade union groups of Social Democrats in each profession thereby linking together the trade union groups of Social Democrats in different enterprises.

All of these groups must be tied to the local party centre and must conduct their work in close organizational association with it.

5   As regards such legal societies as mutual aid societies, temperance societies, etc., tightly knit groups of Social Democrats must be formed in them for party work among the broadest possible masses of the proletariat. In such cases, it must be made clear that legal societies cannot take the place of militant trade unions and that the organized activities of the proletariat cannot be restricted to within the limits of these societies.

6   Illegal unions must struggle subbornly for legal recognition, but this legal existence as such ought not to minimize the militant tasks of the proletariat's trade organizations.

1.74
[On Co-operatives]   March 1908

... Social Democrats must bind the co-operatives to the trade unions and the party through lengthy and persistent work. This tie is especially necessary in view of the novelty of the co-operative movement and its mass character. Social Democrats must not disappear without trace inside these organizations but must, on the contrary, group themselves together so as to achieve a unified effect. In the co-operatives, Social Democrats must, of course, constantly recruit members for the party and for trade unions. They must act in accordance with the strictest democratic principles, thus ensuring the spontaneity of the masses and the mass character of the movement ... The immediate tasks of Social Democrats in the co-operatives are to struggle against high dividends on shares and premiums on loans, to agitate for more cultural and educational work by cooperatives, to appeal to the party and the trade union movement for help, and to support the workers during strikes and other actions ... Close relations between co-operatives and trade unions would be extremely useful for both sides. In some localities trade unions themselves are undertaking to open co-operatives with their own funds, the result being that under present conditions the trade unions may go bankrupt. While we consider it eminently desirable that the trade unions, as entities, do everything possible to establish new co-operatives and strengthen existing ones, we would at the same time warn trade unions against expending their own funds in this manner. The trade union treasury is to be expended for militant purposes. The funds of co-operatives are to be made up of the dues of individual members of trade unions and the other members of the co-operative which, of course, is not limited to persons of just one trade.

The co-operative must be a proletarian organization not only by the nature of its activity but also in its membership. This does not mean that it must consist absolutely and exclusively of workers. It only means that the general character of the co-operative and the bulk of its membership should be proletarian. Non-proletarian elements may be admitted to co-operatives on the condition, one share – one vote, and if this does not compromise the independent action of the workers.

The only persons who should not be admitted to co-operative membership or to its management are those working in the factory administration or upon whom the workers are directly dependent and who could exert undesirable pressure. The co-operative must be a school for training the proletariat in autonomous activity. This must be manifested not only in the full accountability and publicity of the management of all co-operative affairs but also in the manner of financing the co-operative. It is better for a co-operative to develop slowly than to take steps which from the very beginning tie down the workers or compel them to look for outside assistance. In this connection we would warn comrades against taking advances from management or accepting contributions which involve any sort of obligation.

Attempts are already being made to centralize the co-operative movement. In particular, an all-Russian congress of co-operative societies is scheduled to take place [in Moscow] in the near future [April 1908]. This centralization should be promoted and participated in actively. Social Democrats should discuss ahead of time the questions which are to be examined at the congress and should appear at the congress as a tightly knit group. But active participation in the co-operative movement does not mean that Social Democrats should forget for one minute the huge responsibility incumbent upon them as the only reliable leaders of this movement – especially in those places where they are also its initiators. In such cases any mistake not only leads to the collapse of the particular workers' organization, which is extremely valuable in itself, but also causes the masses to be dissatisfied with the Social Democrats as the ones supposedly responsible for this collapse. That is why we are confronted with the particularly urgent task of explaining the necessary conditions for the correct development of the co-operative movement (political liberty, development of the other aspects of the workers' movement, more or less adequate wages, a high level of mass consciousness, etc.) and also of remaining extremely careful in our actions. In undertaking to organize a co-operative one must prepare the ground beforehand among the working masses, collect sufficient funds, find suitable leaders, etc.

Rapid growth is often a morbid and baneful phenomenon. Only through gradual efforts can we accumulate the experience which we now lack.

The work of the Social Democrats in co-operatives not only places the latter on a firm class basis but also has a favourable impact on the development of the Social Democratic Party itself. By unifying even the most backward levels of the proletariat, the co-operatives pull them into the area of common proletarian interests and develop in them the spirit of autonomous activity and solidarity ...

Proletarii, no. 21 (13 February 1908), 4; no. 26 (19 March 1908), 5

Partiia Bol'shevikov v period reaktsii, 1907–1910 gg. (Moscow, 1961), 199–200, 206–8

Plenum of the Central Committee   11–13 August 1908

The Central Committee elected at the London Congress met several times during 1908 to deal with the continuing scandal caused by expropriations in Russia and the problem of reconstructing party work in the aftermath of Stolypin's coup d'état. Factional animosities and the evenly balanced nature of the Committee, however, reduced the effectiveness of these gatherings. Perhaps the most interesting and constructive plenum met in Geneva during August of that year and was attended by five Bolsheviks, three Mensheviks, one Latvian, one Pole, and two Bundist members of the Central Committee.

The principal difficulty facing the Committee was its own debility inside imperial Russia. The August Plenum, therefore, spent considerable time redefining the Central Committee's responsibilities and restructuring its organization. It created out of its membership two new bodies: a five-man subcommittee (suzhennyi or uzkii sostav) composed of a Bolshevik (Goldenberg), a Menshevik (M.I. Broido), a Pole (A.M. Maletsky), and one member each from the Latvian and Bundist contingents in the Central Committee, which would function inside Russia; and a subordinate three-man Foreign Bureau (Zinoviev, L. Tyszka, N.V. Ramishvili) which would co-ordinate party activities abroad. It also established a Press Commission composed of Bogdanov, Zhordaniia, V.K. Taratuta, and three national representatives to oversee the activities of the Central Organ. The latter, which had published only one issue in Russia since December 1906, was moved abroad in the summer of 1908 and assigned new editors, Lenin and B.I. Goldman, by the plenum. When neither they nor the Press Commission were successful in resolving the paper's difficulties, the next plenum meeting in Paris in December altered the factional balance of the editorial board to include three Bolsheviks (Lenin, Zinoviev, Kamenev), one Menshevik (Martov) and one Pole (J. Marchlewski). *Sotsial-demokrat* finally began appearing regularly in February 1909.

Martov tried to raise at the August Plenum the question of Bolshevik complicity in recent expropriations and especially their role in disposing of the bank notes obtained in the Tiflis robbery. With Polish and Latvian help, Lenin managed to take this embarrassing question out of the hands of the Menshevik-controlled Central Bureau of Foreign Groups (which was replaced by a new Foreign Central Bureau consisting of four Bolsheviks, four Mensheviks, and two German Social Democrats) and to pigeonhole it in an Investigatory Commission headed by his close associate, Zinoviev.

The plenum closed by calling for the quick convocation of a new party conference.

1.75
The Organization of the Central Committee

I   Plenary meetings of the Central Committee possess all the rights of the Central Committee itself; regular plenary meetings are convoked once every three months, extraordinary meetings – at the demand of six members of the [Central Committee] or of the majority of the subcommittee of the Central Committee working in Russia. Plenary meetings are valid if eight members are present and if the others who expressed a desire to come have been given the financial assistance to do so.

II   During intervals between plenary sessions, current work in Russia is conducted by the subcommittee of the Central Committee.

   I   This subcommittee is made up of five Central Committee members; an arrested member is to be replaced immediately by his candidate member.

Upon the initiative of the subcommittee, questions that cannot be postponed may be resolved by polling all members of the Central Committee.

Questions which directly affect the national organizations may be resolved only at plenary sessions of the Central Committee.

2 Tactical questions of a general nature are to be resolved by the subcommittee only if they are extremely urgent; in such cases the subcommittee will take steps to bring the matter to the immediate attention of all Central Committee members.

In important matters, especially when new questions of tactical principle arise, the five [members of the subcommittee] will postpone a decision until a meeting of the plenum unless the matter is extremely urgent.

3 The subcommittee of the Central Committee is charged with leadership of the Social Democratic Duma fraction.

4 Within the above limits, the subcommittee acts for the Central Committee as a whole and takes its place, endowed with all of its rights.

5 The subcommittee is to send written reports on all of its activities as frequently as possible to the Foreign Bureau of the Central Committee for informational purposes.

III The Central Committee hereby establishes a Foreign Bureau, made up of three members of the Committee, which is subordinate to the Central Committee subcommittee.

1 This Bureau is to be in constant communication with the Central Committee in Russia and with Central Committee members working abroad. It is to send the subcommittee periodic reports on its activities and is subordinate to the five [Central Committee members] in Russia.

2 The [Foreign] Bureau of the Central Committee represents the Central Committee's interests abroad; it supervises the activities of local collaborating groups and their [Foreign] Central Bureau; it is the recipient of foreign contributions to the Central Committee treasury and organizes independent financial undertakings for the Central Committee's benefit.

IV The Central Organ will continue to be published.

1 The editorial board of the Central Organ consists of three members. Two are appointed by the plenum, and the third is delegated by the Central Committee of the Social Democratic Party of Poland and Lithuania according to the Organizational Rules [1.58].

2 A [Press] Commission of six members, who must be members or candidate members of the Central Committee, is appointed to give constant support to the Central Organ. Conflicts of principle arising within the editorial board are, if any editor so demands, transmitted to this Commission for a decision. The Commission's decisions are binding upon the editors.

KPSS v rezoliutsiiakh I, 242–7

December All-Russian Conference of the RSDRP
21–27 December 1908

Preparations for the December or V All-Russian Conference of the RSDRP began shortly after the August 1908 Plenum. Despite this head start, police conditions or factional animosities allowed only two Social Democrats to arrive in Paris with authentic underground mandates. The rest of the sixteen 'local' delegates were either émigré leaders or representatives of the national organizations. There were, in addition, eight delegates (primarily from the Central Committee) who attended in an advisory non-voting capacity. Partly because of this lack of broad representation, the Mensheviks suggested unsuccessfully that the delegates constitute themselves as a 'meeting' without all-Russian significance.

The Mensheviks were also motivated no doubt by the fact that they were considerably outnumbered in Paris. Of the sixteen voting delegates, five were Bolsheviks and an equal number represented their Polish allies while the Mensheviks and the Bundists had only three representatives each. Given their numerical inferiority in the party's central institutions, the Mensheviks decided to adopt Lenin's old scheme of appealing for the convocation of a new party congress on the grounds that one had not been held in a year and a half despite the statutory requirement for annual gatherings. Lenin, in a reversal of positions, opposed this manoeuvre and got the Conference to pass a procrastinating resolution calling for a series of consultations and questionnaires on the practicality of a congress. The Bolshevik leader was probably influenced by the fact that his own house was not in order. Three of his 'local' Bolsheviks at the Conference were Otzovists who strenuously opposed the Conference's support of continued Social Democratic participation in the III Duma (1.76, sec. 5), advocating instead the 'recall' of the party's eighteen deputies. Relations between the Leninists and these left-Bolsheviks headed by Central Committee member Bogdanov became increasingly strained over other operational, ideological, and philosophical questions. In February 1909 contact between the two groups was broken off and at the June meeting of *Proletarii*'s expanded editorial board the Otzovists were put out of the Bolshevik faction (see *KPSS v rezoliutsiiakh* I, 273–6).

The most interesting facet of the Conference was the fact that for the first time since 1905 the party leaders sat back and reflected on their objectives and the broader implications of their activities rather than concentrating on pressing tactical and organizational questions. They finally admitted that the reactionary forces had triumphed in Russia and that the party had to readjust its operations accordingly. They noted the drastic decline in the participation of the revolutionary intelligentsia and the corresponding increased proletarianization of the RSDRP. They also spent considerable time trying to work out the proper balance between operations in the illegal underground and in legal worker organizations. This in turn brought conflict with the Liquidator wing of the Menshevik faction as well as with the Otzovists. Lenin cited, as an example of their attempt to 'liquidate' the underground structure of the party, the refusal of Broido to participate in the work of the subcommittee in Russia (see 1.75), and had his action obliquely condemned by the Conference (1.77).

On either side of the Conference, on 21 December and 27–29 December, a plenum of the Central Committee met which modified somewhat the organizational decisions of the August 1908 Plenum (1.75) and conveniently ratified the decisions of the December Conference.

1.76
On the Tasks of the Party at the Present Moment

... The All-Russian Conference of the RSDRP recognizes that at the present time the party is faced with the following basic tasks:

1 It must explain to the broad popular masses the meaning and significance of the latest [agrarian reform] policy of the autocracy and the role of the socialist proletariat which, while pursuing an independent class policy, must lead the democratic peasantry in contemporary political life and in the forthcoming revolutionary struggle. The goal of this struggle remains, as before, the overthrow of tsarism and the conquest of political power by the proletariat which, with the support of the revolutionary sections of the peasantry, will complete the bourgeois-democratic revolution by convoking a nation-wide constituent assembly and setting up a democratic republic.

2 It must study thoroughly and disseminate widely the experience of the mass struggle in the years 1905–1907, which has provided indispensable lessons confirming the correctness of revolutionary Social Democratic tactics.

3 The RSDRP must strengthen itself along the lines developed during the revolutionary epoch; as before, an implacable struggle must be waged both against the autocracy and the reactionary classes and against bourgeois liberalism; the party must fight against deviations from revolutionary marxism and against attempts to belittle the slogans of the RSDRP which presently are seen in some strength among certain decadent party elements.

4 The economic struggle of the working class must be promoted in every way, in accordance with the resolutions of the London Congress and the [1907] Stuttgart Congress [of the Second International].

5 The Duma and the Duma rostrum must be used for revolutionary Social Democratic propaganda and agitation.

6   The first item on the agenda is the lengthy task of educating, organizing, and consolidating the class-conscious proletarian masses. Following upon this comes the necessary extension of party work to the peasantry and the army, particularly in the form of written propaganda and agitation, with the brunt of the effort being devoted to the socialist education of proletarian and semi-proletarian elements in the peasantry and the army.

1.77
On the Reports to the Conference

1   The Conference hereby states its view that, considering the present unprecedentedly difficult political conditions and the existing intra-party situation, the Central Committee is doing everything possible to implement the political line established by the London Congress [1.62–1.68 above]. The Conference orders the Central Committee to continue to safeguard party unity and integrity in the struggle against the disorganizing tendencies within it which disrupt this unity.
2   Noting that in many places a section of the party intelligentsia is attempting to liquidate the existing organization of the RSDRP and to replace it by a shapeless amalgamation within the framework of legality, whatever this might cost — even at the price of the open rejection of the Programme, tactics, and traditions of the party — the Conference finds it essential to conduct the most resolute ideological and organizational struggle against these liquidationist efforts and appeals to all true party workers, regardless of faction or tendency, to offer the most energetic resistance to these attempts.
3   The Conference feels that the Central Committee can work with complete success only if its minority will submit to party discipline and work loyally within the framework of a single institution and through its executive organs; it notes further that refusal to work in this way constitutes a boycott of the party.

1.78
On the Work of the Central Committee

1   The Conference approves the Central Committee decree which, in the light of the existing situation, provided for the creation in Russia of an organ of reduced membership [i.e., the subcommittee of the Central Committee, see 1.75] endowed with all the rights of the Central Committee plenum.
2   In the view of the Conference, the questions of tactical principle which are again being raised should whenever possible be examined by a

Central Committee plenum, being resolved by the reduced Central Committee only in cases of the most extreme urgency.

3   The Conference orders the Central Committee to reinforce its supervision and its ties with local, regional, and national organizations through more frequent trips by Central Committee members, by dispatching agents from the subcommittee of the Central Committee in Russia, and by improving its correspondence.

4   In view of the significance of the party's work abroad, and also in view of the massive frictions and disorganizing opposition to the Central Committee's work which is found abroad —

The Conference regards as useful and necessary the existence abroad of a representative institution of the entire party in the form of the Foreign Bureau of the Central Committee [which the Menshevik delegates sought to abolish, see 1.75].

1.79
On the Organizational Question

... Considering that:

1   although the victory of the counter-revolution at the present moment has engendered a temporary indifference to the party on the part of those workers who are inclined toward revolution but are devoid of sufficient socialist consciousness, the party none the less remains confronted with the fundamental task of expanding its political and economic agitation and organizational work among the broadest possible working masses;

2   by postponing implementation of the party's democratic slogans, this victory [has resulted in] the departure from the party's ranks of all those unsteady intellectual and petty bourgeois elements which had sided with the workers' movement mainly in the hope of the imminent victory of the revolution;

3   the changed political conditions make it increasingly impossible to contain Social Democratic activity within the framework of the legal and semi-legal workers' organizations;

4   the personnel of the leading party institutions is increasingly being replaced by conscious proletarian elements whose class-consciousness has been deepened by their experience during the years of revolution;

5   present conditions of work make it impossible to apply in full measure the party's democratic organizational principles —

The Conference therefore finds that:

a The party must devote particular attention to the utilization and strengthening of existing illegal, semi-legal and where possible, legal organizations — and to the creation of new ones — which can serve it as strong points for agitational, propagandistic, and practical organizational work among the masses: such organizations being factory meetings, propaganda circles, illegal and legal trade unions, [workers'] clubs, various workers' educational societies, etc. This work will be possible and fruitful only if there exists in each industrial enterprise a workers' committee, consisting solely of party members even if they are few in number, which will be closely linked to the masses, and if all the work of the legal organizations is conducted under the guidance of the illegal party organization.

b In order to unify party efforts at the local level, it is necessary:
i to organize in each region a centre which will not only give technical support to the local organizations but also assist them ideologically and reconstitute them in case of collapse;
ii to establish the very closest ties between local and regional organizations and the Central Committee.

c To ensure the correct and uninterrupted functioning of local organizations, the occasional application of the principle of co-optation is permitted, but such co-opted members are to be replaced at the first opportunity by comrades elected legally on the basis of the Rules [1.62]. As regards the content of organizational work, the Conference finds that, in addition to political and economic agitation connected with the present situation ... the party must devote particular attention to deepening the Social Democratic outlook of the broad circles of party workers and in particular to developing practical and ideological leaders of the Social Democratic movement from among the ranks of the workers.

1.80
On the Unification of National Organizations at the Local Level

1 The Conference orders the Central Committee to take steps to unify the local organizations of our party in all regions where – despite the resolution of the Stockholm Congress [1.59] – this has not yet occurred.
2 In this respect, the Conference finds that such unification must proceed from the principle of the unity of the Social Democratic organizations of each particular locality, and decisively rejects any unification based on the principle of federalism [see also 1.6].

1.81
On the Social Democratic Duma Fraction

In regard to the activity of the Social Democratic Duma fraction, which is one of the auxiliary organs subordinate to the party and to its Central

Committee, the Conference – in order to raise the activities of the fraction to the proper party level and to elucidate correctly for the entire party its agitational and propaganda work – hereby states:

that the fraction's activities in the period under consideration manifested, together with some correct speeches, certain deviations from the political line of our party ...

that the fraction has in no way properly exposed the bourgeois opposition, headed by the Kadet Party, which has de facto set out on an imperialistic course and one of open support for the counter-revolution;

that the fraction on numerous occasions has not carried out the direct orders of the Central Committee.

In view of all of this, the Conference – stating at the same time that the blame for the fraction's deviation does not rest on it alone, since it is working in the particularly difficult conditions of the Black Hundred Duma, but is shared to some extent by all the organizations of the party and by its Central Committee, which have not been doing everything that was necessary and possible for the proper direction of the party's work in the Duma – finds that:

1   In its further activity the fraction must serve the party in the spirit indicated by the London Congress [1.65] and in line with the directives of the Central Committee of the party.

2   The basic task of the fraction in the counter-revolutionary III Duma is to act as one of the organs of the party in matters of Social Democratic propaganda, agitation, and organization; in no way taking the path of so-called positive legislation or pursuing petty sham reforms; and, without restricting itself to speeches only on matters raised by the Duma majority, to strive in every way to raise in the Duma the questions which will agitate the working masses and our party.

3   In the interests of carrying out these agitational and propaganda tasks, the fraction must as soon as possible:

a   introduce in the Duma independent drafts for working-class legislation (concerning an eight-hour working day, freedom to strike and to form unions, workers' insurance, etc.);

b   in one form or another, raise as frequently as possible the question of the advance of capital in the economic realm, tying this in with the changed correlation of forces in the political struggle, the question of unemployment in the cities, and famine in the villages, etc.;

c   introduce a series of draft laws which put forward the demands of our minimum programme, giving these draft laws a popular form which can be understood by broad sections of the population;

d   initiate energetic agitation against the counter-revolutionary foreign policy of the government and of the parties which support it, and also against those imperialist and nationalist trends which the Kadets and a part of the Octobrists are adopting;

e the fraction must expose and brand from the Duma rostrum the nationality policy of the government and the Duma majority; it must devote constant attention to national questions within the state and must energetically support the demands of the party Programme in defence of the rights of the oppressed nationalities;

f must raise, in one form or another, the question of the situation in the army and must defend the demands raised by the soldiers and sailors in the days of the revolutionary upsurge [i.e., in 1905 and 1906];

g in defending the local needs of the population, even if they are petty and limited in nature, the fraction must connect these limited needs with the party's overall demands and must set as its task the exposure before the people of the impossibility of any sort of satisfactory resolution of local needs under the present régime, and must also refuse to support those local demands which are in contradiction with the overall interests of the proletariat;

h with respect to the budget, the Conference is of the view that it is in principle wrong to vote for the budget as a whole. It is also wrong to vote for individual items in the budget of a class state which sanction expenditures on instruments of mass oppression (troops, police, administration, courts, etc.).

In voting for reforms or for items covering expenditures for cultural needs, the point of departure should be that principle in our Programme according to which Social Democrats reject any reforms associated with the tutelage of the police and the bureaucracy over the labouring classes.

Therefore, as a general principle, the fraction must vote against the so-called reforms and the items of expenditure for so-called cultural needs which are introduced into the III Duma.

In those exceptional cases where there is a good chance of improving the position of the workers and the lower salaried employees, or of genuinely satisfying the cultural needs of the broad popular masses, the fraction will, depending on the circumstances, either abstain (giving a special explanation of why it did so) or vote in favour, after preliminary discussion of the matter in the Central Committee with the representatives of party and trade union organizations;

i the fraction must enter into the closest possible relations with all local and national party organizations, with Social Democratic groups operating within the trade unions and other workers' organizations, and with these unions and organizations themselves; it must speak at workers' meetings and must generally expand its activities outside the Duma whenever possible.

The Conference, furthermore, directs the attention of all local and national party organizations and of the party Central Committee to the fact that their hitherto inadequate assistance to the fraction has greatly hampered the latter's activity, and considers it necessary that all party organizations:

a send to the fraction any and all information on the situation of the workers, the actions of the administration and of united capital, materials for interpellations and speeches, the resolutions of workers' meetings and of party groups, and drafts of speeches; give systematic and businesslike suggestions concerning the forthcoming moves of the fraction as well as businesslike criticism of its past actions;

b disseminate among the masses speeches, interpellations, draft laws, and the fraction's reports, expanding and utilizing its speeches for purposes of mass agitation, in leaflets, etc.

[For conspiratorial reasons, the following points were not published in the original version of this resolution.] The Conference directs the attention of the Central Committee, whose duty it is to lead the fraction, to the following:

1   Knowledgeable persons may be admitted to the deliberations of the fraction only by decision of the Central Committee and only in an advisory capacity.

2   The fraction must allocate 10 per cent of its salary for the special purpose of organizing the Central Committee's servicing of the fraction.

3   In view of its responsibility to the party for the fraction's work, the Central Committee must unhesitatingly use its right to veto the fraction's decisions whenever these decisions threaten to harm the party.

4   If the party's work in the Duma does not proceed along the lines set forth by the Conference and approved by the Central Committee, an extraordinary party conference must be convoked (but not before the end of the spring session) to discuss the question of the fraction's continued existence.

Vserossiiskaia konferentsiia *KPSS v rezoliutsiiakh* I, 248–59
Ros. Sots.–Dem. Rabochei Partii
(v Dekabre 1908 goda) (Paris,
1909), 38–47

Plenum of the Central Committee 2–23 January 1910

The January 1910 Plenum of the Central Committee, which met in the Café d'Arcourt in Paris, was attended by some nineteen Social Democrats: fourteen voting members of the Central Committee (four Bolsheviks, four Mensheviks, two Poles, two Bundists, one Latvian, and one Vperedist) and by 5 non-voting representatives (Lenin, Kamenev, Martov, Trotsky, and Bogdanov) from the major émigré newspapers. The plenum came at a very inopportune time for Lenin; indeed he opposed its convocation. Only a month earlier, the former left-Bolsheviks (Otzovists, Ultimatists, God-constructionists) had formed their own Vperedist faction under Bogdanov and were making plans to publish a factional journal *Vpered* and to hold a factional school. Moreover, three of the four Bolshevik representatives on the Central Committee wished to 'conciliate' factional differences. Had the Mensheviks been willing to take advantage of this situation, they might have been able to regain the power they had held at the time of the Unification Congress and perhaps even to remove the Bolshevik leader from all positions of influence. One of the delegates in fact read a list of Bolshevik sins – continued expropriations, the unethical acquisition of $140,000 from the estate of N.A. Shmidt, the Tiflis bank-note scandal, financial manipulations, etc., – that should have been sufficient to bring Lenin before a party court. Instead, in the interests of unity, the plenum merely condemned these 'derogations from party discipline' (1.88) and sought to strip him of his organizational machinery. Lenin had to agree to close down the Bolshevik 'Centre' as well as his factional paper *Proletarii*, and to turn over both his factional treasury and the proceeds of the Shmidt bequest to the Central Committee and to three impartial German 'trustees' (Franz Mehring, Klara Zetkin, Karl Kautsky). He also had to accept Menshevik-Bolshevik parity in the Central Organ (Lenin, Zinoviev, Martov, Dan, Warski), in the Foreign Bureau of the Central Committee (A.I. Liubimov, B.I. Goldman, Tyszka, I.A. Berzin, F.M. Koigen), and in the Russian Board (Kollegiia) of the Central Committee (two Bolsheviks, two Mensheviks and one representative from each of the three national organizations) which replaced the subcommittee of the Central Committee (1.75) made ineffectual by factional animosities and police pressures. In each body, the deciding votes rested with the representatives of the national organizations whose loyalty Lenin increasingly had reason to doubt. The spirit of unity also saved the Vperedists and Liquidators who were condemned indirectly rather than being expelled from the party, as Lenin had wanted, for refusing to accept the orthodox formula of operating in both legal and illegal organizations under the direction of the illegal party (1.79).

The Mensheviks later claimed that they had won a 'moral victory' at Paris but they were to pay dearly for failing to press their advantage. Trotsky felt that the 'unification plenum' was the 'greatest event in the history of Russian social democracy.' Lenin did not agree. From this point on, in the words of Soviet historians, he 'waged a war on two fronts' in an effort to create a 'party of the new type' – an all-Bolshevik party.

1.82
Rules of the Central Committee

1   The Board of Central Committee members functioning in Russia is endowed with all the rights of the Central Committee.
2   All Central Committee members are obliged to carry out any part of the Central Committee's work.
3   The present Central Committee is composed of those members and candidates who were elected at the London Congress.
4   The operative number of members for the [Russian Board of the] Central Committee is set at seven, of which four are [Russian] members and three are representatives of the national organizations (including a member of the Polish Social Democrats) elected [to the Central Committee] at the [London] Congress.
5   In case of the departure [i.e., arrest] of any one of the seven members of the Board, the departing member is replaced by a candidate elected by the London Congress who has expressed the desire to work in Russia; in the absence of such a candidate, replacement is made from among candidates previously selected by the Board who were not elected by the London Congress.
6   New candidates are to be co-opted by a majority of the Russian Board, with no dissenting votes, and are considered to be acting members of the Central Committee until approved by an all-party conference.
7   The candidates elected at the London Congress replace departing members of the Central Committee in the order provided for in the Rules.
   Departing members are replaced by recently co-opted candidates representing the same [factional] tendency or belonging to the same national organization.
   Details of the procedure for replacing departing Central Committee members are to be worked out by the Russian Board.
8   When possible, the Central Committee is to meet once a month; between meetings its business is conducted by the [Foreign] Bureau of the Central Committee elected by the general meeting.
9   The Foreign Bureau of the Central Committee, consisting of five members of the Central Committee and appointed by it, handles work abroad. The Bureau is to contain three representatives of the 'national' Central Committees.
   The Central Committees of the national organizations have the right to appoint to the Foreign Bureau persons who are not members of the [RSDRP] Central Committee. The latter may not participate in plenary sessions of the [RSDRP] Central Committee.
   The Foreign Bureau of the Central Committee controls the party's finances, handles its publishing and technical activities [i.e., transporting and smuggling illegal literature into Russia], represents the party abroad,

and serves as a unifying point for the foreign groups collaborating with the party and as an intermediate link between them and the Central Committee operating in Russia.

The majority of the Foreign Bureau's members must live in the same city.

10   A plenum of the Central Committee's fifteen members is convoked: 1/ by decree of the Russian Board (requiring a two-thirds majority, but not less than five votes); 2/ by unanimous decree of the Foreign Bureau; 3/ in case of the arrest of more than half of the Russian section of the Central Committee when those arrested cannot be immediately replaced by available candidates.

11   The plenary session (of fifteen members) is to include: 1/ the members of the Russian Board; 2/ the members of the Foreign Bureau of the Central Committee except those who are not actually members of the Central Committee; 3/ if a total of fifteen is not thereby attained, the remaining candidates participate in the plenary session in the following order: a/ candidates elected by the London Congress who are engaged in any sort of party activity in Russia; b/ Central Committee members and candidates who are living abroad and engaged in work assigned them by the Central Committee.

In the filling of candidacies, the proportion among the [factional] tendencies is to be maintained. The question of which candidate has the right to be present at the plenary session is decided by the actual members of the Central Committee present at the meeting.

1.83
On the Central Organ

The following recommendation is made to the Central Organ [*Sotsialdemokrat*]: while aiming to have the majority of articles unsigned (i.e., written by the editors), an effort should be made to insert signed articles by individual comrades when the editorial board is in general agreement with them even though disagreeing in particulars – thus making it easier for the representatives of various tendencies in the party to participate in the Central Organ.

The editorial board of the Central Organ is to be made up of two Bolsheviks, two Mensheviks, and one representative of the Polish Social Democratic Party.

1.84
On Factional Centres

In view of the passage of a number of resolutions aimed at creating de facto unity in the party, and in view of the declaration of the Bolshevik comrades [see *KPSS v rezoliutsiiakh* 1, pp. 296–8] that they are disbanding their organizational Centre and closing [their factional newspaper] *Proletarii* —

The Central Committee expresses its full confidence that, in carrying out the resolutions adopted unanimously by the Central Committee, the editorial board of the Central Organ will promote the consolidation of all literary forces without distinguishing among tendencies; it is convinced that the interests of the party and of party unity will be served by the immediate closing of the [Menshevik] newspaper, *Golos Sotsialdemokrata*.

The Central Committee therefore appeals to the Menshevik comrades who are members of the Central Committee and the Central Organ to make every effort to achieve this goal by exerting influence on their close associates.

1.85
On the Newspaper *Pravda*

The Central Committee hereby resolves that a subsidy [of 380 Austrian kronen a month] will be paid to the newspaper *Pravda* [published by Trotsky in Vienna] and that its representative [Kamenev] will be posted to the editorial board in the capacity of third editor.

Any changes in the *Pravda* editorial board must be the result of agreement between the editorial board and the Central Committee.

The question of transforming *Pravda* into an organ of the Central Committee is to be postponed to the next conference.

1.86
On the *Vpered* Group

The Central Committee hereby registers the *Vpered* literary group as a publishing group of the party.

The Central Committee orders the commission on organizational matters to develop draft measures providing for the inclusion of the literary and publishing undertakings of the *Vpered* group within the general system of party literary activity abroad, so that there will be no further need for a separate group.

1.87
On the Party School

The Central Committee resolves that preparations shall be undertaken for organizing a party school abroad.

For this purpose the Central Committee appoints a committee of nine: two Bolsheviks, two Mensheviks, two from the *Vpered* group, one Bundist, one Polish Social Democrat, and one Latvian Social Democrat.

Applications to this school are to be solicited immediately, both abroad and in Russia.

The Foreign Bureau of the Central Committee is hereby informed that it must take exhaustive steps to ensure that Comrade Maksimov [Bogdanov] and others refrain from organizing a separate school and, instead, participate in organizing the Central Committee school in which they will be provided with every opportunity to make full use of their pedagogical and lecturing talents.

1.88
On Derogations from Party Discipline

While expressing its view that since the London Congress events have occurred in connection with the [Shmidt] affair which are in contradiction to party resolutions and that certain comrades have performed acts [i.e., expropriations] which violate party discipline, but at the same time, bearing in mind that:

1 these comrades did not intend to harm party interests;
2 the comrades against whom these accusations are directed were guided only by an incorrect appreciation of party interests;
3 furthermore, with respect to certain matters, this incorrect understanding is to be explained by the atmosphere existing at the moment immediately following the period of militant mass action [i.e., the Revolution of 1905];
4 in some of the above-mentioned matters the violations of the organizational rules and derogations from party discipline are closely linked to the existence of factions and to the intra-party struggle —

The Central Committee decisively condemns such derogations from party resolutions and violations of party discipline and considers it necessary to take all steps to ensure that they not recur in the future.

1.89
On Convening the Next All-Party Conference

In view of the destruction of the regional organizations in most oblasts and the extreme difficulty of convening extensive regional conferences at the present time because of political obstacles [see 1.62, art. 8], the Central Committee recommends that the following procedure be adopted for electing regional delegations [to an all-party conference]:

a after consultation with the local organizations, the Central Committee will determine ... the most important centres of the Social Democratic movement in each oblast. The total number of delegates from the oblast will be drawn from these centres;

  b organizations of the less significant centres of Social Democratic work are to unite with the nearest major centre to elect delegates.

Note 1 This is not to exclude regional conferences if it is possible to convoke them.

Note 2 In this respect, the Central Committee urgently requests comrades in all cases to elect conference delegates from among local party workers.

The Central Committee recognizes the need for preliminary elaboration of agenda items at the local level and recommends that the discussion of these matters be extended not only to the raion, factory, and other party cells, but also to those Social Democratic participants in the legal movement [trade unions, etc.] who are prepared to resume organizational connection with the party. In organizing the elections, *party* groups in the legal workers' movement should be included on the same basis as all other party cells.

Considering that the comprehensive establishment of firm organizational ties among the various forms of local Social Democratic activity involves enormous difficulties that can be overcome only through long and arduous work, and recognizing that the participation of the largest possible number of *party* workers from the legal movement in the forthcoming conference would give a powerful impetus to the accomplishment of this task — the Central Committee recognizes the need for supplementary representation from Social Democratic groups in the legal movement which are prepared to establish firm organizational ties with the local party centres. In giving these additional delegates a consultative voice, the Central Committee postpones to the conference itself the final decision on whether they are to have advisory or voting status.

For the sake of the successful preparation of the forthcoming all-Russian conference and for the further consolidation of Social Democrats in the various areas of the workers' movement into a unified party organization, the Central Committee recommends that the regional and local party centres take on themselves the initiative of convoking local and regional meetings both of party workers in the primary party cells, factory and raion committees, etc., and of Social Democratic groups and individual party activists in the [legal] workers' movement.

The purpose of such meetings should be to discuss the items on the agenda of the party conference as well as any other general questions of current local Social Democratic activity ...

Sotsial-demokrat, no. 11 (13 February 1910), 10-11; except for articles 4 and 8 of 1.82 which were not published for conspiratorial reasons

KPSS v rezoliutsiiakh I, 289-99

Meeting of Members of the
Central Committee 28 May – 4 June 1911

As Lenin had foreseen, the unification dictated by the January 1910 Plenum did not last for long. The Mensheviks refused to close down *Golos Sotsialdemokrata* (see 1.84) since Martov and Dan found it impossible to work within the supposedly 'unified' Central Organ controlled by Lenin. The Vperedists continued to exist as a separate faction (1.86) and carried through with plans to publish their own journal and to hold a factional school at Bologna (1.87). Lenin then used these actions as excuses to delay turning over his factional treasury and to conduct his own school for underground party workers at Longjumeau near Paris. He also instructed the Bolshevik members of the Foreign Bureau (N.A. Semashko) and of the editorial board of Trotsky's *Pravda* (Kamenev; see 1.85) to leave these bodies. More significantly, the proposed conference (1.89) failed to materialize and the Russian Board of the Central Committee was totally hamstrung by the arrest of two sets of Bolshevik representatives and the refusal of the Menshevik Central Committee members in Russia to participate in the Board's work (1.82, art. 4). On the grounds that another plenum was needed to restructure the Board and that the Foreign Bureau refused to exercise its responsibilities (1.82, art. 10) in this regard, Lenin had Rykov summon 'a meeting of Central Committee members living abroad' to take this initiative.

Only eight Social Democrats showed up in Paris for the meeting; two of these (B.I. Goldman from the Mensheviks and M.I. Liber from the Bund) promptly walked out and a third (the Latvian delegate M.V. Ozolin) agreed to participate only in a private capacity. This allowed Lenin, Zinoviev, and Rykov plus their Polish allies, Tyszka and Dzerzhinsky, to proceed unopposed. The original idea of calling a plenum was soon shelved as being too time-consuming, and the little gathering thus took on itself the duty of calling the all-party conference. It created a Foreign Organizational Commission (Kamenev, Semashko, Rykov, Liubimov, Tyszka) and a Technical Commission (Tyszka, M.F. Vladimirsky, M.K. Vladimirov) to make the arrangements for the conference and to assume the legal duties of the Foreign Bureau. While these bodies were entirely Bolshevik or Polish in composition, which augured well from Lenin's point of view for the make-up of the future conference, the Bolshevik leader was less than happy with the conciliatory attitude of some of his colleagues. He was particularly upset that the Mensheviks and Vperedists might be invited to join the Organizational Commission, that the Foreign Bureau was allowed to remain in existence, and that provision was made to hold a joint conference if other tendencies sought to duplicate his efforts. In each instance, he was outvoted by the 'conciliators' – Rykov, Tyszka, and sometimes Dzerzhinsky – who also were well represented on the two newly created and blatantly illegal Commissions.

1.90
On Calling a Party Conference   1 June 1911

The approaching elections to the IV Duma and the stirring in the workers' movement, on the one hand, and the whole situation within the party, on the other, make the immediate calling of an all-party conference a matter of urgent necessity.

In view of the impossibility ... of at once calling a plenum of the Central Committee, which could itself set about convoking the conference —

This meeting of Central Committee members considers that its duty to the party compels it to take the initiative in this matter and therefore resolves as follows:

1   A party conference must be convoked within four months, i.e., by the beginning of October, and that the practical organizational work for its calling must be undertaken *immediately*.

2   The conference must be convoked on the same basis (that is, with the same composition, agenda, electoral procedures, etc.) as was set forth in the resolution [1.89] and letter on the conference of the last plenum of the Central Committee held in January 1910.

3   This meeting elects an Organizational Commission for calling the conference; this Commission, consisting of five members, will have the following tasks:

  a It must *at once* proclaim to the party the necessity of the conference, calling for the immediate election [of delegates] and generally for the preparation of the conference;

  b The Organizational Commission must enlist the services in calling the conference of representatives of local organizations in Russia, as well as influential comrades occupied with activities among the masses, so that they might form as quickly as possible a Russian board [i.e., the Russian Organizing Commission formed in October 1911, see *KPSS v rezoliutsiiakh* 1, 308–12, for its deliberations] to carry out under the general supervision of the Organizational Commission, the practical work of organizing the conference – which means fulfilling the directives set forth in the resolution and the letter of the [January 1910] Plenum;

  c The Organizational Commission should suggest to all regional and local organizations in Russia (as well as to the Duma fraction) that they enter into relations with it.

  d It should suggest to all party organizations abroad that they delegate a representative to the Organizational Commission for work on the immediate convocation of the conference.

Note 1 This invitation must be sent to: the Party Mensheviks [i.e., the followers of Plekhanov], the *Vpered* group, [Trotsky's] *Pravda* group, the Bund, and the Latvian Social Democrats. As regards participation by other tendencies [i.e., the Martov Mensheviks] in the Organizational Commission, a suggestion [to this effect] by one of the above groups is sufficient for their representatives to be invited.

Note 2 If it feels this to be necessary, the Organizational Commission has the right to increase the number of delegates to the Organizational Commission from among the Party Mensheviks [who were then allied with the Bolsheviks] and also to take as a member Comrades Iuri [A.A. Bekzadian] or Mark [Liubimov] who are valuable practical workers.

4   The Organizational Commission is to initiate its work on calling the conference *immediately*.

If other tendencies in the party should decide to convoke another party conference, it is desirable that agreement be reached with the organizers of the latter to ensure that only one party conference takes place [cf. 1.93].

1.91
On Creating a Technical Commission   1 June 1911

Considering that the Bolshevik representative [Semashko] has walked out of the Foreign Bureau of the Central Committee and that the Bolsheviks have categorically refused to entertain any relations whatever with the Foreign Bureau or to recognize it as a party institution and, on the other hand, bowing to the imperative necessity that a number of technical functions connected with party publishing activities, transporting [literature to Russia], etc., must continue to be discharged —

The meeting hereby resolves to create, for the execution of the above tasks until the convocation of the next plenum, a temporary Technical Commission of three members which is to be subordinate to the group of Central Committee members participating with voting status in the present meeting.

'Izveshchenie soveshchaniia tsentral'nogo Komiteta RSDRP' (leaflet, 1911), in *Revoliutsiia i VKP(b) v materialakh i dokumentakh* v (Moscow, 1926), 357–62. For conspiratorial and perhaps factional reasons, the original leaflet omitted note 2 and the last paragraph of 1.90 as well as all reference to precise periods of time, individuals, sizes of bodies and the Duma fraction.

KPSS v rezoliutsiiakh I, 303–7

Bern Meeting   20–23 August 1911

The non-Bolshevik forces, which had been talking about calling a party conference for over a year but had done nothing concrete in this direction, reacted quickly to Lenin's June 'meeting of Central Committee members living abroad.' Trotsky hastened to accuse the Bolshevik leader of 'usurping the name of the party' in an effort 'to demoralize and smash the party' through the calling of his private conference. The Foreign Bureau of the Central Committee responded on 18 July 1911 by issuing an invitation to the leading émigré organizations and newspaper editors to attend a countermeeting in Bern. Plekhanov and Lunacharsky refused in the name of their groups; and Lenin and the Poles simply ignored the invitation. Thus, the six Social Democrats who showed up at the Café Bubenberg – Trotsky, Dan, Liber from the Bund, 'Ludis' from the Latvian organization, and two non-voting representatives of the Foreign Bureau (B.I. Goldman and K.I. Elias) – hardly constituted a more legitimate or representative forum than did the June meeting. They too called for a party conference and authorized an 'Organizational Committee' to implement this decision, all the while criticizing Lenin's parallel Organizational Commission and proposed conference as schismatic. The anti-Bolshevik forces were slow off the mark, however. Their Organizational Committee – consisting initially of G.I. Urotadze from the Caucasian Oblast Committee, Liber from the Bund, a Latvian known as 'Alfred,' and later enlarged to include several émigré and Russian Mensheviks – did not start functioning until January 1912 and the conference it was to call did not meet until the following August. By then Lenin had long since stolen the march at his Prague Conference.

1.92
On the Attitude toward the Technical and Organizational Commissions

The meeting hereby notes that the so-called 'Technical Commission,' as well as the so-called 'Organizational Commission' [see 1.90, 1.91], were set up through a conspiracy between several Bolsheviks abroad and several Polish Social Democrats who supported them, through an internal party coup and a crude violation of all standards of party life as set forth in the party Rules and as defined by the last plenum, and finally, through the seizure of party funds [this probably refers to the fact that Semashko took the party's treasury and records when he left the Foreign Bureau on 13 May] – which is a discredit to the party's honour and dignity.

    The meeting hereby notes that the very existence of these two Commissions represents a split deliberately organized for factional purposes and undermines the entire basis of the party's existence.

In bringing this to the attention of the entire party, the meeting appeals to all Social Democrats who are devoted to their party to repulse decisively the pretensions of the above-mentioned groups to speak and act for the RSDRP.

Since the above-mentioned schismatic institutions contain elements who declare that their aim is to struggle for the restoration of the party and its unity, the meeting hereby places these elements on notice that party unity can be assured only by voluntary mutual agreement of all party tendencies on political objectives and that the indisputable condition of such agreement is the dismantling of the institutions which have arisen through the coup and which exist for schismatic purposes.

1.93
On the Party Conference

The meeting welcomes the initiative of the Caucasian Oblast Committee, the Central Committee of the Bund, the Central Committee of the Latvian Region and of certain local organizations, which set themselves the task of creating, on an urgent basis, an Organizational Committee in Russia for convoking a conference of the entire party following the principles laid down by the last Central Committee plenum [see 1.89].

The meeting regards as essential that such a conference be organized and convoked, with the participation of persons active in all aspects of Social Democratic work, in order to tie together organizationally all Social Democratic work, to enlarge its scope, and, in particular, to organize in a systematic and suitable manner the party's activities in the forthcoming elections to the [IV] State Duma. The political and organizational preparation for such a conference must be in the hands of the Organizational Committee which should be set up as rapidly as possible and should include the most advanced political activists irrespective of their group or factional allegiance.

The meeting, in complete agreement with the decisions of the [January 1910] Plenum, feels that the character of the preparatory work must be essentially that of rallying the progressive workers on the basis of political work under the banner of the Russian Social Democratic Labour Party and expresses its conviction that both the work of the Organizational Committee and that of the conference itself – especially considering the present condition of the party's forces – will be the more fruitful the more it is based not on a striving for mere numerical preponderance of some groups and trends over others but on agreement and concord of all Social Democratic groups which for so long have been working in isolation from one another. This agreement should be reached through the solution of the day-by-day problems put forward by the class movement of the Russian proletariat.

Listok zagranichnago biuro tsentral'ago komiteta, no. 1 (8 September 1911), 4

Prague Conference of the RSDRP   5–17 January 1912

Lenin's machinations during the summer of 1911 (1.90, 1.91) were successful in producing a virtually all-Bolshevik conference. Of the fourteen voting delegates who came to Prague, twelve were Bolsheviks and the other two were Party Mensheviks who at this time were aligned with the Leninists in Russia. In addition, all four of the non-voting émigrés (Lenin, Kamenev, Semashko, and O.A. Piatnitsky) were staunch Bolsheviks. As Trotsky was quick to point out, many of the local mandates were patently fraudulent or were products of artificially splintered groups. Despite their questionable legality, their lack of numbers, and the absence of all their prestigious Social Democratic leaders save Lenin and of any representation from the non-Russian parties, the delegates voted almost unanimously to constitute themselves as 'an all-party conference of the RSDRP – the supreme organ of the party.'

As such, they took it upon themselves to change the party Rules and the composition of the leading party bodies. A new Central Committee was elected consisting of five Bolsheviks (Lenin, Zinoviev, G.K. Ordzhonikidze, S.S. Spandarian, F.I. Goloshchekin), one Party Menshevik (D.M. Shvartsman), one police agent (R.V. Malinovsky), and five candidate members (A.S. Bubnov, M.I. Kalinin, A.P. Smirnov, E.D. Stasova, and S.G. Shaumian). Within a year Lenin used a new provision in the party Rules (1.94, art. 2) to co-opt six loyal Bolsheviks (Stalin, Sverdlov, I.V. Belostotsky, G.I. Petrovsky, A.E. Badaev, and A.S. Kiselev) to full membership in his Committee. Subordinate to it were two all-Bolshevik bodies: a restructured five-man Russian Bureau of the Central Committee to co-ordinate activities inside imperial Russia and a Committee of Foreign Organizations to replace the Menshevik-controlled Foreign Bureau. The Conference also confirmed *Sotsial-demokrat* as the party's Central Organ under a new all-Bolshevik editorial board (Lenin, Kamenev, Zinoviev); named the more popular *Rabochaia gazeta* as the official 'organ of the Central Committee'; approved in principle the establishment of a legal workers' daily in Russia; and terminated the earlier subsidy to Trotsky's *Pravda* (1.85) whose name the new daily was to appropriate four months later.

The Prague delegates declared that the Liquidator-wing of the Menshevik faction had 'once and for all placed itself outside the party' (1.102) and threatened that all other groups not operating through the new Central Committee would be unable to 'use the name of the Russian Social Democratic Labour Party' (1.103). In this sense, the Prague Conference (or the VI Conference in Bolshevik nomenclature) completed the work of the II Congress of the RSDRP in that it brought to an end nine years of sporadic attempts at party unity and finalized the Menshevik-Bolshevik split. The future role of the various national Social Democratic parties within the RSDRP was also called to question. 'Experience has conclusively proven,' noted the delegates, 'that we cannot tolerate a situation where non-Russians working in total isolation from Russian organizations have chosen to set up a federation of the worst type and have ... placed key Russian organizations in such a position that without the support of non-Russian national centres, which for all practical purposes do not concern themselves with Russian affairs, the RSDRP is unable to effect very essential and important party work' (*KPSS v rezoliutsiiakh* 1, 327–8).

The Conference not only laid the groundwork for the monolithic post-revolutionary party but it also was a foreshadowing of future congresses of the CPSU in the uniformity of its composition, in the fact that Lenin authored almost all of the resolutions, and in the ease with which these resolutions were passed.

1.94
Changes in the Organizational Rules of the Party   11 January 1912
[Revises Rules adopted 1907; see 1.62]

Add to article 2:
Co-optation is recognized as permissible – in accordance with the decisions of the December (1908) Conference [1.79].
    Delete article 8 and put in its place:
The Central Committee will convoke conferences of representatives of all party organizations as often as possible.
    Change article 9, third paragraph, concerning representation in the congress, to read:
Norms of representation at future congresses will be set by the Central Committee after preliminary discussions with the local organizations.

1.95
On the Party's Tasks at the Present Moment 12 January 1912

... The Conference confirms the tasks confronting the party as set forth in detail in the resolution of the December 1908 Conference [1.76] and calls particular attention to the task of the conquest of power by the proletariat while carrying the peasantry with it, which remains as before the aim of the democratic revolution in Russia. The Conference particularly directs the attention of comrades to:

1   the fact that the first task on the order of the day remains, as before, the continued work of socialist education, organization, and consolidation of the leading masses of the proletariat;

2   the necessity of intensified work on restoring the illegal organization of the RSDRP, which makes even broader use than before of every kind of legal opportunity, which is capable of directing the economic struggle of the proletariat, and which alone is able to take the lead in the increasing political activities of the proletariat;

3   the necessity of organizing and expanding systematic political agitation and of giving whole-hearted support to the incipient mass movement, securing its development under the banner of the full implementation of the party slogans. Propaganda for a republic, and against the policies of the tsarist monarchy, must be particularly stressed so as to counteract, among other things, the widespread propaganda which is being conducted in favour of curtailing our slogans and limiting ourselves to the existing framework of 'legality.'

1.96
On the Reports from the Local Organizations 7 January 1912

With respect to the reports presented by the local organizations, the Conference states that:

1   everywhere at the local level Social Democratic workers are energetically seeking to strengthen the local illegal Social Democratic organizations and groups;

2   the necessity is everywhere recognized of combining legal and illegal Social Democratic work; Social Democrats everywhere recognize that our illegal party organizations must use all existing legal workers' associations as bases for their activities among the masses. But even so, too little practical Social Democratic work has been done so far in trade unions, co-operatives, clubs, etc., in disseminating marxist literature, in exploiting the speeches of Social Democrats in the Duma, etc.; in these respects, it is

absolutely necessary for underground Social Democratic groups to show greater initiative;

3   everywhere at the local level, without a single exception, party work is being conducted jointly and amicably by Bolsheviks and Party Mensheviks in particular, but also by Russian members of the *Vpered* group wherever the latter exist, and by all other Social Democrats who recognize the necessity of an illegal RSDRP; all work is conducted in the spirit of defending party principles and of fighting against liquidationism.

The Conference expresses its conviction that, with the revival of the workers' movement, energetic work will continue in strengthening the old and building new and sufficiently flexible organizational forms which will help the Social Democratic Party to struggle for the *old* revolutionary goals and methods under *new* conditions.

1.97
On the Character and Organizational Forms of Party Work

Recognizing that the experience of the last three years has definitely confirmed the fundamental provisions of the resolution on the organizational question adopted by the December (1908) Conference [1.79], and assuming that the present revival of the workers' movement will make possible a further development of the party's organizational forms along the same lines – namely, the creation of illegal Social Democratic cells surrounded by the broadest possible network of legal workers' societies of various sorts —

The Conference finds that:

1   illegal party organizations must participate most actively in guiding the *economic struggle* (strikes, strike committees, etc.) and in bringing about co-operation between the illegal party cells and the trade unions – especially with the Social Democratic cells in the trade unions and also with various individuals in the trade union movement;

2   it is desirable that Social Democratic cells in trade unions, which are organized along *occupational* lines, should function wherever local conditions permit in conjunction with party branches organized on a *territorial* basis;

3   the greatest possible initiative must be taken in organizing Social Democratic work in the legal societies; trade unions, reading rooms, libraries, workers' recreational societies of all sorts; disseminating trade journals and guiding the trade union press in the marxist spirit; making use of Social Democratic speeches in the Duma; training legal lecturers from among the workers; setting up workers' and other voters' electoral com-

mittees (in connection with the elections to the IV Duma) for each district, street, etc.; conducting Social Democratic agitation during elections to the organs of municipal government, etc.;

4   energetic measures must be taken to reinforce and extend the number of illegal party cells, seeking out new and extremely flexible organizational forms for these cells, setting up and strengthening the leading underground party organizations in each city, and propagandizing such forms of underground mass organization as party 'exchanges' [i.e., the informal take-over of a particular street or promenade at a specified time so that party members could meet socially and also receive instructions or transfer literature], factory party meetings, etc.;

5   it is desirable to involve propaganda [i.e., study] circles in everyday *practical* work: the distribution of illegal Social Democratic and legal marxist literature, etc.;

6   it must be borne in mind that systematic Social Democratic written agitation, especially the regular and frequent issuance and distribution of an underground party newspaper, may be of great significance in establishing organizational links both among the underground cells and between the underground Social Democratic cells and the legal workers' societies.

1.98
On the Elections to the IV State Duma

I

The Conference recognizes the absolute necessity of participation by the RSDRP in the forthcoming electoral campaign for the IV Duma, of our party's advancing independent candidates, and of forming a Social Democratic fraction in the IV Duma which as a section of the party will be subordinate to the party as a whole.

The principal task of the party in the election, and equally of the future Social Democratic fraction in the Duma itself – a task to which all else should be subordinated – is socialist class propaganda and organizing the working class.

Our party's principal electoral slogans for the forthcoming elections should be:

1   *a democratic republic*
2   *an eight-hour working day*
3   *confiscation of all landed estates.*

In all of our pre-electoral agitation, these demands must be explained as graphically as possible on the basis of the experience of the III Duma and of the government's activity in both the central and the local administration.

All propaganda on the other demands contained in the Social Democratic minimum programme – such as universal suffrage, freedom of association, popular election of judges and officials, governmental insurance for workers, replacement of the standing army by the arming of the people, etc. – must be inseparably linked with the above three demands.

II

The overall tactical line of the RSDRP in the elections must be as follows: the party must conduct a merciless struggle against the tsarist monarchy and the parties of the capitalists and the landowning nobility which support it, at the same time steadfastly unmasking the counter-revolutionary and pseudo-democratic views of the bourgeois liberals (headed by the Kadet Party).

In the electoral campaign, particular attention must be directed to dissociating the position of the proletarian party from that of *all* non-proletarian parties and to explaining both the petty bourgeois essence of the sham socialism of the democratic groups (especially the Trudoviks, the narodniks, and the Socialist Revolutionaries) and the harm which their wavering in matters of a consistent and mass revolutionary struggle inflicts on the cause of democracy.

As regards electoral agreements, the party, adhering to the decisions of the London Congress [1.63, see also 1.60, sec. II], must:

1   put forward its own candidates in all workers' curiae and allow *no* agreements with other parties or groups (i.e., the Liquidators);

2   take care to put forward its own candidates in the second stage [i.e., district electoral] assemblies of urban curia representatives and, where possible, in the peasant curia as well – in view of the considerable agitational significance of merely nominating independent Social Democratic candidates there;

3   in cases of a second ballot (Article 106 of the Electoral Law) for electors in the second stage assemblies of urban curia representatives, agreements may be concluded with the bourgeois democratic parties against the liberals, and then with the liberals against all the governmental parties. One form of agreement could be the compilation of common lists of electors for one or several cities proportional to the number of votes cast in the first stage of the elections.

4   in the five cities (St Petersburg, Moscow, Riga, Odessa, Kiev), which have direct elections [to the Duma] with a provision for a second ballot, in the first elections independent Social Democratic candidates must be put forward for the [less propertied] second curia of urban voters. In case of a second ballot here, because of the clear absence of any Black Hundred threat, agreements are allowable only with democratic groups against liberals;

5   no electoral agreements may involve putting forward a common platform, and they may neither impose any sort of political obligations on Social Democratic candidates nor may they impede the Social Democrats in their resolute criticism of the counter-revolutionary nature of liberalism and of the half-heartedness and inconsistency of the bourgeois democrats;
6   whenever it is essential to defeat the Octobrist–Black Hundred or the government list in general in the second stage of the elections (in the district assemblies of representatives, in the guberniia electoral assemblies, etc.), agreements must be reached concerning the division of deputy seats – first with the bourgeois democratic parties (Trudoviks, Popular Socialists, etc.) and then with liberals, non-party persons, Progressivists, etc.

III

All Social Democrats must undertake *immediate* preparations for the electoral campaign, to this end devoting particular attention to the following:
1   underground Social Democratic cells must immediately be formed everywhere so that they can commence, without further delay, the preparations for the Social Democratic electoral campaign;
2   necessary attention must be devoted to strengthening and extending the legal workers' press;
3   all electoral work must be carried on in close association with the workers' trade unions and with all the other workers' societies – their legality being taken into account in determining the manner of their participation;
4   special attention is to be devoted to the organizational and agitational preparation for elections in the workers' curia of the six guberniias (St Petersburg, Moscow, Vladimir, Kostroma, Kharkov, and Ekaterinoslav) in which a deputy must be elected to the Duma from the workers' curia. All worker electors here and in the other guberniias must without exception be members of the Social Democratic Party;
5   guided by the decision of the underground party organizations, the assemblies of workers' representatives must resolve *precisely whom* is to be elected to the Duma from the workers' curia and compel all electors to withdraw their own candidacies in favour of the party's candidate – or else be boycotted and tried for treason;
6   in view of persecution by the government, the arrest of Social Democratic candidates, etc., it is necessary to work in a particularly restrained, systematic, and careful fashion using every means to react quickly to all police tactics, to nullify all the tricks and acts of violence of the tsarist government, and to elect Social Democrats to the IV State Duma, and consequently to strengthen generally the group of democratic deputies in this Duma;
7   Social Democratic Party candidates are approved, and directives

relating to the elections are issued, by the local underground party organizations and groups, under the overall supervision and guidance of the Central Committee of the party;

8   if, despite all efforts, a party congress or a new conference cannot be convoked before the elections to the IV Duma, this Conference hereby authorizes the Central Committee, or such other institution which it may appoint, to issue concrete instructions on the conduct of the electoral campaign in the individual localities or in accordance with the specific conditions which may arise, etc.

1.99
On the Social Democratic Tasks in the Fight against Hunger 8 January 1912

... The Conference resolves that it is necessary:

a to harness all Social Democratic forces to the extension of propaganda and agitation among the broad popular masses, especially among the peasantry, explaining the connection between the famine and tsarism with all its policies; distributing in the villages for agitational purposes not only the Duma speeches of Social Democrats and Trudoviks, but also of such friends of the tsar as Markov II [N.E. Markov, one of the leaders of the reactionary Union of Russian Men and a deputy to the III Duma]; and popularizing the political demands of social democracy – the overthrow of the tsarist monarchy, the institution of a democratic republic, the confiscation of landed estates;

b to support the workers in their desire to render all possible assistance to the starving, advising them to send contributions exclusively to the Social Democratic Duma fraction, to the workers' press, or to workers' cultural-educational and other societies, etc., as well as forming special cells of Social Democrats and other democrats upon entering groups, committees, and commissions for famine relief;

c to try to direct the democratic excitement aroused by the famine into demonstrations, rallies, mass meetings, and other forms of mass action against tsarism.

1.100
On the Attitude toward the Draft Duma Law
on State Insurance for Workers

1   ...
2   The best form of workers' insurance is *state* insurance, based on the following:
   a it should insure the workers against *all* cases of loss of earning power

(accidents, sickness, old age, permanent disability; pregnancy and child birth coverage for women; compensation for widows and orphans upon the death of the wage earner) and also against loss of earnings owing to unemployment;

   b the insurance should cover *all* wage earners and their families;

   c all insured persons should be compensated on the principle of restoration of their *full* wages, with *all* costs of the insurance being borne by the employers and the state;

   d all forms of insurance should be administered by *uniform* insurance organizations of the *territorial* type based on the principle of *complete* management by the insured.

3   All of these fundamental requirements for a rationally constructed insurance system are sharply contradicted by the government's draft law adopted by the State Duma; this law

   a includes only *two* forms of insurance – insurance against accidents and against illness;

   b covers only a small part (one-sixth – by the most liberal calculations) of the Russian proletariat, leaving outside the system whole regions (Siberia and, in the government's version, the Caucasus as well) and whole categories of workers which are in particular need of insurance (agricultural, construction, railroad, post and telegraph workers, shop clerks, etc.);

   c establishes miserly levels of compensation (the maximum for total disability due to injury is two-thirds of the wage level, and this is calculated on a base which is lower than the actual earnings) and at the same time makes the workers bear the main share of the cost of the insurance ... ;

   d deprives the insurance institutions of any autonomy, placing them under the interlocking supervision of bureaucrats, gendarmes, police, and managers ...

II

On the basis of the foregoing, the Conference resolves as follows:

1   Both the illegal party organizations and the comrades working in the legal organizations (trade unions, clubs, co-operatives, etc.) have the urgent task of developing the broadest agitation against the draft insurance law before the Duma, as this affects the class interests of the entire Russian proletariat and violates these interests in the crudest manner.

2   In the view of the Conference, it is necessary to emphasize that all Social Democratic agitation on the draft insurance law should tie it with the class position of the proletariat in contemporary capitalist society, with a critique of the bourgeois illusions being disseminated by social reformers, and with our fundamental socialist tasks in general; on the other hand, this agitation should tie the character of the Duma 'reform' with the current

political situation and with our revolutionary-democratic tasks and slogans generally.

3   While fully supporting the vote of the Social Democratic Duma fraction against the draft law in the Duma, the Conference directs the attention of comrades to the extensive and valuable material clarifying the attitude of the various classes toward labour reform which these Duma debates furnished ...

4   The Conference most earnestly warns workers against all attempts to curtail or distort Social Democratic agitation by keeping it within the limits legally permitted during this period of dominance by counter-revolutionary forces; on the contrary, the Conference emphasizes that the major theme in this agitation should be to explain to the broad proletarian masses the truth that no real improvement of the workers' position is possible without a new revolutionary upsurge; that anyone wanting to bring about genuine labour reform must struggle above all else for a new victorious revolution.

5   In case the draft bill before the Duma becomes law, despite the protest of the class-conscious proletariat, the Conference calls upon comrades to exploit the new organizational forms which it will establish (workers' sickness funds) to conduct, in these organizational units, energetic propaganda for Social Democratic ideas and thus to transform this law – devised with the aim of oppressing and imposing new shackles upon the proletariat – into a weapon for developing the proletariat's class consciousness, making it organizationally stronger, and intensifying its struggle for full political liberty and for socialism.

1.101
On the Central Organ

The Conference, having heard and discussed the report of the representative [i.e., Lenin] of the Central Organ [*Sotsial-demokrat*], and supporting in principle the line of the Central Organ —
   Expresses the hope that the Central Organ will devote more space to articles of a propagandistic character and that articles will be written in a more popular style so as to make them more intelligible to the workers.

1.102
On Liquidationism and the Group of Liquidators

Considering:

1   that for about four years the RSDRP has been struggling resolutely against the liquidationist tendency [see 1.77]...

2   that, continuing the struggle against this tendency, the plenum of the Central Committee in January 1910 unanimously declared it to be a manifestation of bourgeois influence on the proletariat and set the total break with liquidationism and the final overcoming of this bourgeois deviation from socialism as the preconditions for genuine party unity and the merging of the former Bolshevik and Menshevik factions [cf. *KPSS v rezoliutsiiakh* 1, 291];

3   that, despite all the decisions of the party and despite the commitment undertaken at the January 1910 Plenum by the representatives of all factions, a section of Social Democrats, grouped around the periodicals *Nasha zaria* [Our Dawn] and *Delo zhizni* [The Vital Question], have openly undertaken to defend a trend which the entire party has recognized as the product of bourgeois influence on the proletariat;

4   that the former [Menshevik] Central Committee members, 'Mikhail' [I.A. Isuv], 'Iurii' [P.A. Garvi], and 'Roman' [K.M. Ermolaev], not only refused to join the [Russian Board of the] Central Committee in the spring of 1910 but even refused to attend a single meeting to co-opt new members, declaring openly that they considered the very existence of the party's Central Committee to be 'harmful';

5   that it was precisely after the 1910 Plenum that the chief liquidationist publications mentioned above, *Nasha zaria* and *Delo zhizni*, definitely adopted liquidationism in all its aspects, not only 'disparaging' (despite the resolutions of the plenum) 'the significance of the underground party,' but openly disowning it, declaring that the party was 'extinct,' stating that it has already been liquidated, describing the restoration of the underground party as a 'reactionary utopia,' abusing and slandering the underground party in the pages of legally published periodicals, appealing to the workers to recognize that party cells and their hierarchy are 'outmoded,' etc.;

6   that at a time when party members throughout Russia, without distinction as to faction, have united their efforts for the immediate task of convoking a party conference, the Liquidators have isolated themselves in completely independent groups, [i.e., 'Initiative Groups'], have split off even in those areas where Party Mensheviks predominate (Ekaterinoslav, Kiev), and have definitely refused to maintain any party contacts with the local organizations of the RSDRP —

The Conference therefore declares that by its conduct the *Nasha zaria and Delo zhizni* group has *once and for all placed itself outside the party*.

The Conference appeals to all party members, irrespective of [factional] tendency or shade of opinion, to struggle against liquidationism, to explain the full scope of its harmfulness for the cause of the liberation of the working class, and to strain every nerve to restore and strengthen the underground RSDRP.

1.103
On the Party Organization Abroad   10 January 1912

The Conference recognizes the absolute necessity of the existence abroad of a single party organization rendering assistance to the party under the supervision and guidance of the Central Committee.

The Conference hereby approves the Committee of Foreign Organizations [formed by eleven émigré Bolsheviks in December 1911] as one of the party organizations abroad and appeals to all party elements, without distinction as to faction or tendency, who support an underground party and who are struggling relentlessly with anti-party tendencies (liquidationism), to unite around the Central Committee so as to assist the party in its work in Russia and to create a single organization abroad.

All foreign groups, without exception, may communicate with Russian organizations only through the Central Committee.

The Conference hereby states that groups abroad which do not submit to the Russian centre of Social Democratic activity, that is, to the Central Committee, and which cause disorganization by communicating with Russia independently of the Central Committee, are not able to use the name of the Russian Social Democratic Labour Party.

Vserossiiskaia konferentsiia Ros.   *KPSS v rezoliutsiiakh* I, 325–45
Sots.-Dem. Rab. Partii, 1912
goda (Paris, 1912), 16–31

Paris Meeting   28 February 1912

The reaction of Lenin's rivals to the Prague Conference was not long in coming. On the last day of February 1912 representatives of the Bund, the Party Mensheviks, the Vperedists, the Martov Mensheviks, the Trotsky 'non-factionalists' and the Bolshevik 'conciliators' met in Paris to plan countermeasures. The Prague Conference was roundly condemned for 'usurping the party banner,' local committees were instructed to ignore its decisions, and the earlier call [1.93] for a truly all-party conference was repeated. Lenin even heard a rumour that the meeting was seeking his removal from the International Socialist Bureau as well as protesting his recent schismatic actions to that body. For his response to this meeting, see his letters to G. Huysmans in V.I. Lenin, *Polnoe sobranie sochinenii* XXI, 215–18; XLVIII, 55–7.

1.104
[On the Prague Conference] 28 February 1912

Considering:

1   that this Conference was convoked by the 'Russian Organizing Commission' [see 1.90, sec. 3b] which from its inception has never contained a single representative of any national organization, that the Russian Organizing Commission has not been recognized by a number of local organizations or by the Caucasian Oblast Organization, that its factional activity and its refusal even to add the representatives of other tendencies and organizations to its membership has finally antagonized every national organization and party tendency except the leninist;

2   that only some of the exclusively Russian organizations were represented at the Conference, with the validity of the representation of the more important of these already having been protested by the organizations themselves [see *Pravda*, no. 24, 14 March 1912, 6];

3   that the Conference did not even invite theoreticians representing party tendencies other than Lenin's and put its trust completely in the biased information of schismatics;

4   that despite all this the Conference was audacious enough to christen itself pretentiously an 'All-Russian Conference,' to declare itself the supreme organ of the party, and to elect a Central Committee —

The meeting therefore considers this Conference to be a clear attempt at usurping the party banner by a group of persons who are deliberately leading the party towards a split and expresses its deep regret that certain party organizations and certain comrades should have let themselves be deceived and thus have promoted the policy of splitting and of usurpation on the part of Lenin's group.

The meeting is confident that the whole of the party organization in Russia and abroad will protest resolutely against the coup which has been effected, will refuse to recognize the centres elected at this Conference, and will in every way promote the restoration of party unity by convoking a conference which truly represents the whole party.

The meeting resolves that the present resolution is to be brought to the attention of the International Socialist Bureau, the central committees, and the central organs of the German, French, and Austrian socialist parties, and also of the [German] 'trustees' [see page 135].

'Rezoliutsiia soveshchaniia predstavitelei,' *Pravda*, no. 25 (23 April 1912), 5

August Conference   12–20 August 1912

The August Conference was in many respects doomed before it began. Called primarily by Trotsky in a last effort to unify the party, it failed even to unify the anti-leninist forces. The Bolsheviks, the Polish Social Democrats and the Party Mensheviks refused to attend; the representatives of the Latvians and the Vperedists left before the proceedings were over; while some Menshevik leaders such as Martov considered the whole affair as an exercise in 'empty verbal conciliationism' useful only as a means of putting the onus for division on Lenin. The Conference soon became, in the words of Bertram Wolfe, 'a babel of voices and a jangle of creeds.'

The thirty-three Social Democrats who attended the sixteen sessions in Vienna included eighteen with voting privileges, ten consultants, and five guests. The latter represented the Polish Socialist Party-Levitsa and the Social Democratic Party of Lithuania who were attracted by the Mensheviks' informal acceptance of Karl Renner and Otto Bauer's principles concerning national-cultural autonomy and who sought closer relations with the RSDRP (1.107). Perhaps because the Conference chose to postpone official recognition of national-cultural autonomy (1.114) – that is, autonomy in matters of education, culture, religion, and the press together with the right to personal nationality for every citizen within a multinational state – this merger failed to materialize before the war. Among the eighteen voting delegates, who supposedly represented operative organizations in Russia but in fact were largely from the émigré colony, were two police agents. While recognizing their right to call themslves an 'all-party conference,' as had the Bolsheviks in Prague, the delegates in Vienna were more legalistic and honest in constituting themselves as a 'conference of organizations of the RSDRP.' Just as in 1905, when Lenin had similarly expropriated the 'hard' name of the Central Committee, his rivals in 1912 were left with an 'Organizational Committee.' Not only was it less authoritative in name, it was also less prestigious in composition. The Conference named five of its Menshevik participants (A.N. Smirnov, B.I. Goldman, M.S. Uritsky, Garvi, Urotadze) to its leadership body, leaving the remaining two places to be filled by the Bund and the Latvian Social Democrats.

Lenin also stole the march on his opponents with his choice of election slogans. While the Bolsheviks advocated a straightforward programme of an eight-hour day, confiscation of all gentry-owned land, and the creation of a democratic republic, the August Conference sought to appeal to the voters by seeking 'a revision of agrarian legislation' and 'the sovereignty of the people's representatives.' Just as at their I Conference in 1905, the Mensheviks in 1912 put their emphasis on the avoidance of violence (1.109, 1.113) and on the utilization of legal opportunities so as to create a western-style mass workers' party (1.108). They did not reflect as well as Lenin the new militancy of the labour movement in Russia nor did they provide that movement with effective leadership. The 'August Bloc' of anti-Bolshevik forces created at Vienna was from its inception beset by ideological and personality conflicts. As Trotsky later acknowledged, 'I found myself formally in a "bloc" with the Mensheviks and a few disparate groups of Bolshevik dissenters. This "bloc" had no common political basis' and as such it disintegrated within a year and a half.

1.105
On the Organizational Committee

The Conference hereby resolves to establish the Organizational Committee as a leading [party] institution. It will consist of five members elected by the Conference. Furthermore, one representative of the Social Democratic Party of the Latvian Region and one representative of the Central Committee of the Bund will be delegated to this Organizational Committee. The Organizational Committee thus constituted will have the right to co-opt other members. Such co-operation will be by majority vote but with no more than one member opposed.

The Organizational Committee will have the task of unifying and directing the political activity of the local organizations, and subsequently of rallying all Social Democratic forces within the framework of a single party.

The Organizational Committee must be a board, situated in and operating in Russia.

In case of the arrest of the members of the Organizational Committee and its candidates, its re-establishment will be the task of the Social Democratic Party of the Latvian Region, the Bund, and the Caucasian Oblast Union: these centres will make every effort to obtain the assent of the most important organizations of the Russian part of the party to the membership of the new Organizational Committee.

1.106
On Organizational Unity

The Conference expresses its profound regret that the Organizational Committee's efforts to establish organizational unity among the various parts of the RSDRP should not have been crowned with complete success, and that some groups and party organizations did not find it possible even to appear at the present Conference in order to discuss the question of restoring party unity or at least of conducting the [Duma] election campaign in concert.

The Conference sees in this fact the insufficient awareness by all sections of Russian social democracy of the harm done to the proletarian cause by the party crisis during recent years.

The Conference, for its part, hereby notes that all sections of Russian social democracy recognize one and the same party Programme, that they are all aware or are becoming aware that the main arena of Social Democratic activity, despite the illegal character of its organization at present, is found in the various opportunities for legal political and economic struggle available to the proletariat and, especially, in the State Duma. Therefore, the Conference in no way views as a sufficient basis for schism those disputes over tactical matters and, in particular, over the forms of organization of the proletariat and the party itself, which have served as the principal motive for splitting up the party into factions and subfactions.

Expressing its confidence that the very development of the proletarian movement, and especially its consolidation of the position it has won in the open class struggle, will more and more urgently drive the Social Democratic Party to eliminate the splintering, isolation, and intolerance of the factional groups, the Conference therefore resolves:

1   To recommend that local organizations strive for organizational unity or, at least, for co-ordination of action at the local level by all active Social Democratic groups.
2   To impose upon the Organizational Committee the obligation of immediately reaching agreement with other sections of the party to undertake negotiations for the joint convocation of a party conference or congress.
3   To inform the International Socialist Bureau of the Conference's readiness to accept its mediation in the matter of restoring organizational unity with the other sections of the RSDRP. [This offer of mediation did not come until December 1913; it ultimately resulted in the abortive Brussels Conference of July 1914.]

1.107
On the Polish Socialist Party

Having heard the statement of the delegation of the Polish Socialist Party [Levitsa], the Conference welcomes the decision of its [XI] Congress on the necessity for complete organizational unification with the RSDRP. Considering, like the Congress of the Polish Socialist Party, that the unification of all Social Democratic elements, both in Poland and in Russia as a whole, can be prepared and carried out only through co-ordinated activities in general political work, the Conference urges the Organizational Committee to give thought to ensuring that those of its political acts, which are significant for the country as a whole, should include agreements with the central institutions of the Polish Socialist Party.

1.108
On the Organizational Forms of Party Development

Having discussed the forms and methods of party development, the Conference has reached the following conclusion:

1   The transformation of social democracy into a self-governing organization of the Social Democratic proletariat can be achieved only to the extent that this Social Democratic organization comes into being during the process of attracting the working masses to open socio-political life in all of its manifestations;

2   In view of the changed socio-political conditions, in comparison with the pre-revolutionary epoch [i.e., pre-1905], existing and newly instituted illegal party organizations must adapt themselves to the new forms and methods of the legal workers' movement;

3   Even though its organization on the whole must remain underground, the Social Democratic Party should presently strive to conduct certain aspects of its party work above ground and should aim to set up appropriate [legal] institutions;

4   Since the Social Democratic organization, because of its illegal existence, is unable to bring within its framework the broad strata of workers who are under its influence, it must establish ties with the politically active section of the proletariat (and, through it, with the masses) by forming both various kinds of 'legal' and illegal political organizations and various types of legal covers (election committees, political societies authorized by the Law of 4 March [1906], municipal commissions, societies for combatting inflation, etc.), and also by co-ordinating party activities with those of the non-political workers' organizations.

1.109
On the Economic Struggle

... The Conference appeals to the workers to exploit the conditions of industrial resurgence so as to intensify the development of trade unions; in

places where such organizations exist, it appeals to them to concentrate in their hands the direct or indirect leadership of strikes; and in places where such unions do not exist and cannot be created, to set up:
1   trade union commissions, one of whose principal tasks will be the struggle for legal trade unions;
2   temporary strike committees. Both the trade union commissions and the strike committees should be elected by the workers of the given trade.

The Conference calls particular attention to the need for a broader development and extension of the trade union press. The Conference recommends utilizing the office of shop steward to strengthen the workers' position in the economic struggle.

The Conference – in complete agreement with the position presently adopted by the trade unions – recommends that party organizations devote every effort to the organization and systematization of the economic struggle of the working masses and warns the workers against going out on strike either without taking into due account their own strength and that of their opponents, or without sufficient preparation.

1.110
On Electoral Tactics

Acting as an independent proletarian party, the Social Democratic Party sets itself the following tasks in the election campaign [for the IV Duma]:
1   It should call for a merciless struggle against the monarchist-gentry régime which is supported by predatory groups of the capitalist bourgeoisie and is implacably hostile to the vital interests of the popular masses; it should strike the sharpest possible blow against this régime as embodied in the Black Hundred majority of the III Duma;
2   It should explain to the electorate the true political physiognomy of the various parties engaging in the elections, in particular the non-democratic nature of the various liberal parties – whose hostility to any revolutionary movement makes them indecisive and half-way in their opposition to the régime, causes them to capitulate to the ruling clique, and frequently leads them to perform real services for the cause of the reaction;
3   It should strive to eliminate the influence of the parties of the propertied classes upon those sections of the popular masses which follow them and at the same time should criticize the Trudoviks and other populist groups for being inconsistent in their democracy and utopian in their social demands;
4   It should propagandize the broad masses on behalf of the long and short range goals of the Social Democratic Party, its attitude towards the present social and state order, and ways of struggling against this order; it

should mobilize the broad popular masses around our day-to-day demands; it should rally and unite the unco-ordinated progressive elements of the proletariat and develop their autonomous organizational and political activity;

5   It should elect to the IV State Duma representatives of the Social Democratic proletariat who are capable of using the Duma as a rostrum for a comprehensive struggle in the interests of the working class ...

I.III
On Unity in the Election Campaign

In the view of the Conference the forthcoming election campaign can play a significant role in developing the class consciousness of the workers and particularly in revitalizing the party, only if it is conducted in a unified manner – under the general party banner, on the basis of a common platform, and in support of common candidates.

The Conference directs the attention of all Social Democratic workers, who are answerable to their class for the course and outcome of the electoral campaign as well as for the fate of the party generally, to the threatening danger of dual Social Democratic candidacies – a danger which, in addition to everything else, threatens to deprive the party of the small degree of representation which it can still win for itself on the basis of the [Election] Law of 3 June [1907].

The Conference hereby expresses its conviction that the Social Democratic workers' movement in Russia does not contain such differences of opinion as to in the least justify introducing the kind of discord and chaos into the ranks of the proletariat which will inevitably result from an election struggle between Social Democrats and Social Democrats before the eyes of the broad masses, on the one hand, and the class enemies of the proletariat on the other.

The Conference appeals most energetically to all progressive workers to ensure unity in the electoral campaign by unanimously rejecting all schismatic endeavours, from whatever side they may come, and to press most energetically for the adoption of all measures to achieve agreement among *all* Social Democratic organizations and groups active in a given locality for the submission of a single candidate in the name of the party, casting all responsibility for rivalry among Social Democratic candidates upon those that refuse to follow the path of agreement. [The German Social Democrats had offered 80,000 marks for election campaigns where only one Social Democratic candidate was advanced.]

Whenever party organizations are confronted with the danger of a split in the Social Democratic election campaign or with groups which do not want to unite in its conduct, the Conference recommends, for purposes of maintaining electoral unity, that comrades insist that candidates for electors from the workers' curia and for Duma deputy be designated once and for all by the Social Democratic part of the congress of representatives and that all electors, except the one appointed by it, be compelled to renounce their candidacies for deputy if such candidacy is proposed to them at the guberniia electoral assembly.

The Conference instructs the Organizational Committee immediately to enter into discussions with the Central Committee elected at the leninist conference as well as with representatives of the other sections of the party which are not represented at this Conference, proposing negotiations on the joint conduct of the electoral campaign. At the same time, the Conference places all organizations under the obligation of devoting every effort to achieving agreement among all Social Democratic groups in each locality for purposes of forming common guberniia or city electoral committees ...

1.112
On the Insurance Laws of 23 June 1912

... The Conference appeals to all workers:
1   to achieve the *simultaneous* establishment of [jointly financed and administered] sickness funds [that would partially compensate employees in times of illness] and the general implementation of the insurance laws *everywhere* [see also 1.100];
2   to take into their own hands the working out of sickness fund regulations, compelling the employers to propose for confirmation drafts which have been developed by the *workers themselves* of the respective enterprises;
3   to endeavour from the outset when establishing sickness funds, especially for small enterprises, to set up funds on the largest possible scale so as to serve a number of enterprises, and also to link these sickness funds together;
4   to elect as representatives to joint meetings and as members of sickness fund boards those comrades who are the most worthy and most devoted to the workers' cause – if possible, from among those who in their practical work in workers' organizations have displayed a clear understanding of the interests of the working class, a steadfastness in defending these interests, and the necessary organizational abilities;
5   to support their elected bodies and their representatives in insurance institutions in every way – up to and including strikes;
6   to exert pressure by all available means on factory owners so as to

compel them to transfer the sickness funds, and their administration, into the hands of the insured workers and to renounce the special rights (two-thirds of the votes in the meeting of representatives, almost one-half of the members of the sickness fund administration, chairmanship of the general meeting, custody of the funds, etc.) conferred on the owners by the law;

7   to endeavour to extend the scope of the activities and functions of the sickness funds and, in particular, to have the organization of all medical assistance transferred to the sickness funds (with the employers still paying the costs), as well as the custody and administration of the money and securities in the funds ...

1.113
On the Recent Events in the Army and the Navy

The Conference salutes the heroism and selflessness of the comrade sailors and comrade soldiers who participated in the recent movements in the Black and Baltic Seas [where eighty-three sailors were tried in late June and early July 1912 for allegedly planning armed revolts] and in Turkestan [where over a hundred sappers rebelled on 1 July only to be crushed by cossacks] and who paid with their blood for striving for a better life and for liberty. The awakening of a spirit of indignation in the army and navy is an indication that the 1905–06 rapprochement between the army and the socialist proletariat is reviving despite the Black Hundred agitation in the armed forces and the bloody oppression reigning in the barracks.

While inviting comrades who are in any way informed about barracks life to supply the Social Democratic Duma fraction and press with material exposing the barrack-room oppression in order to help develop the civic and political self-consciousness of the soldiers, the Conference at the same time feels it necessary to direct the attention of comrades to the inadvisability and extreme danger of outbreaks in the army or navy, or of attempts at military uprisings, which are isolated from the national movement.

In the absence of a broad and spontaneous revolutionary movement on the part of the popular masses, such attempts can lead only to heavy and useless sacrifices, to an interruption in propaganda and agitational activity among the troops, and to a needless exacerbation of relations between the progressive soldiers and sailors and the indifferent mass of them upon whom falls the full weight of the reprisals provoked by the unsuccessful outbreak.

The Conference directs the attention of comrades to the fact that when the movement in the armed services assumes serious dimensions the government itself sometimes has an interest in artificially provoking an uprising, thus cutting short the further development of the movement; therefore, it is extremely likely that direct provocation by the Okhrana [the tsarist political police] took place in some of the recent events.

Thus, in the view of the Conference, all conscious socialists in the army and the navy have the heavy but sacred duty of restraining their less conscious and less experienced comrades from exploiting in premature and pointless actions the indignation and despair which the unbearable oppression and individual humiliation presently reigning in the barracks is creating in the masses of soldiers and sailors. In any case, conscious socialists must explain to their comrades that at moments like the present the socialist proletariat may view open rebellion as inevitable only in one extreme case – when the soldiers are confronted with the demand by the authorities to take up arms against the people.

Conveying the expression of its profound sympathy to the comrades who have suffered during the recent outbreaks and honouring the memory of those who perished in the struggle and on the scaffold, the Conference expresses the indignation and revulsion of the Russian Social Democratic proletariat at the bloody cruelty which a cowardly and barbarous government has brought down upon the participants in the military uprisings and the members of the military organizations.

1.114
On the Question of National-Cultural Autonomy

Having listened to the report of the Caucasian delegate stating that at the recent conference of the Caucasian organizations of the RSDRP and in the literary organs of these organizations Caucasian comrades have expressed the view that it is necessary to advance the demand for national-cultural autonomy, the Conference, without speaking to the substance of this demand, notes that such an interpretation of the article of the party Programme recognizing the right of each nationality to self-determination [article 9, second section of 1.3] is not contrary to the article's precise meaning and expresses the hope that the nationality question will be included on the agenda of the next congress of the RSDRP.

Izveshchenie o konferentsii or-
ganizatsii RSDRP (Vienna,
1912), 23–44

Cracow Meeting of the Central Committee   26 December 1912 – 1 January 1913

Lenin had hoped to call another party conference within a year of the Prague Conference. This proved impossible, however, either because of a lack of money or a lack of authentic representatives from the local organizations. He also found it difficult to hold a formal plenum of his new Central Committee since five of its nine members had been arrested during 1912. The best he could do, therefore, was to gather together in Cracow where he was then living the four remaining Central Committee members along with two of their wives, four of the Bolshevik Duma deputies, several underground representatives who did not have mandates from their organizations, and a few émigrés. These 14 Bolsheviks decided to call themselves a 'meeting of the Central Committee of the RSDRP with party workers.' Afterwards, it was often referred to as the 'February Meeting' since Lenin, in an attempt to mislead the police, announced that it had taken place in February 1913. Owing to the presence of Malinovsky, who was a member of both the Central Committee and the Duma fraction as well as of the police, this deception was obviously of little value.

The resolutions of the meeting, all of which were written by Lenin and adopted unanimously, reflected an awareness of the new upsurge in worker unrest as evidenced in the increased number of strikes during 1912, the magnitude of the worker protests which followed the Lena goldfield massacre, the more enthusiastic worker participation in the IV Duma elections, and the warm reception given to the legal daily newspaper *Pravda* which the Bolsheviks began publishing in St Petersburg on 22 April 1912. The meeting also kept up the running battle with Lenin's old factional opponents: the Bund, sections of the Polish and Latvian Social Democratic Parties, the Mensheviks in general, and the Liquidators in particular. There still was the problem, however, of the conciliatory attitude adopted by certain Bolsheviks within key legal organizations. In a secret and unpublished section to a resolution on the Social Democratic Duma fraction (see *KPSS v rezoliutsiiakh* 1, 361–2), the meeting instructed the six Bolshevik deputies to demand voting and representational equality with the seven Menshevik deputies, to stop serving as contributing editors of the Mensheviks' *Luch,* and to take a more active part in illegal party activities outside the Duma. In another secret resolution passed at a closed session of the Central Committee immediately after the Cracow Meeting, the editorial board of *Pravda* was criticized for not flailing the Liquidators sufficiently and for ignoring Central Committee (i.e., Lenin's) instructions from Galicia. It is interesting to note that Stalin, who attended the meeting, was not only one of the guilty editors of *Pravda* but also opposed as 'premature' the demand for Bolshevik Duma equality which was to split the fraction ten months later. To reinforce the Central Committee's ties with and control over these principal legal outlets, Duma deputy Petrovsky was co-opted to the Committee along with the new editor of *Pravda*, Sverdlov, while Stalin was sent to Vienna to study the nationality question.

1.115
On the Revolutionary Resurgence, Strikes, and the Party's Tasks

1 The major fact in the history of the workers' movement and the Russian revolution in 1912 is the remarkable development of both the economic and the political strike movement of the proletariat. The number of political strikers [on May Day, in sympathy strikes, etc.] has reached one million.

2 The character of the strike movement in 1912 is worthy of particular attention. In many cases the workers advanced economic and political demands at the same time; a wave of economic strikes was replaced by a wave of political ones, and then the converse occurred. The struggle with the capitalists for restoration of the gains of the 1905 [Revolution], which had been taken away by the counter-revolution, and the rising cost of living aroused new sections of workers, confronting them with political issues in their most acute form. All these various forms of combining and interweaving the economic and political struggle are the precondition and the guarantee of the movement's power, giving rise to a mass revolutionary strike wave.

3 The beginning of the outbursts of dissatisfaction and of the uprisings in the navy and army [see 1.113], which highlighted the year 1912, was unquestionably tied to the mass revolutionary strikes of the workers; this indicates the increasing discontent and indignation in broad democratic circles and, in particular, among the peasantry who are the principal source of troops.

4 All of these facts, combined with the general swing to the left in the country, which had its effects on the elections to the IV Duma despite the most shameless manipulation by the Black Hundred tsarist government, ultimately made it clear that Russia was again entering an era of open revolutionary struggle by the masses. The new revolution, whose first stage we are now experiencing, is the inevitable result of the bankruptcy of the tsar's Third of June policies [i.e., the autocratic programme that followed the proroguing of the II Duma and the changing of the election law on 3 June 1907]. This policy could not have satisfied even the most obsequious among the large bourgeoisie, while the popular masses, and especially the

oppressed nationalities, were increasingly deprived of their rights, and millions and millions of peasants have once again been reduced to starvation.

5   Under these conditions mass revolutionary strikes are of exceptional importance since they are one of the most effective means of overcoming the apathy, despair, and dispersion of the agricultural proletariat and the peasantry, of arousing their political spontaneity, and of drawing them into broader, more concerted and simultaneous revolutionary initiatives.

6   In broadening and intensifying their agitation for the immediate demands of the RSDRP – a democratic republic, an eight-hour working day, and confiscation of all landed estates for the benefit of the peasants – party organizations must assign one of the top priorities in their activity to the comprehensive support of mass revolutionary strikes and also to the development and organization of all forms of revolutionary action by the masses. It is particularly important to set as an immediate task the organization of revolutionary street demonstrations, both in combination with political strikes and as independent actions.

7   The use by some capitalists of lock-outs (mass dismissals) against the strikers confronts the working class with new tasks. It is necessary to pay close attention to the economic conditions behind strikes in each district, in each branch of industry, in each individual case; to seek new ways of counteracting lock-outs (such as with an Italian [sit-down] strike); and to replace political strikes with revolutionary meetings and revolutionary street demonstrations.

8   Certain legal publications, quite irrespective of their view on any given strike, agitate generally against mass revolutionary strikes. Such agitation emanates not only from the liberal press but also, for example, from a group of Liquidators in the [legal daily] newspaper *Luch* in defiance of a substantial portion of those workers who support this paper in one way or another. In view of this, the task of all Social Democratic party workers is: 1 / to wage a determined struggle against this group; 2 / to explain systematically and persistently to all workers, regardless of their tendency, the full extent of the damage caused by such preachments; and 3 / to rally all proletarian forces for a further development of revolutionary agitation and mass revolutionary action.

1.116
On the Structure of the Illegal Organization

1   In summarizing the results of the workers' movement and of the party's work for 1912, the meeting finds that: the beginning of the new wave of revolutionary action by the masses has completely confirmed the previ-

ous decisions of the RSDRP (and, in particular, that of the January 1912 Conference [1.97]) on the structure of the party. The course of the 1912 strikes, the Social Democratic election campaign for the IV Duma, the progress of the insurance campaign [see 1.119], etc., have demonstrated beyond a doubt that the only correct type of organizational structure in the present epoch is an illegal party, which is the sum of the party cells, surrounded by a network of legal and semi-legal workers' associations.

2   The organizational forms of the underground structure must definitely be adapted to local conditions. A variety of disguises for the underground cells and the greatest possible flexibility in adapting forms of party work to local and general living conditions guarantee the vitality of the illegal organization.

3   At the present time the chief task in the area of organizational work is the creation in all plants and factories of purely party underground factory committees containing the most active elements among the workers. The enormous upsurge in the workers' movement has created conditions which make it possible in most places to restore party factory committees and to strengthen the existing ones.

4   The meeting points out that it has now become essential to form a single leading organization in each centre out of the disconnected local groups.

For example, as a type of city-wide organization there has emerged in St Petersburg a leading City Committee formed by combining the principle of election by raion cells with the principle of co-optation.

Such a type of organization makes possible the establishment of the closest and most direct ties between the leading body and the lower-level cells, and at the same time permits the creation of a highly conspiratorial executive body which is small, very mobile, and has the right to speak at all times for the whole organization. The meeting recommends that this type be adopted by other centres of the workers' movement as well, with appropriate modifications as dictated by local conditions.

5   For purposes of establishing close links between the local organizations and the Central Committee, and also of guiding and unifying party work, the meeting views as urgently necessary the organization of regional centres in the principal areas of the workers' movement.

6   The use of confidential agents is proposed as one of the most important practical techniques in establishing a permanent vital tie between the Central Committee and the local Social Democratic groups, and also in creating flexible forms for directing local work in the major centres of the workers' movement. Confidential agents must be recruited from among the workers in charge of local party work. The central party apparatus locally and throughout Russia can be strengthened and reinforced only by the efforts of the leading workers themselves.

7   The meeting expresses the hope that the Central Committee will organize meetings as frequently as possible with local party functionaries active in various areas of Social Democratic work.
8   The meeting calls attention to the numerous party resolutions stating that a workers' party can only exist on the basis of a regular collection of membership dues and workers' contributions. Without such dues and contributions, especially under present conditions, even the most modest central party institutions (local or national) will be absolutely unable to exist.
9   (Not to be published.) [This point probably referred to the creation of a fund for the use of the legal Bolshevik newspaper *Pravda* and for supporting full-time party workers.]

1.117
On the Attitude toward Liquidationism and on Unity

1   ... The Liquidators are by no means condemned for stressing the necessity for legal work but for renouncing the underground party and for destroying it ...
2   In withdrawing from the underground party and forming groups separate from the local party organizations, the Liquidators brought about a schism which they then formalized by setting up in many places, especially in St Petersburg, the so-called Initiative Groups ...
3   The August 1912 Conference, which called itself a 'conference of organizations of the RSDRP,' turned out in fact to be a liquidationist conference since its leaders and chief participants largely belonged to a literary group of Liquidators which has split away from the party and is alienated from the Russian working masses.
4   The devotion of the overwhelming majority of leading workers to the underground party obliged the August Conference to make seeming concessions to the party's principles by professing to recognize the underground party [see 1.108]. But in fact all the resolutions of this Conference are permeated through and through with liquidationism. ... Thus the party is still confronted with the task of waging a determined struggle against the *Nasha zaria* and *Luch* group of Liquidators and of explaining to the working masses the serious harm contained in their pronouncements.
5   The 'unity' campaign launched by the Liquidators in the legal press skirts and beclouds the chief question of participation and work in the underground party, thus misleading the workers, since the question cannot even be raised in the legal press. In fact, the Liquidators are continuing to act as schismatics ...
6   On the condition that the illegal organization of the RSDRP is recog-

nized and joined, the unity of worker Social Democrats of all shades and tendencies is an absolute necessity dictated by all the interests of the working class movement ...

7   The meeting gives its most energetic support to such unification and recommends that it immediately be undertaken everywhere from below, in factory committees, raion groups, etc., with worker comrades checking on whether or not the illegal organization is in fact being recognized as well as the willingness to support the revolutionary struggle of the masses and revolutionary tactics. The final unification of the party and the complete consolidation at the all-Russian level will be accomplished only to the extent that this unity from below is actually established.

1.118
On the 'National' Social Democratic Organizations

1   The experience of 1912 has fully confirmed the correctness of the resolution of the January (1912) Conference of the RSDRP on this question [see page 147 above]. The Bund's support of the candidacy of a non-Social Democrat, E.I. Jagiello [a member of the Polish Socialist Party-Levitsa], against the Polish Social Democrats, and the violations of the party programme on behalf of nationalism by the August (1912) Conference of Liquidators, Bundists, and Latvian Social Democrats have revealed with particular clarity the total bankruptcy of structuring the Social Democratic Party on federalist principles and the serious harm done to the proletarian cause by detached 'national' Social Democratic organizations.

2   Therefore, the meeting urgently appeals to the workers of all the nationalities in Russia to reject most resolutely the militant nationalism of the reactionaries, to combat all manifestations of a nationalist spirit among the toiling masses, and for Social Democratic workers on the local level to merge into unified organizations of the RSDRP conducting work in each of the languages of the local proletariat and in fact effecting unity from below, as has been done for a long time in the Caucasus.

3   The meeting expresses its deep regret at the schism in the ranks of the Polish Social Democrats [between the dissident Regional Presidium or Rozlamovists of the Warsaw organization and the Main Presidium led by Lenin's current critics, Rosa Luxemburg and Leo Tyszka], which is greatly weakening the struggle of the Social Democratic workers in Poland. The meeting is obliged to state that the Main Presidium of the Polish Social Democratic Party, which at present does not represent the majority of the Social Democratic organizations of the Polish proletariat, is resorting to impermissible techniques in its struggle with this majority (for example, groundlessly suspecting the entire Warsaw organization of being agents

provocateurs). The meeting appeals to all party organizations in contact with the Polish Social Democratic workers to help create genuine unity among Polish Social Democrats.

4   The meeting particularly notes the extreme opportunism and liquidationism of the resolutions of the last (IX) Bund Conference [in June 1912], which dropped the slogan calling for a republic, gave a very low priority to underground work, and showed that it had forgotten the revolutionary tasks of the proletariat. The Bund's resistance to the unification of all Social Democratic workers on the local level (Warsaw, Lodz, Vilna, etc.) deserves similar condemnation, this unification having been insisted upon by the congresses and conferences of the RSDRP on many occasions since 1906 [e.g., 1.80].

5   The meeting salutes the revolutionary Social Democratic workers of the Latvian organization, who are persistently conducting anti-liquidationist propaganda, and expresses regret that the Latvian Social Democratic Central Committee is inclined to support the anti-party moves of the Liquidators [see 1.93].

6   The meeting expresses its firm conviction that the beginning of the revolutionary resurgence, the mass economic and political strikes, the street demonstrations, and the other forms of open revolutionary struggle of the masses will promote the complete consolidation and amalgamation of local Social Democratic workers, without any distinction as to nationality, thus intensifying the onslaught against tsarism, which oppresses all the peoples of Russia, and against the gradually consolidating bourgeoisie of all the nations of Russia.

1.119
On the Insurance Campaign

Noting that the working class and its party, despite all persecutions, have displayed great energy in standing up for proletarian interests in connection with the introduction of the insurance laws—

The meeting concludes that:

1   The most resolute and united struggle must be waged against the attempts of the government and the capitalists to force the workers to elect their representatives to sickness funds blindly through the prohibition of workers' meetings.

2   The workers must strive everywhere to hold unauthorized meetings for the preliminary nomination of the persons they want to be their candidate representatives.

CRACOW MEETING 175

3   The workers must hold revolutionary meetings to protest the violence and mockery which have accompanied the introduction of the insurance laws.
4   In any case, it is necessary beforehand to draw up a workers' list of candidates for representative from among the most influential Social Democratic workers and by concerted effort to put this list across also in places where preliminary meetings cannot be held.
5   The meeting considers a boycott of the elections of representatives to be inexpedient and harmful. At the present time the capitalists are devoting their principal efforts to preventing the workers from taking over certain factory proletarian units – the sort that the workers' sickness funds should become. A boycott, by dividing the workers at the present moment, would only assist the capitalists in their efforts.
6   The struggle for the proper election of delegates to sickness funds should not be interrupted for a moment. While exploiting every favourable opportunity with all material and personnel, not permitting the employers to feel for one minute that the normal course of production is assured, extending and developing the struggle of the workers – at the same time, work should continue in support of the Social Democratic list despite all obstacles. The elections do not preclude the further development of the struggle. On the contrary, by electing staunch Social Democratic workers as delegates, we shall facilitate the subsequent struggle for proper elections – a struggle in which the delegates will give all possible support to the workers.
7   In all places where elections are held without [preliminary worker] meetings it is necessary to agitate, using all means available to the workers, for the re-election of representatives on the basis of worker meetings and genuinely free elections.
8   The Social Democratic Duma fraction should immediately make a new interpellation on the banning of workers' election meetings.
9   All agitation on the introduction of insurance [provisions] should be tied in closely with an elucidation of the whole situation in tsarist Russia, explaining our socialist principles and revolutionary demands.

1.120
On the Reorganization and Work of the *Pravda* Editorial Board

1   The editorial board is insufficiently firm in its party spirit. The editorial board has been persistently urged to observe and execute all party decisions more strictly. Full compliance is obligatory. The Central Com-

mittee is taking steps to reorganize the editorial board. [Shortly after the Cracow Meeting, instructions were sent to Sverdlov that he was to take over as editor, that Badaev was to replace N.G. Poletaev as publisher, and that two three-man boards headed by Bolshevik Duma deputies were to assume all editorial and business responsibilities.]

2   The editorial board responds weakly to the party life of the St Petersburg Social Democratic workers. It is absolutely necessary to present or mention party resolutions in their correct form.

3   The editorial board must devote more attention to explaining the incorrectness and the harmfulness of liquidationism in general and of the *Luch* pronouncements in particular.

4   The editorial board must devote more attention to agitation for newspaper subscriptions and financial collections from among the workers.

5   The Bolshevik portion of the [Duma] deputies must become part of the newspaper's enlarged editorial board and must organize systematic and persistent participation in both the literary and economic aspects of its affairs.

6   The editorial board must treat the Vperedist contributors [e.g., Bogdanov and G.A. Aleksinsky] especially carefully so as neither to hinder the incipient rapprochement nor to allow errors in matters of principle.

7   Every effort must be made to reduce publication expenses and to set up a small guiding board (conducting the whole operation) which must include at least one representative from the six [Bolshevik Duma deputies].

A similar guiding board (economic commission), with the obligatory participation of one of the six, is necessary for conducting the business side of the operation.

8   Articles (with a prearranged signature), which the Central Committee feels must be included, are to be published immediately.

9   While strictly guarding the newspaper's legality, it is necessary to enlist the active participation of workers' societies, unions, committees, groups, and individuals in St Petersburg and the province in the paper's literary work and in its distribution.

10   The initiative of a group of St Petersburg Social Democrats in issuing an anti-liquidationist, general trade union organ is to be supported, and its development on the local level is to be followed up carefully.

11   Steps are to be taken to bring together the literary and economic aspects of the newspaper [*Pravda*] and the magazine [*Prosveshchenie*, a monthly theoretical journal].

12   Energetic efforts must be made to set up in Moscow a daily workers' newspaper [*Nash put'* (Our Path)] as a branch of the St Petersburg newspaper [*Pravda*]. To this end the Moscow group must be connected organi-

zationally with the three [Bolshevik Duma] deputies from the Moscow region.

Izveshchenie i rezoliutsii soveshchaniia TsK RSDRP s partiinymi rabotnikami, Fevral' 1913 (Paris, 1913); 1.120 in G.V. Petriakov, 'Deiatel 'nost' V.I. Lenina po rukovodstvu 'Pravdoi' v 1912–1914 godakh,' *Voprosy istorii*, no. 11 (1956), 7

KPSS v rezoliutsiiakh 1, 358–68

Poronin Meeting of the Central Committee 23 September – 1 October 1913

An expanded version of the Central Committee met again in September 1913, this time in the Galician mountain village of Poronin where Lenin and several of his entourage spent their summers. This gathering attracted twenty-two Bolsheviks: four members of the Central Committee, the wives of Lenin and Zinoviev who served as secretaries of the Central Committee, five Bolshevik Duma deputies, four Polish Rozlamovists who attended in an advisory capacity, plus assorted émigré littérateurs and underground operatives. Among the delegates, half of whom had attended the Cracow Meeting nine months earlier, were police agents Malinovsky and A.I. Lobov. To confuse students of Russian history if not the Okhrana, the conference was known to the party as the 'Summer Meeting' and to the police as the 'August Meeting.'

The first five sessions were given over to hearing encouraging reports from the Central Committee, the local organizations, and the Duma fraction. It was evident from these that worker unrest was still on the rise; that the Bolsheviks' echoing of this militancy was gaining them new adherents in trade unions, insurance councils, and other legal worker organizations; and that *Pravda* was having considerably more success that the Mensheviks' *Luch* in reaching this new generation of discontented Russian workers. Moreover, the conciliatory attitude of the *Pravda* editors and the Duma deputies, which had been evident before the Cracow Meeting, was absent at Poronin. Lenin and Malinovsky, both of whom opposed true party unity but for different reasons, had no difficulty making final arrangements for the splitting of the Social Democratic Duma fraction. On the final day at Poronin they met with the other Bolshevik deputies and decided to issue an ultimatum demanding parity within the fraction as the price for fractional unity. When this was predictably rejected, the Bolsheviks walked out and on 15 November declared themselves to be an independent 'Fraction of the Russian Social Democratic Workers.' The seven Menshevik deputies henceforth were known simply as the 'Social Democratic Fraction.'

Perhaps the most significant of the Poronin resolutions concerned the nationality question. Faced with the revival of nationalist sentiment among all the minorities of eastern Europe and the growing appeal of the 'Austrian heresy' of national-cultural autonomy (1.114), the Bolsheviks were forced to re-examine the party's limited nationality programme adopted in 1903. The delegates decided to recognize the 'full equality of all peoples and languages,' the right of regional autonomy for distinctive ethnic groups, and the right to secede and to form an independent state. Lenin felt, however, that the mere acknowledgement of the right of secession would eliminate the need for its implementation. Indeed, if pressure were brought to bear for self-determination, it would be the party that would determine whether it was 'expedient' and in the 'interests of the proletarian class struggle' to grant the right. Even this all-important reservation, however, was not enough to satisfy the Polish delegates who felt that this re-interpretation violated the principles of proletarian internationalism. Evidently, the resolution was merely meant as a preliminary formulation and to serve as a basis for party discussion since the meeting placed the entire question on the agenda of the forthcoming party congress. But the war prevented this congress from convening; thus, the resolution remained the Bolsheviks' basic statement of nationality policy until they came to power in 1917.

1.121
On the Strike Movement

...

4   The meeting recognizes that the movement has reached the point of considering a nation-wide political strike [on the next anniversary of Bloody Sunday, 9 January 1914]. Systematic agitation in preparation for this strike must be started everywhere immediately.

5   The slogans for this political strike, which must be vigorously disseminated, should be the fundamental revolutionary demands of the moment: a democratic republic, an eight-hour working day, confiscation of landed estates.

6   The meeting calls on all local party workers to develop leaflet agitation and to establish the closest and most correct relations possible between political and other types of workers' organizations in various cities. In the first place, particular attention must be devoted to reaching an agreement between the Moscow and St Petersburg workers so that the political strikes, which may arise from various causes (persecution of the [workers'] press, insurance strikes, etc.), will as far as possible take place simultaneously in both capitals.

1.122
On the Party Press

1   The meeting hereby notes the great importance of the legal press for Social Democratic agitation and organization and therefore calls on party institutions and on all class-conscious workers to give greater support to the legal press by helping to broaden its circulation, and by organizing mass collective subscriptions and regular financial collections. The meeting again confirms that such contributions count as party membership dues.
2   Special attention must be paid to strengthening the legal workers' organ in Moscow [*Nash put'*; see 1.120] and to setting up a workers' newspaper in the south [i.e., the Ukraine] as soon as possible.
3   The meeting hereby expresses its hope that the closest contact possible will be established between the existing legal workers' newspapers through the exchange of information, the holding of meetings, etc.
4   Recognizing the importance of, and need for, a theoretical marxist organ, the meeting hereby expresses the hope that all party organs and trade union papers will acquaint the workers with the magazine *Prosveshchenie*, and will urge them to subscribe to it regularly and to give it systematic support.
5   The meeting directs the attention of the party publishers [i.e., Priboi Publishing House in St Petersburg] to the extreme need for a wide range of popular pamphlets on questions of Social Democratic agitation and propaganda.
6   In view of the recent intensification of the revolutionary mass struggle and of the necessity of reporting it fully and comprehensively, which is impossible in the legal press, the meeting calls particular attention to the need to stimulate the development of underground party publishing ventures; in addition to illegal leaflets, pamphlets, etc., it is absolutely necessary to issue more frequently and regularly the illegal organ of the party (the Central Organ [*Sotsial-demokrat*, which had appeared only five times since the Prague Conference]).

1.123
On the Social Democratic Duma Fraction

The meeting finds that unity of the Social Democratic fraction in Duma work is possible and necessary.

The meeting notes, however, that the conduct of the seven [Menshevik] deputies is a serious threat to the unity of the fraction.

The seven deputies, exploiting their accidental majority of one vote, are violating the elementary rights of the six worker deputies who represent the overwhelming majority of the workers of Russia [by not allowing the six Bolshevik deputies equal chance to speak in Duma debates and equal representation on Duma committees] ...

Therefore, the meeting finds that unity of the Social Democratic fraction in Duma work can be maintained only if the two parts of the fraction possess equal rights and only if the seven deputies renounce their policy of suppression. ...

1.124
On Work in Legal Organizations

1   At the present moment of upsurge in the economic and political struggle of the working class it is especially important to intensify work in all legal workers' associations (trade unions, clubs, sickness insurance funds, co-operatives, etc.).

2   All activities in the legal workers' associations should be conducted, not in a spirit of neutrality, but in the spirit of the decisions of the London Congress of the RSDRP [1.64] and of the [1907] Stuttgart Congress of the [Socialist] International. Social Democrats must bring the broadest possible circles of workers into all workers' societies, inviting all workers regardless of party outlook to become members. But within these societies the Social Democrats must form party groups and by long and systematic work within these societies secure the establishment of the closest relations between them and the Social Democratic Party.

3   The experience of the international and of our Russian workers' movement teaches that it is necessary to ensure from the very inception of such workers' organizations (trade unions, co-operatives, clubs, etc.) that each of these institutions is a stronghold of the Social Democratic Party. The meeting invites all party members to bear in mind this important task, which is especially urgent in Russia where the Liquidators are making systematic efforts to employ the legal associations *against* the party.

4   The meeting finds that in electing representatives to insurance funds, in all trade union work, etc., it is necessary, while upholding the complete

unity of the movement and subordination of the minority to the majority, to implement the party line, to seek the election of party adherents to all responsible posts, etc.

5   In order to evaluate the experience of practical work in legal workers' associations, it is desirable to hold more frequent meetings with persons actively participating in the legal workers' organizations on the local level and also to attract the greatest possible number of representatives of party groups working in these legal societies to party-wide conferences.

1.125
On the Nationality Question

The orgy of Black Hundred nationalism, the growth of nationalist tendencies among the liberal bourgeoisie and the intensification of nationalistic tendencies among the upper strata of the oppressed nationalities, give prominence to the nationality question at the present time.

The situation within social democracy (i.e., the attempts of the Caucasian Social Democrats, the Bund, and the Liquidators to repeal [parts of] the party Programme [see 1.114], etc.) compels the party to devote even greater attention to this question.

Guided by the Programme of the RSDRP [1.3] and in the interests of a correct development of Social Democratic agitation on the nationality question, the meeting advances the following propositions:

1   To the extent that peace among nationalities is possible within a capitalistic society founded upon exploitation, profit, and strife, it may be attained only through a consistently and thoroughly democratic republican form of government which ensures the full equality of all peoples and languages by not having a compulsory state language, by providing the population with schools giving instruction in all native languages, and by including in the constitution a fundamental law prohibiting any special privileges whatsoever for one nation and any infringement whatsoever on the rights of a national minority. Broad regional autonomy and fully democratic local self-government are particularly necessary, with the boundaries of the self-governing and autonomous regions being determined by the local population itself on the basis of its economic conditions, living conditions, national make-up of the population, etc.

2   A division of the school system by nationality within the limits of a single state is unquestionably harmful from the viewpoint of democracy in general, and the interests of the proletarian class struggle in particular. Precisely such a division is the essence of the plan for so-called 'national-cultural' autonomy or for the 'creation of institutions guaranteeing free

national development' which has been adopted in Russia by all the Jewish bourgeois parties and by opportunistic petty bourgeois elements of the various nationalities.

3   The interests of the working class demand the merging of the workers of all nationalities within a given state into unified proletarian organizations – political, trade union, co-operative-educational, etc. Only such an amalgamation of the workers of different nationalities into single organizations enables the proletariat to wage a victorious struggle against international capital and against the reaction, as well as against the pronouncements and aspirations of the landowners, the priests, and the bourgeois nationalists of all nations who usually carry out their anti-proletarian designs under the slogan of 'national culture.' The world-wide workers' movement is creating and daily developing more and more an international proletarian culture.

4   As regards the right to self-determination of the nations oppressed by the tsarist monarchy, i.e., their right to secede and to form independent states, the Social Democratic Party must unconditionally defend this right. This is required by the fundamental principles of international democracy generally and, in particular, by the unprecedented national oppression of the majority of the population in Russia by the tsarist monarchy which, when compared with neighbouring states in Europe and Asia, is the most reactionary and barbarous régime. Furthermore, this is required for the freedom of the Great Russian population itself which is incapable of creating a democratic state unless it extirpates Black Hundred Great Russian nationalism which is supported by a tradition of bloody suppressions of national movements and is systematically fostered not only by the tsarist monarchy and all the reactionary parties but also by the Great Russian bourgeois liberals who cringe before the monarchy, especially in the epoch of counter-revolution.

5   It is impermissible to confuse the question of the right of nations to self-determination (i.e., the constitutional guarantee of a completely free and democratic method of resolving the question of secession) with the question of the expendiency of secession by any given nation. The Social Democratic Party must decide the latter question quite independently in each individual case, from the standpoint of the interests of overall social development and of the proletarian class struggle for socialism.

Social Democrats must also bear in mind that the landowners, the priests, and the bourgeoisie of the oppressed nations frequently use nationalist slogans to disguise their endeavours to divide and fool the workers, making deals behind their backs with the landowners and bourgeoisie of the ruling nation to the detriment of the toiling masses of all nationalities ...

1.126
On the Organizational Question and the Party Congress

1 Local reports indicate that the most urgent organizational task is not only to consolidate the leading party organizations in each city but also to connect the different cities with one another.
2 As a first step towards regional unification, the meeting recommends the organization of [regional] meetings (and also conferences, wherever possible) of comrades from the various centres in the workers' movement. Every effort must be made to have all branches of party work represented at these meetings: political, trade union, insurance, co-operative, etc.
3 The meeting recognizes the absolute necessity of a system of confidential agents, attached to the Central Committee, for co-ordinating work throughout Russia. The February Meeting's decision about confidential agents [1.116] has just begun to be implemented. Progressive workers on the local level must make sure that confidential agents are appointed at least in each major centre of the workers' movement and in the largest possible number.
4 The meeting places on the agenda the question of convoking a party congress. The growth of the labour movement, the maturing of the political crisis in the country, and the need for unified action by the working class on a nation-wide scale, all make the convocation of such a congress both necessary and possible, after sufficient preparations have been made [see 1.129] ...

All except 1.121, sec. 6; 1.122, sec. 1–5 in *Iz-veshchenie i rezoliutsii let-nego 1913 g. soveshchaniia Tsentral'nago Komiteta RSDRP s partiinymi rabot-nikami* (Paris, 1913)

KPSS v rezoliutsiiakh 1, 380–90

Meeting of the Central Committee 27–29 December 1913

During the crucial eight months before the war, the Central Committee met on at least five occasions in Galicia. Little is known about the composition of these meetings or about the nature of their debates. Indeed, the resolutions of only two of these have been published and these did not come to light until after 1957.

The meeting in Cracow during December 1913 was concerned with the party's two primary legal activities: Duma work and legal journalism. In the absence of a viable underground Russian Bureau of the Central Committee, the new-formed Russian Social Democratic Workers' Fraction with its parliamentary immunities assumed added importance as a de facto Russian centre. The six Bolshevik deputies were told to concentrate on their organizational and informational activities outside the Duma and especially on helping to revive *Pravda*. The party's chief legal newspaper had been hurt by strict censorship, heavy fines, police confiscation, declining subscriptions, a lack of funds, and compromising leadership by police agent M.E. Chernomazov who edited *Pravda* from May 1913 to February 1914. Lenin hoped that between these detailed instructions from the Central Committee and close supervision by the Duma fraction that *Pravda*'s problems could once again be resolved.

1.127
On the Activities of the Russian Social Democratic Workers' Fraction

First of all, the guiding institution [i.e., the Central Committee] notes with pleasure the enormous success in Duma activity of the Russian Social Democratic Workers' [i.e., Bolshevik] Fraction during the first half-session of its existence. During this short and in many respects especially difficult period for the workers' deputies, a number of excellent speeches were made, a number of interpellations were raised, the preliminary steps were taken for the introduction of important bills, etc.

Duma activities during the forthcoming half-session must emphasize the following:

1   in addition to the draft law on the eight-hour day, it is necessary to introduce the basic principles of an independent Social Democratic bill on [workers'] insurance;

2   considering the enormous interest in the position of teachers as a result of the recent congress of public school teachers, it is necessary in one way or another to raise this problem in the Duma – best of all in the form of a short bill that would increase their salaries and provide them with insurance (pension) coverage;

3   by first sending out questionnaires and then publicizing this material in the Duma, it is necessary to arouse interest in the position of various categories of workers and employees – miners, railwaymen, bakery work-

ers, shop clerks, waiters, postal workers, etc. – [which are not covered by workers' insurance];
4   it is desirable to work out and submit an independent Social Democratic bill on regular rest periods and pay of shop clerks;
5   it is desirable, from time to time, to publish the most important and successful [Duma] speeches in the form of special low-priced pamphlets. To do this, the speeches should be stereotyped during the process of printing them in *Pravda*;
6   it is necessary to publish a report on the fraction's activities at the end of the session;
7   it is necessary to give more attention to moving passage to the regular order [as a means of avoiding or ending undesirable debate, etc.];

At the same time, the Central Committee recognizes that, because of the conditions in the workers' movement and the situation within the party, the centre of activity of the six [Bolshevik deputies] must now inevitably shift to work *outside the Duma*.

Therefore, it is urgently necesary that the six now take up the systematic organization of their work *outside the Duma*, mindful of the fact that (on the basis of the February 1913 decision of the Central Committee [see page 168 above]), the six Duma deputies are first of all party organizers, propagandists, and agitators.

The immediate task of the six is to organize the participation of all six deputies in all aspects of party life and of the labour movement – both directly and especially by furthering the work of confidential agents and prominent [party] workers.

It is especially necessary in this regard that any participation in underground work be conducted with maximum observance of the rules of conspiracy.

One of the six must take part in each legal congress but need not make speeches.

But the guiding institution [i.e., the Central Committee] finds it particularly necessary to direct the attention of the Russian Social Democratic Workers' Fraction to strengthening *Pravda*, the position of which has been severely shaken. Without *Pravda*, all Duma work loses 99/100ths of its significance. Everything is now based on strengthening *Pravda*. This, in the most literal sense of the word, is the most urgent and important immediate task. And even if work in the Duma should temporarily suffer (in terms of the number of speeches), the deputies should concentrate their efforts on strengthening *Pravda*.

It is necessary:
1   to keep a strict watch over the legality of the newspaper's content so as to avoid [police] confiscation;

2   to go into all details of the business side of the operation so as to ensure that everything is being done economically;
3   to increase the number of copies printed by whatever means necessary.

I   Newspaper offices must be set up immediately in the workers' districts of St Petersburg. The guiding institution [Central Committee] requests that [Duma] deputies Badaev and Muranov take the lead in implementing this decision.
II   An attempt must be made to establish offices in such major cities as Riga, Moscow, Kiev, Kharkov, Ekaterinoslav.
III   The Russian Social Democratic Workers' Fraction must make several appeals for support for *Pravda* and must circulate letters on this at the local level.
IV   The deputies must divide up the raions in St Petersburg and go in person to influential workers in the largest factories so as to tell them about the paper's crisis and to appeal to them for assistance. Visits of workers to the fraction should also be used for this purpose.
V   The deputies must appeal to wealthy persons who sympathize with the labour movement and ask them to support the newspaper.

1.128
For the Guidance of *Pravda*'s Editors

1   All editorial work must be strictly collective. Censorship is all-important. Three weeks of leadership by Max [M.A. Savelev, who temporarily replaced Chernomazov as editor in December 1913] have shown that confiscation *can* be avoided. All external economies must be effected; otherwise the newspaper will fail.
2   The newspaper must become more varied. For this [the poet and satirist] D. Bednyi must definitely be brought back; more space must be allotted to belles-lettres, poetry, satire, etc.
3   The earlier decree [1.120], that articles sent in and signed with three prearranged letters are to be published at once and without change, remains in effect.
4   The following is resolved with respect to articles of local origin and especially those of a polemical character: such articles must without fail be evaluated by the entire editorial board; if a minority so demands, an article may be set aside and sent abroad; A. Vitomsky [pseudonym of Bolshevik publicist M.S. Olminsky] is personally accorded the same right to demand deferment; the same right is also granted to a person designated by the Russian Social Democratic Workers' Fraction. Articles of a polemical

nature, if they can withstand deferment, should generally be sent for review to ... [the foreign section of the Central Committee (?); words omitted for conspiratorial reasons].

5   Leading local *workers* must be involved in editorial work. Periodic meetings with workers on the conduct of the paper are feasible and necessary.

'Deiatel 'nost' TsK RSDRP   *KPSS v rezoliutsiiakh* 1, 391–5
po rukovodstvu gazetoi
'Pravda,' 1912–1914 gg.,'
Istoricheskii arkhiv, no. 4
(1959), 41–2

Meeting of the Central Committee   2–4 April 1914

Had the First World War been delayed a month, the April or 'Easter Meeting' of the Central Committee in Cracow might not have passed into oblivion. As it is, we know nothing about the composition of this meeting and have only what Soviet historians have acknowledged to be its 'extremely laconic' and conspiratorial resolutions on which to base our judgments.

The principal achievement of this meeting was to make arrangements to call the long-delayed VI Party Congress on 7–12 August 1914. Lenin very astutely used the X Congress of the Second International, scheduled to convene in Vienna on 13 August 1914, as a cover for his own congress in Poronin. By ostensibly working on the former congress, the Bolsheviks could more or less openly raise money, elect delegates, and discuss plans for their own congress. Moreover, they would have been assured of having a timely programme and a strong delegation in Vienna. Lenin's congress was intended to be a predominately Bolshevik affair. While talking about inviting all underground organizations 'regardless of factional adherence,' the meeting decided not to include the émigré factional centres since it would have been 'a hopeless task' to work in concert with them. More importantly, the national organizations, while invited, were relegated to a much more inferior position than they had held in the past. From Lenin's notes and police reports, it would appear that the Central Committee envisaged that only seven or eight out of the 68 to 119 anticipated delegates were to be from the national organizations and it was undecided whether to accord even these voting privileges.

Crucial to the calling of a Bolshevik congress was the creation of all-Bolshevik preparatory bodies. Thus the meeting authorized the establishment of an 'organizational section of the Central Committee,' that would serve as an unofficial Russian centre in St Petersburg while co-ordinating national preparations for calling the congress, and of eight 'oblast organizational commissions' (St Petersburg, Moscow and the Central Industrial Region, the Ukraine, the Caucasus, the Volga Region, the Northwestern Region, the Urals, the North) that would provide regional consolidation while overseeing local arrangements for the congress. To assist in these operations, the Bolshevik Duma deputies were told by the meeting to take advantage of their parliamentary immunities by travelling around the country agitating for the congress. Several of the deputies also participated in the oblast commissions and one of them, Badaev, was co-opted to the Central Committee. By July 1914, nearly all of these arrangements were complete and many of the delegates had been elected.

Apparently, some Mensheviks approached Lenin about forming a 'federated' committee to call a true 'general congress.' Since this is precisely what the Bolshevik leader did not want, the overture was ignored and the Mensheviks instead made half-hearted plans for their own 'all-Russian conference.' The plans for all three of these gatherings, however, had to be scrapped with the outbreak of the Great War.

1.129
On Calling the Party Congress

While the party has done enormous work in the area of agitation and propaganda during the last two or three years of the resurgence, disproportionately little has been done in the area of consolidating the party *organizationally*. As early as the summer of 1913, a party meeting announced the need for convoking a party congress [1.126]. The further events unfold, the greater the demand for the party to resolve important questions and the greater the need for a party congress.

In view of the above, the Central Committee resolved that *preparations are to begin immediately for the convocation of a regular congress of the RSDRP*.

The date of the congress is to be the middle of August 1914. The place is to be either X or Y [Cracow or Poronin]. All work on convoking the congress must be adapted to this date, since the congress of the Socialist International meeting in Vienna will serve as the best 'cover' and will make it possible to attract a larger number of worker delegates. For the time being, the date is to be communicated only to confidential agents.

The congress is to be convoked under the overall guidance of the Central Committee as the body unifying the vast majority of workers.

All Social Democratic underground organizations and party cells in legal organizations, without any exceptions, are invited to the congress.

A number of *oblast organizational commissions* are to be set up on the local level. These commissions are to be elected by the local committees and groups or are to be set up by authorization of the Central Committee ...

These commissions are to be established *immediately*. For this purpose agents of the Central Committee are already making the necessary trips, supplying the commissions with certain funds, etc.

The organizational commissions have the following functions:

By 15 June 1914 they must explain in the most detailed fashion precisely which organizations and groups in each region may and should be represented at the congress. All [election] supervision is in the hands of the organizational commissions. They decide who is to be invited and in this are guided by the principle that *not one* underground party group or organization, regardless of factional adherence, may be left out. Furthermore, the organizational commissions ought to give detailed information to comrades at the local level on the agenda of the congress, help supply them with literature, assist them in preparing resolutions, etc. The organizational commissions should determine the precise number of delegates from each region – within the minimum and maximum limits contemplated by the Central Committee. In agreement with the Central Committee and the local organizations, the organizational commissions should establish precise *norms* [concerning the number of voting members per delegate, etc.] for the elections to the congress. They should be granted the broadest autonomy in this so as everywhere to be able to adapt the elections to local conditions. The organizational commissions must immediately start financial collections for the congress, ascertaining by 15 June precisely what funds the local organizations themselves have available and what sort of subsidy will be needed from the Central Committee. The organizational commissions must inform the Central Committee about all of their efforts. If it turns out to be necessary, there possibly will be a meeting between the representatives of all eight organizational commissions and the Central Committee after 15 June. The organizational commissions should not refuse to assist the day-to-day political work of the local organizations and they should aid in every possible way the political leadership of the Central Committee ...

In addition, the following are invited: the Bund, the Latvian Social Democrats and the Polish Social Democrats (the Main Presidium and the Regional Presidium [see 1.118, sec. 3]). If these organizations agree to participate in the congress, the Central Committee, in consultation with the oblast organizational commissions, will make a special agreement with these national organizations with respect to [the norm of] their representation at the congress. The Armenian and Lithuanian Social Democrats [who were not yet members of the RSDRP] are invited to attend in an advisory capacity.

A rough estimate indicates that the basic expense will be about 100 roubles per delegate. It is desirable wherever possible (St Petersburg, Moscow, Kiev, Kharkov, etc.) that [delegates] be sent by Social Democratic groups in trade unions and workers clubs and that their expenses be paid by trade union treasuries...

1.130
On Establishing an Organizational Section of the Central Committee for the Leadership of Underground Work

In view of conspiratorial conditions, a special section of the Central Committee is to be set up for the direct guidance of underground organizational work.

    General meetings of all sections of the Central Committee [i.e., the foreign section and the organizational section] are held only in extraordinary cases, with special observance of conspiratorial conditions and with the agreement of the representatives of both sections. Usually relations [between these sections] are conducted by authorized individuals.

    As a cover, the organizational section of the Central Committee will be called the Workers' Co-operative Commission.

    This section:

1   directs the work of the St Petersburg Committee, giving it systematic assistance and reconstituting it in case of its collapse;
2   takes care to ensure that in their work all legal organizations are linked together by a sense of the party;
3   searches out special conspiratorial forms of cover for underground relations and operations;
4   unifies work on a nation-wide scale, instituting regular contacts and trips [between local organizations];
5   is principally concerned with guiding the preparations for the party congress in August 1914.

    The Russian Bureau of the Central Committee will appoint three to five persons as members of the organizational section and an equal number, or double the number, of candidate members.

'Zasedaniia TsK RSDRP, 15–17 Aprelia 1914 goda,' *Voprosy istorii KPSS*, no 4 (1957), 115–18

1.129 in *KPSS v rezoliutsiiakh* 1, 396–9

Central Committee on the War   September 1914

The outbreak of the First World War halted the efforts which Lenin had begun three years earlier to build a new, all-Bolshevik party. A combination of popular patriotism and police pressures curtailed the pre-war strike movement, decimated the underground organization, and severely restricted legal opportunities for party operations. This reversal at home apparently did not bother the Bolshevik leader as much as the sudden patriotism of many socialist leaders abroad who found the chauvinistic appeals of traditional nationalism stronger than the ideological demands of proletarian internationalism. Not surprisingly, the war did not elicit a unanimous response from the leaders of Russian social democracy. Some eminent figures, such as Plekhanov and Potresov, became what Lenin called 'social chauvinists' when they advocated support of Russia's war efforts. Martov and Trotsky took a 'centrist' or pacifist position in calling for the end of the war through united socialist pressure. And a few agreed with Lenin that the defeat of tsarist Russia was the 'lesser evil' and that the imperialist war should be transformed into a civil war.

Lenin first spelled out his theses in a report to a Bolshevik meeting in Bern on 24 August, shortly after his arrival from Galicia. In September these theses were expanded into a more readable manifesto on 'War and Russian Social Democracy' which Lenin intended to publish as a leaflet of a 'Group of Social Democrats.' When word reached him on 3 October that the theses had been approved by a meeting of leading Petrograd Bolsheviks, plans were changed so that the manifesto came out in the name of the Central Committee on the pages of the revived Central Organ, *Sotsial-demokrat*. It was subsequently approved, with minor editorial revisions, by a conspiratorial 'all-Russian meeting' which brought together the Bolshevik Duma fraction, a representative of the Central Committee (Kamenev), and some five underground leaders at Ozerki near Petrograd on 2 November 1914. Abroad, a variation of the manifesto was passed by a Bolshevik meeting in Bern in February 1915, but Lenin had less success convincing his fellow anti-war socialists on the correctness of his defeatist position at the subsequent Zimmerwald and Kienthal Conferences.

One is struck when reading this 'classic' of marxism-leninism with Lenin's pessimism and sense of helplessness. He in no way foresaw the imminence of revolution or that the war might bring upheaval first of all to his own country. His attention was more on castigating the leaders of the old International, calling for the creation of a new International, devising appropriate slogans, etc. One of the more interesting of these slogans, which was repeated in both his theses and the manifesto but later repudiated when the manifesto was reprinted in August 1915, concerned the establishment of a 'United States of Europe.' One can only speculate whether Kautsky's and Trotsky's concurrent use of this same slogan or the difficulties he encountered in interpreting the political tasks and economic implications of such a federation caused Lenin to drop it.

1.131
The War and Russian Social Democracy

The European war, which the governments and the bourgeois parties of all countries have been preparing for decades, has broken out. The growth of armaments, the extreme exacerbation of the struggle for markets in the latest – the imperialist – stage of capitalist development in the advanced countries, and the dynastic interests of the most backward eastern European monarchies must inevitably have brought on, and did bring on, this war. The seizure of territory and the subjugation of foreign peoples, the destruction of the competing nations and the plunder of their riches, the distraction of the attention of the toiling masses from the internal political crises in Russia, Germany, England, and other countries, the disunity and nationalistic befuddlement of the workers, and the destruction of their vanguard in order to weaken the revolutionary movement of the proletariat – such is the only real content, significance, and meaning of the present war.

Social democracy bears, first of all, the duty of revealing the true meaning of the war and of mercilessly unmasking the lies, sophisms, and 'patriotic' slogans disseminated by the ruling classes, the landowners, and the bourgeoisie in defence of the war ...

Neither group of belligerents yields in any way to the other in pillaging, atrocities, and the endless brutalities of war; but in order to fool the proletariat and distract its attention from the only real war of liberation – i.e., the civil war against the bourgeoisie both of one's 'own' country and of 'foreign' countries – for this lofty purpose, the bourgeoisie of each country uses empty slogans about patriotism in an attempt to exalt the significance of its 'own' national war and to convince everyone that it is striving to overcome its opponent, not for the sake of plunder and the seizure of territory, but for the sake of the 'liberation' of all peoples other than its own.

But the more zealously the governments and the bourgeoisie of all countries strive to disunite the workers and to incite them against one another, the more violently the system of martial law and military censorship is used for this lofty purpose (even now, during the war, persecuting the 'internal' enemy much more than the external one) – the more imperative is the duty of the class-conscious proletariat to defend its class solidarity, its internationalism, and its socialist convictions in the face of the raging chauvinism of the 'patriotic' bourgeois cliques in all countries. Renunciation of this task by the class-conscious workers would mean renunciation of all their aspirations for freedom and democracy, not to mention their strivings for socialism.

One must note, with a feeling of the most profound disappointment, that the socialist parties of the principal European countries have not fulfilled this duty, and that the conduct of the leaders of these parties – especially of the German party – verges on direct betrayal of the socialist cause. At a moment of the greatest world-wide and historical importance, the majority of the leaders of the present Second Socialist International (1889–1914) are striving to replace socialism with nationalism. As a result of their behaviour, the workers' parties of these countries did not set themselves against their governments' criminal conduct, but instead called upon the working class to *merge* its position with that of the imperialist governments. The leaders of the International have betrayed socialism by voting for war credits, repeating chauvinistic ('patriotic') slogans of the bourgeoisie of 'their own' countries, justifying and defending the war, entering bourgeois ministries of the belligerent countries, etc., etc. The most influential socialist leaders and the most influential organs of the socialist press of contemporary Europe have adopted a point of view which is chauvinistic, bourgeois, and liberal, but in no way socialistic. The responsibility for this disgrace of socialism falls primarily upon the German Social Democrats, who were the strongest and most influential party in the Second International. But neither can one justify the French socialists [J.B. Guesde and Marcel Sembat] who accepted ministerial posts in the government of the same bourgeoisie which betrayed its motherland and allied itself with Bismarck to crush the [Paris] Commune ...

Our party, the Russian Social Democratic Labour Party, has suffered and will continue to suffer great losses as a result of the war. Our entire legal workers press has been annihilated. Most of the trade unions have been closed; a great number of our comrades have been arrested and exiled. Yet our parliamentary representatives, the Russian Social Democratic Workers' Fraction [and also the Mensheviks' Social Democratic Fraction] in the State Duma, felt that it was their indisputable socialist duty not to vote for war credits, and even to walk out of the Duma hall [on 26 July 1914] so as to express their protest more energetically; they felt it their duty to brand the policy of the European governments as imperialist. And, despite the fact that the tsarist government has increased its oppression tenfold, the Social Democratic workers in Russia are already publishing their first underground proclamations against the war, thus fulfilling their duty to democracy and to the International ...

The collapse [of the Second International] must be clearly recognized and its causes understood, in order to make it possible to build a new and more durable socialist coalition among the workers of all countries.

Opportunists have wrecked the decisions of the Stuttgart [1907], Copenhagen [1910], and Basel [1912] Congresses [of the International], which obligated socialists of all countries to struggle against chauvinism in all circumstances, and which obligated socialists to respond to any war started by the bourgeoisie and the governments with intensified propaganda for civil war and social revolution. The collapse of the Second International is the collapse of opportunism ...

It is impossible either to carry out the tasks of socialism at the present time or to effect a genuinely international coalition of the workers without a resolute break with opportunism and without explaining its inevitable fiasco to the masses.

The very first task of the Social Democrats of every country must be to struggle against chauvinism in their country. In Russia the bourgeois liberals ('Kadets'), and a part of the populists (down to the Socialist Revolutionaries) and the 'right' Social Democrats [i.e., Plekhanov and some Liquidator Mensheviks] have been entirely engulfed in this chauvinism ...

In the present state of affairs, it cannot be determined, from the standpoint of the international proletariat, whose defeat – as between the two groups of belligerent nations – would be the lesser evil for socialism. But for us Russian Social Democrats, there can be no doubt that from the standpoint of the working class and the toiling masses of all the peoples of Russia, the lesser evil would be the defeat of the tsarist monarchy, the most reactionary and barbarous of governments, which is oppressing the largest number of nations and the greatest bulk of the population of Europe and Asia.

The immediate political slogan of European Social Democrats should be the formation of a republican United States of Europe; but, in contrast to the bourgeoisie, which is prepared to 'promise' anything in order to draw the proletariat into the general chauvinist current, Social Democrats will explain just how false and meaningless this slogan is without the revolutionary overthrow of the German, Austrian, and Russian monarchies.

Owing to the greater backwardness of Russia, which has not yet completed its own bourgeois revolution, the task of the Russian Social Democrats should remain as before to achieve the three fundamental conditions for consistent democratic reform: a democratic republic (with full equality and self-determination for all nations), confiscation of landed estates, and an eight-hour working day. But in all the advanced countries, the war has raised the slogan of a socialist revolution, and this becomes the more urgent the more the burdens of war weigh on the shoulders of the proletariat, and the more active its future role must become in the restoration of Europe after the horrors of contemporary 'patriotic' barbarism in the midst of the tremendous technical progress of large-scale capitalism. The use by the bourgeoisie of wartime laws to gag the proletariat confronts the latter with the indisputable task of creating underground forms of agitation and organization. Let the opportunists 'preserve' their legal organizations at the price of betraying their convictions – the revolutionary Social Democrats will utilize their organizational experience and ties with the working class so as to create illegal forms of struggle for socialism which are suitable for this period of crisis, and also to unite the workers not with the chauvinist bourgeoisie of their own countries but with the workers of all countries. The proletarian International has not died and will not die. Despite all obstacles, the working masses will create a new International. The present triumph of opportunism will be short-lived. The greater the number of war casualties, the clearer will it be to the working masses that the opportunists have betrayed the workers' cause and that it is necessary to turn their weapons against the governments and the bourgeoisie of every country.

The transformation of the present imperialist war into a civil war is the only correct proletarian slogan, one which is indicated by the experience of the Commune, one which was outlined by the 1912 resolution of the Basel [Congress of the International], and one which is dictated by all the conditions of an imperialist war among highly developed bourgeois countries. However difficult such a transformation may seem at any given moment, socialists will never give up their systematic, persistent, undeviating preparatory work to this end now that the war has become a fact.

Only by following this course will the proletariat succeed in tearing itself away from its dependence upon the chauvinist bourgeoisie and, in one way or another and with greater or lesser rapidity, in taking resolute steps toward the real freedom of nations and toward socialism ...

Sotsial-demokrat, no. 33   *KPSS v rezoliutsiiakh* 1, 403–10
(19 October 1914), 1

Russian Bureau of the Central Committee 28 February – 22 March 1917

The long-awaited February Revolution began with street demonstrations on the 23rd, reached its critical moment with the formation of the Duma's Temporary Committee (which soon became the Provisional Government) and the Soviet of Workers' and Soldiers' Deputies on the 27th, and culminated in the abdication of Nicholas II on 2 March 1917. The reaction of the Social Democrats to these events was hesitant and ambiguous, in part because almost all of their acknowledged leaders were either in exile or in emigration and also because of difficulties inherent in fitting these events into Marx's historical schema.

In the case of the Bolsheviks, a reconstituted Russian Bureau of the Central Committee, composed of A.G. Shliapnikov, V.M. Molotov, and P.A. Zalutsky, attempted to provide a modicum of co-ordination and leadership in Petrograd. However, according to Trotsky, the Bureau's hitherto insignificant members 'did not consider themselves and were not considered by others capable of playing a guiding role in revolutionary events.' It is certainly true that the Bureau neither initiated nor directed the events leading up to the abdication of the tsar. Its first proclamation appeared only on 25 February and then merely called for a general strike which was in fact already in progress. This was followed on the 28th by a manifesto in the name of the Central Committee 'To All Citizens of Russia' (1.132) and on 4 March by a resolution 'On Tactical Tasks' (1.133). These documents called for the overthrow of the new Provisional Government and for the formation of a provisional revolutionary government which would fulfil the party's minimum programme for the bourgeois revolution, end the war, and summon a constituent assembly. The date on which this manifesto was issued is controversial and of considerable importance in understanding the Bolsheviks' initial attitude toward the Soviet of Workers' and Soldiers' Deputies which was to become their chief vehicle to power. The editor of this collection accepts the conclusion of the Soviet historian, E.N. Burdzhalov, that the manifesto, which totally ignores the Soviet, was drafted by two Bolsheviks on the 27th, after the possibility of calling a Soviet had been discussed in party circles; that it was edited by the Russian Bureau on the 28th, when support of the new Soviet could have been inserted; and that it was issued that same day, first as a supplement of *Izvestiia* (News) and then as a separate leaflet. Quite obviously, Shliapnikov and company found it safer to repeat the party's slogans adopted at the time of the 1905 Revolution (see especially 1.20) than to contemplate such doctrinal innovations as advocating all power to the Soviet (especially when it was controlled by the Mensheviks and the Socialist Revolutionaries) or the inauguration of the socialist revolution.

In this militant attitude toward the Provisional Government and in underestimating the revolutionary potential of the Soviets, as well as in calling for turning the 'imperialist war into a civil war' (1.137), the Russian Bureau independently of Lenin adopted a position which was close to that of the émigré Bolshevik leader. It was not, however, a position which all Bolsheviks in Russia shared. More than half of the forty-odd Bolsheviks in the 400-member Petrograd Soviet, for instance, supported the Soviet's 2 March resolution approving the establishment of the Provisional Government and its announced programme. This attitude was confirmed the next day when the Bolshevik Petersburg Committee (which until 1918 adamantly refused to adopt the more Russian sounding title of Petrograd on the grounds that the change in the city's name was an act of wartime chauvinism) voted 'not to oppose the authority of the Provisional Government in so far as its actions conform with the interests of the proletariat.' Since four members of this Committee (Kalinin, V.N. Zalezhsky, M.I. Khakharev, K.I. Shutko) along with five other Bolsheviks (Olminsky, K.S. Eremeev, K.M. Shvedchikov, M.I. Ulianova, A.I. Ulianova-Elizarova) were added to the Bureau on 7–8 March, it is not surprising that the Bureau's next resolution on the Provisional Government (1.136) found that active opposition to rule by the bourgeoisie was no longer advisable. This resolution, however, was apparently revised by Molotov just before submission to the Soviet so as to return the emphasis to the creation of a provisional revolutionary government at the expense of the bourgeois government. This 'editing,' according to the Petersburg Committee, 'discredited bolshevism.'

The Russian Bureau was enlarged again on 12 March following the return from Siberia of Stalin, Kamenev, and M.K. Muranov. By virtue of their seniority in the party, they demanded and received, after some opposition from the Bureau, important positions in the party leadership. Stalin and Muranov were added to the Russian Bureau (1.138) and to its five-man presidium (Muranov, Stasova, Shliapnikov, Molotov replaced by Zalutsky, Olminsky replaced by Stalin); together with Kamenev, they were named to the Executive Committee of the Petrograd Soviet on the 15th; and on that same day they seized control of *Pravda*'s editorial board. This action, which Shliapnikov later called an 'editorial coup d'état,' was taken 'in spite of and contrary to' the decision of the Russian Bureau and made redundant the editorial board it had appointed only two days previously (1.139). Nevertheless, after protesting these 'strong-arm methods' (1.140), the Bureau acquiesced by naming Stalin, Kamenev, and Molotov as editors of *Pravda* and Muranov as its publisher.

Together with some of the members of the Petersburg Committee, they succeeded in moderating still further the Bureau's attitudes toward the Provisional Government, the continuation of the war, and party unity. They also moved further away from Lenin. In response to his telegraphed instructions of 'absolutely no trust in and no support for the new [Provisional] Government,' the Bureau noted on 13 March that 'one bald slogan is insufficient since it permits arbitrary interpretation and causes serious misunderstandings' and on 22 March passed a resolution implying that the Provisional Government might be pressured into granting meaningful reforms (1.143). In contrast to Lenin's instructions of 'no rapprochement with other parties,' the Bureau on 17 March viewed favourably suggestions of union both with the Inter-District Committee (Mezhraionka), which had been formed in November 1913 by some leading Vperedists, Bolshevik 'conciliators,' and followers of Trotsky and Plekhanov to foster party unity, and also with a small, loosely knit group of left-wing Menshevik intellectuals known as the Menshevik Internationalists (1.141). On the war issue, Lenin's and the Bureau's earlier slogans of 'Down with the War' and 'Turn the Imperialist War into a Civil War' were dropped. *Pravda* adopted a more or less defencist position, which caused the Inter-District Committee temporarily to lose interest in unification, and the Russian Bureau suggested that the bourgeois government could be pressured into ending the bourgeois war (1.144), which was 'nonsense' according to Lenin. It is perhaps indicative that only one of Lenin's articles appeared in the Russian press before his return and that this one, his first 'Letter from Afar' in the 21–22 March issues of *Pravda*, was editorially cut by 20 per cent so as to remove his sharp criticisms of the Provisional Government and the other revolutionary parties.

Because the positions of the Bureau during the last half of March and especially of Stalin were contrary to those of Lenin and were subsequently rejected by the party, most of the following documents pertaining to the Russian Bureau were suppressed until 1956.

1.132
To All Citizens of Russia 28 February 1917

CITIZENS! The strongholds of Russian tsarism have fallen. The prosperity of the tsarist band, erected on the bones of the people, has crumbled. The capital is in the hands of the insurgent people. Units of revolutionary troops have come over to the side of the insurgents. The revolutionary proletariat and the revolutionary army must save the country from the final destruction and break-up prepared by the tsarist government.

By gigantic efforts, by blood and lives, the Russian people haś shaken from itself the age-old slavery.

The task of the working class and the revolutionary army is to establish a *provisional revolutionary government* which must stand at the head of the new *republican* régime which is coming into being.

The provisional revolutionary government must undertake to adopt provisional laws defending *all the rights and liberties of the people, must confiscate and hand over to the people the lands of the monasteries, the nobility and the imperial family, must introduce an eight-hour working day, and must convoke a constituent assembly* elected by secret ballot on the basis of direct, equal, and universal suffrage.

The provisional revolutionary government should undertake the task of immediately supplying the population and the army with food; thus, all [private] reserves and also those stored away by the former [national] government and the city administrations must be confiscated.

The hydra of reaction may yet rear its head. The task of the people and of its revolutionary government is to crush all anti-popular counter-revolutionary schemes.

The provisional revolutionary government has the immediate and urgent task of entering into relations with the proletariat of the belligerent countries both for a revolutionary struggle of the peoples of all countries against their oppressors and enslavers, against royal governments and capitalist cliques, and also for an immediate end to the bloody human butchery which has been forced on the enslaved peoples.

Workers in factories and shops and also the insurgent troops should at once elect their representatives to the provisional revolutionary government which must be set up under the protection of the insurgent revolutionary people and army.

Citizens, soldiers, wives, and mothers! All to the struggle. For an open struggle against the tsarist régime and its stooges!

The red banner of insurrection is being raised *all over Russia*! Everywhere in Russia take into your own hands the cause of liberty, overthrow the tsarist stooges, call the soldiers to the struggle.

Set up the government of the revolutionary people in cities and villages all over Russia ... Long live the democratic republic! ...

*Izvestiia Petrogradskogo Soveta
rabochikh deputatov*, no. 1
(28 February 1917), supplement,
p. 1

1.133
On Tactical Tasks 4 March 1917

The present Provisional Government is in essence counter-revolutionary, since it is made up of representatives of the upper bourgeoisie and the nobility, and therefore no manner of agreement with this government is possible. The task of revolutionary democracy is to create a provisional revolutionary government that is democratic in character (i.e., a dictatorship of the proletariat and the peasantry).

Pravda, no. 4 (9 March 1917), 3

1.134
[On the Question of the Publication of a Party Organ]   4 March 1917

On the question of the [party] organ, it was decided that *Pravda* should come out as the organ of the Central Committee of the RSDRP and also temporarily, in view of purely technical and financial considerations, as the organ of the Petersburg Committee. The editorial board will consist of three persons: two from the Bureau of the Central Committee [Molotov and Eremeev] and one from the Petersburg Committee [Kalinin], but named by the Bureau of the Central Committee. All three editors are equally responsible and will resolve questions unanimously; in the event of disagreement concerning a particular article, it is to be set aside and transferred to the Bureau of the Central Committee for discussion ...

1.135
[On the Attitude toward the Soviet]   8 March 1917

On the question of the attitude toward the Soviet of Workers' and Soldiers' Deputies, it was pointed out that the strength presently represented in the Soviet makes it necessary to support it as the body which can and should create a Provisional Revolutionary Government. But it was further noted that the Executive Committee [of the Petrograd Soviet] is considerably more opportunistic than the Soviet itself, and that therefore it is desirable for it to be re-elected and enlarged. Members of the Executive Committee and the Soviet have related what was being done in this direction, but since the question has not been resolved by the Executive Committee or the Soviet, it is suggested that comrade Social Democratic Bolsheviks make every effort to exert the needed pressure on the Soviet in this direction. [On 9 March the Executive Committee duly authorized the Socialist Revolutionaries, the Mensheviks, and the Bolsheviks each to select three additional representatives.]

1.136
[On Relations between the Soviet of Workers' and Soldiers' Deputies and the Provisional Government]   9 March 1917

A resolution, proposed by the Executive Committee [on 8 March], was read [concerning the establishment of formal ties with the Provisional Government and the formation of a special Control or Liaison Commission which would exert pressure for certain reforms and generally exercise control over the actions of the bourgeois government]. This resolution is completely unacceptable since it establishes certain legal interrelationships [between the Soviet and the Provisional Government]. From the debate, it was evident that all members of the Bureau considered it impossible to support the Provisional Government but active opposition to it does not appear feasible since it is impossible to take over the responsibility for governing.

It was further pointed out that we divide forces into two categories: forces promoting the revolution and forces impeding it. In the first is the Soviet of Workers' and Soldiers' Deputies; in the second, the Provisional Government. Since it is desirable to have the opportunity of exerting constant pressure on the Government, legal norms or interrelationships should not be established ... 2 / Our goal is to turn the Soviet of Workers' and Soldiers' Deputies into a General [i.e., All-Russian] Soviet of Workers' and Soldiers' Deputies. 3 / It is necessary to fight for a provisional revolutionary government (i.e., a dictatorship of the proletariat and the peasantry).

1.137
On the War　　　　　　　　　　　　　　　　　　　　9 March 1917

The continuation of the war by the new Provisional Government has as its aim the same expansionist imperialistic policy, one that is in no sense a change from the predatory policy of the overthrown tsarist government, with the sole difference that the new government is striving to utilize the movement of revolutionary democracy – and in particular, the revolutionary army – for its imperialist aims.

Therefore, the Bureau of the Central Committee of the RSDRP, confirming former party decisions on its attitude toward expansionist imperialistic wars [see 1.131], declares that the basic task of revolutionary social democracy is, as before, the struggle to turn the present, antipopular imperialist war into a civil war of the peoples against their oppressors, i.e., the ruling classes.

For the practical execution of this urgent and most important task, it is necessary:

1   to establish contacts with the proletariat and with revolutionary democrats of the belligerent countries in order to put an immediate end to this criminal war that has been foisted upon the peoples;
2   to foster widespread and systematic fraternization in the trenches between the soldiers of the belligerent nations;

3   to democratize the army in rear areas and at the front by electing committees and commanders at the company, battalion and other levels in accordance with Order No. 1 of the Soviet of Workers' and Soldiers' Deputies;

4   to support and strengthen the revolutionary movement of the peoples against the ruling classes and their governments in all countries.

Only at such time as the revolutionary movement of the proletariat and democracy, which will win freedom for the people and repudiate all annexationist imperialist goals, shall be threatened by the expansionist policy of other imperialist governments, only then will revolutionary democracy assume the defence of the country's freedom. This is possible only under a revolutionary dictatorship of the proletariat and the peasantry.

Pravda, no. 5 (10 March 1917), 3

1.138
[On the Return of Stalin, Kamenev, and Muranov]   12 March 1917

The question of new persons [for the Russian Bureau] was raised in connection with the arrival [from Siberia] of Comrades Muranov, Stalin, and Kamenev and also in regard to the suggestion of Comrade Molotov concerning the introduction of Comrade Maksim [G.I. Boky] into the Bureau of the Central Committee as provincial manager. Discussion led to the decision that the Bureau of the Central Committee should include in its ranks all those persons it considered useful by virtue of their political credo but by no means to broaden its ranks in accordance with the performance of certain duties by this or that member.

Thus, the Bureau invites into its ranks valuable theoretical party workers and then distributes work among them. Concerning Comrade Maksim [Boky], it was proposed to include him in the Bureau of the Central Committee since he backed the position of the Bureau of the Central Committee and for a long time fulfilled the duties of dealing with the provincial [organizations] ... The question was then dealt with concerning Comrades Muranov, Stalin, and Kamenev. The first was unanimously invited [to join the Russian Bureau]. Concerning Stalin, it was submitted that he was an agent of the Central Committee in 1912 [in fact, he was then a member of both the Central Committee and the Russian Bureau] and that therefore it would be desirable to have him in the [present] Bureau of the Central Committee; but in view of certain personal traits characteristic of him, the Bureau expressed itself in favour of inviting him to join in an advisory [i.e., non-voting] capacity. As regards Kamenev, in view of his conduct at the trial [of the Bolshevik Duma deputies on 10 February 1915 wherein he dissociated himself from the Bern manifesto (1.131) and adopted a defencist position] and of those resolutions concerning him which were passed both in Siberia and in Russia, it was decided to accept him as a contributor to *Pravda*, if he offered his services, but to demand from him an explanation of his conduct. His articles should be accepted as material [for publication] but he should not be allowed to sign them.

1.139
[On the Question of *Pravda*]   13 March 1917

... On the question of *Pravda*, certain short-comings in it were pointed out: the absence of sufficiently sound theoretical articles, the inaccuracy of its information, and the fact that despite its agitational character it does not give as much guidance as it should. The desirability was noted of the paper's confining itself to our programme, eliminating its light tone (i.e., the ironical stories of Demian Bednyi) ... The composition of its editorial board is changed and enlarged to include Olminsky, Stalin, Ivanov [Kalinin], Eremeev, and Ilina [M.I. Ulianova].

1.140
[On the Editorial Board of *Pravda*]   17 March 1917

The Bureau of the Central Committee and the Petersburg Committee, protesting against the strong-arm methods in the matter of Kamenev's introduction into the editorial board of *Pravda*, transfers the question of his conduct and his participation in *Pravda* to the next party conference.

1.141
[On Party Unity]   17 March 1917

The question of an all-Russian party conference [see 1.152–1.158] is closely tied with that of unification of the Mensheviks and the Bolsheviks, and for that reason Comrade Belenin [Shliapnikov] reported on the suggestion of the Inter-District Committee of whether or not we wish to accept them into our midst. They do not make this subject to any conditions but hope that they would be given one place on the bureau (or commission) for calling the conference and one place on the editorial board of *Pravda* ... After debate about whether a federative or an amalgamative form of organizational unity was preferable, it was resolved as follows:

The Bureau of the Central Committee, having discussed the suggestion of the Inter-District Committee about merger with organizations belonging to the Petersburg Committee, finds this desirable and welcomes [the suggestion]. It transfers, however, the practical solution of this question to the Petersburg Committee and the Inter-District Committee for discussion.

This was passed unanimously with the rider that the Bureau of the Central Committee considers it feasible for the Inter-District Committee to retain temporarily its separate representation in the Soviet of Workers' and Soldiers' Deputies.

As regards the question of unity with the Menshevik Internationalists, this ought to be introduced for the discussion of the Bureau of the Central Committee, the Petersburg Committee, and the writers' groups.

1.142
On Party Membership   18 March 1917

As members are accepted those who recognize the Programme and enter into a [party] organization. Admission takes place upon the recommendation of two party members.

A standard membership card is produced by the Bureau of the Central Committee and distributed through the local organizations which, after affixing their seal, will issue it to their members. The party Rules should be attached to the card.

1.143
On the Provisional Government   22 March 1917

The Provisional Government, which was promoted by the moderate bourgeois classes of society and which is connected by its interests with Anglo-French capital, is incapable of resolving the tasks set by the revolution. Its resistance to the further development and deepening of the revolution is paralysed only by the growth of the revolutionary forces themselves and of their organizations. The focal points for the latter's consolidation should be the Soviets of Workers' and Soldiers' Deputies in the cities and the Soviets of Peasants' and Farmhands' Deputies in the villages which, as embryos of revolutionary power, are prepared at a given moment in the further development of the revolution to implement the full power of the proletariat in alliance with revolutionary democracy so that the demands of the insurgent people may be fully realized. Even now these Soviets must exercise firmest control over all the actions of the Provisional Government and its agents, both at the centre and at the local level, and must take on themselves a number of state and economic functions arising from the complete disorganization of the country's economic life and from the need to take very decisive measures so as to provide for the starving and war-ravaged population.

Therefore, the task of the day is the rallying of forces around the Soviets of Workers' and Soldiers' Deputies as embryos of revolutionary power which alone are capable of repelling the counter-revolutionary attempts of the tsar and the bourgeoisie and of implementing the demands of revolutionary democracy as well as of explaining the true class nature of the present government.

The Soviets' immediate and most important task, the fulfilment of which is the only guarantee of victory over all the forces of counter-revolution and of the further development and deepening of the revolution is, in the party's view, the general arming of the population and, in particular, the immediate creation of a workers' Red Guard throughout the country.

Pravda, no. 18 (26 March 1917), 2

1.144
On War and Peace   22 March 1917

1   The peace which the toilers of the world need can only result from the transformation of the present imperialist war, started by the capitalists to divide up and exploit the world market, into a civil war of all social classes oppressed by capitalism in all countries.

2   The Russian Revolution, the first in a series of revolutions and uprisings by the proletariat which the imperialist war will inevitably engender, can only secure for the peoples of Russia the maximum of democratic liberties and social reforms if it becomes the starting point for the revolutionary movement of the western European proletariat against their bourgeois governments.

3   The revolutionary proletariat of Russia, relying on the country's entire working population which is ravaged by the burden of war, the food crisis, and the rising cost of living, must therefore, in its own interests, which fully coincide with those of the peoples of all countries:

   a appeal directly to the proletariat of all countries and to the oppressed nations, calling on them to rise up against their own governments and thus support the revolutionary movement in Russia and clear the path to universal peace;

   b force the Provisional Government of Russia not only to renounce all annexationist plans but also immediately and openly to formulate the will of the peoples of Russia proposing peace to all warring countries on the basis of the liberation of all peoples who are oppressed, suppressed or who [do not] have equal civil rights (i.e., on the basis of the right to self-determination). This declaration of the will of the peoples of Russia would inevitably incite the toiling masses to rise up against any imperialist governments which opposed the peace proposal and would unify all nations, without distinction, in the struggle for peace which is so necessary to a humanity ruined and enslaved by imperialism.

The Soviets of Workers' and Soldiers' Deputies, which should immediately develop agitation among the broadest masses in the spirit of the above theses, must become an instrument for influencing both the proletariat of the belligerent states and the Provisional Government in the indicated direction.

4 The Social Democratic Party, which is the leader of the proletariat in this struggle for peace, must tirelessly explain the true meaning of the present imperialist war and must struggle undeviatingly both against the imperialist current, which is zealously inculcated and inflamed by the liberal bourgeoisie, and also against the nationalist current in the revolution as represented by the petty bourgeois groups which have adhered to it. Any vacillation in this struggle and, what is worse, any bowing to this nationalist current, would be a betrayal of the tasks of the international proletariat and, thereby, the true interests of both the proletariat and the entire toiling population of Russia.

Pravda, no. 18 (26 March 1917), 2

'Protokoly i rezoliutsii Biuro TsK RSDRP(b) (Mart 1917 g.),' *Voprosy istorii KPSS*, no. 3 (1962), 136–54

I.132, I.143 and I.144 in *KPSS v rezoliutsiiakh* I, 427–31

Menshevik Organizational Committee   March 1917

The Mensheviks were even less organized and unified than the Bolsheviks on the morrow of the February Revolution, but initially at least they were far more influential. Their influence came through participation in the War Industries Committees during the war and in the Petrograd Soviet after the overthrow of the tsar. As orthodox marxists, they saw Nicholas' abdication as Russia's bourgeois revolution which would inaugurate a long period of capitalism under bourgeois rule. This led them to be less ambiguous than the Bolsheviks in their attitude toward both the Provisional Government and the Soviet of Workers' and Soldiers' Deputies. They accepted the right of the former to govern Russia, until the convocation of a constituent assembly, and they were prepared to utilize the latter so as to pressure the government for democratic reforms. The first Menshevik leaders to return to the capital – N.S. Chkheidze, Tseretelli, and, in late March, Dan – accordingly took leading roles in the Petrograd Soviet.

The issue which divided and weakened the Mensheviks was the question of the war. When the revolution broke out, many of the Menshevik leaders were in Switzerland grouped around the Foreign Secretariat of the Organizational Committee. Led by Martov, Akselrod and Martynov, these émigrés were strongly internationalist in their approach to the war. Martov saw the war as an absolute evil and wanted 'peace at any price' through united socialist action. The success of the February Revolution did not cause any alteration in his pacifist position. In Russia, however, the Menshevik leaders of the new Soviet, while largely internationalists before the revolution, now felt that the Provisional Government and the Soviets had the duty to protect the gains of the revolution even if it meant continuing the war. They therefore opposed any attempts to disorganize the army or to encourage fraternization at the front. Martov and the Menshevik Internationalists rejected this 'revolutionary defencism' from afar, but it received first-hand support from the Organizational Committee in Petrograd.

The Organizational Committee, which had been the titular head of menshevism since 1912 (see 1.105), played a role during March 1917 analogous to that of the Bolsheviks' Russian Bureau of the Central Committee. Its composition was equally undistinguished, and surely not of the calibre of either the Foreign Secretariat (which it tended to ignore) or the Menshevik Soviet hierarchy (which it supported). Little is known about its actual activities and membership during the first few months of the revolution: perhaps because it was less organized and less active than its Bolshevik counterpart, perhaps because it was overshadowed by the Soviet, perhaps because history often ignores the losers. In any case, the two resolutions printed below, which Dan introduced in the name of the Organizational Committee at the All-Russian Conference of Soviet Deputies, clearly reflect both the dominant thinking of the Mensheviks then in Russia on the issues of the war and the Provisional Government, and also the differences between menshevism and bolshevism before the return of Martov and Lenin.

1.145
On the Attitude toward War and Peace   25 March 1917

Recognizing that the most important and absolutely urgent task of democracy at the present moment is the struggle for peace without annexations or indemnities on the basis of national self-determination, a struggle for peace on a worldwide scale, we consider it necessary:

1   To mobilize public opinion and to organize pressure on the Provisional Government by the working class and the democracy of the entire country, so as to induce it:
   a   to renounce officially and unconditionally all aggressive plans;
   b   to take the initiative in working out and publicizing a similar collective declaration by all the governments of the Entente countries; and
   c   to take the necessary steps, together with the allied governments, to enter upon the path of peace negotiations.
2   To appeal, with the same aim in mind, to the proletariat of all belligerent countries to exert co-ordinated pressure on their governments in order to induce then to renounce nationally all aggressive aspirations and to enter upon the path of peace negotiations.
3   In confirmation of our decision and our complete readiness to support the Provisional Government in its actions, in so far as they are directed toward developing and consolidating the gains of the revolution, we consider it our duty to declare that we will struggle resolutely against any overt or covert attempt by it to continue an aggressive [foreign] policy.
4   At the same time, we are well aware that Russian military defeats would endanger the Russian Revolution as well as international democracy and, in view of this, consider it necessary to speak out resolutely against all actions leading to the disorganization of the [national] defence.

1.146
[On the Attitude toward the Provisional Government]   1 April 1917

... [The Organizational Committee] associates itself with the decision of the Petrograd Soviet of Workers' and Soldiers' Deputies to recognize the Provisional Government which was created by the revolution and has assumed state power until the convocation of a constituent assembly.

The [Committee] recognizes that, under pressure from the proletariat and democracy as a whole, the Provisional Government to date has by and large been discharging the obligations it assumed in the matter of liquidating the tsarist régime and securing the gains of the revolution, and at the same time has taken a first step [in its proclamation of 27 March] toward renouncing an annexationist policy.

The [Committee] finds it necessary that the working class and democracy as a whole, in the form of its plenipotentiary bodies – the Soviets of Workers' and Soldiers' Deputies – should henceforth, without taking upon itself the functions of state power and without assuming responsibility for all governmental activity, exert continuous pressure on the government by organizing its own forces for political control on the one hand and for exchanging information on the other [through the Control or Liaison Commission; cf. 1.136].

The [Committee] appeals to all democratic elements to give effective support to the Provisional Government in so far as it continues to act in the spirit of the revolution, to struggle resolutely against the remnants of the old régime and against any counter-revolutionary attempts, and in so far as it continues to stand firmly for universal peace without annexations or indemnities on the basis of national self-determination.

Rabochaia gazeta, no. 16 (25 March 1917), 4; no. 25 (7 April 1917), 2

All-Russian Meeting of Party Workers   27 March–2 April 1917

The All-Russian Meeting of Party Workers or 'March Conference,' as it is sometimes called, is one of the most obscure gatherings in party history. For a long time it was assumed that the minutes and resolutions of the meeting had been destroyed during the July Days. This situation was not inconvenient for stalinist historians since it allowed them to ignore their leader's questionable role during March 1917. In 1932, however, Trotsky published the partial protocols for the last five sessions in his *Stalin School of Falsification*. The accuracy of these was confirmed when post-Stalin historians rediscovered and published for the first time in the Soviet Union a nearly identical protocol. These documents cast interesting light on the Bolsheviks' first national conference since the February Revolution and on the first legally convened gathering in the party's history.

The rationale for the meeting was to define party positions on questions to be discussed at the All-Russian Conference of Soviets of Workers' and Soldiers' Deputies scheduled to convene in Petrograd on 29 March. Originally planned as a purely preliminary meeting, the more than 120 Bolshevik delegates representing individual Soviets, local party organizations, and central party institutions met intermittently in the palace of the tsar's favourite ballerina, Mathilda Kshesinskaia, throughout the life of the Conference of

Soviets. While all of the delegates were Bolsheviks, they tended to fall into three distinct groups: the hard-liners of the original Russian Bureau (Molotov, Zalutsky), moderates who openly supported the Provisional Government (V.S. Voitinsky, P.N. Sevruk, and several others who shortly joined the Mensheviks), and the centrist majority (Stalin, Kamenev, Nogin, Rykov) who leaned toward Social Democratic unity and who were willing to follow the lead of the Menshevik-Socialist Revolutionary-controlled Executive Committee of the Petrograd Soviet in dealings with the Provisional Government.

The Russian Bureau of the Central Committee introduced its own resolutions on the key questions of the war and the Provisional Government which, in each instance, the centrist majority succeeded in moderating. The resolution adopted by the meeting on the war, for example, rejected the Russian Bureau's earlier call to disorganize the army (1.137) and instead appealed to all soldiers and workers 'to remain at their posts and to maintain complete order.' In reporting on the Bureau's resolution concerning the Provisional Government, Stalin noted that the government was 'the fortifier of the gains of the revolutionary people'; that it was inadvisable to frighten the bourgeois democrats; and that, therefore, he personally supported an alternate resolution of the Krasnoiarsk Soviet which called for 'support of the Provisional Government ... in so far as it follows a course of satisfying the demands of the working class.' The meeting initially agreed to this formulation, but then changed its mind and decided not to state openly its support of the government. Nevertheless, the resolution which it finally adopted on 31 March omitted the Russian Bureau's earlier description of the Soviets as 'embryos of revolutionary power' as well as its call for the creation of Red Guard units and for the arming of the people (1.143). Neither of these resolutions fared very well at the Conference of Soviets: 'On the War' received only 57 votes compared to 325 for the Executive Committee's more defencist position; 'On the Attitude toward the Provisional Government' was first read by Kamenev and then withdrawn, despite contrary instructions from the meeting, in favour of the Executive Committee's formula which overtly supported the government. The latter received the unanimous backing of the deputies.

The meeting also spent considerable time discussing the possibility of unity with the Mensheviks. After an initial meeting with Menshevik representatives to explore the chances for a joint submission on the war question, Tseretelli proposed that both factions meet to discuss a merger and a unification congress. Stalin supported this suggestion: 'we ought to go ... unification is possible along the lines of Zimmerwald-Kienthal ... we will live down minor differences of opinion within the party.' Since almost half of the local delegates to the Bolshevik meeting came from united organizations, the objections of the hard-liners were soon overcome and it was agreed both to attend the joint meeting for purposes of information and without a formal programme and also to create a commission (Stalin, Kamenev, Nogin, Teodorovich) to help arrange a subsequent unification conference. On the morning of 4 April, in what was in effect an extension of the March Conference, fifty Bolsheviks, forty-seven Mensheviks, seventeen non-factionalists, and three representatives of national Social Democratic parties attended Tseretelli's meeting at the Tauride Palace. One of those in attendance was Lenin, who had arrived the night before at the Finland Station. After several speakers praised Tseretelli's proposal, Lenin rose and delivered his famous April Theses. According to Trotsky, his speech 'passed over the work of the [March] Conference like a wet sponge of a teacher erasing what had been written on the blackboard by a confused pupil.' He attacked any form of defensive war, any type of support for the Provisional Government, and any notion of unity with the Mensheviks. Unlike either the Russian Bureau or the March Conference, he said that the bourgeois revolution was over and that the time had come to advocate the transfer of power to the Soviets. He concluded by suggesting that the Social Democratic Party should be renamed the Communist Party. Shortly after his speech, the majority of the Bolsheviks joined him in walking out of the joint meeting. Without them the call for a unification congress, which the meeting confirmed, was virtually meaningless.

1.147
On the War   28 March 1917

The present war arose out of the imperialist (aggressive) aspirations of the ruling classes of all countries to seize new lands and to subordinate small and backward states. Each additional day of war enriches the financial and industrial bourgeoisie and ruins and exhausts the forces of the proletariat and peasantry of all belligerent countries. In Russia, furthermore, the dragging out of the war seriously endangers the consolidation of the gains of the revolution and the completion of the revolution. The will of the people must put an end to this war which is not needed by the people. Therefore, the revolutionary forces of Russia (the proletariat and the army) set themselves the urgent task of ending the war as quickly as possible on the basis of a peace without annexations or indemnities, and with each nation being granted the right of self-determination.

To this end, Russian revolutionary democracy must immediately appeal to the peoples of all belligerent countries to rise up against their oppressors who bear the guilt for this fratricidal butchery. Then the Russian Revolution, finding its echo in the West, will clear the way for universal peace. The first step along this path was the adoption of the 'Manifesto to the Peoples of the World' at the 14 March meeting of the Soviet of Workers' and Soldiers' Deputies [which called for a revolutionary peace but justified revolutionary defencism until that peace was achieved].

Work must be continued on strengthening international ties with a view to ending the war. It is necessary, in particular, to convoke an international socialist congress in the near future. On the other hand, next on the agenda is the necessity of compelling the Russian Provisional Government not only to renounce all aggressive plans, but also immediately and openly to express the will of the Russian peoples; i.e., to propose to all belligerents a peace without annexations or indemnities and with the right of nations to self-determination.

Only the complete liquidation of the entire foreign policy of tsarism and of the imperialistic bourgeoisie, together with the liquidation of secret international treaties and the real transfer of power into the hands of the proletariat and revolutionary democracy, would signify a change in the imperialist character of the war on the part of Russia and – if any other country should refuse peace – would compel the insurgent people [of Russia], in alliance with the proletariat of western Europe, to take the war into its own hands as a war for national freedom. Until then we, rejecting the disorganization of the army and considering it necessary to preserve its strength as a bulwark against counter-revolution, appeal to all soldiers and workers to remain at their posts and to maintain complete order.

Pravda, no. 20 (29 March 1917), 3

1.148
On the Attitude toward the Provisional Government 31 March 1917

Recognizing that the Provisional Government consists of representatives of the moderate bourgeois classes who are tied to the interests of Anglo-French imperialism; that it is implementing its proclaimed programme only in part and only under pressure from the Soviets of Workers' and Soldiers' Deputies; that the forces of counter-revolution, which are in the process of being organized and which are hiding behind the banner of the Provisional Government with the obvious toleration of the latter, have already launched an attack against the Soviets of Workers' and Soldiers' Deputies [in the form of agitation among front line troops that the Soviets were sabotaging the patriotic war effort]; that the Soviets of Workers' and Soldiers' Deputies are the sole organs of the will of the revolutionary people —

The Conference therefore calls upon revolutionary democracy:

1   To exercise vigilant control over the actions of the Provisional Gov-

ernment on the national and local levels, urging it toward a most energetic struggle for the complete liquidation of the old régime;
2   to rally around the Soviets of Workers' and Soldiers' Deputies which alone are capable, in alliance with other progressive forces, of repulsing tsarist and bourgeois counter-revolutionary attempts and of consolidating and extending the gains of the revolutionary movement. [Several versions of this point exist: the protocol version given in Trotsky and *Voprosy istorii KPSS* (above); the version found in the stenographic reports of the All-Russian Conference of Soviets which includes a clause about the Soviets being 'organizational centres of revolutionary and democratic forces produced by the revolution'; and the *Pravda* (no. 27, 8 April 1917) version, repeated in *KPSS v rezoliutsiiakh*, which omits all mention of other 'democratic' and 'progressive forces' and refers to the Soviets as 'embryos of revolutionary power.']

'Protokoly Vserossiiskogo (Martovskogo) soveshchaniia partiinykh rabotnikov,' *Voprosy istorii KPSS*, no. 6 (1962), 136, 141

KPSS v rezoliutsiiakh 1, 432–3

Central Committee on the April Crisis   20–22 April 1917

The first major crisis between the Provisional Government and the Petrograd Soviet occurred in April 1917 over the question of foreign policy. At the insistence of the Soviet's Executive Committee, the government agreed to communicate its domestic statement of 27 March disavowing aggressive and expansionistic aspirations to the Entente powers. The Note, which Foreign Minister P.N. Miliukov sent on 18 April, however, interpreted this statement in such a way as to reassure the allies that Russia would carry the war 'to a decisive conclusion' in order to obtain certain 'sanctions and guarantees.' The publication of this Note on 20 April provoked in Petrograd a series of spontaneous strikes and demonstrations which Trotsky later described as a 'quarter-insurrection.'

The Central Committee immediately condemned the Note but concluded that nothing better could be expected as long as the Soviet tried to achieve peace solely by pressuring the bourgeois government. Only after 'taking the entire power of the state into its own hands' would the revolutionary proletariat be able to arrive at a 'truly democratic peace.' To Lenin's surprise, rhetoric soon found practical expression and spontaneity received unexpected leadership when a Bolshevik soldier, F.V. Linde, convinced the Finnish Regiment to march on the Provisional Government. By late afternoon on the 20th, some 15,000 troops were calling not only for the ouster of Miliukov but for the overthrow of the government. On the next day, some members of the Petersburg Committee and of the Bolshevik Military Organization distributed leaflets using the slogan 'Down with the Provisional Government.' That afternoon armed clashes took place between the demonstrators and the growing numbers of government supporters. These actions caused the Central Committee to hesitate. Fearing that they would be used to justify suppression of the party and would drive the Soviet into the arms of the government, the Central Committee on the 21st called for purely 'peaceful demonstrations' and on the 22nd supported the Soviet's ban on all demonstrations. The militancy of the Petersburg Committee and the slogan 'Down with the Provisional Government' were condemned as 'adventuristic.'

The April Crisis revealed not only the continued division in the Bolshevik hierarchy and the weakness of the Provisional Government, but also the strength of the Petrograd Soviet. The crowds respected the Soviet's ban on demonstrations; the garrison troops followed its instructions not to engage in any more actions either for or against the demonstrators without precise orders from the Executive Committee; and the Provisional Government agreed on 21 April to send an additional note to the Entente powers 'explaining' that Miliukov's 'sanctions and guarantees' merely meant a limitation of armaments, etc., and not territorial annexations. This repudiation led to the resignation of the Foreign Minister twelve days later and eventually to the formation of the first coalition (see 1.159). Even Lenin, who wrote the three Central Committee resolutions printed below, had to acknowledge the unexpected strength of the Soviet during the April Crisis. He came to realize that the party must temper its rhetoric as well as the violent expressions of mass unrest until it was better organized and especially until after the Bolsheviks had gained control of the key Soviets.

1.149
On the Provisional Government's Note
of 18 April 1917 20 April 1917

The Note of the Provisional Government has shown the complete correctness of the position taken by our party in the resolution of the Petrograd City Conference [on 15 April], namely that:

1   the Provisional Government is imperialist through and through, tied hand and foot to Anglo-French and Russian capital;
2   all the promises which it has made or could make (with respect to

'ascertaining the will of the people for peace,' etc.) are nothing but deceptions;
3   the Provisional Government cannot renounce annexations, regardless of its composition, because the capitalist class is tied in with banking capital in the present war and especially at the present moment;
4   the petty bourgeois policy followed by the narodniks [e.g., Socialist Revolutionaries], the Mensheviks, and most of the leaders of the present Soviet of Workers' Deputies, which consists in encouraging false hopes of being able to 'reform' the capitalists (i.e., the Provisional Government) by 'influencing' them, has once again been exposed by this Note [cf., 1.148].

In view of the above, the Central Committee finds that:
I   Any changes in the composition of the present government (the resignation of Miliukov, the recall of [Justice Minister A.F.] Kerensky, etc.) would be an imitation of the worst practices of bourgeois parliamentary republicanism, *replacing* the class struggle with the rivalry of cliques and the reshuffling of individuals.
II For the mass of the petty bourgeoisie, which is wavering between the capitalists and the working class, salvation can only come by unconditionally joining the revolutionary proletariat, which alone is capable of throwing off the fetters of finance capital and of the annexationist policy. Only by taking the entire power of the state into its own hands – with the support of the majority of the people – will the revolutionary proletariat together with the revolutionary soldiers create, in the form of the Soviet of Workers' and Soldiers' Deputies, the sort of government which will have the confidence of the workers of all countries and which alone will be in a position rapidly to terminate the war by means of a truly democratic peace.

1.150
[On Peaceful Demonstrations]   21 April 1917

... The Central Committee of the RSDRP resolves that:
1   Party agitators and orators must refute the malicious lie of the capitalistic newspapers, and of the newspapers supporting the capitalists, to the effect that we are threatening a civil war ... *At this moment*, any thought of civil war would be naive, senseless, and preposterous; ... should violence occur, the responsibility will fall on the Provisional Government and its supporters ...
4   All party agitators in factories, in regiments, in the streets, etc., must propagandize these views and this proposal through *peaceful* discussions and peaceful demonstrations ...
5   Party agitators must protest again and again against the malicious slander spread by the capitalists alleging that our party stands for a separate

peace with Germany ... We are against negotiating with the capitalists [of any country], we are for negotiating and fraternizing with the revolutionary workers and soldiers of all countries ...

7   We consider the policy of the present majority of the leaders of the Soviet of Workers' and Soldiers' Deputies and of the narodnik and Menshevik parties to be profoundly erroneous, since confidence in the Provisional Government, attempts to compromise with it, horse-trading for amendments, etc., would only mean, in effect, the proliferation of meaningless pieces of paper, pointless delays, and moreover this policy threatens to create a divergence between the will of the Soviet of Workers' and Soldiers' Deputies and that of the majority of the revolutionary soldiers at the front and in Petrograd as well as that of the majority of workers.

8   We appeal to those workers and soldiers, who recognize that the Soviet of Workers' and Soldiers' Deputies must alter its policy and renounce the policy of confidence in and compromise with the capitalist government, to hold new elections for delegates to the Soviet of Workers' and Soldiers' Deputies and to send there only persons who will staunchly adhere to a fixed point of view which is in agreement with the true will of the majority [of the workers].

1.151
[On Dual Power] 22 April 1917

... The slogan, 'Down with the Provisional Government,' is an incorrect one at present because, in the absence of a firm (i.e., a class-conscious and organized) majority of the people on the side of the revolutionary proletariat, such a slogan is either an empty phrase or, objectively, it leads to attempts of an adventuristic nature.

We will favour a transfer of power into the hands of the proletarians and semi-proletarians only when the Soviets of Workers' and Soldiers' Deputies adopt our policy and are willing to take this power into their own hands.

The organization of our party, the cohesiveness of the proletarian forces, have clearly proven inadequate during the days of the crisis.

The slogans of the moment are:

1   explain the proletarian line and the proletarian way to end the war;
2   criticize the petty bourgeois policy of confidence in and compromise with the government of the capitalists;
3   conduct propaganda and agitation from group to group within each regiment, in each factory, and especially among the most backward masses, such as servants, manual labourers, etc., since the bourgeoisie tried to rely upon them in particular during the days of the crisis;

4   organize, organize, and once more organize the proletariat: in each factory, in each district, in each block.

The resolution of the Petrograd Soviet of Workers' and Soldiers' Deputies of 21 April banning all street meetings and demonstrations for two days should be unconditionally observed by all members of our party ...

We call on all workers and soldiers to consider carefully the results of the crisis of the last two days and to send as delegates to the Soviet of Workers' and Soldiers' Deputies and to the Executive Committee only those comrades who express the will of the majority. Whenever a delegate does not express majority opinion, new elections must be held in the factories and barracks.

Pravda, no. 37 (21 April 1917), 1; no. 38 (22 April 1917), 1; no. 39 (23 April 1917), 1

V.I. Lenin, *Polnoe sobranie sochinenii* XXXI (Moscow, 1962), 291–2, 309–11, 319–20

VII All-Russian Conference of the RSDRP

24–29 April 1917

At the VII or April Conference of the RSDRP Lenin completed what Trotsky has called 'the re-arming of the party.' The Conference, which met in the Women's Medical Institute in Petrograd, was attended by 133 voting and 18 consulting delegates from 78 Bolshevik organizations. They represented not only four-fifths of the total Bolshevik membership (100,000) but also a fourfold increase in the faction's size since the February Revolution. Lenin, whose April Theses had been ignominiously rejected by his own Central Committee immediately after his return to Russia, was once again clearly in control of the party. He sat on the Conference's presidium, wrote most of its resolutions, and delivered four of its major reports. The principal tenets of his Theses – no support for the war, no dealings with the Provisional Government, all power to the Soviet – were now accepted almost unanimously (1.152, 1.154, 1.156) even by those who had earlier led the Russian Bureau to moderate its positions on these very same issues (cf. 1.147, 1.148). By virtue of the strength of his own personality and by reflecting the growing militancy of the crowds who had demonstrated in the streets during the April Crisis, Lenin secured what N.N. Sukhanov has termed his 'most important and fundamental victory' during the revolution.

He also succeeded in turning the party's attention for the first time to issues less pressing in Petrograd but of paramount importance outside the capitals.

Recognizing that neither the peasants nor the national minorities had yet to benefit substantially from the revolution and were disinclined to follow the Provisional Government's advice that they wait for the Constituent Assembly to bring them meaningful reform, Lenin resurrected the Bolsheviks' call for the nationalization of all the land (1.157), which the RSDRP had turned down in 1906 (1.51), and also their 1913 resolution (1.125) favouring recognition in theory of the right of all national minorities to self-determination (1.158). He suggested that these basic changes be incorporated into a revised party Programme which the Central Committee was instructed to prepare for the next party congress (*KPSS v rezoliutsiiakh* 1, 455–6).

These victories were not without some opposition, however. Forty-seven right-wing delegates, led by Kamenev and Rykov, opposed or abstained on Lenin's key formulation that the 'objective conditions for a socialist revolution ... had ripened with tremendous rapidity' and that the February Revolution had been 'only the initial stage of the first of the proletarian revolutions which would inevitably result from the war' (*KPSS v rezoliutsiiakh* 1, 452–5). Thirty-four left-wing delegates, led by Dzerzhinsky and G.L. Piatakov, disagreed with his view on the nationality question claiming that any recognition of the right to secession violated the basic principles of proletarian internationalism. On one issue, Lenin even found himself in a minority of one. While the delegates agreed that the Bolsheviks 'should take the initiative in setting up a Third International' and should 'break once and for all with the "defencists,"' they nevertheless refused his demand that they should also break with the Zimmerwald Bloc (*KPSS v rezoliutsiiakh* 1, 450–2).

Perhaps in recognition that some compromise was needed to hold together the various wings of his faction, Lenin uncharacteristically refrained from using his majority to dominate the new central institutions of the party. The nine-man Central Committee, which the Conference elected to replace the one named in 1912, contained five of his supporters (Lenin, Zinoviev, Stalin, Sverdlov, I.T. Smilga) and four so-called 'moderates' (Kamenev, Nogin, V.P. Miliutin, G.F. Fedorov), in addition to five less-significant candidate members.

1.152
On the War   **27 April 1917**

... As regards the most important question of how to end the present capitalistic war as quickly as possible, not by an imposed peace but by a truly democratic one, the Conference recognizes and resolves:

This war cannot be ended by a refusal of the soldiers of one side alone to continue it, by the simple cessation of military actions by one of the belligerents.

The Conference protests again and again against the base slander, disseminated by the capitalists against our party, to the effect that we are in favour of a separate peace with Germany. We consider the German capitalists just as rapacious as the Russian, English, French, and other capitalists, and Kaiser Wilhelm just as much a crowned brigand as Nicholas II or the English, Italian, Rumanian, and all other monarchs.

Our party will patiently but persistently explain to the people the truth that wars are waged by *governments*, that wars are always indissolubly linked with the policies of certain *classes*, that this war can be ended by a democratic peace *only* through the transfer of all state power, in at least several of the belligerent countries, into the hands of the proletarian and semi-proletarian class which is really capable of bringing to an end the oppressive rule of capital.

The revolutionary class, having taken state power into its own hands in Russia, would adopt a series of measures to undermine the economic rule of the capitalists as well as measures rendering them completely harmless politically, and would immediately and openly offer to all nations a democratic peace on the basis of a complete repudiation of all annexations and indemnities. These measures and this open offer of peace would cause the workers of the belligerent countries to have complete confidence in one another and would inevitably lead to uprisings of the proletariat against those imperialist governments which opposed the peace offer.

Until the revolutionary class in Russia has taken all state power into its own hands, our party will support in every way the proletarian parties and groups abroad which are in fact, during wartime, carrying on a revolutionary struggle against their own imperialist governments and their own bourgeoisie. In particular, the party will support the incipient mass fraternization of the soldiers of all belligerent countries at the front, striving to transform this spontaneous manifestation of the solidarity of the oppressed into a politically conscious movement – and one which is as well organized as possible – for the transfer of all governmental power in all belligerent countries into the hands of the revolutionary proletariat.

Pravda, no. 44 (29 April 1917), 1

1.153
On Uniting with the Internationalists against the Petty Bourgeois Defencist Bloc   29 April 1917

Considering:
1   that the parties of the Socialist Revolutionaries, the Menshevik Social Democrats, etc., have, in the great majority of cases, adopted a

position of 'revolutionary defencism,' that is, one of support for the imperialist war by voting for the loan [i.e., the 'Liberty Loan of 1917' approved by the Executive Committee on 7 April whereby the Provisional Government proposed offering 5 per cent bonds in order to raise money for national defence] and by supporting the Provisional Government which represents the interests of capital;

2   that these parties in all their policies advance the interests and the viewpoint of the petty bourgeoisie and pervert the proletariat with bourgeois influence by suggesting that the government's imperialist policy can be altered and that it can be diverted from the path of counter-revolutionary encroachments upon freedom by means of agreements with it, exercising 'control' over it, entering the cabinet, etc.;

3   that this policy encourages and reinforces the trusting unthought-out attitude of the masses toward the capitalists, even though such an attitude is the principal obstacle to the further development of the revolution and raises the possibility of its defeat by the counter-revolutionary forces of the bourgeoisie and the landowning nobility —

The Conference therefore resolves as follows:

1   unification with parties and groups pursuing this policy is absolutely impossible;

2   rapprochement and unification with groups and tendencies which really are internationalist [e.g., the Inter-District Committee] is necessary on the basis of a break with the policy of petty bourgeois betrayal of socialism.

Pravda, no. 46 (2 May 1917), 3

1.154
On the Attitude toward
the Provisional Government   27 April 1917

The All-Russian Conference of the RSDRP recognizes that:

1   the Provisional Government, by its [class] character, is the instrument of the rule of the landowning nobility and the bourgeoisie;

2   the Provisional Government and the classes which it represents are indissolubly tied, both economically and politically, to Russian and Anglo-French imperialism;

3   the Provisional Government is implementing its proclaimed programme only in part and only under pressure from the revolutionary proletariat and a section of the petty bourgeoisie;

4   the counter-revolutionary forces of the bourgeoisie and landowning nobility, which are in the process of being organized and which are hiding

behind the banner of the Provisional Government with the latter's obvious collaboration, have already launched the attack against revolutionary democracy: thus the Provisional Government is postponing the calling of elections to the Constituent Assembly, is hampering the general arming of the people, is opposing the transfer of all lands into the hands of the people and is imposing the landowner's method of resolving the agrarian question, is obstructing the introduction of the eight-hour working day, is conniving at counter-revolutionary agitation in the army (by [War Minister A.I.] Guchkov and Co.), is rallying the high-ranking officers against the soldiers, etc.;

5   while protecting the profits of the capitalists and landowners, the Provisional Government is incapable of adopting a number of revolutionary economic measures (with respect to the food supply, etc.) which are absolutely and urgently needed in view of the imminent economic catastrophe;

6   at the same time, this government is presently relying on the confidence of, and direct agreement with, the Petrograd Soviet of Workers' and Soldiers' Deputies which is still the leading organization for the majority of workers and soldiers, i.e., peasants;

7   each step by the Provisional Government, in both foreign and domestic affairs, will open the eyes of the urban and rural proletariat and semi-proletariat and will force the various strata of the petty bourgeoisie to adopt one political position or the other.

In the light of the foregoing, the Conference resolves as follows:

1   Extensive work must be done to develop the class consciousness of the proletariat and to unite the urban and rural proletariat against the vacillations of the petty bourgeoisie, for only this sort of work will guarantee the successful transfer of all state power into the hands of the Soviets of Workers' and Soldiers' Deputies or of other bodies which directly express the will of the majority of the people (organs of local self-government, the Constituent Assembly, etc.).

2   Such activity requires comprehensive work inside the Soviets of Workers' and Soldiers' Deputies, an increase in their number, a consolidation of their power, and a unification within them of our party's proletarian internationalist groups.

3   For the immediate consolidation and extension of the gains of the revolution on the local level it is necessary, by relying on the solid majority of the local population, to develop, to organize, and to reinforce in every way independent actions aimed at implementing liberties, sweeping out counter-revolutionary authorities, putting into effect such economic measures as control over production and distribution, etc.

4   The political crisis of 19-21 April created by the Provisional Government's Note [see 1.149-1.151] has demonstrated that the govern-

mental party of the Kadets, which as a matter of fact is organizing counter-revolutionary elements both in the army and in the streets, is now making attempts at shooting down the workers. Because of the unstable situation arising from dual power, such attempts are bound to be repeated. The party of the proletariat has the duty to tell the people as forcibly as possible that the proletariat must be organized, armed and allied in the closest manner with the revolutionary army, and that there must be an end to the policy of confidence in the Provisional Government so as to prevent the seriously impending danger of mass shootings of the proletariat such as took place in Paris during the June Days of 1848.

Pravda, no. 42 (27 April 1917), 1

1.155
On a Coalition Ministry   28 April 1917

... The party of the proletariat hereby declares that anyone, regardless of his good intentions, who joins a cabinet carrying on the imperialist war becomes an accomplice of the imperialist policy of the capitalists.

On these grounds the party of the proletariat opposes most resolutely the entrance of representatives of the Soviets of Workers' and Soldiers' Deputies into a coalition ministry [as suggested by the Provisional Government on 26 April but turned down by the Executive Committee by one vote two days later].

The party warns the people against attempts to focus the attention of the population on the question of replacing one person in the cabinet by another or one group of bourgeois politicians by another. Revolutionary social democracy contrasts the unprincipled struggle of parliamentary cliques with the struggle of classes and, in particular, with the question of a radical change in the entire policy of the Soviets of Workers' and Soldiers' Deputies and the transfer of all power to them.

Pravda, no. 44 (29 April 1917), 3

1.156
On the Soviets of Workers' and
Soldiers' Deputies   29 April 1917

Having discussed the reports and communications of comrades working in the Soviets of Workers' and Soldiers' Deputies in various parts of Russia, the Conference states that:

In many provincial areas the revolution is moving forward through the independent organization of Soviets by the proletariat and the peasantry, the spontaneous dismissal of old authorities, the creation of a proletarian and peasant militia, the transfer of all the land into the hands of the peasantry, the institution of worker control over the factories, the introduction of an eight-hour working day, the raising of wages, the maintenance of a steady flow of production, the establishment of worker supervision over food distribution, etc.

This growth in the breadth and depth of the revolution in the provinces is, on the one hand, the growth of a movement for the transfer of all power to the Soviets and for control over production by the workers and peasants themselves; on the other hand, it serves to guarantee the build-up, on an all-Russian scale, of forces for the second stage of the revolution – which must transfer all state power to the Soviets or to other bodies directly expressing the will of the majority of the people (organs of local self-government, the Constituent Assembly, etc.).

In the capitals and in certain large cities the task of transferring state power to the Soviets is particularly difficult and demands especially lengthy preparation of the proletarian forces. This is where the largest forces of the bourgeoisie are concentrated. Here the policy of compromise with the bourgeoisie is observed more strikingly, a policy which often hampers the revolutionary initiative of the masses and weakens their independence, a policy which is especially dangerous in view of the importance of these Soviets as leaders for the provinces.

Therefore, the proletarian party has the task, on the one hand, of giving comprehensive support to the above development of the revolution at the local level and, on the other, of fighting systematically within the Soviets (through propaganda and re-election of deputies) for the victory of the proletarian line. The party must direct all its efforts and all its attention toward the mass of workers and soldiers; toward separating the proletarian line from the petty bourgeois line, the internationalist line from the defencist, the revolutionary line from the opportunist; toward organizing and arming the workers; and toward preparing their forces for the next stage of the revolution.

The Conference states once again that what is needed is comprehensive work inside the Soviets of Workers' and Soldiers' Deputies, an increase in their number, a consolidation of their power, and a unification within them of our party's proletarian internationalist groups.

Pravda, no. 46 (2 May 1917), 3

1.157
On the Agrarian Question   28 April 1917

... The Conference resolves as follows:
1   The party of the proletariat will fight with all its strength for the immediate and complete confiscation of all landed estates in Russia (and also of all crown, church and state owned lands, etc., etc.).
2   The party decisively favours the immediate transfer of all lands to the peasantry organized in Soviets of Peasants' Deputies, or in other organs of local self-government elected on a completely democratic basis and completely independent of the landowning nobility and the bureaucracy.
3   The party of the proletariat demands the nationalization of all lands in the state; nationalization, which signifies the transfer of the right of ownership of all land into the hands of the state, places the right to administer the land in the hands of local democratic institutions.
4   The party must struggle resolutely against the Provisional Government which, through the mouth of [Minister of Agriculture A.I.] Shingarev and in its collective utterances, is imposing on the peasants 'voluntary agreements with the landowners' [concerning food supply, leaseholds on vacant land, etc., through agrarian conciliation chambers which the government announced it was setting up on 11 April] (i.e., actually, a landlord-type reform) and is threatening to punish the peasants for 'arbitrary actions' [taken before the Constituent Assembly] (i.e., a minority of the population – the landowners and the capitalists – is resorting to violence against the majority). The party must also struggle against the petty bourgeois vacillations of the majority of the narodniks and Menshevik Social Democrats who are advising the peasants not to seize all the land before the Constituent Assembly.
5   The party advises the peasants to take over the land in an organized manner, not allowing the slightest damage to property and taking care to increase production.
6   Agrarian reforms generally can be successful and lasting only if the whole state is fully democratized: i.e., after the abolition of the police, the standing army, and the privileged bureaucracy on the one hand, and after the creation of broad local self-government, entirely free of supervision and tutelage from above, on the other.
7   It is necessary to undertake immediately the separate and independent organization of the agrarian proletariat everywhere, both in the form of Soviets of Deputies of Agricultural Labourers (as well as special soviets of deputies of the semi-proletarian peasantry) and also in the form of proletarian groups or fractions in the general Soviets of Peasants' Deputies, in all bodies of local and municipal government, etc., etc.
8   The party must support the initiative of those peasant committees

which, in many localities of Russia, are handing over the livestock and implements of the landowning nobility to the peasants who are organized in these committees, for socially regulated use in the cultivation of all the land.

9   The party of the proletariat must advise the rural proletariat and semi-proletariat to endeavour to convert each landed estate into a fair-sized model farm which can be run on the public account by the Soviets of Deputies of Agricultural Labourers under the guidance of agronomists and using the best technological methods.

Pravda, no. 45 (30 April 1917), 1

1.158
On the Nationality Question   29 April 1917

The policy of national oppression, inherited from the autocracy and the monarchy, is maintained by the landowners, the capitalists, and the petty bourgeoisie in the interests of preserving their class privileges and of dividing the workers of different nationalities. Contemporary imperialism, intensifying the drive to subjugate weaker nations, is a new factor in the exacerbation of national oppression.

To the extent that such national oppression can be eliminated in a capitalistic society, it is possible only through a consistently democratic republican system and state administration which ensures the complete equality of all peoples and languages.

Every nation forming a part of Russia must be recognized as having the right to secede freely and to form an independent state. The denial of such a right or the failure to adopt measures guaranteeing its practical implementation is equivalent to maintaining a policy of aggrandizement or annexation. Only the proletariat's recognition of the right of nations to secede ensures complete solidarity of the workers of different nations and promotes a genuinely democratic rapprochement of nations.

The conflict which has recently arisen between Finland and the Russian Provisional Government [when the Finnish Diet asked for complete autonomy and the government replied that this must await the calling of the Constituent Assembly] shows in a particularly graphic way that denial of the right to free secession leads to a direct continuation of the policy of tsarism.

The question of the right of nations to free secession should not be confused with that of the expediency of the secession of one nation or another at any given moment. The party of the proletariat must decide the latter question quite independently in each individual case, from the standpoint of the interests of overall social development and of the proletarian class struggle for socialism.

The party demands broad regional autonomy, the abolition of supervision from above, the abolition of a compulsory official language, and the determination of boundaries of the self-governing and autonomous regions by the local population itself on the basis of its economic conditions, living conditions, national make-up of the population, etc.

The party of the proletariat resolutely rejects so-called 'national-cultural autonomy,' i.e., the removal of educational matters, etc., from state direction and their transfer to some sort of national diet [see 1.114]. National-cultural autonomy artificially divides the workers living in a given locality, and even working in the same factories, according to their various 'national cultures'; i.e., it strengthens the tie between the workers and the bourgeois culture of the particular nation, whereas the aim of social democracy is to strengthen the international culture of the world proletariat.

The party demands inclusion in the constitution of a fundamental law prohibiting any special privileges whatsoever for one nation and any infringement whatsoever on the rights of a national minority.

The interests of the working class demand the merging of the workers of all nationalities of Russia into unified proletarian organizations – political, trade union, co-operative-educational, etc. Only such an amalgamation of the workers of different nationalities into single organizations enables the proletariat to wage a victorious struggle against international capital and bourgeois nationalism.

Soldatskaia pravda, no. 13 (3 May 1917), 3

Petrogradskaia obshchegorodskaia i Vserossiiskaia konferentsii RSDRP(bol'shevikov) v aprele 1917 (Moscow, 1925), 156–69

KPSS v rezoliutsiiakh I, 437–57

All-Russian Conference of Menshevik and United Organizations of the RSDRP 7–12 May 1917

The Menshevik Conference which met in Petrograd during May 1917 stood in marked contrast to the Bolshevik April Conference. Rather than uniting the faction around one leader, the Conference resulted in a further polarization of the faction and in the virtual repudiation of Martov, its principal pre-war spokesman.

The meeting was attended by eighty-eight voting delegates, representing twenty-seven purely Menshevik organizations and an equal number of united local groups, and by thirty-five non-voting delegates. It claimed to speak in the name of 44,830 party members. 'The central problem of the whole Conference' and the one that was to prove 'fatal,' according to Sukhanov, was the entry of two leading Mensheviks (Tseretelli and M.I. Skobelev) into the first coalition cabinet on 5 May 1917. After a debate of only two or three hours, the delegates accepted the fait accompli by a 51 to 12 vote (with 8 abstentions) and called on all Social Democrats 'to render full and unconditional support to the new Provisional Government' (1.159). This, says Sukhanov, 'decided the fate of Menshevism in the revolution.' When Martov arrived back in Petrograd a day later, he immediately and bitterly attacked this decision as contrary to the Mensheviks' 1905 resolution to remain a 'party of extreme revolutionary opposition' (1.33) and as one that would make them responsible for the policies of an essentially bourgeois government. Martov also assailed the Conference's decision 'to promote in every way the strengthening of the army's combat readiness' (1.160) and announced that he and his fellow Menshevik Internationalists would not be bound by a policy of 'revolutionary defencism.' Nor would they sit on the new seventeen-member Organizational Committee (Akselrod, Ermolaev, Garvi, Krokhmal, Dan, Khinchuk, Isuv, Makadziub, B.I. Goldman, A.N. Smirnov, B.S. Tsetlin, F. Iudin, B.O. Bogdanov, O.A. Kogan, A.B. Romanov, S.M. Zaretskaia, S.O. Ezhov) which the Conference elected as its 'central guiding institution.' For his trouble, Martov was shouted down by the party that he had once led. Rather than leaving the Menshevik ranks or attempting to split the faction, as Lenin probably would have done, Martov chose to remain inside and to try to recapture control. By the time he succeeded, the October Revolution was lost.

Also in notable contrast to the Bolsheviks in April, the Mensheviks in May failed to come up with concrete proposals to attract either the peasantry or the national minorities. Attempts to arrive at a definitive agrarian programme bogged down in debate and as a result the Conference passed only a 'tactical resolution' which called for certain 'temporary adjustments in land tenure arrangements,' pending the convocation of the Constituent Assembly. Discussion of a formal nationality programme was deferred to the next party congress, but in this case even the suggested 'tactical resolution' was left undiscussed 'owing to a lack of time' and perhaps to the presence of irreconcilable differences within the faction. It might also be noted that while the Bolsheviks had more or less assumed that they now represented a separate political party, with possibilities for unification existing only with a few small groups of left-wing Menshevik intellectuals, the Menshevik Conference still held to the old illusion that broad party unity was both desirable and feasible.

1.159
On the Attitude toward
the Provisional Government
8 May 1917

1   In the process of a revolution that had touched off profound social conflicts, the [Provisional] Government set up during the first days of the revolution proved unable to cope with the disruption of the country's entire economy and the disorganization of its army caused by a protracted war. Incapable either of taking sufficiently energetic and revolutionary steps in the area of internal construction or, in particular, of consistently implementing a policy of peace in the field of international relations, it aroused the distrust of the broad democratic masses. Therefore, it did not have the absolute authority it needed.

2   The governmental crisis that resulted brought to the fore the question of creating a powerful revolutionary régime. This crisis could be resolved neither by a seizure of power by the Soviets of Workers' and Soldiers' Deputies, an action for which objective conditions were not ripe and that would have alienated important segments of bourgeois democracy and the peasantry from the revolution; nor by the setting up of a government responsible for the interests of the proletariat and the revolution without the participation of the Social Democrats in that government; nor by a transfer of power into the hands of bourgeois elements further to the right, which would have confronted the country with a threat of civil war.

3   Under these conditions, despite all the political dangers connected with the entry of socialists into a bourgeois government, a refusal by revolutionary social democracy to take an active part in the Provisional Government on the basis of a resolutely democratic platform in foreign and domestic affairs would have threatened the revolution with collapse and would have been contrary to the interests of the working class and of all revolutionary democracy.

4   The socialist entry into the government on a platform of an aggressive policy aimed at the earliest possible conclusion of a general peace based on democratic principles should prove to be a major factor in ending the war in the interests of international democracy.

5   Therefore, the Conference considers it necessary to render full and unconditional support to the new Provisional Government, which guarantees a stable policy aimed at realizing the demands of democracy within the country and in the field of international relations, and appeals to the working class and to party organizations to work actively and systemati-

cally to consolidate the power of the new revolutionary government both nationally and locally.

6   In assuming responsibility for the activities of party members who enter the government at the behest of the Soviet of Workers' and Soldiers' Deputies, the Conference considers it necessary that Social Democratic ministers be responsible not only to the Soviet, but also to the party in the person of its central institutions.

1.160
On the War   9 May 1917

... The Russian Social Democratic Labour Party, functioning in the context of a victorious revolution, recognizes:

1   that until such time as an end has been put to the war by the efforts of the international proletariat, all revolutionary democracy is obliged to promote in every way the strengthening of the army's combat readiness for the all-around defence of the front against the external dangers that threaten it;

2   that in fostering the defence of the country against the danger of a total military defeat, it is also necessary to promote a very extensive and energetic struggle for a general peace.

In this struggle, the Russian Social Democratic Labour Party sets itself the following, immediate tasks:

a   to weld the proletariat of Russia, which stands at the head of all revolutionary democracy, into an independent force capable of assuring the resolute and consistent conduct of the policy already announced by the Soviet of Workers' and Soldiers' Deputies and adopted by the Provisional Government [on 6 May] of seeking to conclude as quickly as possible a peace with no annexations or indemnities on the basis of national self-determination;

b   to appeal persistently to the proletariat of all belligerent countries to bring strong pressure to bear on their governments and parliaments so as to induce them to adhere to the programme of the Russian Provisional Government and thus make possible both a review of the treaties of alliance as well as the opening of peace talks;

c   to enlist in this struggle not just socialist, but all democratic organizations and sections of the population that have an interest in ending the war as quickly as possible;

d   to convene an international socialist congress and restore the [Socialist] International in order to unite and co-ordinate the efforts of the proletarians of all countries in the struggle for peace.

1.161
On Fraternization 9 May 1917

Noting that the wish to fraternize with the enemy, which has become apparent among widespread segments of the Russian revolutionary army, expresses the intense desire of democratic Russia for peace and brotherhood among nations – a desire that sometimes finds a response in enemy ranks – the Conference at the same time recognizes:

1   that fraternization can in no way serve as a means for attaining social democracy's goal of a general peace which can only be achieved by a systematic political struggle on the part of a united international proletariat;

2   that in the absence of a victorious revolutionary movement in Germany and Austria, and given the continuing unconditional subservience of the Austro-German army to its reactionary leaders, fraternization could lead, and in fact is leading to the disintegration of the Russian army and could expose it to the danger of a total defeat.

Therefore, the Conference opposes the preaching of fraternization as a method of struggle for peace and calls on soldiers of the revolutionary army to support energetically social democracy's struggle to unite proletarians of all countries as the only way to attain a general peace.

1.162
**On the Attitude toward the Soviets of Workers'
and Soldiers' Deputies** 10 or 11 May 1917

1   The revolutionary period, the period of the revolution's struggle for supremacy and for the consolidation of its gains, poses a two-fold task for social democracy: on the one hand, in order to carry the revolution forward, Social Democrats must act in the Soviets of Workers' and Soldiers' Deputies in a compact bloc with semi-socialist parties and even with parties that are only superficially socialist (the Popular Socialists, the Trudoviks) and carry with it the non-socialist masses in the name of purely democratic gains; on the other hand, it cannot and must not forget that it is a class party of the proletariat and as such must implement its own class policy and must ensure for itself maximum class independence during the revolutionary period.

2   Being the organ of self-government for broad segments of democracy which are largely undefined politically, the Soviets show a tendency – in their struggle against those segments that have remained outside the Soviets and against the political parties that represent them – to assume the role of some sort of a party of revolutionary democracy, substituting

themselves for the individual political parties that actually make up the Soviets.

3   For the sake of the entire subsequent political development of Russia, for the purpose of clarity and precision in the class struggle, as well as for the sake of asserting its independent class position, social democracy must fight against this tendency and eliminate the political practice of the Soviets deputizing for the party.

4   Specifically, during elections both to organs of local self-government and, in particular, to the Constituent Assembly, social democracy must in no case dissolve itself in a left bloc attached to the Soviets, but must take an independent stand wherever there is no counter-revolutionary danger; and even where such danger forces it to act in concert with the left bloc in election campaigns, social democracy should advance its own particular class line along with the common line of the bloc.

5   The implementation of this independent political line outside the Soviets must be matched by corresponding action inside the Soviets. Acting within the Soviets, social democracy must be organized as an independent fraction and must, in all its actions, be subject to the supervision and direction of an independently organized and independently operating Social Democratic Party.

1.163
On Labour Policy   10 or 11 May 1917

... As immediate tasks in the area of labour policy, the Conference sees:

a the elaboration, in close conjunction with worker organizations, of a well-conceived plan for comprehensive labour legislation to be implemented by the Constituent Assembly;

b the immediate promulgation of a decree on the complete freedom of association which is fundamental to the free class struggle of the proletariat;

c the immediate promulgation of decrees establishing the eight-hour working day, but permitting overtime work during the war with the concurrence of the workers' organizations; setting up institutions to establish minimum wages for the most poorly paid and most backward strata of workers; radically reorganizing the system of factory inspection to one of labour inspection with the participation of representatives elected by the workers and paid by the state; eliminating the most prominent shortcomings in the workers' insurance laws, pending the preparation of a general law on all aspects of social insurance and, in particular, on disability and unemployment insurance;

d the immediate adoption of measures to combat unemployment;

e the creation by decree of a number of socio-political institutions (labour exchanges, labour courts, conciliation boards);

f the immediate preparation of a plan for measures to be taken, in connection with the demobilization of the army and industry, so as to prevent or moderate imminent mass unemployment and the grave worsening of the labour situation by the possible intensification of economic dislocation during the reconversion of industry to peaceful production ...

1.164
On Agrarian Policy   12 May 1917

1   The Conference of the Russian Social Democratic Labour Party, adhering to the party's basic agrarian programme [1.51] until such time as it can be revised by a party congress, instructs the Organizational Committee to draw up a draft agrarian programme for presentation at the next party congress.

2   The Conference considers that land reform can be carried out only by the Constituent Assembly and that at the present time – pending the carrying out of such a reform – only temporary adjustments in land tenure arrangements are possible through the offices of local democratic institutions (land committees, food committees).

3   The Conference calls on all party workers to implant this idea in the consciousness of the peasant masses by means of verbal and written agitation and to combat energetically any anarchistic seizures of land or other arbitrary solutions of the question, explaining to the peasant masses that resolving the agrarian question by such methods can only lead to internecine strife within the ranks of the peasantry itself as well as paving the way for counter-revolution.

4   To facilitate the successful carrying out of land reform by the Constituent Assembly, the Conference considers it necessary for the Provisional Government to adopt immediately a decree forbidding all types of private transactions in land or timber without the permission of the land committees.

5   With a view toward adjusting land tenure in the interests of peasants and workers, pending the implementation of land reform by the Constituent Assembly, the Conference calls on [party] workers at the local level:

a to promote energetically the earliest possible formation of guberniia and uezd land committees [that would collect information needed for land reform, execute decisions of the Ministry of Agriculture and mediate local land disputes] in conformity with the recently adopted law [of 21 April], and to agitate energetically for the formation everywhere of volost land committees, the formation of which is left, under the law, at the discretion of local initiative;

b to set up Social Democratic fractions in these committees;

c to fight everywhere for the creation in these committees of a cohesive democratic majority and for [the selection of] class-conscious representatives from the peasantry and workers;

d to direct the activities of the land committees toward a compulsory regulation of leasing and hiring agreements in the interests of the peasants and workers, pending a final solution of the land question by the Constituent Assembly;

e to work energetically in the food committees to obtain the transfer by the committees of all lands not under crops (winter wheatfields) to the local peasantry to be worked by them, including provision for the temporary use of privately owned implements necessary for working the land.

1.165
On Party Unity   10 or 11 May 1917

1   The Russian Revolution, from its very outset, has revealed the gigantic ideological influence of the Social Democratic Party, establishing it – during the course of the revolution's subsequent development – at the head of the overall revolutionary movement.

2   The absence of an organizationally cohesive party was and is in sharp contradiction with the ideological influence of social democracy.

3   The solution of all the crucial political and social problems created by the revolution demands the political and organizational unity of the Social Democratic Party, a unity constructed on a general understanding of the tasks and tactics of the proletariat during the revolution.

4   The Conference recognizes that the tasks and tactics of the Social Democratic Party can be successfully ascertained only at a general congress of all sections of the party and, assuming that the decisions and positions taken by the party constitute a platform which is best able to unify all Social Democratic elements, therefore considers that at the present moment the only way to unify all sections of the party is to call a general party congress on the basis of recognition of the party Programme and Rules.

5   The Conference instructs the central guiding institution elected by it [i.e., the Organizational Committee] to make immediate contact with the Bolshevik Central Committee, proposing to it the formation of a special bureau to call a party congress; this bureau is to be made up of an equal number of representatives from both sections of the party and is to be impressed with the necessity of attracting to its ranks representatives from

Social Democratic organizations which are not associated with either the Organizational Committee or the Central Committee.

6   The Conference feels that only after exhausting all possibilities for agreement with the Central Committee concerning the calling of a party congress on the basis of recognizing the Programme and Rules of the party, should the central guiding organ form a special bureau for convoking a unification congress on the same basis by inviting to participate in this [latter] bureau the representatives of those Social Democratic organizations which recognize the necessity of calling a unification congress on the principles adopted by this Conference.

7   The Conference instructs the central guiding organ in this case to work out, in collaboration with the bureau for calling the congress, an appropriate manifesto to all party organizations.

8   The Conference expresses its firm conviction that the proposal of its elected central guiding organ to the Bolshevik Central Committee concerning the calling of a unification congress of the party will be received most sympathetically and will find broad support in all party organizations.

9   The Conference salutes all those Bolshevik and Menshevik organizations which have already unified at the local level and suggests that party organizations everywhere strive for unification.

Rabochaia gazeta, no. 51 (9 May 1917), 3; no. 52 (10 May 1917), 2–3; no. 54 (12 May 1917), 3; no. 55 (13 May 1917), 2

Central Committee on Worker Control of Industry 24 May 1917

The April Conference said very little about the Bolsheviks' proposed labour policy other than that the war had dislocated the economy and that there was a need for some kind of 'control over the production and distribution' of goods (1.154). The Mensheviks, however, produced a far more detailed plan for labour reform at their May Conference (1.163). This disparity, plus the forthcoming Conference of Shop Committees in Petrograd, probably induced Lenin to elaborate on the Bolsheviks' labour slogans. His chief conclusion was that there should be 'worker control' over all major enterprises rather than leaving them in the hands of their original capitalist owners or transferring supervision of them to the state. This control was to be

WORKER CONTROL   235

exercised primarily through the various 'shop committees' that had grown up in March 1917 and over which the Bolsheviks had very considerable influence. The resolution which incorporated these points was hastily written by Lenin, confirmed by the Central Committee on 24 May, and introduced by Zinoviev at the First Conference of Shop Committees on 30 May. The appeal of 'worker control' was obvious to the delegates who, on 3 June, approved a more coherent version of the Central Committee's resolution by a vote of 297 to 21 with 44 abstentions. The Conference also established a Central Council of Factory and Shop Committees which the Bolsheviks used to offset Menshevik control of the Petrograd Soviet and as a competing spokesman for the Petrograd proletariat.

1.166
On Measures to Cope with Economic Dislocation   24 May 1917

...

3   The only way to escape from an [economic] catastrophe is to establish genuine worker control over the production and distribution of goods. For such control it is necessary, in the first place, that the workers have a majority of not less than three-fourths of all votes in all key institutions and that the owners who have not fled and the technical and scientific personnel be obliged to participate; secondly, that factory and shop committees, central and local Soviets of Workers', Soldiers' and Peasant Deputies, and trade unions should have the right to participate in this control and should have at their disposal all commercial and banking books as well as all other available information; thirdly, that the same right be extended to the representatives of all the major democratic and socialist parties.
4   Worker control, which has already been recognized by the capitalists in a number of instances of conflict, should be immediately developed – through a series of carefully thought-out measures that are implemented gradually but without delay – into the complete regulation of the production and distribution of goods by the workers.
5   Worker control should also be extended on the same basis to all financial and banking operations with the aim of clarifying the entire financial situation and with the participation of councils and congresses of bank, syndicate, and other employees that are to be organized forthwith.
6   To save the country from [economic] catastrophe it is necessary first of all that by deeds rather than words the workers and peasants be instilled with full and absolute confidence that national and local governing institutions will transfer to the people the bulk of the profits, income, and property of the large banking, financial, commercial and industrial magnates of the capitalist economy. Without implementing this measure, it is impossible

either to demand or to expect that the workers and peasants will carry out genuinely revolutionary measures or will make a genuinely revolutionary effort.

7 In view of the complete disruption of the whole financial and monetary system and the impossibility of returning it to normal as long as the war continues, the goal of the state organization should be to organize on a broad regional scale, and subsequently on a country-wide scale, the exchange of agricultural tools, clothes, boots, and other goods for grain and other agricultural products. Urban and rural co-operatives are to be extensively involved in this exchange.

8 Only when these measures have been carried out will it be possible and necessary to introduce universal labour conscription. This measure, in turn, requires the establishment of a workers' militia, in which workers will serve without pay over and above their eight-hour working day, followed by the transition to a national people's militia in which workers and employees are paid by the capitalists. Only such a workers' militia, and the people's militia growing out of it, can and should implement universal labour conscription – not bureaucratically or in the interests of the capitalists, but in the interests of truly saving the people from [economic] catastrophe. And only such a militia can and should institute truly revolutionary discipline and obtain from all the people the supreme effort needed to avert a catastrophe. Only universal labour conscription is capable of bringing about maximum economy in the use of the national labour force.

9 Among the measures for saving the country from catastrophe, one of the main tasks must be the large-scale transfer of workers to the production of coal and raw materials and into transport services. Equally necessary is the gradual transfer of workers from military production to the manufacture of products needed to restore the economy.

10 The systematic and successful implementation of all these measures is possible only if the entire power of the state is transferred into the hands of the proletariat and the semi-proletariat.

Sotsial-demokrat, no. 64 (25 May 1917), 2

KPSS v rezoliutsiiakh I, 458–60

Central Committee on the June Demonstrations
9–10 June 1917

The non-demonstration of 10 June is one of the more curious episodes in the Russian Revolution. The idea for a joint demonstration by the workers and soldiers of Petrograd to coincide with the I All-Russian Congress of Soviets originated in the Bolsheviks' Military Organization on 1 June 1917. The Central Committee, however, was hesitant about the proposal: Stalin and Smilga favoured a show of Bolshevik force against the Provisional Government, Kamenev and Zinoviev feared a repetition of the April Crisis, while Lenin apparently approved of a 'political probing action' but not of an armed clash. The divided Committee sought more information on rank-and-file attitudes and more opinions from the party leadership. A subsequent meeting on 8 June of the Central Committee, the Petersburg Committee, the Military Organization, the Central Council of Factory and Shop Committees, and representatives of various Bolshevik trade unions and newspapers revealed that the mood of the Petrograd masses was indeed increasingly militant and that some kind of demonstration seemed inevitable. This meeting thus authorized, by a vote of 131 to 6 with 22 abstentions, the calling of a peaceful demonstration for the afternoon of 10 June. The next day posters and leaflets appeared in the working class districts listing the Bolshevik slogans (1.167).

On the evening of 9 June, Chkheidze informed the Congress of Soviets of a planned demonstration by armed military units under Bolshevik influence. Despite the fact that the march was to be peaceful and was perfectly legal, the Congress decided to ban all demonstrations for three days. This posed a dilemma for the Bolsheviks since they recognized the Soviets as the legitimate source of authority and feared an illegal demonstration might be used as a pretext for massive counter-action by right-wing forces. Lenin, moreover, still opposed premature and hastily organized moves against the Provisional Government as long as the Bolsheviks were a minority within the key Soviets. The Central Committee, after more hesitation and debate, agreed at 2 a.m. to call off the demonstration scheduled for that afternoon. The previous appeal, which was already typeset for *Pravda*'s morning edition, was withdrawn and replaced with a full front-page presentation of the cancellation resolution (1.168). The printers of the Military Organization's *Soldatskaia pravda* (Soldiers' Truth), however, doubting the authenticity of similar telephoned instructions, published several thousand copies of the original appeal to the understandable confusion of Bolshevik readers.

Despite the fact that no demonstrations took place on 10 June, not everybody was happy with the Central Committee's actions. Some local Bolshevik organizations passed resolutions condemning the cancellation and demonstratively returned their membership cards. The Congress of Soviets, while rejecting Tseretelli's plea to disarm the Bolsheviks as 'plotters against the revolution,' censored the planning of the march and approved Dan's suggestion for an 'official demonstration' that would show the unity of the revolutionary forces and the workers' acceptance of Soviet policies. Not surprisingly this gave the Bolsheviks a chance to recoup their losses, to re-issue their 9 June appeal, and to re-use the banners prepared for the tenth. On 18 June, 400,000 workers and soldiers marched peacefully and legally through the streets of Petrograd. In the resulting clash of slogans, the Bolsheviks' call for 'Down with the Ten Capitalist Ministers,' 'All Power to the Soviets,' and 'Bread, Peace, and Liberty' proved far more popular than the Soviets' appeal for revolutionary unity, support of the Provisional Government, and faith that the Constituent Assembly would ultimately bring reform.

1.167
Appeal to All Toilers, Workers, and Soldiers of Petrograd   9 June 1917

... COMRADES! Such things [as the continuation of the war, increased unemployment, food shortages, the threat of counter-revolution, and official restrictions on forms of public protest] can no longer be tolerated in silence! After all of this it would be criminal to be silent!

Protest is already beginning in the hearts of the workers.

We are free citizens, we have the right to protest, and we must avail ourselves of this right before it is too late.

We have the right to demonstrate peacefully. Let us demonstrate peacefully and make our needs and desires known!

Let the victorious banners unfurl today [i.e., 10 June] and put fear into the enemies of freedom and socialism!

Let our battle-cry, the battle-cry of the sons of revolution, spread today over all Russia to gladden all who are oppressed and enslaved!

Workers! Join the soldiers and support their just demands. Do you not remember how they supported you in the days of the revolution?

Into the streets, comrades!

Soldiers! Reach out your hands to the workers and support their just demands. The strength of the revolution lies in the union of the soldiers and the workers. Not one regiment, not one company, should remain in the barracks today!

Into the streets, comrades!

March in orderly ranks through the streets of the capital.

Calmly and confidently, as befits the strong, state your desires:

Down with the tsarist Duma!
Down with the State Council!
Down with the ten capitalist ministers!
All power to the All-Russian Soviet of Workers', Soldiers', and Peasants' Deputies!
Revise the 'Declaration of the Rights of Soldiers' [so as to remove the right of commanders to use force against insubordination and to appoint or dismiss officers without consulting soldiers' committees]!

Annul the 'orders' against soldiers and sailors!
Down with anarchy in industry and the lockout capitalists!
Long live [worker] control and organization in industry!
The war must be stopped! Let the Soviet of Deputies announce conditions for a just peace!
Neither a separate peace with [Kaiser] Wilhelm nor secret treaties with the French and English capitalists!
Bread! Peace! Liberty!

1.168
[On the Cancellation of the Planned Demonstration]   10 June 1917

In view of the fact that the Congress of Soviets of Workers' and Soldiers' Deputies together with the Executive Committee of the Soviet of Peasants' Deputies has resolved, after having recognized the very exceptional circumstances, to ban all demonstrations, even peaceful ones, for a period of three days:

The Central Committee of the Russian Social Democratic Labour Party resolves to cancel the demonstration it had scheduled for 2 p.m. on Saturday, [10 June].

The Central Committee calls on all party members and sympathizers to carry out this decision.

Soldatskaia pravda, no. 41
(10 June 1917), 1; *Pravda*, no. 78
(10 June 1917), 1

Revoliutsionnoe dvizhenie v Rossii v mae–iiune 1917 g.: Iiun'skaia demonstratsiia (Moscow, 1959), 494–5, 498

Central Committee on the July Days   3–6 July 1917

The pattern of events that occurred in April and June 1917 was repeated during the July Days but with more intensity and greater consequences. Once again the discontented and militant masses of Petrograd, responding to Bolshevik agitation, took to the streets only to find that the Central Committee was hesitant to put its theories into practice.

The immediate causes of the July Days were the Kerensky Offensive, which threatened to pull the garrison troops up to the front, and the resignation on 2 July of four Kadet ministers over concessions to the Ukraine. The next day, elements of the First Machine Gun Regiment, reacting no doubt to fear of front-line duty and to long-standing suggestions of the Bolshevik Military Organization, decided that the slogan 'All Power to the Soviets' ought to be implemented rather than acquiescing to yet another cabinet shuffle. By evening they had found numerous supporters from among the other regiments and the striking Putilov workers, many of whom started to besiege the Central Executive Committee at the Tauride Palace.

The soldiers not unnaturally sought leadership for their endeavours from the Central Committee. That body, however, was hesitant to sponsor the armed uprising which the agitation and planning of their own Military Organization had caused, especially in the absence of Lenin who was vacationing in Finland. Throughout 3 July they tried to restrain the demonstrators. But, faced with the growing hostility of their own followers and with the possibility that they might seek leadership elsewhere, the Central Committee around midnight reluctantly issued a leaflet calling for a 'peaceful and organized demonstration' in favour of a transfer of power to the Soviets (1.169).

The next day the size of the milling crowd grew to 400,000 and its militancy was enhanced by the arrival of the Kronstadt sailors. Many of the armed demonstrators gathered in front of the Tauride Palace trying to force the Soviet to take power against its wishes. Others engaged in random looting and occasional shooting which left several hundred dead. Both the Soviet and the Provisional Government appeared powerless on 4 July; power, in Lenin's words, was 'lying in the streets' but the Bolsheviks were afraid to pick it up. That evening many of the frustrated and tired demonstrators started drifting home as troops loyal to the government began arriving in the capital. The Central Committee, meeting in a second all-night session with the Petersburg Committee, the Military Organization, and the Inter-District Committee, once again reversed itself and called for an end to the demonstration (1.170).

Unlike during the April and June crises, this time the government, which was backed by the Soviet, decided to act resolutely against the Bolsheviks. Helped by some documents purporting to prove that Lenin was a German agent, orders were issued on the fifth and sixth for the closure of *Pravda*, the seizure of the Bolshevik headquarters, and the arrest of the party leaders. The 'semi-insurrection,' as Trotsky called the July Days, ended with Lenin and Zinoviev in hiding in Finland, Kamenev and Trotsky in jail, and Kerensky firmly in power as premier of the Provisional Government with a virtual mandate from the hapless Soviet to restore law and order.

1.169
Appeal to the Workers and Soldiers of Petrograd   4 July 1917

COMRADE WORKERS AND SOLDIERS OF PETROGRAD! Since the counter-revolutionary bourgeoisie has openly come out against the revolution, let the All-Russian Soviet of Workers', Soldiers', and Peasants' Deputies take all power into its own hands.

Such is the will of the revolutionary populace of Petrograd, which has the right, by means of a *peaceful* and *organized* demonstration, to make its will known to the Executive Committees of the All-Russian Soviet of Workers', Soldiers', and Peasants' Deputies now in session.

Long live the will of the revolutionary workers and the revolutionary soldiers!

Long live the power of the Soviets!

The coalition government has collapsed: it fell apart because it was incapable of carrying out the tasks for which it was created. Gigantic and most difficult problems confront the revolution. A new authority is needed which, together with the revolutionary proletariat, the revolutionary army and the revolutionary peasantry, will resolutely set about to consolidate and to extend the gains of the people. Such authority can only be that of the Soviets of Workers', Soldiers', and Peasants' Deputies.

Yesterday the revolutionary garrison of Petrograd and the workers demonstrated in favour of the slogan, 'All Power to the Soviets!' We call on this movement, which has broken out in the regiments and factories, to become a peaceful and organized expression of the will of all the workers, soldiers and peasants of Petrograd.

1.170
On the Demonstration 5 July 1917

COMRADES! On Monday [3 June] you came out into the streets. On Tuesday you decided to continue the demonstration. We called you to a *peaceful* demonstration yesterday. The object of this demonstration was to show to all the toiling and exploited masses the power of our slogans, their weight, their significance, and their necessity for the deliverance of the people from war, hunger, and destruction.

The object of the demonstration has been achieved. The slogans of the vanguard of the working class and the army have been put forth in an impressive and suitable manner. The scattered shots fired by counter-revolutionaries at the demonstrators could not disturb the general character of the demonstration.

Comrades! During the course of the present political crisis, our goal has been achieved. Therefore, we have resolved to end the demonstration. Let everyone discontinue the strike and the demonstration in a peaceful and organized fashion.

We will now await the further development of the crisis. We will continue to prepare our forces. Life is on our side; the course of events proves the correctness of our slogans.

Pravda, no. 99 (5 July 1917), 4

1.171
[On Accusations That Lenin Is a German Agent]   6 July 1917

An unheard-of accusation has been lodged against *Comrade Lenin* – that he received and is receiving money for his agitation from German sources. The newspapers have already publicized this monstrous slander. Underground leaflets are now being printed containing reference to [accusations by] the former [Social Democratic] deputy [to the II Duma] Aleksinsky [that a confessed German agent, Lt Yermolenko, had been told that Lenin was also a spy]. Appeals are now being heard to kill the Bolsheviks. Lists of persons to be exterminated are already in the hands of deceived soldiers.

The aim is clear: the counter-revolution wants to behead the revolution in the simplest way by sowing discord among the masses and by inciting them against their most popular leaders – the honoured fighters of the revolution.

We hereby declare that everything which has been said about monetary or other ties of Comrade Lenin with the ruling classes of Germany is a lie and a slander.

Aleksinsky, the initiator of this affair, is a notorious slanderer who has accused a whole series of persons of accepting bribes from the Germans. He has already been condemned for dishonourable acts by the Union of Russian, English, Italian, and Neutral Journalists in France; expelled for malicious slander by all democratic organizations in Paris; and barred from the Petrograd Soviet of Workers' and Soldiers' Deputies.

We demand that the Provisional Government and the Central Executive Committee of the Soviet of Workers' and Soldiers' Deputies make an immediate and public investigation of all the circumstances behind this base plot by the pogromists and hired slanderers against the honour and lives of the working-class leaders.

Full light must be cast upon this whole affair. And this investigation will convince all the people that there is not a single blemish on the revolutionary honour of Comrade Lenin.

To court with the slanderers and spreaders of slander! To the pillary with pogromists and liars!

Sotsial-demokrat, no. 102 (8 July 1917), 1

Revoliutsionnoe dvizhenie v Rossii v iiule 1917 g.: Iiul'skii krizis (Moscow, 1959), 17–18, 33–4, 148–9

Menshevik Organizational Committee 9 July 1917

The appraisal of the current situation made by the Menshevik Organizational Committee stands in marked contrast to the concurrent one of the Central Committee (1.173). Moreover, a comparison of the two positions reveals how far apart the two wings of Russian social democracy had grown since March 1917 (cf. 1.145, 1.146, 1.147, 1.148).

The July Days, which the Organizational Committee blamed solely on the Bolsheviks, frightened the Mensheviks, drove them further to the right, and consolidated their belief in evolutionary bourgeois democracy. They now equated the Bolsheviks with counter-revolutionaries and feared that their actions would cause the masses to turn on all socialists. They therefore dissociated themselves from their fellow Social Democrats and stopped seeking a panacea in party unity. The most interesting aspect of the Menshevik appraisal is its refutation of the various Bolshevik slogans: 'Bread, Peace, Land,' 'All Power to the Soviets,' and 'Down with the Capitalist Ministers.' While they effectively pointed out the contradictions in the Bolsheviks' platform and the dangers posed the revolution by war and economic dislocation, they nevertheless were in the dilemma of knowing what not to do but of being unable to tell their followers what to do other than to accept the status quo while awaiting the Constituent Assembly.

1.172
[On the Current Situation] 9 July 1917

COMRADES! The sad and dreadful events in Petrograd, which have in part spread into the provinces and to the front, should compel all of us to give deeper thought to the fate of the Russian Revolution and to the tasks of the working class.

What happened in Petrograd during the days of 3–5 July?

An armed demonstration of several regiments led by irresponsible agitators from the Bolshevik Party, and in some cases simply by certain suspicious individuals, brought part of the workers into the streets. Together they demanded in a threatening fashion the overthrow of the revolutionary Provisional Government and the transfer of all power into the hands of the Soviets of Workers', Soldiers', and Peasants' Deputies.

The Tauride Palace, where the Central Executive Committees of Workers', Soldiers', and Peasants' Deputies were in session, was besieged by [men armed with] bayonets and machine guns. Violence was used against some members of the Committees and even against Comrade Chernov [the Minister of Agriculture and leader of the Socialist Revolutionaries who was saved from possible lynching only by the intervention of Trotsky].

Groups of soldiers, joined by notorious spies and agents provocateurs, drove back and forth through the city in confiscated automobiles shooting at citizens with rifles and machine guns.

As a result, dozens were killed and hundreds wounded, enormous losses were suffered from the strike, stores and private apartments were looted, the hatred of the workers by the petty bourgeoisie was intensified, and the counter-revolutionary forces were alarmingly strengthened.

Those who used threats to demand the transfer of power to the Soviets showed that they did not respect these Soviets. The Bolsheviks and anarchists at first did everything possible to undermine confidence in the Soviets, refusing to recognize their decisions and fighting against them in every way, and then they demanded that these same Soviets seize all power in the country. Advancing the slogan 'Down with the Capitalist Ministers,' they actually incited the uninformed masses against the Soviets, which are supporting the Provisional Government, as well as against the socialist parties and their leaders ...

The Leninists promised the masses an early peace and bread, and the masses followed the Leninists. Now these same masses, disenchanted with the Leninists, may well turn their wrath against all socialists and begin to listen to those who in the same manner whisper all kinds of promises in their ears and lay the blame for all the ills and misfortunes at the door of the democratic parties, the Soviets, and the revolution.

The revolution is in danger, comrade workers. You started it, and you must save it, for there is no class to whom the liberties won by the revolution are as necessary, as essential, as to the working class.

What is the greatest threat to the revolution?

It is the war – the main cause and source of all the misfortunes we are experiencing.

But everyone in Russia agrees that it is impossible to end the war by a separate peace with Germany. Peace must be universal. Only such a peace will serve the common interests of all peoples. Therefore we should not seek peace, as the Leninists have been doing, either by calling for the repudiation of the [Kerensky] Offensive now in progress or by disorganizing the army. Their tactic was a direct stab in the back of those who are dying by the thousands on the battlefield, it has already led to grave military defeats, it will provoke mutual bitterness and fratricidal hatred among the soldiers at the front, it will bring about the disintegration of the revolutionary army and, perhaps, a new advance by [Field Marshal Paul von] Hindenburg.

No, now that the entire Russian democratic movement and the Russian government have come out in favour of peace on democratic principles, our incessant appeals must all be directed not to our army, which is fulfilling its difficult duty to the revolution and which we are obliged to assist as much as possible, but to the European democratic movement, to the workers of the Entente countries and to those fighting against us, so that ultimately they will force their governments to accept our peace conditions.

Not fraternization at the front, but fraternization of the proletariat of all countries at an international socialist conference and a common struggle for peace – this is what will end the war and toward this all of our efforts should be directed.

The second danger threatening the revolution is internal chaos, the disruption of the entire economy, the imminent famine, and unemployment. Will that seizure of power which the Leninists are proposing to us be of any help here? No, for no seizure of power will give bread to the people; on the contrary, it will only add to the general disintegration by provoking a panic, that is, an absurd senseless fear, a mutual suspicion and hatred.

And the slogan which many workers are following – 'All Power to the Soviets' – is a dangerous slogan. For the Soviets are supported by a minority of the population, and we must strive with all our strength to ensure that those bourgeois elements which are still able and willing to defend with us the gains of the revolution, will also help to shoulder the burdensome legacy of the old régime and the enormous responsibility for the fate of the revolution which we bear in the eyes of the nation ...

Therefore, rejecting the seizure of all power, we should in our economic struggle take into account the growing economic chaos and the bankruptcy of the state which is threatening the country. We must carefully weigh the demands which have been advanced and act, not in an uncoordinated fashion, but only at the direction of our trade unions so that the struggle with the industrialists will not turn into the destruction of industry.

Therefore, our immediate task is to assist the state in its struggle against economic chaos by the regulation and control of industry. You won't get bread just by criticizing and shouting 'Down with the Capitalists!'

Pressure must be exerted on the organs of power, but we ourselves must also display independence, initiative, and creativeness.

Therefore, our principal means of combatting [economic] chaos is organization – the rallying of everyone around their own organizations, around the Soviets, around their own delegates in the city dumas.

Finally, the third danger threatening our revolution and our liberty is the union of all the dark forces, of all the overt and covert counter-revolutionaries.

But the counter-revolution is strong only with mass support. Without such support the counter-revolutionaries do not present a danger to us. And to prevent the masses from succumbing to the agitation of the enemies of the people and of the revolution, unceasing educational and organizational work is needed.

Extensive and active participation in trade unions, educational societies, co-operatives, and especially in our Social Democratic Party, is both the best way to overcome the ignorance and lack of awareness in our own midst and the most reliable way to render the counter-revolution harmless.

We Menshevik Social Democrats have always warned you, comrade workers, against the ruinous tactics of the Leninists and the anarchists.

You have become convinced that we were right. Enter, then, into the ranks of our Menshevik organizations. Only as a large, well-organized, and powerful party shall we be able to save the country and lead it successfully to the Constituent Assembly.

Only then, in the Constituent Assembly which will decide the fate of Russia for many years to come, will the voice of the working class resound forcefully and loudly. On with the job, comrades! Everyone join the trade unions and our party!

Long live the Russian Social Democratic Labour Party!

Rabochaia gazeta, no. 102 (9 July 1917), 1–2

Expanded Meeting of the Central Committee   13–14 July 1917

In the aftermath of the July Days, those members of the Central Committee not in hiding or in jail met illegally in Petrograd to discuss the current situation with representatives of the Petersburg Committee, the Military Organization, the Moscow party groups and probably the Inter-District Committee. In the absence of Lenin, Zinoviev, and Kamenev, leadership of the meeting fell to Stalin and Sverdlov. The meeting is most notable for what it did not say and for its inability to give clear guidelines to the party during this difficult period. No concrete resolutions were passed other than to set a date for the forthcoming VI Congress and to confirm an earlier decision that Lenin was not to appear before a government court.

On the key question of relations with the Soviet, the Central Committee chose to sit on the fence by telling party members not to withdraw from the body but at the same time not to subordinate themselves to it. Unlike Lenin, who came to the conclusion that the 'peaceful development of the Russian Revolution was no longer possible' and that the slogan 'All Power to the

Soviet' should be replaced by 'All Power to the Revolutionary Proletariat,' this meeting apparently concluded that the correct path to power was still a peaceful one through the Soviet.

1.173
On the Current Situation

1   The spontaneous action of the worker and soldier masses in Petrograd on 3–5 July was caused by dissatisfaction with the Provisional Government which has followed a policy of agreement with the landowning nobility, the capitalists, and the foreign imperialists and for that reason has been absolutely unable to satisfy the urgent needs of the country. The departure of the Kadets from the cabinet [on 2 July], because they wanted to untie their hands for a counter-revolutionary coup, served as the external stimulus for the events which occurred.
2   Despite all attempts to prevent the impending spontaneous outburst, our party was confronted with the fait accompli. Being a mass party of the revolutionary proletariat, it had to intervene in the course of events so as to give the movement an organized and peaceful character.
3   Instead of meeting the mass movement halfway and trying to give it a degree of organization, the representatives of the Menshevik and Socialist Revolutionary parties (which hold the majority in the Soviet) used all their strength and authority against the Petrograd workers and soldiers, declared the latter's demonstration for the sovereignty of the Soviets to be an uprising against the Soviets, unmuzzled counter-revolutionary elements with the aim of crushing the internationalist wing of the proletariat, and added their voices to the chorus of the filthy yellow press.
4   Such a policy on the part of the Soviets and the Provisional Government accelerated and facilitated the mobilization of the forces of counter-revolution which, led politically by the so-called Kadet Party, is supported socially by the imperialist bourgeoisie and the landowning nobility and derives its military power from the top levels of the army high command.
5   The present government (the dictatorship of Kerensky [Premier and Minister of War], Tseretelli [Minister of the Interior and of Posts and Telegraphs], Efremov [Minister of Welfare after 23 July]) has a dual character: on the one hand, it represents the peasant petty bourgeoisie and a part of the workers which has not yet become disillusioned with the petty bourgeois democrats; on the other, it represents those sections of the bourgeoisie and the landowning nobility which are tied to Entente capital and are heading toward an imperialist counter-revolution. At present these governmental factions are bargaining, while the representatives of the petty bourgeoisie (both in the cabinet and in the Soviets) – by their coward-

liness, their betrayal of revolutionary principles, and their open treachery to the revolutionary proletariat – are steadily strengthening the position of classes which are hostile to the revolution.

6   The counter-revolution, which has become more brazen thanks to the connivance of the Mensheviks and Socialist Revolutionaries, is already moving from attacks on the Bolsheviks to attacks on the Soviets and on the parties of the Soviet majority. Anxious to rescue its positions from the onslaught of the counter-revolution, the petty bourgeoisie cannot bring itself to give battle but prefers to reach an agreement with this counter-revolution and to yield one position after the other. As a result, the proletariat has in fact been placed 'outside the law,' the role of the Soviets is declining, and the organs of revolutionary power are being replaced by institutions (a revived State Duma, the Moscow congress [i.e., the Moscow or State Conference which the Provisional Government announced on 12 July it was convening in mid-August for the purpose of effecting a 'rapprochement between the state power and all the organized forces in the country'], etc.) in which the decisive influence belongs to all the propertied groups which are under the hegemony of imperialism. On the other hand, by helping the counter-revolution (through repressive actions, arbitrary administrative measures, field courts-martial, persecuting the proletarian press, restoring the death penalty, and reviving the punitive articles of the tsarist criminal code), the Provisional Government will inevitably provoke a very powerful rebuff by the popular masses.

7   The so-called government for 'saving the revolution' is incapable of accomplishing a single one of the fundamental tasks of the revolution. Under the pressure of foreign capital it continues the policy of imperialist war pursued by previous governments which, as recently seen in the attempted offensive and in the complete absence of the promised struggle for peace, has already had ruinous consequences. In the economic and political realms, it is incapable of undertaking a single genuinely revolutionary measure to struggle against economic breakdown and counter-revolution. The crisis of this authority thus becomes inevitable.

8   Only a state authority which will be supported by the proletarian masses and the poorest strata of the peasantry and which will resolutely and firmly implement the programme of the workers, i.e., by taking decisive steps to end the war, breaking off any conciliation with the bourgeoisie, transferring the land to the peasants, establishing worker control over production and distribution, destroying all the bulwarks of the reaction, etc. – only such an authority will be viable.

9   Seeking the concentration of all power in the hands of the revolutionary proletarian and peasant Soviets, we maintain that this authority can carry out the tasks of the revolution only by implementing the above programme.

10   Under such conditions the proletarian party has the task of unmasking any counter-revolutionary measures, of criticizing relentlessly the reactionary policy of the petty bourgeois leaders, of strengthening the positions of the revolutionary proletariat and its party, of preparing its forces for the decisive struggle to implement the party Programme – if the course of the crisis permits – on a genuinely national scale. This period of preparation and building up forces requires that the party use all of its organizational opportunities.

11   In the process of the further development of the revolutionary proletarian movement and in view of the growing resistance of the bourgeois counter-revolution, the Russian proletariat will be increasingly confronted with purely socialist tasks, and the revolutionary struggle of the Russian workers will be very closely tied with the developing revolution in western Europe.

Rabochii i soldat, no. 1 (23 July 1917)   *KPSS v rezoliutsiiakh* 1, 480–2

VI Party Congress   26 July–3 August 1917

The VI Congress of the RSDRP, which was largely organized by Sverdlov and orchestrated by Stalin, met under difficult conditions. Not only were a half-dozen of the party's leaders in jail or like Lenin still in hiding, but fear of government suppression forced the Congress to meet in three different places in the working class districts of Petrograd and to rely on the dubious protection of armed Red Guards. And yet, the mood of the delegates was optimistic, even militant, despite the setbacks suffered in the aftermath of the July Days. There was a growing sense of strength in their own numbers: the 157 voting and 110 consulting delegates from 162 local organizations claimed to represent 176,750 party members. From their reports, Sverdlov concluded that the Bolshevik ranks had increased almost two and a half-fold since the April Conference, numbering now some 240,000 members. Much of this growth was in the provinces where the repercussions of the July Days were less severe than in Petrograd.

The Congress opened by sending warm greetings to the 'victims of counter-revolution' – Lenin, Trotsky, Zinoviev, Lunacharsky, Kamenev, A.M. Kollontai – and by debating at some length whether Lenin should return to face spy charges arising out of the July Days (see 1.171). Initially, he had agreed to do so but now he said he would answer only to the Constituent Assembly. Several delegates, however, felt that Lenin should surrender himself, if only to refute the charges and to use the resulting trial as a Russian 'Dreyfus Affair' so as to embarrass the government. Stalin apparently concurred, if certain guarantees for Lenin's safety could be obtained from the Soviet. It is interesting to note that N.I. Bukharin's resolution implicitly rejecting any trial, which the Congress ultimately adopted by a 'huge majority' (1.182), has been omitted from all editions of *KPSS v rezoliutsiiakh* since 1927.

Recognizing the possibility of premature closure, the delegates then decided to elect a new Central Committee before proceeding with the planned agenda. The size of the body was increased from fourteen to thirty-one: twenty-one of these were full members (Lenin, Kamenev, Zinoviev, Stalin, Sverdlov, Smilga, Nogin, Miliutin, Trotsky, Berzin, Bubnov, Bukharin, Dzerzhinsky, Kollontai, N.N. Krestinsky, Muranov, Rykov, F.A. Sergeev, Shaumian, G.I. Sokolnikov, Uritsky) and ten were candidates. Many of these new members were not proven Leninists: Trotsky and Uritsky, for instance, represented the Inter-District Committee whose four thousand members joined the Bolsheviks only at the time of the Congress; Dzerzhinsky, Bukharin and Madame Kollontai had remained noticeably outside of Lenin's close-knit circle before the war; Rykov and Sokolnikov reinforced the conciliatory wing of the Committee elected the previous April. It is perhaps for this reason that many members of this new and heterogeneous Central Committee played leading roles in the opposition movements that grew up after 1918.

In what would have been heresy five months earlier, almost all of the delegates agreed with Lenin that the proletarian revolution might take place in Russia before it occurred in the more advanced West (1.175). But they did not agree on what would happen after the seizure of power. Bukharin suggested that 'we will wage a holy war in the name of all the proletariat ... By such a revolutionary war we shall light the fire of world socialist revolution.' E.A. Preobrazhensky postulated that, without socialist revolution elsewhere, Russia would be unable to proceed with the building of socialism. While both of these amendments were turned down, they nevertheless foreshadowed the Brest-Litovsk and 'socialism in one country' debates that were to rage in the next decade. Another contentious issue was the temporary discarding of the Soviets as the Bolsheviks' vehicle to power (1.176), as Lenin had earlier demanded. More than a few of the delegates expressed qualms about losing the support of the peasantry or the party's non-marxian role inherent in espousing the 'dictatorship of the proletariat' rather than 'all power to the Soviets.'

It is curious that while the delegates had agreed on a seizure of power in theory, they did little to facilitate it in practice. One looks in vain through the resolutions of the VI Congress for clues as to the organizational machinery for the seizure of power or the tactics party members should use to achieve it.

Instead, much attention was given to the mechanics of the election campaign for the Constituent Assembly (1.179) and to the naming of Lenin, Zinoviev, Kollontai, and Lunacharsky as official candidates, even though there is no indication that the party viewed the Assembly as anything more than a convenient slogan. One of the Congress' more constructive pieces of legislation was to adopt new party Rules to replace those made obsolete by the revolution. Revision of the 1903 party Programme, however, which had been recommended by the April Conference, was postponed to a later extraordinary congress because of a lack of time, insufficient preparation, and perhaps the absence of the party's chief ideologue.

1.174
Rules of the Russian Social Democratic Labour Party 2 August 1917
[Replaces Rules adopted 1907 and revised 1912; see 1.62 and 1.94]

1   [Revises 1.62, art. 1] A member of the party is one who recognizes the party Programme, belongs to one of its organizations, submits to all party decisions, and pays membership dues.
2   [New] New members are accepted by local party organizations upon the recommendation of two party members and are approved at the next general meeting of members of the organization.
3   [New] Membership dues are set by the local organization at a rate of not less than one per cent of wages.
   New members pay an entrance fee of 50 kopeks.
Note Party members, who for no valid reason have not paid dues for three months, are considered to have left the organization, and the general meeting is to be so informed.
4   [New] The question of expelling a party member is resolved at the general meeting of the local organization of which he is a member. The decision of the general meeting may be appealed to a higher party institution, to the raion conference, or to the oblast conference (in the capital, to the city conference).
   The party congress is the highest [appellate] body.
Note Notice about the expulsion of party members is published in the party organs.
5   [As in 1.62, art. 2] All party organizations are built on the principles of democratic centralism.
[*Note* Included among 'party organizations' are 'party fractions in governmental, municipal, Soviet and other institutions' which are further obliged 'to subordinate themselves to all party decisions and to their respective leading party centres.']
6   [As in 1.62, art. 3] All organizations are autonomous with respect to

their internal activities. Every party organization has the right to issue party literature in its own name.

7   [New] Party organizations are consolidated at the raion and oblast levels. Raion and oblast committees are elected at raion and oblast conferences.

The boundaries of raions and oblasts are determined at raion conferences. In case of misunderstanding between adjacent oblasts, the question is submitted to the Central Committee.

8   [Revises 1.62, art. 4] New party organizations are approved by the oblast committee or in its absence, by the Central Committee. The Central Committee possesses supervisory power over such approvals. Each new organization is announced by the Central Committee in the party press.

9   [Revises 1.62, art. 6] All local organizations must assign to the Central Committee 10 per cent of all membership dues and other income which is not for some special purpose.

Note In localities where the organization is divided into raions and subraions, the raion or subraion committee is considered to be the local organization.

10   [Revises 1.62, art. 9, and 1.94, art. 9] The congress is the supreme organ of the party. Regular congresses are summoned annually. Extraordinary congresses are convoked by the Central Committee on its own initiative or at the demand of not less than one-third of the members represented at the last party congress. The convocation of a party congress and its agenda are announced not less than one and a half months before the congress. Extraordinary congresses are to be convoked within two months. A congress is considered valid if not less than one-half of all party members are represented at it.

Norms of representation at a party congress are established by the Central Committee in agreement with the oblast committees and take into account the principle of proportional representation.

11   [Revises 1.62, art. 9, paragraph 2] If the Central Committee does not call an extraordinary congress within the period set forth in article 10, the organizations demanding it have the right to form an Organizational Committee endowed with all the rights of the Central Committee with respect to convening the congress.

12   [New] A congress: *a* / hears and approves the reports of the Central Committee, the Auditing Commission, and other central institutions; *b* / reviews and amends the party Programme; *c* / establishes the party's tactical line on current issues; and *d* / elects the Central Committee and the Auditing Commission.

13   [Revises 1.62, art. 7] The Central Committee is elected annually at the congress. For current work, the Central Committee appoints certain of its members to serve as a subcommittee of the Central Committee. [Stalin,

Dzerzhinsky, Miliutin, Sverdlov, Muranov, Bubnov, Smilga, Sokolnikov, Uritsky, A.A. Ioffe, and Stasova were appointed to the subcommittee on 5 August.]

Plenary meetings of the Central Committee convene not less than once every two months. The Central Committee represents the party in relations with other parties and institutions; it organizes various party institutions and guides their activities; it appoints the editorial board of the Central Organ [see 1.183] which works under its supervision; it organizes and conducts undertakings of significance for the party as a whole; it allocates party funds and personnel, and has charge of the central party treasury.

Members leaving the Central Committee are replaced by candidates elected by the congress and in the order established by the congress.

14 [New] The Auditing Commission is elected annually at the party congress; it audits the treasury and all Central Committee undertakings and submits its report to the next party congress.

1.175
On the Current Situation and the War   2 August 1917

...

2   The most dangerous situation for the imperialists of all countries is the Russian Revolution – the first mass action which threatens to turn into a spontaneous mass action against the war and against imperialism and to involve the proletarian masses of other countries in this struggle. ...

8   The Soviet's campaign for peace by means of 'pressuring' the Entente governments and entering into agreements with social-imperialists, while in fact refusing to break with the imperialists, was bound to be a complete failure. This failure confirmed the correctness of the view of revolutionary social democracy that only a revolutionary mass struggle in all countries against imperialism, only an international proletarian revolution, can lead to a democratic peace.

9   The liquidation of imperialist rule sets before the working class of that country which first realizes the dictatorship of the proletariat and the semi-proletariat, the task of supporting by any means (including armed force) the struggling proletariat of the other countries. In particular, such a task stands before Russia if, as is likely, the new and unavoidable upsurge of the Russian Revolution brings to power the workers and the poorest peasants before revolution takes place in the capitalistic states of the West.

10   Therefore, the only effective way to liquidate the war democratically is for the international proletariat to seize power, and in Russia for the proletariat and the poorest peasants to seize power. Only these classes are

able to break with the capitalists of all countries and contribute in fact to the growth of the international proletarian revolution which must liquidate not only the war but capitalist servitude as well.

1.176
On the Political Situation   3 August 1917

...

6   At the present time state power [in Russia] is, in fact, in the hands of the counter-revolutionary bourgeoisie supported by the military clique. It is precisely this imperialist dictatorship which has carried out and is carrying out ... the destruction of political liberty, the coercion of the masses, and the ruthless persecution of the internationalist proletariat – while the central institution of the Soviets, the Central Executive Committee, remains totally impotent and inactive.

The Soviets, suffering in painful agony, are disintegrating as a result of the fact that they did not at the right time take all the power of the state into their own hands.

7   The slogan of transferring power to the Soviets, which was advanced during the initial upsurge of the revolution, and propagated by our party, was a slogan of the peaceful development of the revolution, of the painless transfer of power from the bourgeoisie to the workers and peasants, of the petty bourgeoisie's gradual overcoming of its illusions.

At the present time such peaceful development and painless transfer of power to the Soviets has become impossible, since power has in fact already passed into the hands of the counter-revolutionary bourgeoisie.

The correct slogan at the present time can only be the complete liquidation of the dictatorship of the counter-revolutionary bourgeoisie. Only the revolutionary proletariat, on the condition that it is supported by the poorest peasants, has the strength to carry out this task – which is the task of the new revolutionary resurgence.

8   The success of this upsurge depends upon whether or not the majority of the people become aware, sufficiently rapidly and firmly, of how disastrous are the hopes expressed and supported by the Socialist Revolutionary and Menshevik parties of conciliation with the bourgeoisie. These hopes are being proven unfounded with exceptional brutality by the course of events.

The party must take on itself the role of the foremost fighter against counter-revolution; it must defend energetically all the rights and liberties won; it must defend all mass organizations (the Soviets, the factory and shop committees, soldiers and peasants committees) and above all the Soviets of Workers', Soldiers', and Peasants' Deputies against counter-revolutionary encroachments; with all its might it must preserve and strengthen the positions in these organs won by the internationalist wing [of Russian social democracy]; it must struggle energetically for influence in these organs, welding around itself all elements which are coming over to the point of view of a constant struggle against counter-revolution.

9   The proletariat should not give in to provocation by the bourgeoisie which at the present moment would greatly love to challenge it to premature battle. It must devote all its efforts to organizing and preparing its forces for the moment when the national crisis and the broad upsurgence of the masses will create conditions favourable for the coming over of the town and village poor to the side of the workers, thus putting them against the bourgeoisie.

10   It will then be the task of these revolutionary classes to devote all efforts to taking state power into their own hands and to guiding the state, in alliance with the revolutionary proletariat of the advanced countries, toward peace and the socialist reconstruction of society.

1.177
On the Economic Situation   3 August 1917

...

5   The only way out of the critical [economic] situation is to terminate the war and to organize production, not for war, but for the reconstruction of everything that has been destroyed by it; not in the interests of a handful of financial oligarchs, but in the interests of the workers and poorest peasants.

Production in Russia can be regulated in this way only by an organization which is in the hands of the proletariat and semi-proletariat and which presupposes the transfer of state power into their hands as well. In this connection, it is necessary to carry out a number of decisive revolutionary measures.

6   It is necessary to intervene in production for the sake of the planned regulation of production and distribution, but it is also necessary to nationalize and centralize the banking institutions and to nationalize a number of syndicated enterprises (for example, oil refineries, coal mines, sugar refineries, metallurgical plants, and also transport).

7   A proper exchange of goods between the city and the countryside must be organized by relying on co-operatives and food committees in order to supply the cities with the necessary agricultural products and the villages with the necessary manufactured products, agricultural implements, machines, etc.

8   Genuine worker control must be established. A majority of the

members in the organs of control must be representatives of Soviets of Workers' Deputies, of trade unions, and of factory and shop committees. Technical and scientific personnel must also be involved in the organs of control.

9   Worker control must be developed, through gradually implemented measures, into the complete regulation of production.

10   Such control necessarily involves, as preliminary measures: the abolition of commercial secrecy – the books of merchants, industrialists, and bankers must be open for inspection. The concealment of documents must be declared punishable under criminal law. Reserves must be inventoried periodically and information on quantity of reserves and the enterprises possessing them should be broadly publicized.

In order to struggle against covert and overt lockouts, a law must be promulgated prohibiting the closure of factories or the curtailment of production without the permission of the Soviets of Workers' Deputies, the trade unions, and the Central [Council of] Factory and Shop Committees.

11   The following measures are necessary in the struggle against financial collapse: an immediate cessation of issuing paper money; a repudiation of government debts, both foreign and internal, with due regard, however, for the interests of small creditors; a transformation of the entire tax system through introduction of a property tax, a property gains tax, and high indirect taxes on luxury goods; a reform of the income tax and the establishment of property income assessment under effective national and local control.

12   Productivity must be increased through the proper distribution of the labour force: labour must be transferred from enterprises and branches of industry working on war production to enterprises and branches working for the needs of the country.

13   When all of these conditions have been met and power has been transferred into the hands of the proletariat and the semi-proletariat, it will be necessary to introduce universal labour conscription in order to ensure the correct distribution of labour and to increase production. Only under these conditions will universal labour conscription make possible the largest increase in productivity and not serve as a new technique for enslaving the workers.

14   It must be the task of the workers' organizations (the trade unions, factory and shop committees, Soviets of Workers' Deputies) to encourage the local implementation of such measures, to develop initiative in this direction, and to accelerate the general adoption of such steps on a national scale.

15   Adoption and implementation of all of these measures is possible only if the workers will make every possible effort – with the support of the poorest section of the peasantry – to implement them and to combat and

rebuff decisively the policy of the imperialist bourgeois régime and its counter-revolutionary pressure.

1.178
On the Party and the Trade Union Movement 3 August 1917

... The international socialist labour movement, as a result of many years' experience before the World War, came to the conclusion that true trade union neutrality in the political struggle was, in the first place, impossible; and in the second place, if it were feasible, it would be extremely harmful to the cause of socialism [cf. 1.57] ...

The All-Russian Congress of the RSDRP urges all party members working in trade union organizations:

1 To promote in every way the mobilization and the unification of the working class into trade unions.
2 To advocate the principle of the reciprocal representation in trade unions and the party; to implement this representation in the unions which already accept the revolutionary-internationalist viewpoint and to prepare for its implementation in the remaining trade unions through disciplined work in these unions by party fractions operating in close contact with the party organizations.
3 To influence unions to take the initiative in recreating an international trade union organization made up only of those unions which have refused and still refuse to support the imperialist war and which have not abandoned the class struggle.
4 The Congress insistently urges all party members to enter trade unions, and at the same time invites all class-conscious workers in the trade union movement to enter the party of the proletariat and to work in party organizations.

1.179
On the Electoral Campaign for the Constituent Assembly 3 August 1917

I CAMPAIGN ORGANS
1 The Central Committee will organize a Central Electoral Commission to which the oblast organizations will delegate their representatives. [On 6 August the Central Committee named Uritsky, Sokolnikov, and Stalin to this Commission and instructed Bolshevik groups in the Central Executive Committee and the trade unions, as well as national Social Democratic organizations, to send their representatives.]
2 Each oblast organization will set up an oblast electoral commission to which the local organizations will delegate their representatives.

3   At all lower levels of party associations and organizations, each such association or organization is urged to set up a similar local electoral commission for campaign activity under the guidance of the general [party] collective.

4   In the major industrial centres it is desirable that associations of fellow-countrymen be organized among the workers (and soldiers) for the same activity.

II FINANCING

5   Funds for the electoral campaign are to be made up as follows:
   a by organizing the deduction of a day's wages on one occasion only;
   b by collecting contributions (through collection boxes and subscriptions), by holding lectures, concerts, and soirees where admission is charged, by issuing one-day newspapers, etc.

6   The funds thus collected are to be distributed as follows:
   a 40 per cent to the Central Commission treasury;
   b 60 per cent to the local organizations.

III AGITATION

7   Written:
   a publication of a peasant newspaper;
   b issuance of pamphlets and leaflets setting forth in an easily understood form all of the basic slogans of our platform;
   c publication by the Central [Electoral] Commission of a handbook for agitators indicating the format and content of speeches and also listing the necessary literary sources. In addition, this handbook must set forth the basic provisions of the electoral law, its features, and campaign techniques.

8   Oral: oral agitation must be conducted by cadres of trained party workers. To this end, short-term courses for agitators must be organized through the Central [Electoral] Commission and at the local level; furthermore, during the campaign period class-conscious workers and soldiers should be sent out on a regular basis into the countryside.

IV BLOCS AND AGREEMENTS

9   Blocs may be formed only with parties supporting internationalism and which have broken, not in words but in deeds, with the defencists.

10   Agreements may also be made with non-party revolutionary organizations (for example, Soviets of [Workers' and Soldiers'] Deputies, land committees, committees of sowers, etc.) *which accept our platform completely.*

11   Electoral agreements must be sanctioned by the Central Committee.

V   LISTS OF CANDIDATES
12   Candidates are nominated by guberniia [party] conferences or by local organizations.
13   The Central Committee has the right to reject a candidate.
14   The Central Committee does not have the right to impose its candidates on local organizations.

VI   CAMPAIGN WORK IN THE ARMY AND AT THE FRONT
15   The Congress hereby expresses the hope that the Military Organization of the Central Committee will immediately start working out a plan for the party's election campaign in the army and especially at the front.

1.180
On Propaganda 2 August 1917

The growth of the party organization, which from the first days of the revolution has attracted broad masses of workers into its ranks, has confronted the party in an acute way with the question of the proper presentation of propaganda and agitation.

The flow of the intelligentsia out of the ranks of the proletarian party, which started in 1905, became massive after the February Revolution when the class content of our party's activities inevitably determined the attitude of non-proletarian elements to it.

In order to extend the consciousness of the masses which are united in our party and affiliated with it, and in order to consolidate the influence created by the political situation and the historical role of our organization, the [Congress] considers it essential constantly to clarify the Programme of our party through talks, courses, and lectures. In the present instance, special attention should be devoted to [workers'] clubs which play an important role in extending and deepening the understanding of our Programme.

In order to develop active party workers from among the proletarian intelligentsia, the [Congress] considers it necessary:
1   to establish party schools in which the workers could learn to operate independently;
2   to publish popular-scientific booklets from which workers could draw materials for speaking on the current situation and on sections of our Programme.

1.181
On Party Unification   3 August 1917

The split between the social patriots and the revolutionary internationalists in Russia – a split which has been confirmed on the international level as well – becomes deeper and deeper every day. The Mensheviks, who started with defencism, have ended with a most shameful alliance with the counter-revolutionary bourgeoisie, inspiring and sanctioning the persecution of internationalist organizations, the workers' press, etc., etc. Transformed into lackeys of Russian and Entente imperialism, they have ultimately joined the camp of the enemies of the proletariat.

Under such circumstances, the very first task of revolutionary social democracy is to persist in exposing to the broadest masses of workers the treacherous policy of the Menshevik-imperialists and their utter isolation from even the least revolutionary elements in the working class. Therefore, any attempt at reconciling the imperialist and revolutionary-internationalist elements of socialism by means of a 'unification congress' aimed at creating a single Social Democratic Party (the project of a group of free-floating intelligentsia centred around *Novaia zhizn* [New Life, a non-factional daily founded by Maxim Gorky which called a meeting on 18 June of Social Democratic delegates to the I Congress of Soviets to discuss the possibility of convening a 'unification congress'; see page 264]) constitutes a severe blow against the interests of the proletariat. Recognizing the necessity of a full and irrevocable split with the Menshevik-imperialists, the Congress expresses its most resolute opposition to any such attempts. In contrast to the dangerous slogan of 'Unity of Everyone,' social democracy advances the revolutionary class slogan – unity of all internationalists who have in fact broken with the Menshevik-imperialists. Believing such unity to be necessary and inevitable, the Congress summons all revolutionary elements of social democracy without delay to break organizational ties with the defencists and to join forces around the RSDRP.

1.182
On Comrade Lenin's Failure to Appear before the Court   27 July 1917

Considering that the techniques of police-Okhrana persecution now in practice and the activities of the procurator's office recall the customs of the Shcheglovitov régime [I.G. Shcheglovitov, arch-reactionary Minister of Justice from 1906 to 1916], as the Central Executive Committee of the Soviet of Workers' and Soldiers' Deputies admits; believing, furthermore, that in such conditions there is absolutely no guarantee not only of unprejudiced legal proceedings but even of the elementary safety of persons brought before the court; the Congress of the RSDRP hereby vehemently protests against the outrageous persecution of the leaders of the revolutionary proletariat by the procurator's office and the police spies, sends its warm greetings to Comrades Lenin, Zinoviev, Trotsky, and others, and hopes to see them again in the ranks of the party of the revolutionary proletariat.

Protokoly VI s''ezda RSDRP(b), 26 iiulia–3 avgusta 1917 g. (Moscow, 1919)

KPSS v rezoliutsiiakh I, 484–502; except for 1.182 which is in *VKP (b) v rezoliutsiiakh* I (3rd ed.; Moscow, 1927), 197

Central Committee on the Subordination of the Military Organization   4–16 August 1917

One factor complicating the Central Committee's attempts to control the mass demonstrations during June and July 1917 was the autonomy and militancy of the Bolshevik Military Organization. The Military Organization had been resurrected in late March by the Petersburg Committee to conduct agitation and propaganda among the garrison troops of the capital and the sailors of the Kronstadt naval base. In April it was made an auxiliary of the Central Committee and its scope broadened to include front line and reserve troops throughout the country. By the time the first All-Russian Conference of Military Organizations was held in June 1917, there were some 26,000 Social Democrats enrolled in party cells in over 60 military units. This same Conference established a Central Bureau of Military Organizations to coordinate the body's rapidly expanding activities and to publish its independent organ, *Soldatskaia pravda*.

The fact that the Military Organization existed parallel to the local party organizations, as well as having its own conferences, newspapers, and central executive, gave it an unusual degree of autonomy from the Central Committee. Moreover, because the military units were armed and had good reason to avoid going to the front, they tended to be more militant than the rank and file of the party. Under the enterprising and independent leadership of N.I. Podvoisky and V.I. Nevsky, the Military Organization pressured the Central Committee into reluctantly approving mass demonstrations on 10 and 18 June. Many delegates at its June Conference favoured the immediate overthrow of the Provisional Government at a time when the Central Committee was urging restraint and caution. There also is ample evidence that the July Days were the direct result of planning and agitation on the part of the

Military Organization, operating independently of and often at cross-purposes with the Central Committee.

It is not surprising, therefore, that some leading Bolsheviks blamed the Military Organization for causing the suppression of the party that followed the failure of the July Days and demanded its strict subordination to the Central Committee. There even was discussion at the VI Congress about disbanding the body but eventually the delegates accepted the recommendation of their military section that the Military Organization be allowed 'to guide the everyday work of the party in the military forces under the direct and constant supervision of the Central Committee.' The new Central Committee set out immediately to implement this decision. On 4 August it turned the Military Organization's newspaper *Rabochii i soldat* (which replaced *Soldatskaia pravda* after the latter was suppressed on 23 July and for a while was the party's only national newspaper) into the Central Organ of the party, took control of its publication funds, and prohibited a separate military publication (1.183). Despite the latter injunction, the Central Bureau on 13 August brought out a new newspaper, *Soldat* (The Soldier), which the Central Committee promptly tried to take over (1.184). When the Military Organization sought to discuss these matters with Stalin and Smilga, it was told that the terms were not negotiable. The Military Organization protested that these decisions 'clearly exceeded the rights of the Central Committee' and that Stalin's conduct was 'absolutely intolerable.' On 16 August the Central Committee relented on the publication of *Soldat* but reconfirmed that the Central Bureau could not exist 'as an independent political centre.' Dzerzhinsky and Sverdlov were instructed to oversee the actions of the Bureau and to ensure that its militancy and autonomy henceforth remained within bounds (1.185). Judging from Sverdlov's report (1.195), this subordination of the Military Organization was successful and indeed its members soon became the core of the new Military Revolutionary Committee and as such were instrumental in planning the October Revolution.

1.183
[On *Rabochii i soldat*]   4 August 1917

It is resolved:

[1]   that *Rabochii i soldat* is the organ of the Central Committee;

[2]   that the editorial board shall consist of three members [of the Central Committee – Stalin, Sokolnikov, Miliutin], plus a representative of the Military Organization, plus a representative of the Petersburg Committee [M.M. Volodarsky];

[3]   that for the time being neither the Central Committee nor the Military Organization will have a separate organ;

[4]   ... that the editorial board should follow the line of the Central Committee *undeviatingly* ...

[5] that all funds and expenses for *Rabochii i soldat* be consolidated in the Central Committee.

1.184
[On the Publication of *Soldat*] 13 August 1917

It was decided to change the name of *Soldat* to *Proletarii* and to transfer it to the Central Committee for conversion into the Central Organ. This resolution was passed because of doubts about the feasibility of publishing *Proletarii* on the 'Trud' Press; that is, for [purely] technical reasons. Stalin was instructed to carry out this decision.

On the question of terminating the affairs of *Rabochii i soldat* [which had been suppressed on 10 August], it was decided to demand a detailed accounting of all income and expenses [from the Military Organization] and to transfer the balance to the Central Committee's treasury.

1.185
[On the Central Bureau of Military Organizations] 16 August 1917

With respect to the [Central] Bureau [of Military Organizations], it was decided that the Bureau is an organization leading work among the soldiers. In this regard, it was resolved that according to the party Rules no independently led party organization can exist parallel with another party organization. This applies both to local and to all-Russian organizations. Therefore, the All-Russian Bureau of Military Organizations cannot be an independent political centre.

The desirability of publishing a soldiers' newspaper is recognized. *Soldat* is to remain just such a newspaper [see 1.184]. The Central Committee entrusts the publication of this newspaper to the present editorial board and hereby appoints to it a Central Committee member [Bubnov] with the right of veto. The Central Committee is empowered to appoint the editorial board. The Military Bureau may propose one or another editors for Central Committee approval. Sverdlov and Dzerzhinsky are appointed to negotiate with the Military Bureau and to establish proper relations between it and the Central Committee. They are also charged with temporarily supervising the editing of *Soldat*.

Protokoly tsentral'nogo komiteta
RSDRP(b): avgust 1917–fevral
1918 (Moscow, 1958), 4, 20, 22–3

Menshevik 'Unification' Congress   19–26 August 1917

The 'Unification' Congress of 1917 unified neither the Social Democratic Party nor its various non-Bolshevik components. Originally proposed in June by the *Novaia zhizn* group of left-wing Mensheviks, the actual calling of the Congress was taken over by the more orthodox Menshevik Organizational Committee. The Bolsheviks and their Inter-District allies, at the extreme left of the Social Democratic spectrum, boycotted the gathering; the 'social patriots' around Plekhanov, at the extreme right, were not invited. The result was a purely Menshevik Congress of 222 delegates from 146 organizations claiming to represent 193,172 Social Democrats. Unlike the Bolsheviks' nearly concurrent VI Congress, the Unification Congress in Petrograd attracted substantial representation from the various national minorities: thirty-nine delegates from the Caucasus, thirty-two from the Bund, etc. While the membership of the party had increased in absolute terms since May and was not notably inferior in relative terms to that of the Bolsheviks in August, the influence of menshevism as a political force in Russia was clearly on the wane. Throughout August their commanding position in the various Soviets was steadily eroded or the Soviets themselves lost their local authority. As Lenin had foreseen, as soon as the influential Menshevik leaders of the Petrograd Soviet joined the first coalition, they became responsible for the unpopular policies of the Provisional Government.

This trend might have been reversed had the Mensheviks at their Congress adopted new and dynamic policies or united in a firm and disciplined party organization. One of the principal reasons for their failure in October was that they achieved neither of these objectives in August. While explicitly recognizing that the policies of the Provisional Government had been unsuccessful, the Congress agreed to continue to support and participate in Kerensky's régime. The policies which the delegates sought to have the government implement with respect to the war and internal reconstruction were essentially the same policies the Menshevik Conference had advocated in May and which the government had either ignored, postponed, or diluted in the interim. On the key questions of land reform and nationality policy, the Congress like the earlier Conference found it expedient to pass no resolutions at all. If, as Israel Getzler has concluded, these decisions marked 'a decisive victory for Tseretelli,' then one would have to agree with Trotsky that 'Tseretelli's victory in the [Menshevik] party hastened the defeat of the party in the masses.'

Moreover, the divisions noticeable in the Menshevik ranks in May were even more pronounced in August. More than one-third of the delegates backed *Novaia zhizn* (the 'United Internationalists') or Martov (the Menshevik Internationalists) in opposing the Tseretelli-Dan majority. The debates were particularly bitter in discussing 'The Political Situation and the Tasks of the Party.' After defeating Martov's resolution demanding the recall of the Social Democratic ministers, the Congress agreed by a vote of 114 to 58 with 15 abstentions to remain within the second coalition. When the majority sought to rub salt in the minority's wounds by pushing through another resolution approving the work of the previous Menshevik ministers, the Internationalists demonstratively resigned from the Congress' presidium. In contrast to the Bolshevik concept of organization, the Menshevik version of democratic centralism encouraged this type of factional in-fighting. The Rules adopted by the Congress gave local organizations greater autonomy, made no mention of expulsion from the party, and allowed proportional representation in all party bodies. Thus, the new twenty-five-man Central Committee elected by the Congress had an orthodox majority (Akselrod, Tseretelli, Chkheidze, Dan, Liber, Khinchuk, Isuv, Ermolaev, Kolokolnikov, Iudin, Tsetlin, Garvi, Zaretskaia, B.I. Goldman, L.I. Goldman, A.N. Smirnov, A.I. Chkhenkeli) but allocated one-third of its seats to the Menshevik Internationalist opposition (Martov, Martynov, Abramovich, Rozhkov, Ezhov, S.I. Semkovsky, E.L. Broido, V.I. Iakhontov). The latter, who also received one-third of the eighteen candidate positions, stated openly that they reserved the right not to be bound by the decisions of the Committee. The United Internationalists went one step further in refusing to vote for or to sit on their own Central Committee and shortly after the Congress left the Menshevik ranks altogether.

1.186
On the Organization of the Party   24 August 1917

Taking into account the fact:
that each form of the workers' movement must have an autonomous organization structured in conformity with its own demands and needs;
that the unity of the workers' movement, which is necessary for the proletariat both in its day-to-day class struggle as well as in the struggle for its ultimate ideal, is expressed not in the subordination or in the absorption of one form of organization by another, but in close ideological and, under certain conditions, organizational ties between them;
and that the complete freedom of association won during the days of the revolution has made it possible to carry out a division of labour between the various forms of organizations;
 The Unification Congress of the Russian Social Democratic Labour Party therefore finds:
1   That the party organization must serve primarily as the political form of the movement.

2   That in structure it must be adapted to the existing forms of the state system in the country, which determine the conditions of the daily political struggle of the working class.

3   That it must be built on the principles of democratic centralism so as to use most systematically and expediently the organized forces of the proletariat both for the realization of its ultimate goal and for the operation of its bodies under present conditions.

Proceeding from these general considerations, the Rules of the party organization must be constructed on the following basis:

1   A member of the party is one who accepts the party Programme, submits to party decisions, and pays fixed dues to the party treasury.

2   The norm for amalgamating local party organizations is the electoral district.

3   The district organization specified in article 2 is divided into raion organizations, local conditions permitting.

4   Every member of the party belongs to a local organization and participates in party life as a member of that local organization.

5   The governing body of the district organization is the district party conference of delegates elected by all members of the district on the basis of norms established by the organization itself; its executive body is the district committee.

The principle of proportional representation applies during elections if it is demanded by not less than 20 per cent of those entitled to vote; the same principle applies to all elections.

6   District organizations can amalgamate at congresses and conferences into oblast [organizations] on such basis as they themselves establish.

7   The general party congress is the supreme organ of the party; delegates to the congress are elected by all party members and, wherever possible, by direct elections at the rate of one delegate per thousand members of the organization; organizations numbering between 500 and 1000 members are entitled to one delegate. Regular congresses are convened annually. Extraordinary party congresses are called, when necessary, by decision of the Central Committee of the party or by resolution of a general party conference adopted by a two-thirds majority.

8   General party conferences of representatives from oblast party organizations and from large organizations that are part of oblast organizations are convened not more than once every three months by decision of the Central Committee of the party on the basis of one delegate per 5000 members of the organization.

9   The congress elects a Central Committee made up of 25 persons; election is by absolute majority vote. The Central Committee appoints the editorial board of the Central Organ [*Rabochaia gazeta*]. The Central Committee is elected on the basis of proportional representation.

10   The resolutions of a congress and the directives of the Central Committee are binding on all organizations; local organizations are autonomous in their activities within the bounds of general party decisions.
11   The parliamentary fraction is autonomous in its activities and is answerable for them only to the congress and the conferences. Its relations with party executive bodies are formed on the basis of co-operating and concurring on work. The Soviet, Duma, and zemstvo fractions are autonomous in their activities; they receive overall guiding instructions on questions of general political importance from local party committees and are answerable for their activities to local [party] conferences.

ADDENDUM TO THE RESOLUTION ON PARTY ORGANIZATION
1   Local organizations of the Bund send representatives in proportion to the number of their members to all local RSDRP organizations which unite and direct local [party] work (i.e., all-city conferences, all-city committees, guberniia conferences and committees, etc.).
2   Decisions by the above-named institutions on questions that concern the entire proletariat of a given locality are adopted by a simple majority vote and are binding on all local organizations.
3   The Bund has its representatives in the Central Committee of the party.
4   The Bund is represented at general party conferences and at congresses in proportion to its membership.

1.187
On the Political Situation and the
Tasks of the Party   23 August 1917

1   The present situation of the revolution, in the circumstances of a protracted world war, is characterized by an extreme exacerbation of the external and internal crisis that threatens to undermine the very foundations of the country's existence and to ruin the revolutionary cause. The growing military defeat and the breakdown of all economic life threatens the country with disintegration, gives rise to grave internal complications, makes the crisis of revolutionary power appear chronic, and creates a fertile soil for increasing the danger of counter-revolution.
2   The revolution, having inherited the heavy legacy of tsarism which brought on the economic crisis, has as yet proven unable, in conditions of war and economic dislocation, to ensure full and rapid satisfaction of the people's vital needs. The resistance that the representatives of capital are putting up against the carrying out of the economic and financial reforms advanced by democracy exacerbates still further the economic crisis.

Among the masses of the people there is a growing undercurrent of dissatisfaction with the situation as it has evolved; one sees ever stronger attempts by individual groups to stand apart and fight for their own narrowly conceived interests, and against this background, differences are beginning to emerge among the various sections of labour democracy: between the peasantry and the working class, and between the bulk of the soldiers and the peasants and workers. These differences, which are being consciously exploited by counter-revolutionary forces to sow discord among democrats, are being further reinforced and fed by the growth of anarchistic and rebellious sentiments and methods of struggle on the part of various sections of democracy. All this creates confusion in the ranks of united democracy and a danger of isolation for the working class.

3   In addition, broad sections of the propertied classes show signs – particularly marked since the events of 3–5 July – of wanting order at all costs and are taking their lead from influential bourgeois circles that are conducting an irresponsible policy and are stubbornly resisting the democratic, revolutionary gains of the people. These circles, in league with the counter-revolution that is being organized, are attempting to utilize the country's military reverses and internal difficulties to set up a strong anti-democratic régime with the aim of destroying the democratic organizations in rear areas and at the front, and of reducing the popular masses, the proletariat, and the army to submissiveness. The influence of these irresponsible bourgeois circles that – for the sake of their own mercenary interests – are leading the country toward destruction and the collapse of its productive forces, can be nullified only through a resolute struggle against them by the combined forces of democracy and through constructive work in strengthening revolutionary Russia at the front and in the rear areas.

4   The confusion in the ranks of democracy and the irresponsible policy of influential bourgeois circles in connection with the country's overall situation have up to now rendered the revolutionary Provisional Government largely impotent and have put a brake on its constructive work in carrying out a democratic programme. Added to this have been mistakes and divergences from a resolute revolutionary and democratic line in the field of domestic and foreign policy on the part of the Provisional Government itself, which failed to show sufficient energy in the struggle against the counter-revolution and against the influences of irresponsible bourgeois circles, which permitted the use of repressive methods in the struggle against one of the democratic tendencies [i.e., the Bolsheviks], and which has been insufficiently consistent and resolute in basing its policies on the guidance of organized democracy.

5   Recognizing the dangerous and disastrous consequences of a policy of isolating the proletariat, which would inevitably lead to its defeat and to a complete and unquestionable destruction of the country and the revolu-

tion, the Social Democratic Party must rally round itself all the forces of the working class; it must combat harmful elements in its own midst, strengthen its own class organizations and, while conducting an independent class policy, it must at the same time unite and lead all the country's democratic forces so as to deliver a resolute rebuff to the counter-revolutionary forces and to resolve the basic task of the moment: the energetic defence of the country against the external danger and the intensified struggle for a general peace; and also to direct the government's activities along the path of the democratic foreign and domestic policy proclaimed in its 8 July platform [which promised to summon an allied peace conference in August, to hold elections to the Constituent Assembly on 17 September, to prepare sweeping agrarian changes, and to hasten reforms in local self-government, civil equality, and labour legislation] and toward the consolidation of complete sovereignty before the Constituent Assembly.

6 Since the time of the Moscow [State] Conference [12–15 August, see 1.173, sec. 6] – where [formerly] illegal revolutionary organizations joined side by side on a common platform with democratic organs of local self-government, trade unions, co-operatives and democratic national groups – there has existed a broader basis for conducting a firm and resolute democratic policy.

7 Only by adhering in all foreign policy statements to the principles proclaimed by the Russian Revolution and by applying all its force to the realization of those principles; only by carrying out decisive reforms in the areas of labour protection and the regulation of production, transport and distribution, as well as in the area of finance; only by directing its land policy in the interests of the working people and of providing the country with food; only by waging a ruthless struggle against any counter-revolutionary intrigues and plots whatsover, regardless of their source; and, finally, only by basing all its activities both in the rear areas as well as at the front on organized democracy, only by filling all responsible government posts with persons who are true to the revolution, and only by preparing energetically for the convening of the Constituent Assembly by the fixed date [28 November] and without the slightest additional delay [it had originally been scheduled for 'the middle of the summer' and then moved back to 30 September] – only in this way can the revolutionary Provisional Government create and strengthen the power of revolutionary Russia, protect the country from destruction and defeat, lead it to a democratic international peace, enlist in this cause all elements of the bourgeoisie that are capable of following a resolutely democratic policy which is the only course that can save the country, and assure itself of the firm support of the proletariat.

8 The representatives of the Social Democratic Party, with a view

toward a more energetic implementation of revolutionary and democratic policy, can participate in the coalition government only under these conditions.

1.188
On War and Peace 24 August 1917

1   The mighty champion of peace and of a rebirth of the people's freedom, the Russian Revolution, is threatened with ruin and destruction. The blows dealt by [Kaiser] Wilhelm's troops to the Russian revolutionary armies at the front, blows that fall directly and with full force on democratic Russia, are the most potent threat to the cause of general peace on the principles declared by Russian revolutionary democracy. On the day that the Russian Revolution falls under the onslaught of troops doing the will of German imperialism and under pressure from the Russian counter-revolution, the cause of general peace will be lost and the revival of the international proletariat will be set back many years. In this tragic hour, when democratic Russia is mustering her last forces to save the country, the Congress has not lost its conviction that the international proletariat will fulfil its socialist duty and will make the cause of our revolution its own cause by breaking with the policy of civil peace in the interests of the revolutionary struggle for peace. It is confident that the European proletariat, in recognition of its responsibility for the future of the international workers' movement, will courageously hurry to the aid of Russian revolutionary democracy in its struggle for a general peace and for the salvation of the republic, born in the torment of a world war, from destruction by the imperialist forces of Austria and Germany.

2   In accordance with our previously stated attitude toward war and peace [1.160], the Congress believes that in the present circumstances the only path to general peace on principles acceptable to democracy lies through the restoration of the unity of the international proletariat in order to make a concerted struggle for peace and through a most resolute defence of the Russian Revolution – that most powerful factor for peace – against external and internal destruction.

3   In summoning the proletarians of all countries to a persistent struggle for general peace – a peace without annexations or indemnities on the basis of national self-determination – and to an energetic resistance against imperialists of all countries, who are dragging out the war to the point of complete exhaustion of the peoples in the hope of imposing their will on the vanquished by force of arms, social democracy at the same time rejects the idea of a separate peace, which would deal a major blow to the unity of the international proletariat and would lead to the humiliation and enslavement

of free Russia to world imperialism and would, in actual fact, bring the people not peace but forced participation in the war on the side of the present enemy coalition.

4   In saluting the socialist parties who have agreed to participate [during September 1917] in the Stockholm [or Third Zimmerwald] Conference and in expressing its solidarity with all socialist parties and national minorities that are waging a relentless class struggle against imperialism, the Congress protests against the obstacles being placed in the way of the conference by the imperialist governments and expresses the firm conviction that through the efforts of the international proletariat, which will be able to ensure for itself the free expression of its will, all obstacles to the calling of the conference will be surmounted.

5   The heavy blow that has been dealt the revolutionary army by the German troops on the Riga front [Riga fell to the Germans on 21 August] reveals once again with full and terrifying clarity the danger that a complete military defeat would represent for the country and for the cause of peace. In their efforts to force Russia to conclude a separate peace and to ensure the triumph of military force over the international struggle of the proletariat, the German imperialists have launched their troops against Petrograd, the heart of the Russian Revolution, in order to kill with a single blow both the Russian democratic republic and the struggle of the international proletariat for universal peace. In such circumstances, the entire will of the Russian proletariat must be directed toward repulsing the enemy invasion and toward saving the country and the revolution. The Congress summons the socialist proletariat and all democrats at this decisive hour to rally more closely around the country's defence in order to ward off the fatal blow that is hanging over revolutionary Russia.

1.189
On Election Tactics and the Organization
of the Election Campaign   25 August 1917

I

1   The tasks of the party in the forthcoming elections to the Constituent Assembly are agitation, the polling of votes, the strengthening of our party organization, and the formation in the Constituent Assembly of a fraction that is strong both quantitatively and especially qualitatively.

To this end, the party is putting forward its own candidates in all electoral districts where there is a party organization, regardless of whether it has a chance of winning in that district.

2   In view of the fact that the first three tasks listed above are the most important, and that the desire to increase the number of deputies should not

play a decisive role for the party, the Unification Congress of the RSDRP considers it necessary to retain complete independence both in the electoral campaign and in proposing its own lists of candidates everywhere.

3   Only in places where local conditions make it absolutely necessary is it permissible to conclude agreements on electoral lists with socialist parties that belong to the [Socialist] International, and then only with the concurrence in each case of the Central Elections Committee.

But even in cases where such agreements have been concluded, party organizations retain their right to independence in the pre-election fight and to reject candidacies.

Moreover, while opposing the nomination of independent lists by non-party workers' organizations, the Social Democratic Party enters into agreements with them on support for party lists.

Finally, in the interests of utilizing the so-called electoral residue, the Congress recommends the combining of lists, which is permitted under the law, with all democratic parties up to and including the Trudoviks and the Popular Socialists, where such combination does not interfere with the independence of each party during the elections.

II

1   For the organization of the electoral campaign it is necessary to set up immediately guberniia and, where possible, uezd election committees, elected at conferences of the guberniia and uezd party organizations.

Groups of Social Democratic workers in local municipal, cooperative and trade union organizations should be invited to participate in the electoral campaign.

In places where there are no uezd organizations, the election campaign is to be run by representatives of the guberniia election committee.

The Central Elections Committee is to be in charge of the entire election campaign.

2   The tasks of the Central Elections Committee and of the local committees include: conducting of oral and written agitation, arranging of election gatherings, giving attention to all legal aspects of the elections, and collecting money for the election campaign.

With a view toward the most widespread use of written agitation, the Central Committee is publishing a number of popular leaflets on all questions of the election platform and is placing them at the disposal of local organizations for reprinting.

In order to put together the necessary contingent of travelling agitators, lecturers, and instructors for the elections, the Central Elections Committee and the local committees must immediately set up short-term courses on the elections to the Constituent Assembly. The Central Elections Committee will work out the general programme of the lectures and the practical training as well as providing, as far as possible, lecturers for the courses.

Finally, to create the necessary campaign fund, the Congress resolves that all members of the party shall donate one day's earnings, and also that there will be mass collections, lectures where admission is charged, etc.

3   The Central Committee of the party is assigned the job of drawing up and publishing the election platform.

4   The lists of candidates are drawn up by the guberniia conferences with the Central Committee reserving the right to reject local candidates.

Moreover, the Central Committee has the right to name a group of candidates whose election is regarded as necessary and important for the party. These candidates will be proposed by the local organizations, with their concurrence, so that they may occupy first place on the lists.

Rabochaia gazeta, no. 142 (25 August 1917), 3; no. 143 (26 August 1917), 3; no. 144 (27 August 1917), 2–3

Central Committee on the Korinilov Revolt 26–30 August 1917

In the course of 1917 General L.G. Kornilov had held posts as commander of the Petrograd garrison during the April Crisis, commander on the southwestern front during the Kerensky Offensive, and commander-in-chief after the July Days. He had won the reputation of being a man of action, a disciplinarian, and a champion of social order. Many conservative elements in Russia looked to him to save the country from anarchy, bolshevism, and misrule by the Provisional Government. Even Kerensky apparently thought that he might serve as a useful counterweight to the Soviets. In any case, the premier allowed his military commander to move his troops into position between Petrograd and Riga at a time when Kornilov was telling associates that he was merely waiting 'for a demonstration by the Bolsheviks to take place so as to deal with these traitors as they deserve.' He confidently expected that such a demonstration would take place on Sunday, 27 August, the half-year anniversary of the February Revolution.

Even though the capital was largely and unexpectedly tranquil, the 27th was the turning point of the abortive revolt. On that day the Kadet ministers withdrew from the Provisional Government, Kerensky relieved Kornilov when he learned that the latter planned to purge the Provisional Government as well as the Soviet, and Kornilov replied by ordering his troops to march on Petrograd. The helpless Kerensky could only turn to the Soviet for help. The Central Executive Committee responded by creating the Committee for the Struggle against Counter-Revolution which promptly began re-arming the Red Guard, releasing imprisoned revolutionaries, and sending agitators to deflect Kornilov's slowly advancing troops. By 1 September the 'revolt' was over and Kornilov under arrest.

The reaction of the Bolsheviks to these events is rather difficult to document since no records exist of Central Committee meetings between 23 and 30 August. From an appeal published on the 26th (1.190), it is evident that the party sought to avoid giving Kornilov a pretext to intervene. The party hierarchy also sought to keep its militant followers under strict control in order to avoid premature outbreaks of the type that had occurred in April and July. While Kornilov was successfully and bloodlessly repulsed, no effort was made to turn the masses against the Provisional Government. The Bolsheviks' attitude toward the Committee for the Struggle against Counter-Revolution was one of weary exploitation. While agreeing to participate (1.191), they refused to be bound by the decisions of a body in which they were in a decided minority. In a subsequent attempt to pre-date active Bolshevik opposition to Kornilov, some Soviet historians have claimed that the Central Committee's 'Appeal to All the Toilers, Workers and Soldiers of Petrograd' (1.193) came out as a leaflet on 27 August as well as on the pages of *Rabochii* three days later. This, however, is inconsistent with internal evidence and with the tone of other proclamations. The Bolsheviks, nevertheless, were the most active and efficient of the forces opposing Kornilov and, as a result of the failure of the revolt, they regained with interest the prestige and influence lost in July. Lenin's evaluation of the political situation had been proven correct, his followers were now armed, his lieutenants were freed, and his chief enemy – the Provisional Government – was discredited by its impotency and isolated from the moderate right as well as the extreme left.

1.190
[Appeal Not to Yield to Provocation]   26 August 1917

Suspicious individuals, supposedly speaking in the name of our party, are spreading rumours about a demonstration being prepared for Sunday [27 August] and are conducting provocative agitation.

The Central Committee of the RSDRP urges workers and soldiers not to yield to provocative calls for a demonstration and to maintain complete self-restraint and calm.

Rabochii, no. 2 (26 August 1917), 1

1.191
[Telegram to Local Party Organizations] 28 August 1917

In order to repulse the counter-revolution, we are exchanging information and collaborating technically with the Soviet [through the Committee for the Struggle against Counter-Revolution], while maintaining a completely independent political line.

The meaning of events [so far is that] the conciliatory policy has completely collapsed; in order to save the revolution, power must be organized on the basis of a complete break with the bourgeoisie.

1.192
[On Activities in the Committee
for the Struggle against Counter-Revolution] 30 August 1917

It was decided to conduct a campaign everywhere for meetings that would pass resolutions demanding the release of those arrested in connection with the events of 3–5 July and the return to their posts of the persecuted leaders of the working class – Lenin, Zinoviev, and the others. Members of the Central Committee who are also in the Committee for the Struggle against Counter-Revolution have the duty of raising there as well the question of the persecution [of Bolshevik leaders] for the events of 3–5 July. In this connection, the question was raised of walking out of the Committee for the Struggle. But the decision to walk out was not adopted. In general, this decision may only be taken [if adverse decisions are reached in the Committee] on the questions of arming the workers and of power.

1.193
Appeal to All the Toilers, Workers, and Soldiers
of Petrograd 30 August 1917

The counter-revolution is advancing against Petrograd. That betrayer of the revolution and enemy of the people, Kornilov, is leading troops he has duped against Petrograd. The entire bourgeoisie, headed by the Kadet Party which has been incessantly sowing slander against the workers and soldiers, now welcomes the traitor and betrayer and is ready to applaud with all its heart when Kornilov reddens the streets of Petrograd with the blood of the workers and revolutionary soldiers, when with the hands of the benighted people he has duped he crushes the revolution of the workers, peasants, and soldiers. To make it easier for Kornilov to shoot down the proletariat, the bourgeoisie has concocted the idea that a workers' uprising has supposedly triumphed in Petrograd. Now you see that the rebellion is not by the workers but by the bourgeoisie and the generals headed by Kornilov. The triumph of Kornilov would mean the destruction of liberty, the loss of land, the triumph and unlimited power of landlord over the peasant, the capitalist over the worker, the general over the soldier.

The Provisional Government collapsed with the very first move of Kornilov's counter-revolution. This government, in which a part of democracy has repeatedly expressed its confidence and to which it entrusted absolute power, turned out to be unable to fulfil its first and immediate task: to uproot the counter-revolution of the generals and the bourgeoisie. Attempts to reach agreement with the bourgeoisie have weakened democracy, aroused the appetite of the bourgeoisie, and emboldened it to resolve on an open revolt against the revolution, against the people.

The salvation of the people, the salvation of the revolution, is in the revolutionary energy of the masses of proletarians and soldiers themselves. We can rely only on their strength, their discipline, their organization. We entrust the leadership of the decisive struggle for the salvation of the whole revolution, its achievements and its future to that power which will unconditionally, whole-heartedly, and exclusively undertake to implement the demands of the proletarian and peasant-soldier masses. Only this power will save the revolution, save it from the counter-revolutionary attack, save it in spite of the waverings, shakiness, and lack of character of the vacillating part of democracy.

PEOPLE OF PETROGRAD! We call you to the most decisive struggle against the counter-revolution! Behind Petrograd stands all revolutionary Russia!

SOLDIERS! In the name of the revolution – forward against General Kornilov!

WORKERS! In serried ranks guard the city of revolution against the onslaughts of the bourgeois counter-revolution!

SOLDIERS AND WORKERS! In fraternal alliance, cemented by the blood of the February days, show the Kornilovs that it is not they who will crush the revolution but the revolution that will overwhelm and sweep from the earth attempts at bourgeois counter-revolution.

In the name of the interests of the revolution, in the name of proletarian and peasant power in liberated Russia and throughout the world – as a united family, in closed ranks, hand in hand, all as one, meet the enemy of the people, the betrayer of the revolution, the assassin of liberty!

You were capable of overthrowing tsarism – show that you will not stand for the rule by that henchman of the landowners and the bourgeoisie – Kornilov.

Rabochii, no. 8 (30 August 1917), 1

Revoliutsionnoe dvizhenie v Rossii v avguste 1917 g.: Razgrom kornilovskogo miatezha (Moscow, 1959), 85–6, 473–5, 497

Central Committee on Preparations for the October Revolution 31 August–24 October 1917

The Bolshevik recovery from the July Days became evident on 1 September when the Central Committee's draft resolution 'On Power' (1.194), blaming the Provisional Government for the Kornilov debacle, was passed by the Petrograd Soviet 279 to 115 with 51 abstentions. To Lenin, who was still in hiding in Finland, this change in the political balance meant that the pre-July slogan 'All Power to the Soviets' was once again valid and that 'armed insurrection in Petrograd and Moscow must now be placed on the order of the day.' These momentous decisions should have been discussed and approved by another party congress or at least by a broadly representative conference. But because of the hostility of the government, the illegality of the measures advocated, and a division of opinion within the party hierarchy itself, implementation of these commands was left to the Central Committee. The Committee met semi-conspiratorially nineteen times during the eight weeks preceding the October Revolution. Attendance records, which are available for seventeen of these meetings, indicate that twenty-four Central Committee members attended at least one session: Sverdlov was at all of them; Uritsky, Dzerzhinsky, Bubnov, Sokolnikov, Ioffe, and Trotsky made at least twelve; Stalin curiously attended only ten, Zinoviev four, and Lenin two. The records of these meetings are fragmentary at best. Outside of several well-publicized resolutions (1.194, 1.203, 1.208, 1.210), there exist only the incomplete and telegraphic protocols published in 1958. Three salient facts emerge from these notes: the opposition of the Central Committee to much of Lenin's wishes, its failure to agree on a date for the revolution, and its total silence on how this seizure of power was to be implemented.

On 15 September Lenin's two letters calling for armed insurrection were read 'with bewilderment,' according to Bukharin. After deciding to burn all but one copy of each, the Central Committee members with the July Days still fresh in their minds decreed that 'no demonstrations whatsoever' were to occur in the capital (1.197). Moreover, contrary to Lenin's wishes, they decided later in September to participate in both the Democratic Conference (1.198) and the Pre-Parliament (1.201 and 1.203), by which the more moderate elements were attempting to shore up the régime, and to reject Lenin's suggestion that the Bolshevik delegates at the Democratic Conference should constitute themselves as a party congress which would 'decide the fate of the revolution.' Lenin was beside himself. On 22 September he wrote that 'at the top of our party we note vacillations that may become ruinous' and a week later, in an effort to force the Central Committee's hand, he threatened to resign and to take his case to the rank and file of the party. The Committee's response was to summon him back to Petrograd (1.206). Clean-shaven, wearing a wig and glasses, and looking ten years younger, Lenin arrived on the 7th and on the 10th attended the historic all-night session in Sukhanov's apartment which finally approved in principle by a vote of 10 to 2 his call for insurrection (1.208). Six days later he attended a second and larger meeting with representatives of the Central Committee, the Petersburg Committee, the Petrograd Soviet, and the Military Organization which confirmed the 10 October resolution (1.210), this time by a vote of 12 to 2 with 4 abstentions. In each instance, the negative votes were cast by Zinoviev and Kamenev who on 11 October circulated privately a statement criticizing the Central Committee decision. On the 17th, a Menshevik journalist cited their statement when attacking the rumoured Bolshevik coup; this in turn led Kamenev to state openly on the pages of *Novaia zhizn* the reasons for his opposition. Lenin, who spent the week before the dénouement of the Provisional Government secluded in Madame Fofanova's apartment, concentrated his energies not on planning the long-sought revolution but on denouncing Kamenev and Zinoviev for 'strike-breaking' and demanding that they be expelled from the party. It is perhaps indicative that this demand was rejected by the Central Committee and also that the renegades' staunchest defender was Stalin (see 1.212).

On the question of when the insurrection was to occur, the Central Committee also dragged its feet. As early as 27 September Lenin had urged that power be seized before the convocation of the II Congress of Soviets scheduled for 20 October. At the meeting of 10 October, he advocated immediate action in opposition to Zinoviev and Kamenev who wanted to wait until after the Congress of Soviets and perhaps the Constituent Assembly. Trotsky apparently favoured the action to coincide with the II Congress. In any case, none of the anticipated moves took place in the six days after the meeting in Sukhanov's apartment and on the 16th the Central Committee merely noted that it or the Soviet would 'at the proper time indicate the favourable moment.' It did, however, reject by a vote of 15 to 6 with 3 abstentions Zinoviev's resolution expressly prohibiting insurrectionary activity before the II Congress, whose convocation had been pushed back to the 25th in light of rumours concerning the Bolshevik coup. There is no evidence in the protocols to support John Reed's contention that the Central Committee approved on 21 October Lenin's timetable purporting to call for revolution on the 25th.

The protocols of the Central Committee are equally uninstructive on the question of how power was to be seized. The two resolutions calling for an armed uprising say nothing about tactics. The Committee did indeed spend much of its time creating a number of co-ordinating bodies (1.207, 1.209, 1.211), which conceivably could have planned an insurrection, but which apparently never functioned. On the 20th it gave its support to the Military Revolutionary Committee of the Petrograd Soviet (1.213) which met for the first time the next day and, according to Soviet historiography, produced a revolution four days later. During the week preceding the fall of the Provisional Government, the Central Committee itself seemed more concerned with heading off the government's anticipated counter-moves than with planning aggressive action of its own. The postponement of the II Congress, suspicious troop movements, and cabinet changes led the Committee to fear a 'second Kornilov' plot. Its deliberations on the 24th were almost entirely defensive in character: protection of the party press, of the Smolny Institute, of its own membership (1.216, 1.217); and arrangements for an auxiliary headquarters should Smolny be taken over by the government (1.218). Initial moves by the Military Revolutionary Committee were in the same direction; that is, to protect the bridges, to restore telephone services, and to forestall government actions which to everyone's surprise were slow in coming and ineffectual in implementation. When Lenin finally emerged from hiding and made his way on foot to Smolny on the night of 24 October, it took only a little firm leadership to turn his 'preventive insurrection' into the 'Great October Socialist Revolution.'

1.194
On Power   31 August 1917

Confronted with the counter-revolutionary revolt of General Kornilov, which was prepared and supported by the parties and groups (headed by the Kadet Party) whose representatives are to be found in the Provisional Government, the [Central Committee] considers that it is duty-bound to proclaim that henceforth any vacillation in the organization of power must be resolutely curtailed. Not only must the representatives of the Kadet

Party, who were openly involved in the revolt, and the representatives of the propertied elements in general be removed from power, but there must also be a radical change in the whole policy of conciliation and irresponsibility which gave rise to the very possibility of converting the high command and the apparatus of the state power into a locus and an instrument of the plot against the revolution.

Neither the exclusive powers of the Provisional Government nor its irresponsibility may be tolerated further. The only way out is to create a régime, consisting of representatives of the revolutionary proletariat and the peasantry, whose actions will be based on the following:

1   The decreeing of a democratic republic. [This was done on 27 September].
2   The immediate abolition, without compensation, of the holdings of the landowning nobility and the transfer of this land to peasant committees for management until a decision is taken by the Constituent Assembly, making sure that the poorest peasants are provided with stock and equipment.
3   The institution at the state level of worker control over production and distribution. The nationalization of the most important branches of industry, such as oil refineries, coal mines, metallurgical works; the ruthless taxation of big capital and property holdings and the confiscation of war profits, in order to save the country from economic collapse.
4   A declaration that secret treaties are null and void and the immediate offer of a general democratic peace to all the peoples of the belligerent states.

The following should be decreed as immediate measures:

1   The cessation of all repressions aimed against the working class and its organizations. The immediate abolition of the death penalty at the front and the restoration of all democratic organizations in the army and of complete freedom of agitation therein. The purging of all counter-revolutionary commanders from the army.
2   The election of commissars and other officials by local organizations.
3   The genuine implementation of the right of the peoples living in Russia to self-determination; and in the first instance, satisfaction of the demands of Finland and the Ukraine.
4   The dispersal of the State Council and the State Duma. The immediate convocation of the Constituent Assembly.
5   The abolition of all class privileges (for the nobility, etc.), the complete equality of citizens.

Rabochii, no. 10 (1 September 1917)

1.195
[Report of the Organizational Bureau] 31 August 1917

The Organizational Bureau [established by the Central Committee on 6 August] has submitted a report indicating that the treasury of the Central Committee is in an extremely precarious state (about 30,000 roubles on hand), that some party undertakings [e.g., publishing houses] keep their records badly, and that it is therefore very difficult to determine the financial condition of the Central Committee.

At the present time, the Military Organization is not an independent political organization but a military commission under the Central Committee. The work of the Military Organization is thus generally becoming closely aligned with regular party work. All work in the Military Organization is under Central Committee guidance: Comrade Bubnov is working with [the editorial board of] *Soldat*, and the work [of the Organization] in general is being supervised by Comrades Dzerzhinsky and Sverdlov [see 1.185]. Fifty thousand copies of [the Central Organ] *Rabochii* are being published, while *Soldat* is printing 15,000 to 18,000 copies.

The Central Committee was instructed [on 6 August] to organize a group [under Sverdlov] for unifying all party work in trade unions. Certain steps have been taken along these lines: the group has already been formed but has not yet received its final structure. A Municipal Group is being formed [under Sverdlov to co-ordinate party work in the various city Dumas], and steps are being taken to set up an insurance group. At the insurance congress, the Central Committee report was presented by Comrade Smilga; and at the [II] Conference of Factory and Shop Committees [held in Petrograd, 7-12 August], all work was carried out under the guidance of the Central Committee which was represented by Comrade Miliutin.

Efforts have been made to expand and strengthen relations with [party organizations elsewhere in] Russia, but this is being impeded by the poor functioning of the mail. In the debate on this report it was indicated that the Central Committee's work on the all-Russian scale must be expanded, since up until now, for purely technical reasons, the Central Committee's work has mainly been concentrated on St Petersburg. To implement this policy, a board of travelling agents must be set up; this is especially necessary in order to organize the Northwestern and Southern regions and along the Volga where party cohesiveness is lacking.

1.196
[On a New Presidium for the
Soviet of Workers' and Soldiers' Deputies] 6 September 1917

The Central Committee resolves that the presidium [of the Petrograd

Soviet presently dominated by the Mensheviks and the Socialist Revolutionaries] should be a coalition based on proportionality, and that the new presidium should therefore contain seven representatives of the Bolsheviks in addition to seven persons proposed by the Mensheviks and the Socialist Revolutionaries. [On 25 September a new presidium consisting of four Bolsheviks, two Socialist Revolutionaries, and one Menshevik was established.]

1.197
[On Lenin's Suggestion to Seize Power]   15 September 1917

It is resolved in the very near future to devote a meeting of the Central Committee to the discussion of tactical questions.

Comrade Stalin proposes circulating the letters [in which Lenin concluded that 'having obtained a majority in the Soviets of Workers' and Soldiers' Deputies in both of the capitals, the Bolsheviks can and *must* take state power into their own hands' and outlined how this was to be done] to the most important [party] organizations with the instructions that they are to be discussed. It is resolved to postpone this matter to another Central Committee meeting in the very near future. A vote is taken to determine those in favour of keeping only one copy of the letters. In favour – 6, against – 4, abstentions – 6.

Comrade Kamenev proposes adopting the following resolution: After discussing Lenin's letters, the Central Committee rejects the practical proposals contained in them, calls on all organizations to follow only the directives of the Central Committee, and reaffirms that at the present moment the Central Committee finds street demonstrations of any kind totally impermissible. At the same time, the Central Committee requests that Comrade Lenin spell out in a special pamphlet the question of evaluating the current situation and of the party's policies which he raised in his letter. This resolution is rejected.

Finally, the following resolution is adopted: Members of the Central Committee working in the Military Organization and in the Petersburg Committee are instructed to take steps to ensure that no demonstrations whatsoever occur in the barracks and the factories.

1.198
[On Participation in the Democratic Conference]   21 September 1917

With respect to the Democratic Conference [which met in Petrograd under the auspices of the Central Executive Committee from 14 to 22 September to consider prospects for a permanent socialist government], it is resolved not to walk out of it but only to recall the members of our party from its presidium. As regards the Pre-Parliament [or 'Council of the Republic' which was to serve as a deliberative and consultative body until the convocation of the Constituent Assembly], it was resolved by nine votes to eight not to participate. Considering that the vote is evenly divided, the final decision is left to the party meeting presently being organized from among the [Bolshevik] fraction gathered at the Democratic Conference [which subsequently voted 77 to 50 to take part in the Pre-Parliament; see 1.201].

1.199
[On the Peace Declaration of the
Democratic Conference] 23 September 1917

The adherence of the Democratic Conference, which has not repudiated the alliance with the imperialists and has not condemned the policy of taking the offensive, to the principles of a democratic peace represented a hypocritical demonstration in the spirit of the frequent declarations of the French, English, and American parliaments. It was incumbent upon the Social Democratic fraction [at the Conference] to submit an amendment making this declaration more specific, an amendment carrying the obligation to take certain actions; and, in case this amendment was rejected, to brand the declaration as the hypocrisy of political groups subservient to imperialism, this subservience being concealed from the masses by a deceitful declamation borrowed from the socialist dictionary. The adherence by our fraction to this declaration and the associated demonstration of unity in foreign affairs of so-called democratic forces is a repetition of the 'union sacrée' policy which is capable of compromising even our party in the eyes of the revolutionary proletariat of the West ... With respect to the commission elected at the Democratic Conference to work out the text of an appeal to all nations, it is resolved to take part in the commission and to oppose the appeal of the defencists with one of our own.

1.200
[On Use of the Term 'Comrade'] 23 September 1917

Having listened to a report that Comrade Riazanov had called [Menshevik leader] Tsereteli 'comrade' when reading a declaration [at the Democratic Conference], the Central Committee orders comrades not to use the term 'comrade' when referring in public speeches to those persons concerning whom such a form of address might offend the revolutionary feelings of the workers.

I.201
[On the Pre-Parliament]　　　　　　　　　　　　　23 September 1917

After a general exchange of views on the work of the Pre-Parliament, a number of proposals were submitted with respect to its first meeting [scheduled for 7 October].

1　If [Menshevik leader] Chkheidze is elected chairman, it will be necessary to vote against him and to explain the reasons for so voting. This speech is assigned to Shaumian. [A Socialist Revolutionary, N.D. Avksentev, was in fact elected.]

2　It was resolved to enter the presidium and to demand proportional representation. Rykov, Trotsky, and Kamenev [are assigned] to the presidium.

3　In response to the report of the commission elected by the Democratic Conference for negotiations with the ministers [concerning the formation of a third coalition, it is resolved], if agreement has already been reached, to criticize it and to submit our own declaration [attacking any form of coalition with the 'counter-revolutionary bourgeoisie' and calling for the transfer of power to 'a people's government based on the Soviets']. This speech will be made by Trotsky.

4　It was resolved to suggest to the Left Socialist Revolutionaries that they submit a proposal on the inviolability of the members of the Pre-Parliament.

5　It was resolved to prepare a resolution on the Pre-Parliament for a party meeting. Sokolnikov, Bubnov, Rykov, and Trotsky were instructed to do so.

I.202
[On the Soviet of Workers' and
Soldiers' Deputies]　　　　　　　　　　　　　　24 September 1917

It was resolved to transfer Rykov to Petrograd for work in the Soviet as well as to transfer to Soviet work several other comrades, including Volodarsky. Trotsky is to be made chairman of the Soviet, and Rykov is to be brought into the presidium [see 1.196].

　...　With respect to the II Congress of Soviets [which the Central Executive Committee announced the day before would not meet until 20 October], it is resolved to conduct everywhere an extensive campaign and to pass resolutions in various Soviets demanding the immediate convocation of a congress. Sverdlov is delegated to the commission for convoking the congress, and Yurenev is to be his assistant. It is desirable to call district and oblast congresses of Soviets beforehand.

1.203
On the Current Situation and the
Tasks of the Proletariat   24 September 1917

1   From the point of view of class groupings, the current situation is characterized by: a / the uniting of all bourgeois groups, including the kulak upper strata of the peasantry and cossacks, under the ideological and organizational hegemony of finance capital (the Kadet Party); b / the final freeing of the proletariat from bourgeois ideological influence; c / the overcoming, by the poorest peasants and soldiers, of their last illusions as is evident in the formation and growth of the left-wing of the Socialist Revolutionaries and in the growing influence of the party of the proletariat on these segments.
2   Under such circumstances, the ruling classes in their struggle must rely to an ever larger extent solely on the use of naked physical force by the apparatus of oppression still in their hands (the army high command, part of the cossacks, etc.) and on support from international imperialism interested in imperialistic plundering of Russia and in stifling the Russian proletariat which is now prepared to take power. This is expressed in the policy of repressions (punitive expeditions, martial law), in the organization of military plots and their active support by international capital and, finally, in the desire to end a predatory war by an equally predatory peace for the sole purpose of starting an immediate general war against the Russian proletariat.
3   Therefore, the tactics of the bourgeoisie are at a turning point. The policy of exploiting the unconscious trust of the masses in the bourgeoisie and the conciliationism based on this, which placed the forces of these masses at the disposal of the bourgeoisie, is becoming objectively impossible. The Democratic Conference – which was the last attempt at such a conciliation – ended in failure since it proved to be incapable of bringing the broad masses into the service of bourgeois interests. Under such circumstances, bourgeois policy inclines toward civil war against the popular masses.
4   Foreseeing that this will happen, the party of the proletariat must devote all its efforts to mobilizing the broad popular masses as organized in the Soviets of Workers', Soldiers' and Peasants' Deputies which are now militant class organizations and whose assumption of power has become

the slogan of the day. The work of the party should be in this direction; its activities in the Pre-Parliament should be of a purely auxiliary character and wholly subordinated to the tasks of the mass struggle.

5   To this end, it is necessary to strive to develop the activities of the Soviets and to increase their political importance until they assume the role of organs opposing bourgeois state power (the [Provisional] Government, the Pre-Parliament, etc.). The indispensable conditions for this are: close ties between local Soviets; establishment of contact with other revolutionary organizations of the proletariat, the soldiers, and the peasants; changes in the organizational structure of the Soviets (the elimination of obstacles to re-elections, the possibility of recalling members of the Central Executive Committee and of local executive committees); the immediate convocation of oblast congresses; convocation in the very near future of the [II] Congress of Soviets.

6   The victory of the workers, soldiers, and peasants can be achieved only by welding together all the forces of the broad masses organized in the Soviets. Only by their victory can a democratic peace be achieved and the cause of the international revolution move ahead rapidly.

Rabochii put', no. 23 (29 September 1917)

1.204
[On Calling an Extraordinary Party Congress]   28 September 1917

Having discussed the [question] of convening an extraordinary party congress, the Central Committee has resolved to convoke it on 17 October in Petrograd, several days before the [II] Congress of Soviets, which will open on 20 October. The Central Committee's decision was supported by a party meeting of the representatives of the various party organizations present at the Democratic Conference. [On 5 October the Central Committee changed its mind and postponed the congress 'for a short time' in light of differences with Lenin; it next met four months after the revolution.]

The Organizational Bureau of the Central Committee has worked out the following norms of representation at the congress:

Organizations with 3000 to 5000 members will send one delegate; larger organizations will send one more delegate for each additional 5000 members.

Organizations with less than 3000 members will combine [with other smaller organizations] to send a delegate.

Oblast committees are ordered to assume the responsibility for arranging such combinations of small organizations.

The combining of mandates to the extraordinary party congress and to the Congress of Soviets is both permissible and desirable. Representatives of organizations with less than 3000 members and comrades specially invited by the Central Committee may attend in an advisory capacity.

The agenda of the [party] congress: 1 / revision of the party Programme, 2 / organizational matters.

The Central Committee orders local organizations to hold conversations and discussions on the local level about questions of the party Programme.

At the same time, the Central Committee orders a campaign to be conducted for elections to the Congress of Soviets.

It is necessary immediately to hold re-elections of Soviet representatives, if this is possible; to convoke district and oblast [conferences of] Soviets; to pass resolutions demanding the immediate convocation of a congress of Soviets; and to telegraph these resolutions to the Central Executive Committee of the Soviet, with a copy to us.

Considering it necessary to time the congress of trade unions and that of factory and shop committees to coincide also with the Congress of Soviets, we have reached an agreement with the Central Councils of these organizations which have agreed, on their part, to take appropriate steps to convoke their congresses ...

I.205
[On Bolshevik Candidates for the Constituent Assembly] 29 September 1917

The proposal to print a list of 25 [official Bolshevik candidates], with an indication of the districts for which they are standing, was accepted; at the same time it was resolved to expand the list of recommended candidates to 100 and to print it. The [Central] Electoral Commission for the Constituent Assembly [see 1.179], with the addition of several comrades, was charged with the compilation of the list. It was resolved that Kamenev will stand from Petrograd; and that the Military Bureau of the Central Committee will be entrusted with submitting candidates for the front. Lenin and Zinoviev will stand from the Baltic Fleet and the Army.

I.206
[On the Situation in Moscow and the Return of Lenin] 3 October 1917

1 The report of Lomov [on the situation in the Moscow region] was heard. It is becoming increasingly clear that the mood in the region is

extremely tense. In many places we have a majority in the Soviets. The masses are demanding some sort of concrete measures. Everywhere we are taking a 'wait and see' position. It was resolved not to debate the report.
2   It was decided to suggest to Ilyich [Lenin] that he move to Petrograd so that continuous and close contact will be possible.

1.207
[On Establishing a Bureau for Information on the Struggle against Counter-Revolution]   7 October 1917

Comrade Bubnov reported that the Executive Commission of the Petersburg Committee had elected two [members] to a bureau for ascertaining the mood of the masses and [maintaining] close ties between the masses and the party centres.
    After examining and discussing the question of the need for coordinating activities and acquiring precise information, it was resolved to establish a Bureau of the Central Committee for Information on the Struggle against Counter-Revolution. To this Bureau the Central Committee elects three persons: Trotsky, Sverdlov, and Bubnov who are charged with setting up the Bureau itself.

1.208
[On an Armed Uprising]   10 October 1917

The Central Committee recognizes that both the international situation of the Russian Revolution (the mutiny in the German Navy [in August 1917] as an extreme manifestation of the growth throughout Europe of the world-wide socialist revolution, together with the threat of peace among the imperialists for the purpose of stifling the revolution in Russia) and also the military situation (the undoubted decision of the Russian bourgeoisie and of Kerensky and Co. to surrender Petrograd to the Germans [as seen in the cabinet decision of 4 October concerning moving the capital to Moscow]), as well as the acquisition of a majority in the Soviets by the proletarian party – all this, combined with the peasant uprising and the shift in popular confidence toward our party (e.g., the Moscow election [where the Bolsheviks gained control of 11 of the 17 district dumas on 24 September]), and finally the obvious preparations for a second Kornilov affair (the withdrawal of troops from Petrograd, the bringing of cossacks to Petrograd, the surrounding of Minsk by cossacks, etc.) – all this places armed uprising on the order of the day. Recognizing therefore that an armed uprising is inevitable and that the time for it is fully ripe, the Central

Committee instructs all party organizations to act accordingly and to discuss and resolve all practical questions (the Congress of Soviets of the Northern Region [which met in Petrograd from 11–13 October], the withdrawal of troops from Petrograd, the reaction of the people in Moscow and Minsk, etc.) from this point of view.

1.209
[On Establishing a Politburo]   10 October 1917

Comrade Dzerzhinsky proposes that a Political Bureau of Central Committee members be set up in the very near future for purposes of political leadership.

After an exchange of views, the proposal is adopted. A Political Bureau of seven persons is created: the editorial board [of *Rabochii put'* – Trotsky, Stalin, Sokolnikov, Kamenev], plus two [Lenin and Zinoviev], plus Bubnov.

1.210
[On the Armed Uprising]   16 October 1917

The meeting heartily welcomes and fully supports the Central Committee resolution [of 10 October; see 1.208]; it calls on all organizations and all workers and soldiers to undertake comprehensive and intensive preparations for the armed uprising, and to support the [Military Revolutionary] Centre which the Central Committee is creating for this purpose [see 1.211]. It expresses its complete confidence that the Central Committee and the Soviet will at the proper time indicate the favourable moment and the appropriate methods for the attack.

1.211
[On the Military Revolutionary Centre]   16 October 1917

The Central Committee hereby organizes a Military Revolutionary Centre with the following membership: Sverdlov, Stalin, Bubnov, Uritsky, and Dzerzhinsky. This Centre is [to be] part of the revolutionary committee of the Soviet [i.e., the Military Revolutionary Committee which the Executive Committee of the Petrograd Soviet approved in principle on 12 October and the full Soviet endorsed on the 16th; see 1.213].

1.212
[On the Actions of Zinoviev and Kamenev]   20 October 1917

It is decided to resolve immediately the question of K[amenev] and Z[inoviev remaining in the party]. Kamenev's resignation [from the Central Committee] is accepted. For – 5, against – 3.

[Stalin's proposal] to defer making a decision until a plenum is turned down.

K[amenev] and Z[inoviev] are placed under the obligation of refraining from issuing statements against the decisions of the Central Committee and its projected line of work [i.e., 1.208]. For – 6.

Comrade Miliutin's proposal, that no member of the Central Committee has the right to speak out against the decisions of the Central Committee, was adopted unanimously.

Comrade Stalin states that he is leaving the editorial board [of *Rabochii put'*]. In view of the fact that Comrade Stalin's statement in today's issue [criticizing the 'sharp tone' of Lenin's attack on Zinoviev and Kamenev and expressing the hope that the issue could now be dropped and reconciliation achieved] was made in the name of the editorial board and should be discussed by the editorial board, it is resolved, without discussing Comrade Stalin's statement and without accepting his resignation, to pass on to other matters.

1.213
[Debate on the Military Revolutionary Committee]   20 October 1917

Comrade Ioffe proposes adopting the following resolution:

The proposal of the Central Bureau of Military Organizations is rejected, since all who want to work can join the revolutionary centre of the Soviet [i.e., the Military Revolutionary Committee].

Comrade Trotsky submits an amendment to the effect that all our organizations can join the revolutionary centre and, in our fraction there, discuss all questions of interest to them. (Adopted as amended.)

Comrade Uritsky reports on the situation in the [Security] Commission [of the Petrograd City Duma] with reference to the scheme for organizing a voluntary guard. He asks whether he should remain in this Commission.

Comrade Trotsky proposes informing the Commission about the need to be in contact with the Military Revolutionary Committee of the Soviet. If they refuse, then [Uritsky should] resign.

Comrade Sverdlov proposes not resigning from the Commission, but advocating instead a plan for universal service in the militia. Adopted.

1.214
[On the Executive Committee of the Petrograd Soviet]   21 October 1917

Comrade Dzerzhinsky reports on the total disorganization in the Executive Committee [of the Petrograd Soviet, which after 25 September contained twenty-two Bolsheviks, sixteen Socialist Revolutionaries, and six Mensheviks] and proposes that all Bolshevik members of the Executive Committee be obliged without fail to work in the Executive Committee or to leave it.

It is resolved that the following will be brought into the work of the Executive Committee: Comrades Volodarsky, Yurenev, Miliutin, Skalov, Pakhomov, Zorin, Dzerzhinsky, Stalin, Lashevich, Ioffe.

1.215
[Debate on the II Congress of Soviets]   21 October 1917

Comrade Sokolnikov proposes that the [II] Congress [which was scheduled to convene on 20 October but had been postponed five days on the 17th], definitely open on the 25th.

Comrade Trotsky speaks on the question of the presidium, considering that the method adopted at the last congress for forming the presidium was disadvantageous to us, and proposes forming the presidium on the basis of one member for each 100 delegates.

Comrade Sverdlov considers it necessary to hold a preliminary meeting of the [Bolshevik] fraction, which will require special work; for this work in the fraction, he nominates Sverdlov, Stalin, and Miliutin. Ilyich [Lenin] must be involved in preparing the theses of the reports [for this meeting].

Comrade Stalin proposes sending a comrade to Moscow to demand the immediate arrival of the Moscow delegation. He outlines a range of questions requiring theses:
On land, on the war, on power – to be assigned to Comrade Lenin;
On workers' control [of industry] – to Comrade Miliutin;
On the nationality question – to Comrade Stalin;
On the current situation – to Comrade Trotsky.
Comrade Miliutin proposes an additional report on the rules of procedure [for the congress] and that it be assigned to Comrade Sverdlov.

All of the above is approved.

1.216
[On Defensive Preparations] 24 October 1917

Comrade Kamenev proposes that today no member of the Central Committee be allowed to leave the Smolny [Institute] without special permission of the Central Committee. Arrangements are to be made with the Executive Commission [of the Petersburg Committee] to guard both Smolny and the Petersburg Committee. Adopted ...

It is resolved to dispatch a guard immediately to the printing press [which had been closed down by the Provisional Government during the early morning hours of the 24th] and to make sure that the next issue of the newspaper [*Rabochii put'*] comes out at the proper time.

1.217
[Debate on Relations with the Central Executive Committee and on the Assignment of Central Committee Members] 24 October 1917

Comrade Nogin insists on the necessity of clarifying relations with the Central Executive Committee bureau since the railwaymen obey the decrees of the Central Executive Committee and, in the event of disagreement with the latter, we would be cut off from the rest of Russia. Other comrades do not share this apprehension regarding the railwaymen.

Comrade Trotsky proposes putting two Central Committee members at the disposal of the Military Revolutionary Committee in order to adjust ties with the postal and telegraph workers and the railwaymen; and a third member of the Central Committee to watch over the Provisional Government. With respect to the Central Executive Committee, he suggests that it be announced at today's meeting, regardless of who is there, that the Central Executive Committee – whose powers have long since expired – is undermining the cause of revolutionary democracy.

Comrade Vinter [Berzin] objects to the risky dispersal of the Central Committee; it is better to enlist other than Central Committee members.

Comrade Kamenev considers it necessary to take advantage of yesterday's negotiations with the Central Executive Committee [concerning forestalling punitive action by the Provisional Government before the II Congress of Soviets], which now have been violated by the closing of *Rabochii put'* [see 1.216]; therefore, the break with the Central Executive Committee should take place precisely on this ground. He further considers it necessary to enter into negotiations with the Left Socialist Revolutionaries and to make political contact with them.

Comrade Sverdlov ... proposes that our comrades in the Central Executive Committee bureau immediately announce their lack of solidarity with the latter.

A vote is taken on Comrade Trotsky's first proposal to delegate Central Committee members to the following functions: 1 / the railroads, 2 / post and telegraph, 3 / food supply. Adopted.
Comrade Bubnov – to the railwaymen.
Comrade Dzerzhinsky – to the postal and telegraph workers ...
Comrade Miliutin is charged with organizing the food supply.
Comrade [Sverdlov] is assigned to organize the observation of the Provisional Government and its actions ...

It is proposed to assign three persons to conduct negotiations with the Left Socialist Revolutionaries; they propose one person. This assignment is given to Comrade Kamenev and Comrade Vinter [Berzin].

Comrades Lomov and Nogin are assigned to inform Moscow about everything that is going on here.

1.218
[Debate on Establishing an Auxiliary Headquarters]   24 October 1917

Comrade Trotsky proposes establishing an emergency headquarters in the Peter and Paul Fortress and appointing one Central Committee member there for this purpose.

Comrade Kamenev considers it necessary to have a base of operations on the [cruiser] *Aurora*, in case of the seizure of the Smolny [Institute]; Uritsky submits an amendment favouring a destroyer.

Comrade Trotsky insists that the political base should be the Peter and Paul Fortress.

Comrade Sverdlov suggests assigning overall control [at the fortress] to Comrade Lashevich [a leading member of the Bolshevik Military Organization and the Military Revolutionary Committee], and not to a member of the Central Committee.

It is resolved that all Central Committee members are to be assigned passes to the fortress. General control is entrusted to Lashevich and Blagonravov. The maintenance of constant communication with the fortress is entrusted to Sverdlov.

Protokoly tsentral'nogo komiteta RSDRP(b): avgust 1917 – fevral 1918 (Moscow, 1958), 37–121; except for 1.204 in *KPSS v bor'be za pobeda velikoi oktiabr'skoi sotsialisticheskoi revoliutsii: sbornik dokumentov* (Moscow, 1957), 65

1.194, 1.203, 1.208, 1.210 in *KPSS v rezoliutsiiakh* 1, 509–18

Index

Abramovich, R.A., 92, 265
admission of party members, 11, 56, 82, 93–4, 109, 204, 251, 266
agents provocateurs, 9, 146, 159, 168, 174, 177, 184, 244
agitation and propaganda, 13–14, 15, 16, 50, 58, 71, 79, 129, 148, 179, 258, 259
   College of Propagandists, 12
   kruzhkovschchina (circle work), 13–14, 50, 150
   leaflets, 9, 13, 179
   meetings, 14
agrarian policy, 4–5, 28, 38, 44–5, 55, 63, 67, 77–9, 87–8, 93, 95–7, 218, 224–5, 227, 232–3, 264
Akselrod, P.B., 39, 59, 66, 108, 207, 227, 265
Aleksinsky, G.A., 176, 242
'Alfred,' 144
Amsterdam, 68
anarchism and syndicalism, 113
April Crisis, 28, 213–7, 221, 237, 240, 273, 274
armed forces, 47, 52, 69, 101, 133, 212, 216, 229, 239, 259, 261–3 (*see also* Central Committee, Military Organization of); unrest in, 166–7, 169, 241
Armenia, 74, 99
Armenian Social Democratic Workers' Organization, 22, 108, 190
associations of fellow countrymen, 258
Auditing Commission, 25, 252, 253
August Bloc, 160
Aurora, 293

Austria, 230, 270
Avksentev, N.D., 284

Badaev, A.E., 146, 176, 186, 188
Bakhmetev, B.A., 92
Baku, 74
Baltic Fleet, 287
Baltic Sea, 166
Basel, 194, 195
Bauer, Otto, 159
Bazarov, V.A., 89
Bebel, August, 67
Bednyi, D., 186, 203
Bekzadian, A.A. (Iuri), 143
Belostotsky, I.V., 146
Bern, 8, 144, 191, 203
Bernstein, Eduard, 19
Berzin, I.A. (Vinter), 135, 250, 292, 293
Bismarck, Otto von, 193
Black Hundreds, 15, 61, 62, 81, 88, 98, 99, 110, 111, 112, 113, 114, 151, 152, 166, 169, 181, 182
Black Sea, 166
Blagonravov, G.I., 293
Bloody Sunday, 13, 15, 178
Bogdanov, A.A. (Maksimov), 10, 55, 92, 107, 108, 116, 125, 127, 135, 139, 176
Bogdanov, B.O., 227
Boky, G.I. (Maksim), 202
Bologna, 141
Bolsheviks, 3, 16, 20, 67, 108, 116, 118, 124, 127, 135, 139, 149, 200, 243, 244, 264, 273, 282
Bolshevik Centre, 118, 135, 138

Boycotters (*see* Vperedists)
Broido, E.L., 265
Broido, M.I., 125, 128
Brussels, 39, 161
Bubnov, A.S., 146, 250, 253, 263, 277, 281, 284, 288, 289, 293
Bukharin, N.I., 250, 277
Bulgakov, S.N., 19
Bulygin Duma, 61, 73, 79–81, 90, 116
Bund (*see* General Jewish Workers' Union of Poland, Lithuania, and Russia)
Bureau for Information on the Struggle against Counter-Revolution, 288
Bureau of the Committees of the Majority, 68
Burdzhalov, E.N., 196

Caucasian Oblast Committee, 144, 145, 158
Caucasian Oblast Union, 55, 160
Caucasus, 6, 45, 93, 102, 154, 167, 173, 181, 188, 264
cell (iacheika), 11, 14, 171, 189
Central Bureau of Foreign Groups, 125
Central Committee, 7–9, 14, 18, 28, 34, 36–7, 46–7, 54–5, 56–7, 64, 70, 80, 82, 83, 86, 89, 90, 92, 94, 104, 105, 107, 108, 109, 114, 116, 118–19, 120–6, 129–30, 132, 134, 146, 153, 156, 157, 158, 165, 171, 172, 176, 190, 196, 214, 217, 218, 233, 234–5, 237, 239, 240, 250, 252, 253, 258–9, 286, 290 (*see also* Orgburo; Politburo; Secretariat)
  candidate members of, 7, 108, 109, 125, 136, 146, 218, 250
  confidential agents of, 171, 183, 185, 188
  co-optation to 7–8, 39, 47, 58, 83, 94, 136, 147, 188
  Foreign Bureau of, 8–9, 125, 126, 130, 135–7, 139, 141, 143, 144, 146
  foreign section of, 187, 190

Menshevik Central Committee (1917), 24, 25n, 265, 266, 272–3
Military Bureau, 287
Military Organization, 12, 25, 29, 99, 214, 237, 240, 246, 259, 261–3, 278, 281, 282, 293; Central Bureau of, 261–3, 290; All-Russian Conference of, 261
Organizational Section (Workers' Co-operative Commission), 188, 190
plenums and meetings of: 1908, 8, 124–6, 128; 1910, 8, 18, 20, 134–40, 141, 142, 144, 145, 156; 1911, 8, 141–3, 144; 1912, 168–77, 183, 185; 1913, 177–87; 1914, 187–90; 1917, 246–9, 277–93
Press Commission of, 125, 126
Russian Board of, 8, 135–7, 141, 156
Russian Bureau of, 8, 16, 24, 146, 184, 190, 196–206, 207, 210, 211, 217; presidium of, 24
subcommittee of, 8, 19, 125–6, 128, 129–30, 135, 252–3
Trade Union Co-operative Commission of, 121
Unified Central Committee (1906), 82, 89–91, 92
Central Industrial Region, 10, 188
Central Organ, 9–10, 13, 25, 46, 49, 59, 82, 83, 86, 89, 90, 103, 125, 126, 135, 137, 138, 141, 146, 155, 179, 262, 263, 266, 281
Chernomazov, M.E., 184, 186
Chernov, V.M., 243
Chkheidze, N.S., 207, 237, 265, 284
Chkhenkeli, A.I., 265
city committee, 57, 60, 69, 70, 171, 267
City Duma, 245, 251
  Moscow, 288
  Petrograd, 290; Security Commission of, 290
combat agreements, 64, 98
commissars, 280

INDEX

Committee for the Struggle against
 Counter-Revolution, 274-5
Committee of Foreign Organizations, 9,
 57, 146, 157
committee of sowers, 258
'conciliators,' 22, 135, 141, 157, 198,
 250
conference, party, 6-7, 23, 55, 109, 125,
 139-40, 141-3, 147, 266
 Conference of the Majority (I, 1905),
  7, 18n, 85-8, 89
 I All-Russian (II, 1906), 105-7
 II All-Russian (III, 1907), 115-17,
  118, 121
 III All-Russian (IV, 1907), 117-20
 December All-Russian (V, 1908),
  127-34, 147, 148, 149
 Prague (VI, 1912), 7, 8, 9, 20n, 22,
  144, 146-57, 158, 159, 168, 171, 173,
  179
 VII All-Russian (April, 1917), 23n,
  24, 217-26, 234, 249, 251
 I All-Russian Menshevik Conference
  (1905), 7, 11, 20n, 66-79, 89, 227
 II All-Russian Menshevik Conference (1905), 7, 11, 20n, 82-4, 85, 89
 August Conference (Vienna, 1912),
  5, 7, 20n, 22n, 23, 159-67, 172,
  173
 All-Russian Menshevik Conference
  (1917), 23n, 24, 25, 27, 28, 226-34,
  264
 Riga Conference (1905), 79-81
 All-Russian Meeting of Party Workers (March Conference, 1917), 23n,
  24, 209-13
congress, legal, 18, 123, 184, 185
congress, party, 6, 7, 23, 37, 45, 56, 83,
 86, 93, 94-5, 105, 110, 127, 147, 178,
 183, 187-90, 210, 232, 233, 234, 251,
 252, 260, 266, 278, 286-7
 Control Commission of, 6
 Electoral Commission for, 86

297

 Mandates Commission of, 6
 Organizational Committee for, 56,
  94, 110, 252
 I (1898), 3, 6, 7, 9, 33-7, 39
 II (1903), 3, 4, 5, 6, 9, 14, 17n, 19, 20,
  22, 38-54, 55, 58, 64, 66, 93, 147
 III (1905), 5, 7, 15, 19, 20n, 54-65, 66,
  67, 89, 92
 Unification (IV, 1906), 5, 7, 17, 21,
  22, 92-104, 105, 106, 115, 116, 120,
  131, 135
 London (V, 1907), 7, 17, 22n, 107-15,
  116, 118, 119, 120, 121, 124, 128, 129,
  132, 136, 137, 139, 151, 180
 VI (1917), 23n, 26, 187, 246, 249-61,
  262, 264
 Menshevik Unification (1917), 23n,
  24n, 25n, 27, 264-73
Constituent Assembly, 25, 28, 45, 60,
 61, 67, 72, 73-4, 77, 79, 81, 88, 90, 97,
 101, 106, 113, 128, 196, 199, 207, 208,
 218, 221, 223, 224, 225, 227, 231, 232,
 233, 238, 243, 246, 249, 251, 269,
 271-3, 278, 280, 283, 287
 Bolshevik Central Electoral Commission, 257, 258, 287
 Menshevik Central Elections Committee, 272
 oblast electoral commissions, 257
 guberniia electoral commissions, 272
Constitutional Democratic Party
 (Kadets), 96, 105, 111, 112, 116, 117,
 132, 133, 151, 194, 222, 239, 247, 274,
 276, 279, 285
Control (Liaison) Commission, 201,
 209
co-operatives, 18, 112, 121-4, 148, 180,
 236, 246, 255, 269, 272
Copenhagen, 107, 194
cossacks, 117, 285, 288
Council of the United Nobility, 111
Cracow, 168, 184, 187, 188
Crimea, 10

Dan, F.I., 10, 66, 89, 92, 107, 116, 135, 141, 144, 207, 227, 237, 264, 265
Danishevsky, K.K., 92, 108
Declaration of the Rights of Soldiers, 238
Delo zhizni (The Vital Question, Moscow, 1911), 156
democratic centralism, 82–3, 87, 90, 91, 94, 109, 251, 265, 266
Democratic Conference, 278, 282–5, 286
Desnitsky, V.A., 92
dictatorship of the proletariat, 4, 41, 200, 201, 202, 250, 253
Dnevnik Sotsial-demokrata (Diary of a Social Democrat, Geneva, 1905–12), 10
Donets Basin, 10, 11n
Dubrovinsky, I.F., 108
dues, party, 9, 11, 172, 179, 251, 266
Duma (*see* State Duma; city dumas; Bulygin Duma)
Dzerzhinsky, F.E., 92, 108, 141, 218, 250, 253, 262, 263, 277, 281, 289, 291, 293

Economists, 17, 38, 39, 64
Efremov, I.N., 247
Ekaterinoslav, 11n, 33, 152, 156, 186
elections
 Constituent Assembly, 231, 257–9
 Duma, 85, 91, 93, 105–7, 117, 145, 150–2, 161, 163–5, 168, 169, 171
 Soviet, 287
Elias, K.I., 144
Eremeev, K.S., 197, 200, 203
Ermolaev, K.M. (Roman), 156, 227, 265
Executive Commission, 70
expropriations, 15, 93, 100, 105, 108, 114–15, 118, 124, 125, 135, 139
expulsion of party members, 58, 251
Ezhov, S.O. (Tsederbaum), 227, 265

factory and shop committees, 235, 254, 256
 Central Council of, 235, 237, 256, 287
 Conference of, 234–5, 281, 287
Fedorov, G.F., 218
French socialists, 158, 193
fighting squads, 13, 98, 108, 115
Finland, 225, 277, 280
Finnish Workers' Party, 20
Fofanova, M.V., 278
food committees, 233, 254
Foreign Bureau (*see* Central Committee)
Foreign Central Bureau, 125, 126
Foreign League of Russian Revolutionary Social Democrats, 9, 39, 47, 54, 57
Foreign Organizational Commission, 9, 141–3, 144
fraction (party group within a non-party organization), 251, 257, 267, 271 (*see especially* State Duma)
fraternization, 27, 201, 207, 216, 219, 230, 245

Galicia, 168, 183, 191
Garvi, P.A. (Iurii), 156, 159, 227, 265
General Jewish Workers' Union of Poland, Lithuania, and Russia (Bund), 11, 21, 33, 36, 38, 39, 48–9, 64, 79, 80, 92, 103, 104, 105, 108, 109, 116, 118, 124, 127, 135, 139, 142, 145, 157, 159, 160, 168, 173, 174, 181, 189, 264, 267
Geneva, 66, 124
German Social Democrats, 125, 158, 164, 192–3
Germany, 230, 270, 288
Getzler, Israel, 264
God-constructionists (*see* Vperedists)
Goldenberg, I.P., 108, 125
Goldman, B.I. (Gorev), 125, 135, 141, 144, 159, 227, 265

INDEX

Goldman, L.I., 92, 265
Goloshchekin, F.I., 146
Golos Sotsial-demokrata (Voice of a Social Democrat, Geneva-Paris, 1908–11), 10, 11n, 138, 141
Gorky, A.M., 107, 260
Grille, D., 20n
Grintser, I.M., 66
guberniia (province, administrative level of party), 11n, 259, 267
Guchkov, A.I., 221
Guesde, J.B., 193
'guiding institutions' (*see* Central Committee)
Gutovsky, V.N. (Maevsky), 66, 79

Helsingfors (Helsinki), 117
Hindenburg, Paul von, 244
Huysmans, G., 157

Iakhontov, V.I., 265
industry, worker control over (1917), 28, 234–6, 255–6, 280 (*see also* labour policy)
Initiative Groups, 156, 172
Inter-district Committee (Mezhraionka), 26, 298, 203, 204, 220, 240, 246, 250, 264
International Socialist Bureau, 68, 103, 157, 158, 161
Investigatory Commission, 125
Ioffe, A.A., 253, 277, 291
Iordansky, N.I., 89
Iskra (The Spark, Leipzig-Munich-London-Geneva-Vienna, 1900–5), 6, 9, 19, 38, 39, 49, 59, 71, 82, 89
Isuv, I.A. (Mikhail), 108, 156, 227, 265
Iudin, F. (Aizenshtadt, I.L.), 227, 265
Iuzhnyi rabochii (The Southern Worker, Ekaterinoslav, 1899–1903), 13
Izvestiia (of the Petrograd Soviet) (News, Petrograd, 1917–), 196

Jagiello, E.I., 173
Jews, 33, 36, 39, 48, 182 (*see also* pogroms)
July Days, 26, 27, 209, 239–43, 246, 247, 249, 261, 262, 268, 273, 274, 275, 277, 278

Kadets (*see* Constitutional Democratic Party)
Kalinin, M.I. (Ivanov), 146, 197, 200, 203
Kamenev, L.B., 10, 29, 55, 125, 135, 138, 141, 146, 191, 197, 202–3, 210, 211, 218, 237, 240, 246, 249, 250, 278, 282, 284, 287, 289, 290, 292, 293
Kautsky, Karl, 135, 192
Kerensky, A.F., 27, 215, 240, 247, 248, 264, 273, 274, 288
Kerensky Offensive, 239, 244, 273
Khakharev, M.I., 197
Kharkov, 11n, 152, 186, 190
Khinchuk, L.M., 66, 92, 227, 265
Khrustalev-Nosar, G.S., 82
Kienthal Conference, 191
Kiev, 33, 151, 186, 190
Kiselev, A.S., 146
knizani, 45
Kogan, O.A. (Ermansky), 227
Koigen, F.M., 135
Kotka, 116
Kollontai, A.M., 249, 250, 251
Kolokolnikov, P.N., 92, 265
Kornilov, L.G., 24, 273–7, 279
Kostroma, 152
Krasin, L.B., 55, 89, 92, 108
Krasnoiarsk Soviet, 210
Kremer, A.I., 92
Krestinsky, N.N., 250
Krokhmal, V.N., 89, 92, 227
Kronstadt, 240, 261
Krzhizhanovsky, G.M., 39
Kshesinskaia, Mathilda, 209
kulak (relatively prosperous peasant), 285

labour conscription, 236, 256
Labour Group (see Trudoviks)
labour policy, 4, 28, 43-4, 231-2, 234-6, 254-7 (see also trade unions; workers' insurance; industry)
Lalaiants, I.K., 89
land committees, 232-3, 258
Lashevich, M.M., 291, 293
Latvian Social Democratic Labour Party (see Social Democratic Party of the Latvian Region)
left-Bolsheviks (see Vperedists)
Legal Marxists, 19, 38
Lena massacre, 13, 15, 168
Lengnik, F.V., 39
Lenin, V.I. (Ilyich), 8, 9, 10, 18, 19, 20, 21, 22, 24, 26, 29, 38, 39, 54-5, 64, 66, 82, 85, 89, 90, 92, 93, 105, 108, 116, 118, 125, 127, 128, 135, 141, 144, 146, 147, 155, 157, 158, 168, 177, 178, 187, 188, 191, 192, 197, 198, 207, 211, 213, 214, 217, 218, 234-5, 237, 240, 242, 246, 249, 250, 251, 260-1, 264, 274, 275, 277, 278, 279, 282, 286, 287, 288, 289, 290, 291
  Polnoe sobranie sochinenii (Complete Collected Works), 17n, 157
  Two Tactics of Social Democracy in the Democratic Revolution, 8, 9
  What Is To Be Done?, 20
Letuchii listok Sotsial-demokrata (Leaflet of a Social Democrat, St Petersburg, never published?), 71
Liber, M.I. (Goldman), 141, 144, 265
Linde, F.V., 214
Liquidators, 19, 20, 22, 128, 129, 135, 147, 149, 151, 155-6, 157, 168, 170, 172, 173, 174, 176, 180, 181, 194
Lithuanian Social Democratic Party, 22, 108, 159, 190
Liubimov, A.I. (Mark), 135, 141, 143
Lobov, A.I., 177
Lodz, 174

Lomov, G.I., 287, 293
London, 39, 55
Longjumeau, 141
Luch (The Ray, St Petersburg, 1912-13), 18, 168, 170, 172, 176, 177
'Ludis,' 144
Lunarcharsky, A.V., 89, 144, 249, 250
Luxemburg, Rosa, 173

Machists (see Vperedists)
Makadziub, M.S. (Panin), 66, 227
Maletsky, A.M., 125
Malinovsky, R.V., 146, 168, 177
Marchlewski, J. (Markhlevsky, I.I.), 125
Markov, N.E., 153
Martov, I.O., 10, 27, 38, 39, 59, 66, 89, 92, 125, 135, 141, 143, 157, 159, 191, 207, 227, 264, 265
Martynov, A.S., 66, 89, 92, 108, 207, 265
Marx, K., 3, 5, 14, 20, 196
Maslov, P.P., 92, 93
May Day, 13, 14, 36, 169
Mehring, Franz, 135
Menshevik Internationalists, 26, 27, 198, 204, 207, 227, 264, 265
Mensheviks, 20, 24, 28, 55, 64, 65, 108, 116, 118, 124, 127, 135, 139, 188, 196, 200, 203, 210, 215, 216, 219, 224, 246, 247, 248, 254, 260, 282, 291 (see also conferences, party)
  meetings: Bern, 8, 144-6; Paris, 157-8
Mezhraionka (see Inter-District Committee)
Military Organization (see Central Committee)
Military Revolutionary Centre, 25, 289
Military Revolutionary Committee (see Soviet, Petrograd)
militia (workers', people's, etc.), 43, 78, 223, 236, 291

INDEX

Miliukov, P.N., 213, 214, 215
Miliutin, V.P., 218, 250, 253, 262, 281, 290, 291, 293
Ministry of the Interior (tsarist), 53
Minsk, 33, 288-9
Molotov, V.M., 196, 197, 200, 202, 210
Monarchist Party, 111
Moscow, 33, 85, 116, 123, 151, 152, 176, 179, 186, 188, 190, 287, 288, 289, 291, 293
Moscow (State) Conference, 248, 269
Municipal Groups, 281
municipalization, 5, 93, 95
Muranov, M.K., 186, 197, 202, 250, 253
Muslims, 74, 99, 117
mutual aid societies, 18, 122

Narodnaia Volia (People's Will), 36
narodniks (catch-all term used by Lenin for Socialist Revolutionaries, Popular Socialists, Trudoviks), 151, 215, 216, 224
Nash put' (Our Path, Moscow, 1913), 176, 179
Nasha zaria (Our Dawn, St Petersburg, 1910-14), 17, 156, 172
nationality policy, 4-5, 28, 104, 133, 169, 178, 181-2, 218, 225-6, 227, 264
national-cultural autonomy, 5, 159, 167, 178, 181, 226
Nevsky, V.I., 261
Nicholas II, 196, 206
Nikifor, 108
Nikolaev, 11n
Nogin, V.P., 108, 210, 211, 218, 250, 292, 293
'non-factionalists,' 22, 157, 211
Northwestern Region, 188, 281
Noskov, V.A., 39
Novaia zhizn (New Life, Petrograd, 1917), 260, 264, 278

oblast (region, administrative level of party), 10, 70, 71, 87, 94, 109, 131, 139-40, 171, 183, 252, 266, 286
oblast organizational commissions, 188-90
October Manifesto, 80, 82, 88, 90
Octobrists (*see* Union of the 17th of October)
Odessa, 55, 151
Okhrana (imperial security organ), 167, 177
okrug (district, administrative level of party), 11n
Olminsky, M.S. (Vitomsky), 186, 197, 203
Ordzhonikidze, G.K., 146
Organizational Bureau (Orgburo), 23, 281, 286
Organizational Commission (Menshevik), 66, 67, 68, 70, 79, 82, 83, 86, 89, 90, 118 (*see also* Foreign Organizational Commission)
Organizational Committee (Menshevik), 24, 27, 144-5, 159, 160, 161, 162, 206-9, 227, 232, 233, 234, 243-6, 264 (*see also* congress, party)
Foreign Secretariat of, 207
Osvobozhdenie (Liberation, Stuttgart-Paris, 1902-5), 51
Otzovists (Recallists; *see* Vperedists)
Ozerki, 191
Ozolin, M.V., 141

Pakhomov, P.L., 291
Paris, 125, 126, 135, 141, 222, 242
Paris Commune, 193, 195
Partiinye izvestiia (News of the Party, St Petersburg, 1906), 89
party cards (membership), 204, 237
party Council, 7n, 39, 45, 46, 54, 55
party exchange, 150
Party Mensheviks, 22, 142, 143, 146, 149, 156, 157, 159
Party of Commerce and Industry, 111

Party of Peaceful Reform, 111
party schools, 15, 135, 138-9, 141, 259
peasants (*see also* kulaks; agrarian policy)
  committees, 44, 63, 78, 97, 224, 254, 280
Peasant Union, 96
Peter and Paul Fortress, 293
Petersburg Committee, 171, 190, 197, 200, 204, 214, 237, 240, 246, 261, 262, 278, 282
  Executive Commission of, 288, 292
  conference of, 214
Petrograd, 191, 213, 216, 217, 226, 227, 238, 239, 249, 284 (*see also* St Petersburg)
Petrovsky, G.I., 146, 169
Piatakov, G.L., 218
Piatniksky, O.A., 146
Plekhanov, G.V., 3, 4, 10, 27, 33, 37, 38, 39, 55, 59, 66, 68, 92, 93, 118, 142, 144, 191, 194, 198, 264
Podvoisky, N.I., 261
Pogroms, 99, 111
Poland, 35
Poletaev, N.G., 176
'police socialism,' 39, 53
Polish Social Democratic Party (*see* Social Democratic Party of Poland and Lithuania)
Polish Socialist Party, 21n, 22n, 103, 117, 162
  Polish Socialist Party-Levitsa, 22, 159, 161, 173
Politburo (Political Bureau), 25, 289
Popular Socialists, 111, 117, 152, 230, 272
Poronin, 177, 187, 188
Postolovsky, D.S., 55
Potresov, A.N., 27, 39, 59, 66, 92, 191
'practical centres' (*see* Central Committee and Organizational Commission, Menshevik)

Prague, 146
Pravda (Truth)
  Lemberg-Vienna (1908-12), 10, 138, 141, 142, 146, 158
  St Petersburg (1912-14), 18, 146, 168, 169, 172, 175-7, 184-7
  Petrograd (1917-), 25n, 197, 198, 200, 203, 213, 237, 240
Preobrazhensky, E.A., 250
Pre-Parliament (Council of the Republic), 278, 283, 284, 286
presidium
  Petrograd Soviet, 281-2, 284
  Congress of Soviets, 291
press
  émigré, 10, 13
  illegal, 13, 129
  legal, 16, 17-18, 179, 193
Press Commission (*see* Central Committee)
Priboi Publishing House, 179
Programme, party, 3-5, 24, 33, 38, 39-45, 60, 93, 181, 218, 251, 287
Progressivists, 152
Proletarii (The Proletarian)
  Geneva (1905), 9, 59, 82, 89
  Vyborg-Geneva-Paris (1907-09), 10, 118, 127, 135, 138
  Petrograd (1917), 25n, 263
propaganda (*see* agitation and propaganda)
proportional representation, 12, 82, 252, 265, 266, 282
Prosveshchenie (Enlightenment, St Petersburg, 1911-14), 17, 176, 179
Provisional Government, 26-9, 72-3, 196-201, 204, 205, 206, 207, 208, 209, 210, 211, 212, 213, 214, 216, 217, 220, 221, 222, 224, 225, 227, 228-9, 232, 237, 238, 240, 242, 243, 244, 247, 248, 261, 264, 268, 273, 274, 276, 279, 286, 292, 293
provisional revolutionary government,

26, 55, 60–1, 65, 196–201
Putilov Works, 240

Rabochaia gazeta (The Worker's Newspaper)
  Kiev (1897–8), 9, 33–4, 36, 37
  Paris (1910–12), 146
  Petrograd (1917), 25n, 266
Rabochii (The Worker, Petrograd, 1917), 25n, 274, 281
Rabochii i soldat (Worker and Soldier, Petrograd, 1917), 25n, 262, 263
Rabochii put' (Worker's Path, Petrograd, 1917), 25n, 289, 290, 292
Radchenko, L.N., 92
raion (district, administrative level of party), 12, 69–70, 83, 252, 266
Ramishvili, N.V., 125
Red Cross (political), 19
Red Guard, 205, 210, 249, 274
Reed, John, 279
Renner, Karl, 159
Revolution
  1848, 34
  1905, 10, 15, 19, 55, 62, 121, 139, 169, 196
  1917, 22–9, 196–293
'revolutionary defencism,' 27–8, 207, 212, 220, 227
Revolutionary Ukrainian Party, 21n, 22n, 80
Riazanov, D.B., 283
Riga, 79, 151, 186, 271, 273
Romanov, A.B., 227
Rozanov, V.N., 92
Rozhkov, N.A., 108, 265
Rules, party, 6–12, 23, 38, 45–7, 55, 67, 69–70, 82, 90, 93–5, 109–10, 146, 147, 251–3, 265–7
Russian Board of the Central Committee (*see* Central Committee)
Russian Bureau of the Central Committee (*see* Central Committee)

Russian Organizing Commission, 142, 158
Rykov, A.I., 55, 92, 108, 141, 210, 218, 250, 284

St Petersburg, 6, 15, 33, 35, 70, 71, 82, 89, 151, 152, 168, 172, 176, 179, 186, 190, 249, 281 (*see also* Petrograd)
St Petersburg Committee (*see* Petersburg Committee)
Sammer, I.A., 89
Savelev, M.A. (Max), 186
Secretariat, 25
Semashko, N.A., 141, 143, 144, 146
Sembat, Marcel, 193
Semkovsky, S.I., 265
Sergeev, F.A., 250
Sevruk, P.N., 210
Shaumian, S.G., 146, 250, 284
Shcheglovitov, I.G., 260
Shidlovsky Commission, 61
Shingarev, A.I., 224
Shliapnikov, A.G. (Belenin), 196, 197, 203
Shmidt, N.A., 135, 139
shop committees (*see* factory and shop committees)
Shvartsman, D.M., 146
Shvedchikov, K.M., 197
Shutko, K.I., 197
sickness funds (*see* workers' insurance)
Skalov, S.I., 291
Skobelev, M.I., 227
Smelov, 82
Smilga, I.T., 218, 237, 250, 253, 262
Smirnov, A.P., 146
Smirnov, A.N., 159, 227, 265
Smolny Institute, 279, 292, 293
Social Democratic Party of the Latvian Region, 11, 21, 80, 92, 105, 108, 109, 116, 118, 124, 135, 139, 142, 145, 159, 160, 168, 173, 174, 189
Social Democratic Party of Poland and

Lithuania, 11, 21, 80, 92, 102–3, 105, 108, 109, 116, 118, 124, 126, 127, 135, 136, 139, 144, 159, 168, 173, 174
  Regional Presidium (Rozlamovists), 173, 177, 178, 189
  Main Presidium, 103, 173, 189
Socialist (Second) International, 68, 121, 128, 180, 187, 188, 192–5, 229, 272 (*see also* International Socialist Bureau)
Socialist Revolutionary Party, 39, 51, 64, 96, 111, 117, 151, 194, 196, 200, 219, 247, 248, 254, 272, 282, 291
  Left Socialist Revolutionaries, 284, 285, 292, 293
Sokolnikov, G.I., 250, 253, 257, 262, 277, 284, 289, 291
soldiers' committees, 254
Soldat (The Soldier, Petrograd, 1917), 262, 263, 281
Soldatskaia pravda (Soldier's Truth, Petrograd, 1917), 237, 261, 262
Sotsial-demokrat (The Social Democrat)
  Geneva (1904–5), 71
  Vilna-Paris-Geneva (1906–17), 9, 10n, 11n, 92, 108, 119, 125, 137, 146, 155, 179, 191
Southern Region, 281
Soviet
  All-Russian Conference of, 207, 209, 210, 213
  Central Executive Committee, 240, 242, 243, 254, 257, 260, 274, 282, 284, 286–7, 292
  congresses of, 21n, 237, 239, 260, 278–9, 284, 286–7, 291, 292; Northern Region, 289
  of Deputies of Agricultural Labourers, 224–5
  Moscow, 26
  Petrograd, 26, 28, 197, 206, 214, 217, 221, 235, 242, 247, 277, 278; Executive Committee of, 197, 200, 210, 213, 214, 217, 220, 222, 289, 291; Order #1, 202; Manifesto to the Peoples of the World, 211–12; Military Revolutionary Committee of, 25, 262, 279, 289, 290, 292, 293
  of Peasants' Deputies, 97, 224, 239
  of Peasants' and Farmhands' Deputies, 204
  of Workers' Deputies (1905), 82, 108, 112–13
  of Workers' and Soldiers' Deputies, 26, 196–7, 200, 201, 202, 204–5, 206, 208, 212–13, 215, 216, 222–3, 228–9, 230, 235, 238–9, 241, 243, 245, 250, 254, 256, 258, 264, 285, 286
Spandarian, S.S., 146
Spilka (*see* Ukrainian Social Democratic Union)
Stalin, J.V., 25, 85, 93, 107, 146, 168, 169, 197, 198, 202, 203, 210, 211, 218, 237, 246, 249, 250, 252, 257, 262, 263, 277, 278, 282, 289, 290, 291
Stasova, E.D., 25, 146, 197, 253
State Council, 238, 280
State Duma, 8, 15, 16, 85, 88, 90, 97, 100–2, 105–6, 113–14, 116–17, 127, 128, 148, 150–4, 161, 163–5, 180, 184–6, 238, 248, 267, 280
  Russian Social Democratic Workers' Fraction (Bolshevik), 178, 184–6, 188, 193, 203
  Social Democratic Fraction (Menshevik), 178, 193
  united Social Democratic fraction, 16, 23, 101, 107, 113, 114, 126, 131–4, 142, 166, 168, 169, 175, 176
Stockholm, 92, 271
Stolypin, P.A., 124
strikes, 13, 35, 149, 163, 168, 169, 170, 178–9, 191, 213
  strike committees, 149, 163
Struve, P.B., 19, 33, 51

INDEX 305

Stuttgart, 194
Sukhanov, N.N., 217, 278
Sverdlov, I.M., 25, 146, 169, 176, 218, 246, 249, 250, 253, 262, 263, 277, 281, 285, 288, 289, 291, 292, 293

Tammerfors, 85, 105
Tarasevich, A.A., 66, 89
Taratuta, V.K., 125
Tauride Palace, 211, 240, 243
Technical Commission, 9, 141, 143, 144
Teodorovich, I.A., 108, 211
Tiflis, 125, 135
Tovarishch (Comrade, St Petersburg, 1906–7), 118
trade unions, 12, 15, 16–17, 53–4, 62, 67, 75–6, 92, 97, 102, 112, 115, 116, 120–3, 148, 149, 152, 162–3, 176, 180, 182, 190, 193, 226, 235, 237, 245, 246, 256, 257, 269, 272, 281, 287
  Central Bureau of (1905), 82
Trotsky, L.D., 10, 29, 107, 135, 138, 141, 142, 144, 146, 147, 157, 159, 160, 191, 192, 196, 198, 211, 213, 217, 240, 244, 249, 250, 260, 264, 277, 278, 284, 288, 289, 290, 291, 292, 293
  Stalin School of Falsification, 209
Trudoviks (Labour Group), 111, 117, 151, 152, 153, 163, 230
Trud Press, 263
'trustees,' 135, 158
Tseretelli, I.G., 25, 207, 210, 211, 227, 237, 247, 264, 265, 283
Tsetlin, B.S., 227, 265
Turkestan, 166
Tyszka, Leo (Tyshko), 125, 135, 141, 173

uezd (district, administrative level of party), 232, 272
Ukraine, 179, 188, 239, 280
Ukrainian Social Democratic Labour Party, 22n

Ukrainian Social Democratic Union (Spilka), 21, 79
Ulianova, M.I. (Ilina), 197, 203
Ulianova-Elizarova, A.I., 197
Ultimatists (*see* Vperedists)
Union of Russian, English, Italian, and Neutral Journalists, 242
Union of Russian Social Democrats Abroad, 9, 37, 39
Union of Russian Men, 110, 153
Union of Struggle for the Emancipation of Labour, 6, 33, 35, 36
Union of the 17th of October (Octobrists), 111, 116, 123, 152
unions (of party organizations), 10, 45–6
United Internationalists, 264, 265
'United States of Europe,' 192, 194
Urals, 10, 188
Uritsky, M.S., 159, 250, 253, 257, 277, 289, 290, 293
Urotadze, G.I., 144, 159

Vienna, 138, 159, 187, 188
Vilna, 174
Vladimir, 152
Vladimirsky, M.F., 141
Vladimirov, M.K., 141
Voitinsky, V.S. (Woytinsky), 210
Volga, 188, 281
Volodarsky, M.M., 262, 284, 291
volost (district, administrative level of government), 79, 232
Vpered (Forward, Paris, 1910–11), 10, 135, 138
Vperedists (Boycotters, Otzovists, Ultimatists, God-constructionists, Machists, left-Bolsheviks), 20, 127, 128, 135, 139, 141, 142, 149, 157, 159, 176, 198

War Industries Committees, 206
Warsaw, 173, 174

Warski, A.S., 92, 108, 135
Wilhelm II, 239, 270
Winter Palace, 29
Wolfe, B.D., 159
workers' clubs, 19, 76, 148, 180, 190, 259
Workers' Congress, 108, 112–13
'Workers' Co-operative Commission' (*see* Central Committee, Organizational Section of)
workers' insurance, 15, 18, 153–5, 165–6, 174–5, 184, 231
    congress of (1917), 281
    sickness funds, 18, 155, 165–6, 174, 180
World War, First, 187, 188, 191–5

Yermolenko, Lt., 242
Yurenev, K.K., 285, 291

Zalezhsky, V.N., 197
Zalutsky, P.A., 196, 197, 210
Zaria (Dawn, Stuttgart, 1901–2), 49–50
Zaretskaia, S.M., 227, 265
Zasulich, V.I., 39, 59, 66
Zemskii Sobor, 61
zemstvo, 39, 267
Zetkin, Klara, 135
Zhordaniia, N.N., 93, 108, 125
Zimmerwald Conference, 191, 210, 218, 271
Zinoviev, G.E., 10, 29, 108, 125, 135, 141, 146, 177, 218, 235, 237, 240, 246, 249, 250, 251, 260, 275, 277, 278–9, 287, 289, 290
Zorin, S.S., 291
Zubatov, S.V., 53
Zvezda (Star, St Petersburg, 1910–12), 18

www.ingramcontent.com/pod-product-compliance
Lightning Source LLC
Chambersburg PA
CBHW020352080526
44584CB00014B/1001